PUBLIC POLICY FOR WOM
THE STATE, INCOME SECURITY, AND LABOUR MARKET ISSUES

Edited by Marjorie Griffin Cohen and Jane Pulkingham

Through an examination of the state, income security, and labour market issues, the essays in this volume provide an in-depth and wide-ranging perspective on public policy and the changing roles of women. The twenty-four contributors are academics and social activists who have worked within the feminist movement to advance more women-oriented public policy. The topics include some of the more controversial policy issues of today, and in developing their analyses, the authors explore alternative strategies and policies to meet women's needs.

The book is organized into three sections: Restructuring Public Policy in the Canadian State, Reimagining Income Security for the Most Vulnerable, and Rethinking Labour Market and Employment Support Policy. An underlying theme in all the chapters is the importance of designing income, labour, and service supports in a way that recognizes women's dual responsibilities as income earners and caregivers over the course of their lives and the lives of those for whom they provide both financial support and care. With the transformation in gender relations and the gender contract over the past several decades, and the concurrent political constraints brought about by neoliberal policy changes, new policy problems have emerged, requiring new approaches. Taking these developments into account, the authors address a range of possibilities for pursuing more equitable public policies for women.

(Studies in Comparative Political Economy and Public Policy)

MARJORIE GRIFFIN COHEN is a professor in the Departments of Political Science and Women's Studies at Simon Fraser University.

JANE PULKINGHAM is chair and an associate professor in the Department of Sociology and Anthropology at Simon Fraser University.

Studies in Comparative Political Economy and Public Policy

Editors: MICHAEL HOWLETT, DAVID LAYCOCK, STEPHEN MCBRIDE, Simon Fraser University.

Studies in Comparative Political Economy and Public Policy is designed to showcase innovative approaches to political economy and public policy from a comparative perspective. While originating in Canada, the series provides attractive offerings to a wide international audience, featuring studies with local, subnational, cross-national, and international empirical bases and theoretical frameworks.

Editorial Advisory Board

For a list of books published in the series, see page 419.

EDITED BY MARJORIE GRIFFIN COHEN
AND JANE PULKINGHAM

Public Policy for Women

The State, Income Security, and Labour Market Issues

UNIVERSITY OF TORONTO PRESS
Toronto Buffalo London

© University of Toronto Press Incorporated 2009
Toronto Buffalo London
www.utppublishing.com
Printed in Canada

ISBN 978-0-8020-9332-5 (cloth)
ISBN 978-0-8020-9500-8 (paper)

Printed on acid-free paper

Library and Archives Canada Cataloguing in Publication

Public policy for women : the state, income security and labour market
issues / edited by Marjorie Griffin Cohen and Jane Pulkingham.

ISBN 978-0-8020-9332-5 (bound). – ISBN 978-0-8020-9500-8 (pbk.)

1. Women – Government policy – Canada – History – 20th century.
2. Women – Canada – Economic conditions.   3. Poverty – Canada –
History – 20th century.   4. Feminism – Canada – History – 20th century.
5. Canada – Social policy.   I. Cohen, Marjorie Griffin, 1944–
II. Pulkingham, Jane

HQ1236.5.C2P82 2009   362.830971   C2008-906585-9

University of Toronto Press acknowledges the financial assistance to its
publishing program of the Canada Council for the Arts and the Ontario
Arts Council.

University of Toronto Press acknowledges the financial support for its
publishing activities of the Government of Canada through the Book
Publishing Industry Development Program (BPIDP).

This book is dedicated to Linda Sperling (trade unionist) and Michelle Swenarchuk (lawyer), two feminists who worked courageously throughout their lives for public policy changes.

Contents

PART TWO: REIMAGINING INCOME SECURITY FOR THE MOST VULNERABLE

PART THREE: RETHINKING LABOUR MARKET AND EMPLOYMENT SUPPORT POLICY

Preface

This book arises from research associated with the Economic Security Project (ESP). The ESP is a multiyear research initiative funded by the Social Sciences and Humanities Research Council's grant to foster a 'Community-University Research Alliance' (CURA). The principle partners in the CURA are the Women's Studies Department at Simon Fraser University and the Canadian Centre for Policy Alternatives-B.C. Twenty-three academic and twenty-three community-based researchers are involved in the five-year ESP.

The main purpose of the ESP is to understand the changes that have occurred with the conservative shift in public policy in British Columbia and in Canada and to understand the implications of these changes for vulnerable populations. The initial phases of the project worked to examine the extent of the changes and their effects on specific groups with the intent of ultimately proposing policy alternatives that would best meet the economic security needs of these groups.

Most of the chapters in this book were presented and discussed at the ESP's first conference in Vancouver entitled 'Imagining Public Policy for Women.' About 250 women from across Canada and from other countries attended the conference and discussed the features of public policy objectives that would be appropriate for meeting women's economic security needs in the twenty-first century. This was the first time in a great many years that a large national event in Canada seriously discussed the public policy crisis facing women. The intent of the conference, as well as the book, was to 'imagine' and analyse effective public policy for women. While some critique of existing policy inevitably occurs, the main point is to try to advance a progressive agenda for the future.

The authors are grateful to the SSHRC for its funding for the ESP and the work involved in producing this book. We also would like to acknowledge the funding for the conference received from the SSHRC, the Women's Studies Department and the Vice-President Academic at Simon Fraser University, the funding received from Status of Women Canada to bring women to the conference, and the organizational help received from the CCPA-B.C. We would particularly like to thank Thi Vu (ESP Project Manager) and Seth Klein (CCPA-B.C., ESP co-director with Marjorie Griffin Cohen), for their support for this project, and the many student and community-based researchers who helped with specific research projects in this book. Margaret Manery has provided the index and has piloted the edition through to its completion and we thank her for her gracious and expert help.

Contributors

Stephanie Baker Collins, Associate Professor, School of Social Work, York University, focuses her research on social policy, poverty, and women's provisioning work. Her research examines the impact of policies on the lives of the poorest persons in society and includes their participation in her research and works for changes in public policy that affect the quality of their lives.

Shauna Butterwick is an adult educator, researcher, and Associate Professor in the Department of Educational Studies at the University of British Columbia. Much of her research has focused on women's learning, particularly in relation to paid work, and the enabling and disabling aspect of policies and programs.

Lea Caragata is an Associate Professor at Wilfrid Laurier University teaching in the areas of social policy and community development, including marginalization and oppression, and most recently is focused on labour market changes and welfare state retrenchment. She is the Principal Investigator on a Community University Research Alliances (CURA) project funded by SSHRC.

Marjorie Griffin Cohen is an Economist and Professor of Political Science and Women's Studies at Simon Fraser University. She writes on various issues dealing with the Canadian economy, public policy, women, labour, international trade agreements, and deregulation of the electricity sector.

Penny Gurstein is a Professor and Director of the School of Community and Regional Planning at the University of British Columbia. She specializes in the sociocultural aspects of community planning with particular emphasis on those who are the most marginalized in planning processes.

Jill Hanley, Assistant Professor, McGill School of Social Work, is a researcher and community activist whose work has concentrated on community organizing around immigration and antipoverty issues. Her current research explores access to social rights (labour, health, social services) for migrants with precarious immigration status, as well as migrants' collective strategies to improve their social conditions.

Olena Hankivsky is an Associate Professor in the Public Policy Program and Co-director of the Institute for Critical Studies in Gender and Health at Simon Fraser University. She specializes in gender and social and health policy and is the author of *Social Policy and the Ethic of Care* (2004) and co-editor of *Women's Health in Canada: Critical Perspectives on Theory and Policy* (2007).

Andrew Jackson is National Director of Social and Economic Policy with the Canadian Labour Congress and author of the 2005 book, *Work and Labour in Canada: Critical Issues*. He is also a Research Professor in Political Economy at Carleton University, and a Fellow of the School of Policy Studies at Queen's University.

Jane Jenson holds the Canadian Research Chair in Citizenship and Governance at the Université de Montréal, where she is professor of Political Science. She was elected a Fellow of the Royal Society of Canada in 1989. Her research interests cover social citizenship and policy change in Canada and Europe.

Lee Lakeman works with the collective at Vancouver Rape Relief and Women's Shelter and with the Canadian Association of Sexual Assault Centres (CASAC). A front-line worker since 1973, she also served as chair of the NAC Committee Against Male Violence and recently authored *Obsession, with Intent, Violence against Women*, an account of five years of research conducted by CASAC.

Martha MacDonald teaches economics at Saint Mary's University. Her research areas include gender and economic restructuring, income security policy, work-life balance, and gender and restructuring in rural resource-based communities in Atlantic Canada. She is President (2007) of the International Association for Feminist Economics.

Wendy McKeen is an Associate Professor at the School of Social Work, York University, where she teaches in the areas of Canadian social policy and social justice issues. Her current research focuses on the politics of welfare and single mothers in Ontario.

Arlene Tigar McLaren is a Professor Emerita of Sociology in the Department of Sociology and Anthropology and an Associate Member of the Department of Women's Studies at Simon Fraser University. She is also a Research Associate of the Canadian Centre for Policy Alternatives. Her areas of specialization focus on feminist sociology and critical policy studies (education, family, immigration, health, labour, and transportation).

Margaret Menton Manery, who has a master's degree in political science from Simon Fraser University, is an independent researcher. She has conducted post-graduate research for various organizations in British Columbia and most recently for the Columbia Institute on the *Implications of Banning Mandatory Retirement for Low- and Medium-Income Workers*.

Sheila Neysmith, Faculty of Social Work, University of Toronto, has published extensively on how policies affect the caring labour that women do. Her books include: *Telling Tales: Living the Effects of Public Policy; Restructuring Caring Labour: Discourse, State Practice and Everyday Life; Critical Issues for Future Social Work Practice with Aging Persons and Women's Caring: Feminist Perspectives on Social Welfare*.

Elaine Porter is an Associate Professor of Sociology at Laurentian University in Sudbury, Ontario. She specializes in the sociology of the family. Her research includes a study of women's workload as they managed the effects of their spouse's permanent lay-off in a single-industry mining town. Recently she has published on the obstacles faced and strategies used by women entrepreneurs in India.

Jane Pulkingham is Associate Professor of Sociology and Chair of the Department of Sociology and Anthropology at Simon Fraser University.

Her research interests are in critical policy studies focusing on: gender and the state, welfare state restructuring and inequality, women and income security, and poverty studies.

Marge Reitsma-Street is a Professor in Studies of Policy and Practice in the Faculty of Human and Social Development at the University of Victoria. She is also the Principal Investigator of the WEDGE Women, Provisioning and Community Research Project funded by SSHRC. Her scholarship and activism are in the areas of poverty, housing for women, community organizations, and women's work.

Eric Shragge is an Associate Professor and Principal of the School of Community and Public Affairs, Concordia University. His teaching, research, and writing areas include community organizing and social policy. He is active in the Immigrant Workers' Centre in Montreal.

Diane-Gabrielle Tremblay is Canada Research Chair on the Socio-organizational Challenges of the Knowledge Economy, co-chair of the Bell Chair on Technology and Work Organization, and is a Professor at Télé-université, Université du Québec à Montréal.

Emily van der Meulen is a doctoral candidate in Women's Studies at York University, Toronto. She is also a board member at Canada's oldest sex worker-run organization, Maggie's: The Toronto Prostitutes' Community Service Project. Her dissertation is an action research study of sex work policy and labour organizing in Toronto.

Silvia Vilches is a Ph.D. Candidate in the School of Community and Regional Planning at the University of British Columbia and CIHR Strategic Training Fellow, Public Health and Agriculture Rural Ecosytem (PHARE).

Leah F. Vosko is Canada Research Chair in Feminist Political Economy, York University, Toronto. She is author of articles and books, including *Temporary Work: The Gendered Rise of a Precarious Employment Relationship* (2000), *Self-Employed Workers Organize: Law, Policy and Unions* (with Cynthia Cranford, Judy Fudge, and Eric Tucker) (2005), and editor of *Precarious Employment: Understanding Labour Market Insecurity in Canada* (2006).

Margot Young is an Associate Professor in the Faculty of Law at the University of British Columbia. She teaches and writes in the areas of constitutional law, equality rights and theory, and social welfare law. Her latest publication is as co-editor of the volume entitled *Poverty: Rights, Social Citizenship and Legal Activism* (2007).

PART ONE

Restructuring Public Policy in the Canadian State

Introduction: Going Too Far? Feminist Public Policy in Canada

MARJORIE GRIFFIN COHEN AND JANE PULKINGHAM

Soon after the B.C. Liberal government was elected in 2001, it proceeded with what was widely perceived to be a targeting of women through its initiative to improve 'flexibility' in government industries. The most dramatic event was the mass firing of hospital support staff (laundry, cleaning, and food services workers) and the tearing up of their negotiated collective agreement.[1] This was the first time in Canada that a government had passed legislation to set aside completely a properly negotiated collective agreement in the public sector, and it resulted in the largest firing of women in Canadian labour history: about 8,000 workers, who were disproportionately women of colour, older women, and immigrant women, lost their public sector health care jobs (Cohen and Cohen 2004).[2] The public was outraged and throughout the province support for the workers was strong – even from unlikely sectors (like unions comprised of mostly male workers in the private sector). Nevertheless, the government succeeded with this attack on women,[3] continually justifying itself by saying that spending on health care was out of control and that the cost of hospital support work was too high.[4] The B.C. government's general message was that labour relations needed to be 'modernized' to make work more 'flexible' in order to reverse a notion that 'labour relations hinder investment' in British Columbia (Fairey 2005: 11). Modernization and flexibility, when translated into the specifics of this case, meant reversing all of the equal pay gains that women hospital support workers had made through the collective bargaining process over twenty years.[5]

This blatant targeting of women was not an isolated incident in Canada, and while it was one of the most egregious examples of a government's attempt to unravel the progress women had made since the

1970s, it is illustrative of the shift in government thinking about women and public policy in Canada that has occurred since the mid-1980s[6] (Bashevkin 1998; Bezanson 2006; Brodie 1996). How did this change come about? More importantly, does this signify a permanent change – tantamount to a shift in a 'gender order' in Canada in the twenty-first century, as is frequently asserted to be occurring in other countries affected by neoliberal globalism (Sharp and Broomhill 2007; Sainsbury 1999)? This introduction will try to answer these questions, and their implications for future public policy for women. It will examine the dominant approaches to public policy in Canada, how and to what extent these approaches changed to accommodate the distinct needs of women, and subsequently, how gendered-based policy capacity has been influenced by the dictates of neoliberal ideological and economic policy choices. It also will explain the economic and political forces that have undermined the gains women made in the last quarter of the twentieth century and try to indicate where positive directions for change are likely.

Public Policy

There is an important distinction to be made between public policy and social policy. One workable definition of public policy is 'whatever governments choose to do or not to do' (Dye 1978). Two issues related to this definition are crucial for understanding public policy and women. First, both acting and not acting constitute public policy, and not acting is more often than not the public policy approach of governments towards meeting women's needs. Not acting itself can be either a conscious or unconscious decision. When governments decide not to institute a progressive policy that is available elsewhere (like pay equity or universal day care), this is a conscious decision. Canadian governments today are more likely to reject in an automatic way (i.e., without reflection, in an 'unconscious' way) calls for any type of policy decision that affects what are considered to be systemic problems. Problems that are systemic in nature are those that are not a result of isolated inappropriate behaviours towards a specific group, but are built into the way the entire system is constructed. The inequalities that result are consistent and recurring and appear to defy minor adjustments through specific policy initiatives directed at their amelioration.

Addressing systemic issues usually requires many-pronged initiatives that are beyond the scope most politicians want to tackle – unless they are forced to through some kind of sea change in thinking. In this

case the term 'unconscious' may be less appropriate than 'studied ignorance.' The latter is a term that Sheila McIntyre (2000) used to describe
the reaction of administrators at the University of British Columbia that
allowed them to deny and ignore issues of racism and sexism that were
uncovered in the Political Science Department. What she means is that
by refusing to recognize systemic injustice and the way entire structures
support unjust actions, and by insisting that any claims of injustice can
only be narrowly interpreted and substantiated through specific accusations of individual persons' actions, those in power can conveniently
ignore the enormity of the real issue. Although McIntyre was specifically talking about the power structures in academic institutions, the
observations about 'studied ignorance' are equally appropriate to the
way that governments are inclined to behave with regard to women
and disadvantaged minorities. When the problem is the result of how
a large system functions, rather than the behaviour of an individual,
governments, with 'studied ignorance,' are able to see no discrimination – so nothing can be done.

The second important issue with regard to the definition of public
policy as it relates to women is that public policy includes all that governments do – social policy, military policy, economic policy, immigration policy, labour policy, environmental policy, and all of the myriad
types of policies that deal with day-to-day living. It is important to
emphasize that these are all women's issues and have been treated as
women's issues by feminist movements in Canada (Bashevkin 1991).
Over time, feminists in Canada, as elsewhere, shifted their emphasis
'from making women in welfare states visible in the analysis to gender
as a dimension of the analysis' (O'Connor 1996: 104). Governments in
this country, however, have been most comfortable with women's demands when they focus on what governments themselves perceive to
be 'women's issues.' These include things like education, health care,
violence against women, child care, equal pay, social assistance, abortion: issues that are more readily defined as related to social policy.
Women are 'going too far,' and their views are much less welcome,
when they recognize that the impact of policies that have made Canada
pursue specific neoliberal directions restrict genuine collective choices
about how to live in this country. These wider issues include Canada's
relationships with the rest of the world, governments' perceptions of
how to best serve the interests of corporations, and who is in control of
decision-making at all levels of government; that is, the democratic or
undemocratic nature of all decision-making.

Policy for Women – Background

For the period from the early 1970s to the beginning of the 1990s Canada had one of the most vibrant and effective national feminist movements in the world (Rebick 2005). It was exceptional in its ability to make feminist issues prominent in national, provincial, and local debates and to bring about changes in public policy so that women's distinct conditions and needs could be recognized.[7] This is why, according to Janine Brodie, Canada became a leader in Western countries "in the development of policies and agencies designed to enhance the status of women in all sectors of society and to provide them with points of entry into the policy-making process" (2007: 167). This feminist success required the ability to organize, but it also required two related factors for feminist organization to be effective: (1) the detailed knowledge of the conditions that women in different kinds of circumstances face in their everyday lives and (2) a vision of what was needed in public policy and in other realms to improve conditions for women living under different types of situations. The research that mapped the problems with existing public policy – problems that reinforced the patriarchal and unequal nature of Canadian society – brought women's issues to the public consciousness. This unmasking of the problems began in a structured way with the Royal Commission on the Status of Women (RCSW), which issued its report in 1970. At the time the 167 recommendations of this Commission were perceived (correctly) to threaten the power of established privileged groups in Canada. Its recommendations for social policy changes included paid maternity leave, abortion when needed, a national day care program, pensions and paid vacations for housewives, a guaranteed annual income for all one-parent families, liberalization of divorce laws, equal pay, equal job and promotion opportunities, and an end to sex-stereotyping in the classroom (Cohen 1993: 35). The Commission did not however, call for wholesale shifts in the structures of Canada's economic and political systems, and because of this was criticized by many feminists who understood that the root of the problem of achieving genuine equality was bound to a system that was structured to perpetuate inequality. Although initially the work of the Commission was treated as an expensive joke by most of the country's journalists and politicians (Newman 1969), the detailing of the unequal conditions that women faced initiated a long-term and serious project that was carried out by popular sector groups, like the National Action Committee on the Status of Women (NAC),[8] the National Association of Women and the Law (NAWL), Women's Legal Education and Action Fund (LEAF), the Canadian Abortion Rights League (CARAL), the Canadian Day Care Advocacy Association, provincial Status of Women groups, the federal government's Status of Women Canada,[9] specific issue groups (dealing with topics like violence against women), and various individual researchers in academic institutions, many trade unions, and community groups who represented either specific locations or groups of women.

As the most blatant unfairness of Canadian legislation and public policy was exposed, slowly public policy was forced to shift to recognize women's interests in some areas. This happened largely because the political situation was ripe for feminist changes. Feminist ideas were thriving in North America and Europe, with a mutually reinforcing effect on governments. In large part this was a result of the expanding provision of social services that began after the Second World War and the justification by John Maynard Keynes' economic theories of the beneficial effect that would ensue from governments' direct involvement in the economy. With the memory of the misery of the Great Depression, an economic disaster that was exaggerated because of orthodox economic analysis that promoted balanced budgets and reduced government expenditures, governments in the postwar period were emboldened to not only tax and spend, but also sometimes to create debt in order to confront periodic economic underperformance and to stimulate growth in a permanent way. This allowed a great many social services to be instituted, and in the process of their creation and an expanding economy, feminist ideas gained some currency.

In the United States, Betty Friedan's (1963) book, *The Feminine Mystique*, and the President's *Roundtable on Women* set in motion a powerful surge that served as a 'demonstration effect' for Canada's governments to begin to take women's issues seriously.[10] Then, as now, U.S. government approaches were a legitimizing example for Canada to move into new areas. Ultimately, however, it was the actions of women in Canada who were demanding change, as became all too evident through the hearings of the Royal Commission on the Status of Women, and it was these women who provided the vision for what was needed in Canada (Vickers, Rankin, and Appelle 1993).

The patriarchal nature of Canadian society was an obvious target for initial action, and early efforts to change public policy in the 1970s focused on reducing outright and outrageous discrimination against women: overt discrimination and the sheer unfairness of the way competition was supposed to work was the first target for action. This is in contrast to both earlier public policy approaches to women, which tended to deal with women as residual citizens or casualties of life, and later initiatives, which tried to focus on the more systemic nature of women's disadvantage and press for substantive equality (Radbord 2004).

Focusing on women's distinct needs – particularly as mothers or women needing protection – had long been a feature of social policy related to women. The very meagre social assistance that was introduced first in local governments in Canada helped destitute women, particularly those who were widows with children. Minimum wage laws were originally enacted during the First World War (Ramkhalawansingh 1974), and became a permanent feature of labour policy during the Great Depression of the 1930s: these minimum wage laws applied only to women and girls, those perceived to be the most exploited groups in the labour force, and only later were they extended to men (Guest 1980). At various times day care was initiated for a small number of destitute mothers who were expected to work, only becoming more generally available to working mothers during the Second World War, when the war effort desperately needed female labour: these day care services were withdrawn immediately after the war, when men returned and women were expected to take their traditional place in the home (Pierson 1986; Stephen 2007).

Both in the early and postwar periods the focus of social policy for women was built on principles that relied heavily on individual self-sufficiency and the assumption that, under most circumstances, women would be dependent on males. In this sense, the male became the archetype for the design of 'universal' social policy, and when women conformed to this archetype, they too would be beneficiaries of the public policy. This was particularly evident in employment-based programs, such as Unemployment Insurance (now Employment Insurance) and the Canada Pension Plan (Porter 2003). But the establishment of universal access to some types of social benefits, such as education, health care, and old age pensions was particularly beneficial to women, and is one of the reasons feminist groups have continually supported maintaining and providing more universal programs.

Early public policy for women had its mean and controlling side: public policy almost always relates to moral notions of the appropriate ways for women to live and behave at particular points of time (Little 1998). The moral codes are usually unstated, but serve as far-reaching rules that inform the nature of public policy: they include all of the hierarchies, racial prejudices, sexism, and other prejudices that function as common sense at a particular point in time. Some of the most shameful and oppressive policies focused on the most disadvantaged women and included actions like the apprehending of Aboriginal children and the sterilization of those women considered a burden on the state or inappropriate mothers. The eugenics movement is a good example of the way public policy could be affected by ideas of the time: it embodied distinct notions of what constituted a healthy or intelligent individual who should be allowed to procreate, and this usually affected those marginalized by the dominant population with specific emphasis on excluding the disabled, Aboriginal women, those with addictions, and the poor from having children. It was a movement that became part of public policy in many places in the country because it was based on accepted notions of 'common sense' about what was 'normal.' Eugenics was so widespread a notion that it attracted support even from some avowed feminists and progressive political leaders[11] (McLaren 1990).

Even when the policies were not blatantly punitive, the state's ability to control through its policy initiatives was the downside of programs designed to alleviate hardship for some groups. This enabling, but controlling nature of the welfare state is part of the struggle that women have with initiating social policy, and it is a topic that is continually debated by feminists interested in political tactics (Evans and Wekerle 1997). Nevertheless, however much the patriarchal structure and nature of the welfare state is recognized and criticized, it is through the programs of the welfare state that women in North America and Europe have been able to see some progress towards social and redistributive justice. As Elizabeth Wilson notes, in one of the first books written on women and the welfare state, despite the "ambivalent nature of welfare provision under capitalism, nevertheless an inadequate or punitive social security minimum is preferable to no minimum at all" (1977: 39).

Welfare State

The welfare state was a feature of Canada's public life before a strong feminist movement could insist that meeting women's needs should be as central to the functioning of modern society as meeting men's needs. The rise of the welfare state in the period after the Second World War greatly accelerated the areas of the state's involvement in social life – to increase the 'welfare' of the population. It was not a static institution either initially or subsequently, but was continually negotiated, and shifted shape to accommodate the needs of the public, but also with the interests of the most dominant groups in mind. The capitalist system in Canada was in very sorry shape before the beginning of the war. The prolonged economic crisis of the 1930s, which only ended with the economic stimulus of war, was indicative of how little a nation could rely on the actions and interests of the corporate private sector to ensure economic stability and to provide an economy that functioned well enough to employ most of those who needed work. That is, the capitalist class after the Second World War, when the foundations of the welfare state were being set, was not in a position to make great demands on the state to formulate social policy in its interests. It is not that the institution of the welfare state at this stage was perceived to be a hindrance to the capitalist class in Canada. Crown corporations, for example, provided public funding for establishing an infrastructure that was too ambitious and expensive for the private sector, but one that this sector, in particular, needed. This included public hydroelectric projects, airlines, railroads, ports, and highways, but also a social infrastructure that would educate a workforce and maintain the workers and their families when the private sector had less need for labour and one that would provide benefits, such as health care, that the private sector would or could not fund.

Most significant was the shift in the very role of the state: its role now would encompass the social in a way that radically distinguished it from other periods.[12] How this would be done and by which level of government, provincial or federal, was a constant issue. Many provinces, during the Great Depression, were unable to afford to provide essential public services, yet most social services were the responsibility of the provincial governments, not the federal government. The Rowell-Sirois Royal Commission of 1937 examined these issues: it recommended establishing a national standard for social programs and suggested a way for the federal government to equalize the fiscal capacity of the provinces. Both issues were crucial to the subsequent shape of the welfare state in Canada (Rice and Prince 2000). Without some kind of equalization between the provinces, the idea of national standards in social programs simply could not be realized.

The social security system that developed in the postwar period was based on a series of reports, including the one that is considered to be the most influential, *The Report on Social Security for Canada* by Leonard Marsh (1943 [1975]), and focused on six main areas: unemployment, health care, disability, retirement, old age, and income support for families with children. Once the national health care system came into being, in 1968, the major features of the social security network were in place. Women's entitlement to the benefits of the various programs tended to be distinct from that of men, a feature of social policy that became a point of contention at various times. Unemployment Insurance (UI), for example, while initially available to anyone covered who lost a job, was eliminated for married women in the early 1950s. This occasioned a fierce campaign to have married women reinstated, a campaign championed by Conservative MP Ellen Fairclough in the House of Commons and supported by CCF MP Stanley Knowles. Yet, even in later years when married women had been reinstated, the UI system, by being designed around the characteristics of work more normally associated with male labour force participation (full-time, full-year work), provided many women with less coverage and smaller benefits than those received by most men (Evans 1997). The Family Allowance, introduced federally in 1945 for families with children, was distinct from other major programs because it provided allowances that were paid only to mothers.[13] Commonly referred to as the 'baby bonus,' it went through various incarnations until it ultimately included a monthly payment for all children in Canada under the age of 18 years (including Inuit and Indian children, who had been excluded until 1947). The important feature of the Family Allowance is that it was a universal program, paid each month for each child: for many women it was the only income they received. This was a taxable benefit (by 1992 worth $35 per child per month), but unlike any other taxable benefits, although it was paid to the mother, the tax was paid by the highest-income parental earner in the family, which was almost always the father. Although all other features of the early social welfare system remain in place today, if in a changed form, the Family Allowance was abolished by Brian Mulroney's Conservative government in 1992.[14]

The development of the mature welfare state, that is, the period when programs were expanded and more groups were included as having legitimate claims on the benefits of social citizenship – was a relatively short period. Basically it grew from 1945 until the mid-1980s, or for about forty years. During this time ideas about appropriate social claims for women expanded considerably. This was significant for the following reasons: (1) the notion of which groups could rightfully lay claims to social citizenship expanded; (2) women's social contributions, which had been systematically devalued, began to be recognized;

and (3) ideas about equality shifted from formal ones, in the sense that equality implied identical treatment, to substantive ones that focused more on outcomes than on processes.

Inclusion in Social Citizenship

As many feminist analysts have noted, the exclusions from the benefits of the welfare state privileged men over women, but also some groups of women over others. These privileges normally related to social class and racial hierarchies; however, they could also be related to other factors such as age, ethnicity, ability or disability, place of birth, and location of residence. Formally excluded from the protections of citizenship at various times were Aboriginal women, who were governed by a different set of laws, and immigrants, who did not have full civil and political protections (Stasiulis and Bakan 2005). Women in Quebec were formally excluded from provincial citizenship, by not being allowed to vote until 1940. Even more women were excluded, however, when 'social citizenship' is the measure by which the state's actions are judged. Social citizenship is distinguished from citizenship itself in that it extends the obligations of the state beyond political and civil rights. This can be understood as the obligation of people collectively, through the state, to ensure that material conditions exist for all people to live full lives and to have the means to participate within the wider community.[15] Social exclusion and outright deprivation are the usual results of circumstances where the state fails to provide the benefits of social citizenship to all groups and individuals. Understanding who is excluded and in what ways from the benefits of social citizenship has been a major task of feminist political analysis and action. Initially this action focused on achieving gains for the generic 'woman.' The advances both in law and in social policy were considerable, although certainly not sufficient, in recognizing that people are being excluded from the protections of citizenship and social citizenship because of their group identity and that this exclusion is wrong (Young et al. 2007).

To make public policy more inclusive it was crucial to build a policy capacity within government that is able to analyse policy from a gender perspective (Brodie 2007; Chappell 2002). This process gained considerable strength, as ideas about social policy and social citizenship became more prominent, and government's knowledge of women's issues needed to be developed.

Recognizing the Distinct Contributions and Needs of Women

Social inclusion of women in general, and of distinct groups of women in particular, requires the recognition that women contribute to society in significant ways that are not usually recognized in public policy. Particularly important is the understanding that women in different circumstances , such as older women or immigrant women, have distinct needs. 'Social reproduction' is the term now frequently used to refer to the labour involved in the daily and long-term maintenance and reproduction of the population (Crossman and Fudge 2002; Bezanson and Luxton 2006). Historically, the contribution of women to 'social reproduction,' has been implicitly recognized in many social policies, particularly those that based benefits on family units. Women have been frequently termed 'dependents'; however, behind this term lay the assumption that women's household work is a contribution to the family and, in this sense, essential and that these women, therefore, could not be expected to work outside the household.[16] The concept of the 'family wage' included in it a notion that the family was an economic and social unit with a paid worker (almost always male) and an unpaid worker (inevitably female). Labour-related public policy, for example, recognized this type of family structure, and through it privileged male work in the benefit schemes of various types of programs, usually by paying those with 'dependents' more than they paid those without 'dependents.'

Two issues brought about significant changes in thinking about benefits associated with family obligations and the family wage. One relates to shifts in the economic base in society, which resulted in a massive increase in married women's labour force participation after the 1960s. Married women returned to the household immediately after the Second World War, after their unprecedented labour force participation during the war; however, because of the dramatic changes in the economies of capitalist countries in the West, this return was temporary. Capitalist economies grew dramatically during the 1950s and 1960s, and this growth required ever more labour. At the same time, the nature of the economy was changing, from one dominated by manufacturing and primary industries to one where the services sector gained prominence. Much of this change was a result of the marketization of many economic activities that until then had been household-based. The obvious changes related to more market-oriented food and clothing preparation, but also to the increase in the marketization of caregiving: the tasks related to the care of the household in general, but also specifically the tasks related to care of the ill, the elderly, and children. Some of the increased demand for labour was provided through immigration. The need for labour was immense, however, and the latent female labour force within households was the most obvious source for meeting this need. Hiring women had the specific advantage of also keeping labour costs down: the cost of women's labour was less than the cost of men's labour, even when women were doing the same work. The large supply of female workers potentially available managed to keep male wages from rising too rapidly. Women's massive entry into the labour force highlighted their unequal treatment as workers and stimulated public policy to eliminate differential pay between men and women.[17]

As women with dependents themselves increasingly became part of the labour force, the second important factor in changing attitudes towards women and social policy came to the fore: change in ideas about care work.[18] The value of the care work that women perform in the household and in the marketized sector became more visible, albeit largely through the efforts of feminists to have its significance recognized in public policy (Corman and Luxton 2007). Feminists, both in scholarly analysis and in political action, demonstrated the strong relationship between care work and the general economy, with a specific focus on the ways that the economy benefited from women's unpaid labour in taking care of the personal needs of people (Armstrong and Armstrong 1994; Luxton 1980). More recently the focus on care work and public policy has put emphasis on the poor conditions of paid care work done by immigrant women in Canadian households and institutions, as well as on the lack of recognition of the unpaid work of mothers on social assistance (Arat-Koc 2002; Young et al. 2007). Feminist analysis is emphatic about the ways that public policy does not recognize the reality of care work, either in the private or the public sphere, and how this lack of recognition places unfair burdens on women who perform this work, and thereby harms society more generally.

Substantive Equality

Social policy towards women has also been affected by shifts in ideas about equality, which have expanded from 'formal equality' (the strictly equal treatment of men and women) to notions of 'substantive equality.' The elimination of discriminatory language in laws was accomplished during the early 1980s, but this in itself did not mean that government policy became more egalitarian. As the feminist movement grew, it became more knowledgeable, experienced, and effective, and through these changes it also changed its understanding of the roots of unfair treatment of women in public policy. Substantive equality gradually became a significant objective: one that would not simply accept 'equal opportunity' as a goal, but rather, recognized that the choices people make are conditioned by social constraints that do not make opportunities equal.

The push for substantive equality took ideas about women's contributions to society, which require distinct treatment, and wove them together with a wider understanding of how equality needs to be more than a process. Equality requires substantive outcomes. This idea was harder to institute in public policy than was the idea of 'equal opportunity,' because instituting substantive equality means recognizing that social and economic structures have been built with inequality as an inherent component in their design. Nevertheless, there were some significant breakthroughs that allowed people to talk about 'systemic discrimination' within institutions, and that ultimately led to some changes in policy within the institutions, and even within the state itself. The problem with this, though, is that systemic discrimination is extremely difficult to prove in law, because as has been frequently noted, systemic discrimination is the 'norm,' making it hard to demonstrate the relationship between patterns of inequality and structures (Buckley 2007; McIntyre 2000).[19]

Public policy did change in significant ways, for a variety of reasons. These reasons are connected to the changes in the economy, the political activism of women, and changes in ideas about what just policies for women would look like, and all of these affected changes over time in the cultural norms of society. Advances were made in the economic security of women, in claims for social citizenship, their demands for distinct treatment for women who are disadvantaged because of their cultural histories, and legal support for a more substantive justice. Particularly important in establishing a more women-oriented public policy was building the analysis of public policy within the feminist movement, but so was developing a gender-based policy apparatus within government (Brodie 2007; Chappell 2002). Both of these capacities were critically affected by the neoliberal ideology that has pervaded Canadian public policy since the mid-1980s. Initially associated with Brian Mulroney's Progressive Conservative government, these neoliberal ideas persisted and even intensified throughout the Liberal governments of Jean Chrétien and Paul Martin, and were further deepened with Stephen Harper's Conservative government. This persistence of neoliberal policies indicates that the neoliberal shift is deeply rooted and not simply associated with a particular political party in Canada, or with an economic downturn.

Neoliberal Globalism[20] and Public Policy

Neoliberalism refers to a set of policies, ideas, and practices (Larner 2000) associated with a particular Western philosophy of governance that shapes state, civil society, and market relations (Brodie 2002; Kingfisher 2002). Neoliberal ideology, rooted in a philosophy of liberal individualism, rests in the theory that the best approach to securing and protecting human well-being is through individual economic and social freedoms and that state interventions in market activities should be kept to a minimum (Harvey 2005: 2). Neoliberalism was put into practice in the early 1980s in the United Kingdom through Margaret Thatcher's governments and in the United States beginning when Ronald Reagan was elected President. Initially neoliberalism was pursued in opposition to Keynesian-era policy and governance and as a return to pre-Keynesian approaches. The primary focus of neoliberalism continues to be to change the nature of government. It is accomplished through various policies such as: the use of monetary policy to deal with inflation, rather than levels of employment; the privatization of institutions in the public sector, reducing regulation of the private sector; reducing the power of trade unions and other popular sector groups; and redesigning government social programs to reduce their cost and scope.

This Western neoliberal approach to both economic and social policies increasingly became part of a world order. It began initially through Structural Adjustment Policies forced on poor counties by institutions such as the World Bank and the International Monetary Fund (Benería 2003). These neoliberal notions to promote the private sector and constrain governments were extended on a global scale to include industrialized countries through what is often referred to as the Washington Consensus (Cohen and Clarkson 2004). This supposed 'consensus' used international trade agreements like the North American Free Trade Agreement (NAFTA) and the World Trade Organization (WTO) to codify neoliberal policy. Today neoliberal discourse permeates all levels of government policies within nations and affects not only economic policy, but also all issues dealing with the social.

The initial neoliberal shift in Canada appeared to be based more in economic than in social policy. This relatively soft neoliberalism indicated to some analysts a certain resilience of the welfare state in Canada that was distinct from what was occurring in the United States – a resilience attributed to Canada's historical support for government intervention in social programs and the economy (Mishra 1990; Myles 1988). Canada's governments aggressively pursued neoliberal economic policies from the mid-1980s and began to assess their actions mainly on whether they would be good or bad for business interests. Canada, however, had a social safety net that the public supported, and it seemed clear the electorate would not condone the direct privatization of public services, a reduction in public funding for them, or their outright elimination. In hindsight, this relaxed notion of the implications of neoliberalism on social citizenship and the welfare state demonstrated an optimism that could not be sustained as the neoliberal program unfolded.[21] The shift in the state's actions from anything resembling its historical role of mediating between competing interests in public policy initiatives was profound: governments resolutely embarked on radical restructuring in the interests of the corporate sector. The political strategy was to proceed cautiously on an incremental basis in the reshaping of social policy, while simultaneously asserting the good intentions of government towards supporting social services. Initially even business interests talked about neoliberal measures as ways of strengthening the economy to provide services for people in the future, although this type of rhetoric was later abandoned, once the idea that business interests should be paramount in policy initiatives became more ingrained in governments' subconscious. It became clear that the priorities of neoliberal economic structures would have negative implications for the way women and other vulnerable populations would be treated in public policy.

The tactics that governments and business interests used to redirect public policy towards neoliberal objectives were fairly obvious in their intent. The major strategy was to create a crisis that needed a solution, and through this process of fixing a purported problem, governments were able to institute substantial changes that the public did not want. For example, the 'crisis' of inadequate access to U.S. markets was the justification for entering the first free trade agreement with the United States, while the spectre of the United States making Mexico its major trading partner justified the negotiation of the North American Free Trade Agreement (NAFTA). Government debt was the primary crisis that drove a major campaign to convince the public that Canada could not afford its 'expensive' social programs. This was the message despite the fact that the costs of social programs were not the reason that the government's debt had escalated.[22] At the same time, business interests managed to convince governments that their taxes were too high and that this approached a crisis that affected their ability to be competitive in international markets. The result was a focus on tax reductions, resulting in further calls for cutbacks in social programs and privatization initiatives. Currently negotiations over 'deep integration' with the United States are in process because Canada is said to have a crisis with regard to its level of productivity and it must become more efficient: the aim of these negotiations is the harmonization of major policies between the two countries (Grinspun and Shamsie 2007; Dobson 2002).[23]

A great deal has been written about the effects of neoliberal globalism and restructuring on women and much about its specific impact on women in Canada (Bakker 1996; Bashevkin 1998; Day and Brodsky 1998; Crossman and Fudge 2002). The intent here is not to provide a detailed list of the policy changes that have occurred, because they are massive, but rather to touch on some of the major changes and to indicate the strategies that governments have used to institute them. The erosion of social programs began with a major federal budget initiative under the Mulroney government in 1985 to cut the size of the civil service (affecting primarily women workers), cut allocations to various social programs (including the first steps in the abandonment of the federal government's role in social housing), and to begin the process of the privatization of public assets. These kinds of initiatives were accompanied over the next ten years by increasing and continual tax cuts, particularly for corporations and higher-income individuals, and replacing these with increases in various kinds of sales taxes. By 1990 the politically punitive aspect of government changes became obvious through their focus on feminist activists who were opposing the governments' neoliberal policies. In that year the federal government severely cut grants to advocacy groups and funding for women's programs within government (Burt 1995; Cohen 1997). Women's centres that provided front-line social support to vulnerable women were closed around the country. These funding cuts, both within government and to community-based women's organizations, restricted women's communication networks, making critical opposition much more difficult.[24]

These kinds of budget initiatives, indicating the government's neo-liberal policy directions, were supported by a major shift in the federal government's financial arrangements with the provinces. This occurred when Paul Martin ended the Canada Assistance Plan Act (CAP) in 1996, replacing it with the Canada Health and Social Transfer (CHST), followed in 1999 with the establishment of a Social Union Framework Agreement that set the parameters for the relationship between the federal government and the provinces and territories regarding social program negotiations (Cameron 2007; Mosher 2007). These changes greatly affected the way that social programs within provinces were treated because they had an impact on both the level of funding and the ability to have 'national standards' in social programs. While 'national standards,' which had ensured that Canadians across the country received similar treatment within social programs, formally continued to exist, the shift in the nature of the share of federal government funding of the programs crucially affected federal government monitoring and control over national standards. The change in funding consisted of both a drastic reduction in the direct (cash) contribution of the federal government to provincial social program funding and a shift in the nature of funding so that it was not tied to specific programs.[25] The federal government basically gave away its ability to maintain 'national standards,' and allowed provincial governments to increasingly diverge in their funding of social programs and in their guarantees of accessibility to these programs. This greater control on the part of the provinces had a negative impact on women – and, often on the most vulnerable women (Pulkingham and Ternowetsky 1996; 2006). Most prominent, because they were so devastating to those involved, were the changes that occurred with respect to social assistance funding: the programs became increasingly punitive and restrictive. Lone parents, for example, most of whom are female, became the target for social assistance restructuring, with the increasingly accepted notion that those mothers who were not permanently disabled should be working, even if their children were very young.[26] This work requirement, and the introduction of time limits to welfare funding, are policies designed to reduce welfare rolls based on similar policies that were instituted in the United States during Bill Clinton's presidency. These policies have been much admired by governments in Canada (Bashevkin 2002; Klein and Long 2003).[27] Gradually the more right-wing governments in Alberta, Ontario, and British Columbia began cutting back on social assistance benefits and instituting 'workfare' as a condition for receiving social assistance (Mosher 2007; Klein and Long 2003).[28]

Cuts to government programs were not the sole signifier of a new era in public policy in Canada. The dismantling of the Keynesian economic and regulatory apparatus, which had tried to reconcile social reproduction with the interests of capital, affected the way the economy functioned and thus people's economic security. The deregulation of labour markets in particular made life more precarious for many workers (Vosko 2006; Fairey and McCallum 2007). This deregulation included more restrictive unemployment insurance at the federal level, a reduction in employment standards in most provinces, a very large reduction in the real minimum wage across the country, and a weakening of labour protections and their enforcement, so that a more tentative type of employment could flourish. Both employers and governments were shedding their responsibility for social reproduction while in the process creating a labour market that made full-time, full-year work an anomaly. The precarious nature of work increasingly demanded multiple income earners within families, and governments began to treat this as the norm within social policy: rather than ensuring that all workers received a living wage, the expectation developed that workers with precarious employment would have the gap in their incomes filled by another family member.

Changes in public policy that disadvantaged women and other vulnerable groups were tolerated because of the delegitimization of progressive and particularly feminist voices. Janine Brodie documents how this process proceeded with a disparaging of feminists and their ideas, and particularly by labelling equality-seeking organizations as 'special interest groups': this invoked the implication that women's interests were very narrow and contrary to the common good (Brodie 2007). The term 'politically correct' was increasingly used in a disparaging way to counter any critiques of government or corporate actions by feminists or antiracist activists (McIntyre 2000: 159). These types of delegitimization exercises coincided with the ascendancy of neoliberal governing practices, but heralded as well a broader wave of social conservatism that was affecting Western democracies (Brodie 2007). As Brodie shows, the delegitimization of women's progressive voices paved the way for the dismantling of policy capacity within government to deal with women's issues. This happened at both the federal and provincial levels through budget cuts, the elimination of key policy personnel, and abolishing outright the ministries and programs that dealt specifically with women. This led to the "disappearance of women as an analytic category in public policy development, and, in turn, the erosion of women's equality as a central goal of Canadian governments" (Brodie 2007: 177).

Gender Order Changes

During the period when women lost considerable ground in public policy considerations, there were a few significant gains. There were advances in the recognition of gay and lesbian rights throughout Canada, including the ability for gay and lesbian couples to marry in some provinces. In social programs there were relatively few advances, but the increase of maternity/parental leave benefits to one year was a major improvement for many women who had paid employment (Pulkingham and van der Gaag 2004). These examples show that the dominant direction of social conservatism in Canada can be contested by political activism, and the trajectory of globalization need not necessarily be confined to the social policies of neoliberal globalism (Cohen and Brodie 2007). The question remains, however, about how permanent are the changes that have been instituted in economic and social policy directions in Canada, and whether these constitute a change in the 'gender order.'

The major structures of employment alone would seem to indicate that a change in the gender order of social reproduction occurred in the last quarter of the twentieth century (see Appendix 1). This proceeded in two stages: The first had the male breadwinner model as the base, with the increased provision of universal social programs, and an economy that was managed to support the social as the ideal. The second stage shifted to an 'employability' model in which government economic intervention to support social reproduction shifted towards a more individualistic and market-oriented approach.

The welfare state was initiated on a specific idea of an active state with an important role in stabilizing economic activity to ensure the economic security of most of the population. The welfare state is integral to patterns of social equality and inequality.[29] A specific gender order was associated with this initial stabilization regime, and this gender order was implicit in the social supports that developed (Cameron 2006). The gendered social order encompassed more than a notion of the household comprised of a male 'breadwinner' and a female housekeeper; it also included the fiscal and monetary policy to support a smooth functioning economy so that the 'breadwinner' could work. This economic intervention in the economy was particularly important for the quality of social rights because it provided the means for expanding ideas about who could be entitled to consideration in public policy. As Diane Sainsbury notes, the principles of entitlement are crucial in determining "whether policies reinforce existing gender relations or transform them" (Sainsbury 1999: 1). Gender relations were transformed both because of changes in the nature of the economy itself and because of political actions that supported policy for women through the welfare state.

The early gender order of the Keynesian liberal state was clearly a male breadwinner model, but this changed to become a dual-earner family model as more women entered the labour force. This happened over time, and the ability of social programs to keep pace has been slow, particularly with regard to the necessary support for child care and time for family maintenance. Since the mid-1980s, the dual-earner family model appears to have been shifting to become more associated with an individualist social welfare state, where benefits are apportioned by governments largely on the basis of individual labour-market participation. This shift, in recent years, has become so striking that employability itself has become the defining feature of the gender order.

It is important not to overemphasize the extent to which the welfare state in Canada ever actively supported gender equity in public policy. Nevertheless, there was a more activist interest in gender equity through public policy before the shift to neoliberal economic policies dominated the government's approaches to social policy. The shift now is to a more passive or reactive type of social policy that de-emphasizes direct state intervention and prefers to see social services provided either privately or as cash transfers to households, rather than through the direct provision of services (Bussemaker and van Kersbergen 1999). This is occurring at all levels of government in Canada. The welfare state certainly continues to exist, but the egalitarian gender order in public policy that the feminist movement envisioned, and that appeared to be a goal that was progressively part of public policy, has changed. This egalitarian order depended on an approach to economic policy that actively pursues market outcomes by taking into consideration social, in addition to corporate interests.

Advancing feminist public policy is extremely difficult under neoliberal economic and social conditions. Developing effective strategies will require Amazonian efforts to make women's voices loud enough to be heard by governments; nevertheless, feminist persistence has been a characteristic of significant change in the past, even under poor circumstances. This book hopes to make a contribution to a future progressive public policy by providing a vision for some new policy initiatives. As noted at the outset of this chapter, feminist social change requires a great many different kinds of conditions, including both a detailed examination of the existing problems and a clear agenda for what needs to change. The authors in this book provide the material to help develop a vision for policy objectives that meet women's immediate needs and for restructuring our society into the future.

Themes and Content

Through an examination of the state, income security, and labour market issues, the contributors to this book provide in-depth and wide-ranging perspectives on public policy and gender order changes. The authors of the sixteen chapters are academics and social activists, who have worked for years within the feminist movement and to advance a more women-oriented public policy. The selected topics include some of the more controversial policy issues of our day, and in developing their analyses, all of the authors broach the subject of what it means to promote alternative strategies and policies to meet women's needs.

The book is organized into three related parts. In the first part, Restructuring Public Policy in the Canadian State, the authors underscore the importance, theoretically and politically, of understanding the full ideological force of neoliberalism in policy practice. These chapters invite the reader to think critically and conceptually about neoliberalism, the various ways in which the policy literature has taken up this concept, and the political ramifications of different – and sometimes competing – understandings of it. How we think about neoliberalism plays into how we see policy impacts and the prospects for advancing women's equality. Jane Jenson's analysis of Quebec's early childhood education and child care system, implemented in 1997, points to two important insights about neoliberalism and policy developments: (1) neoliberal state practices play out very differently across jurisdictions, and (2) Quebec's progressive child care policy is a significant, albeit exceptional, example in North American jurisdictions of the actualization of a more progressive post-neoliberal set of practices. At the same time, progressive social politics are vulnerable to roll-backs, and political developments in Quebec since 2003 threaten to undermine, if not reverse, the recent advances in family policy that "explicitly recognized the multidimensionality of the challenges"[30] that women, especially poor women, face in juggling paid work and family care responsibilities.

Although a more progressive universal model of early childhood education and child care developed in Quebec in the 1990s, this did not occur at the national level. Wendy McKeen shows how the National Children's Agenda (NCA), spearheaded by the federal government in the late 1990s, hastened the unravelling of universalistic principles in child and family policy at the federal level. McKeen argues that the NCA initiated a distinctive shift in the role of the federal government, involving it more directly in setting program priorities for provincially based support services provided to 'families at risk.' This policy development reveals the enduring, although not static, nature of neoliberalism. The NCA entrenched traditional neoliberal priorities (residual, individualistic policy solutions). However, McKeen argues that this set of policies also reveals the way neoliberal practices transform how people think about themselves in relationship to the state and its citizens: by administering and financing self-help programs for 'at risk' populations, the NCA constructs the responsible, self-governing citizen. Ideas about civic engagement and the functions of civil society are central to neoliberal constructions of the self-governing citizen. Sheila Neysmith, Stephanie Baker-Collins, Elaine Porter, and Marge Reitsma-Street argue that in an era of declining public/state responsibility for social provisioning, policy discourse about civil society engagement interlocks with debates about the balance between work and one's personal life in the new economy in a problematic way, effacing the extensive providing role performed by women, especially by marginalized women. Examining supportive services for elderly persons by way of example, they argue that an alternative approach to social provisioning, anchored in a universal caregiver model, is possible but requires changes to current assumptions about the value of different types of work, how state provisions can support the work done by women, and what the nature of the care would look like.

The Canadian feminist movement's earlier success in advancing a more women-oriented public policy in part lay in its two-fold capacity to undertake public policy analysis and to build a gender-based policy apparatus within the government sector. Today, we can see evidence of this strategy in the adoption of gender mainstreaming (GM), or gender-based analysis (GBA), a policy framework designed to integrate gender considerations into policy in order to effect substantive equality. As

Olena Hankivsky explains, beginning in the mid-1990s the Canadian federal government made a series of commitments to gender-based analysis. What is the potential of gender mainstreaming, however, given the largely regressive policy changes that we have witnessed over the past ten years? Is GBA being co-opted, and can it ever be an effective policy tool within a neoliberal policy context? Hankivsky argues that there is an alternative approach to gender mainstreaming than that currently used, one that is potentially much more transformative. This approach requires a "shift from the often technical exercise of scrutinizing already proposed policies and programs against GM tools and checklists to considering and evaluating the broader contexts that inform government agendas and mould gender relations."[31] Moreover, for those of us who engage in critical analyses of neoliberal government policies, Hankivsky suggests that we turn our attention to considering the "underlying values, political goals, and trade-off choices of the government" that frame policy problems across sectors, rather than focus on "specific cuts in particular policy areas."[32]

Given the penchant, in government circles, for more narrowly scoped 'policy relevant' research inputs and a silo mentality about what are 'women's issues,' the ongoing challenge facing feminist political activists and analysts is how to get politicians and government bureaucrats to be receptive to 'deeper' forms of policy evaluation. Even though there is no easy solution to this problem, feminists are not dissuaded by the challenge – and having shifted the emphasis of their analyses to situate 'women's issues,' and the scope of the policy field, within the broader political, social, and economic contexts – they continue to produce work that extends the boundaries of conventional policy research. As virtually every chapter of this book indicates, the specifics of women's issues are intricately related to wider issues about how the economic and political systems of this country are constructed. In this respect, the authors represented here are upholding what is now a strong tradition in feminist policy-related research.

In the second part of this book, Reimagining Income Security for the Most Vulnerable, the authors provide this kind of contextualized analysis when examining specific policy issues (e.g., welfare reform, prostitution laws) and the implications of an intensification of gendered processes under neoliberalism for particular groups of women – those considered the most vulnerable economically and politically. Lee Lakeman considers the issue of prostitution and women who are prostituted. She argues that solutions sought through existing laws and law reform (criminalization, decriminalization, and legalization) fall short because they fail to understand that the transnational scale of the trafficking of women and children, and the reality that prostitution, as the sexual enslavement of women, is both economically exploitative and a form of violence against women. In seeking policy initiatives that would support the abolition of prostitution, Lakeman points to the need for a range of domestic policies that "are consistent with the goal of effecting global economic fairness and international human rights laws designed to reduce all forms of violence against women, including sex trafficking and sex tourism."[33] In arguing that these policy interventions would be beneficial for all women, and not just prostituted women, Lakeman also makes an important point about feminist politics, one expressed by other authors as well. Even while neoliberal practices attempt to discredit feminist concerns as yet another example of 'special interests' at work, and feminism itself is evolving to better understand the intersection of multiple oppressions and the diversity of women's experiences, there is power in a politics that recognizes a distinctive shared dimension of women's experience: "feminism is a politics that recognizes that women are largely treated in society as a group. While feminism increasingly stresses the differences among women, it also recognizes that many issues confront women as a group and tries to advance the interests of the group, women, so that women collectively and therefore individually are not oppressed."[34]

Four of the chapters in Part 2 of this book focus on the circumstances of some of the poorest of Canadian women, lone mothers in receipt of welfare, and policy solutions to the economic and social inequality that they experience. The authors (Lea Caragata, Shauna Butterwick, Margot Young, and Penny Gurstein and Silvia Vilches) of these chapters examine the welfare policy dynamic that perpetuates the bind in which lone mothers find themselves, the kinds of supports available to lone mothers within the context of prevailing welfare-to-work income assistance policies, and the ways that public policy can better support them. As Lea Caragata underlines, there is an oppressive and powerful collective interest at play when it comes to lone mothers, and consciously or otherwise, we all contribute to its perpetuation. We do so through 'sets of values and social practices that are insufficiently explored and explained, "stories" we tell ourselves about who "these people" are and why they cannot meet their own needs. The problem with the policy and programs that currently impoverish and stigmatize lone mothers – by gender, race, and social class – is that they are driven by certain discourses that remain embedded rather than consciously acknowledged and constructed.'[35] As Caragata explains, pervasive negative public perceptions about lone mothers and the problems that they encounter play out in myriad ways to socially exclude and marginalize them. While not all of those who are vilified or 'othered' by prevailing discursive constructions come to assimilate dominant discourses through processes of subjective exclusion, many do, and for those 'resistors' who do not, the policy response is to criminalize and stigmatize.

Given the unique sets of challenges facing a lone mother, who must straddle the dual-role of financial provider and caregiver to her children, how effective are welfare-to-work policies and what alternatives are there? To identify ways to best support lone mothers' transition from welfare into paid work, Shauna Butterwick reviews evaluation studies of welfare reforms undertaken in a number of jurisdictions. Her analysis challenges conventional evaluation approaches that measure the success of welfare-to-work transitions in terms of employability outcomes alone. Instead she argues that a successful transition is one where mothers are supported to move into "forms of employment that pay a living wage." Butterwick also identifies policy components implemented in different jurisdictions that are "effective in not only reducing welfare expenditure and moving single mothers into paid work, which is the focus of contemporary welfare reforms in most provinces, but also are effective in reducing poverty."[36] But paid work, even if it provides a living wage, is not always the answer, and for some feminist activists today, the idea of a livable income as a solution to women's, especially lone mothers,' poverty and economic and social inequality is gaining popularity.

Although the idea of a basic or guaranteed annual income (GAI) is not new, there is renewed interest in this policy concept, particularly at the grassroots level. Margot Young provides a feminist appraisal of the idea of a guaranteed annual income, revisiting a policy debate initiated thirty-five years ago with the Royal Commission on the Status of Women and again twenty years ago at the time of the Macdonald Commission Report. Giving careful consideration to a wide range of feminist perspectives on the debate, Young ultimately concludes that a GAI would be "too risky and incomplete a political strategy," given "the current political climate and the complex nature of women's economic and social exclusion."[37] One of the strong arguments against the GAI is the pragmatic concern that support for it from the right would likely come at the expense of other welfare state provisions: "Other publicly provided income security benefits will be folded into the GAI and other publicly provided benefits and services – like child care, and so on – will have no political viability."[38] Moreover, given the complexity of women's lives, there will always be the need for a diverse range of supports and services.

Penny Gurstein and Silvia Vilches draw our attention to the complexities of the environment of support for lone mothers. They argue that the problem for lone mothers is not only income poverty, it is also the way that regulatory welfare regimes are imbricated in the complex webs of social supports that lone mothers rely on, and the way that neoliberal regulatory processes intensify the fragility and precariousness of these supports. Drawing on longitudinal qualitative research with lone mothers in British Columbia, Gurstein and Vilches suggest that while extreme poverty is a serious issue, "it is not the foundational impediment in these women's lives." In terms of mothers' everyday experiences, they argue that cuts to service supports and "the government requirement that women exhaust all available capacity in their social networks ... amplifie[s] the gendered impacts of their position as caregivers ... rendering them even more vulnerable to future dependence on the state and to exploitation."[39]

In the third and final part of this book, Rethinking Labour Market and Employment Support Policy, the authors consider the nature and ramifications of gendered labour market insecurity in terms of a number of existing and alternative labour market practices and employment support policies. The ramifications of reconfigurations in the gender contract are perhaps nowhere more evident than in Employment Insurance (EI), one of the leading income security programs in Canada. Examining changes to this program over the past decade, Martha MacDonald illustrates how the state is struggling to grapple with the competing tensions inherent in an adult worker model that relies on women's caregiving activities, even while the model itself creates "a vacuum in caregiving created by women's labour force attachment, state funding cuts, and an aging population."[40] EI provides a range of income benefits to compensate workers for periods of time out of the labour force. Historically, the program was designed to provide wage replacement for periods of unemployment resulting from the loss of permanent or seasonal jobs. Over time, the program expanded to incorporate benefits for periods of sickness and maternity leave. What is most interesting about more recent changes to EI is that, within a relatively short period, changes that reduced eligibility for regular benefits (and that reinforced the requirement to work for women more than for men) were counter-posed by the expansion and introduction of special benefits (parental leave and the Compassionate Care Benefit) that benefited women as mothers and caregivers, underscoring the state's reliance on women's responsibility for care. At the same time, the parameters of eligibility for caregiving benefits remain tied to the male work norm that underpins regular EI benefits – with the result that many women do not qualify for the benefits, and the benefits that they do qualify for are inadequate. Looking to ways to alter this dynamic and promote gender equality through EI, MacDonald suggests that changes need to be made to both types of benefit (regular and special), and she points to recent develop-ments in Quebec's parental leave policy as offering a promising way forward for the federal program operating in the rest of Canada.

The new Quebec Parental Insurance Plan (QPIP), implemented in 2006, is part of a broader model for work-family balance pursued in Quebec, and as Diane-Gabrielle Tremblay explains, this model differs considerably from the model pursued by the current federal Conserva-tive government (a non-interventionist or laissez-faire approach) and its Liberal predecessors (the work-family alternating model). In Quebec the work-family balance (or cumulative) model is signalled by a paren-tal leave policy designed to create flexibility for parents by improving income replacement rates, length of leave options, and leave provisions available exclusively to fathers to encourage greater gender balance in the actual time devoted to the care of children. In addition, child care and day care centres, providing highly subsidized services (costing the parent just $7 a day per child, also discussed in the chapter by Jane Jen-son) are a lynchpin of the work-family balance policy platform. Looking at Canada and Quebec family and work policies within an international comparative perspective, Tremblay concludes that, while it has a way to go to catch up with the more progressive situation in the Scandina-vian countries, "Quebec nevertheless clearly stands apart from the rest of Canada, and even more so from the United States."[41] As such Quebec offers Canada an alternative and more progressive model for balancing the employment and caregiving nexus.

Flexibility is a key word in debates about employment restructuring and policies to promote family-work balance. While English-speaking Canada can learn important lessons from Quebec in terms of imple-menting policies to facilitate greater family-work balance, it remains the case that the balance of the flexibility scale is tilted decidedly in fa-vour of employment practices that leave individual workers (especially women) as the system's shock absorbers. The degree to which women, and especially immigrant and racialized women, are concentrated in jobs that serve this flexibility function is examined in detail in a number of the chapters in this book. In looking at alternative ways that governments can respond to the deleterious consequences of these kinds of flexible employment practices, Andrew Jackson considers the role that wage supplements might play in answering the problems facing working-poor women. As he reflects, "a central underlying question is whether governments should respond to the reality of low-paid and precarious jobs by topping up low family incomes, or intervene directly to ensure that there are better paid and more secure jobs for individual workers."[42] The current popularity of wage supplements as a policy solution to working poverty represents a "welcome turn from the punitive orthodoxies that dominated Canadian social policy from the mid-1970s through the 1990s." But from a gender equity perspective, Jackson argues, wage supplements are problematic. One of the dilemmas posed by wage supplements is that they are promoted and designed to deal with family rather than individual poverty, a fact that can create employment disincentives for individuals who work part-time and earn relatively little. In jurisdictions where they exist (the United States and the United Kingdom), some people (especially women and young people) face very high taxes on their individual earnings because even with very low earnings, their income pushes the family income to levels where the supplement is "quickly lost ... militating against the economic independence of women."[43] Wage supplements are also an expensive policy strategy that potentially crowd out political support for funding other programs and services. Therefore, if wage supplements are to be used, Jackson would rather see them play a 'back-up' role, as part of a broader strategy to increase employment wages – through enhanced unionization and minimum wage legislation – and investments in public and social services.

Margaret Menton Manery and Arlene Tigar McLaren provide the reader an opportunity to consider the ways in which employment arrangements for working-aged women are critical to women's social and economic security in older age and to women's ability to retire. Considering the issue of mandatory retirement, Manery and McLaren point out the broader social policy implications of seemingly narrow employment contract arrangements between employer and employee and the ways in which workers in more precarious forms of employment, especially women, are disadvantaged both by the existence of mandatory retirement arrangements and equally, if not more so, by the abandonment of such arrangements. Government legislation to remove mandatory retirement may help women in jobs that pay well and offer private pensions. Manery and McLaren are concerned, however, about the potential slippage in support for public pensions at age sixty-five among workers who are economically and politically advantaged and what this might portend for the accessibility of programs such as Old Age Security and the Guaranteed Income Supplement: 'Any discussion about eliminating mandatory retirement needs to address the right to social security for seniors, the majority of whom are women. The "right to work" after age sixty-five should not become an '"obligation to work" in conditions that jeopardize the health and well-being of seniors … It is also important to ensure that those in decent jobs who want to have the choice to continue working in old age are not speaking on behalf of everyone else including those in non-standard jobs or those who have no private pension plans.'[44] With an aging population and workforce, they suggest the need for a task force or royal commission for older workers to examine a range of employment and labour standards and pension provisions.

Many of the chapters in this book point to the importance of listening directly to the voices and experiences of marginalized groups of women when considering public policy impacts and developing policy recommendations. For Emily van der Meulen, when it comes to the issue of prostitution, "the most important people in the policy equation, and the most frequently overlooked, are sex workers, the true policy experts and policy analysts." After reviewing policies on the sex industry in Canada and cross-nationally in several other jurisdictions, van der Meulen looks to the kinds of changes demanded by sex workers and advocacy organizations working with and on behalf of sex workers in Canada. Drawing on submissions to the Subcommittee on Solicitation Laws of the Standing Committee on Justice and Human Rights (SSLR), she suggests that the overwhelming consensus of these individuals and groups is that the laws surrounding sex work in Canada should be repealed, with the vast majority supporting decriminalization.[45] In arguing that "sex work is work," van der Meulen locates prostitution as a legitimate form of work that should be treated within the framework of labour laws and regulations and suggests that "in order to increase the health, safety, and economic security of sex workers three major transformations are necessary: labour legitimacy, social change, and decriminalization."[46]

Jill Hanley and Eric Shragge consider what to do about the position of workers in precarious forms of employment vis-à-vis the labour market and employment policy based on their advocacy work in a community setting. Exploring the limitations of labour protection legislation and policy for migrant women workers, they bring attention to the relationship between 'precarious immigration status' and economic insecurity. Drawing on interviews with women represented by a migrants' rights organization in Quebec, Hanley and Shragge trace the way experiences of human trafficking and gender and age discrimination shape migrant workers' experience of paid employment in Canada, the difficulties of trade union organization within the employment sectors where these workers are concentrated, and the fracturing effect of federal-provincial jurisdictional responsibility for labour and immigration policy. They conclude by suggesting that, in the past, unionization "provided an important basis for defending workers," but today the experiences of more recent waves of immigrant workers suggest that "if women migrants' rights are to be protected, changes need to be made in the areas of workplace regulation, worker income security programs [such as EI and workers' compensation], and immigration programs."[47]

In the final chapter, Leah F. Vosko suggests that, given the spread of forms of employment that are more likely to be precarious (solo self-employment, part-time, temporary, and casual work in the social service sector), women, especially immigrant women from racialized groups, are especially vulnerable to high levels of labour market insecurity. As Vosko points out, precarious forms of employment are different from the normative "standard employment relationship" (SER) around which employment policy in Canada in the twentieth century was organized, and the "gendered labour market [today] is a product partly of a series of fractures between the organization of employment policy, which takes the SER as a norm, and the realities of the labour market exacerbated by the drive for employer-centred flexibility."[48] Vosko examines three alternative models for arranging labour and social protections, assessing each in terms of how well it responds to women's economic security needs and the current lack of fit between labour market trends and the organization of employment policies. Two of these alternatives, elements of the "flexible SER model" and the "beyond employment model," appear to hold the most promise for "adjusting the employment norms organizing policy but also embracing a gender contract characterized by shared work and valued care."[49]

An underlying theme in all of the chapters is the importance of fashioning income, labour, and service supports in ways that recognize and value women's dual responsibilities as income earners and caregivers over the course of their lives and the lives of those for whom they provide care and financial support. As Martha MacDonald argues, "the new configuration of the welfare state relies heavily on women's work of social reproduction, as well as on their labour force participation."[50] In this sense, the principle of a welfare state that provides from 'cradle to grave' remains as important today as it was a half century ago. But equally, given the transformation in gender relations and the gender order, the problems and policy solutions identified are changed. Recognizing that we need new ways to do things, and cognizant of the political constraints brought about by neoliberal policy changes, the authors pinpoint a range of possibilities for pursuing more equitable public policies for women. Can significant egalitarian social change occur within the boundaries of neoliberalism? The consensus seems to be that this is probably not a realistic outcome. This reality, however, does not mean that change cannot occur and that more equitable policies and outcomes cannot be actualized, so that people's lives are positively affected in tangible ways. This change, in itself, can bring about conditions for a more critical approach to neoliberal policies in general.

While we often look to far away places, such as the Scandinavian countries, for inspiration when it comes to envisioning more progressive public policies for women, we can actually look much closer to home to see that national and global neoliberal politics are not always insurmountable impediments to implementing more women-friendly public policies, in particular, family and employment policies.

APPENDIX 1: CHARACTERISTICS OF WOMEN IN CANADA*

- Lone female-headed families are a full 20 per cent of Canadian families with children (up from 16% in both 1981 and 1991).
- Birth rates have dropped continually since the 1960s. In 2002 there were 41 births for every 1,000 women in Canada between 15 and 49 years of age. This is one-third of what it was in 1959, when there were 116 births per 1,000 women of child-bearing age. The drop has accelerated since 1991. The current birth rate is 29 per cent lower than in 1990.
- Women are waiting longer to have their first child: the average

---

*Source: Statistics Canada (2006).

age in 2002 was 27 years (26 years in 1990, and 23 years in the late 1960s).
- Life expectancy: Female children born in 2001 will live 82 years (compared with 77 years for a males). This is up considerably from those born in 1981 (79 years) and 1961 (74 years). The long-term life expectancy gap between males and females is now five years, – in 1921 it was two years (55).

Education

Women in Canada now constitute almost one-half of those with a university degree, a proportion that is likely to increase in the future. In 2001–02, 57 per cent of all full-time university students were females (up from 52% in 1992–93 and 37 per cent in 1972–73).
- Women's proportion of enrolments in master's and doctoral programs increased substantially as well. In 2002 women were 51 per cent of the students in master's programs (up from 27% in 1972, and 41% in 1982, and 46% in 1992).
- In 2001–02 women accounted for 46 per cent of doctoral enrolments (35% in 1992, and 31% in 1982, and only 19% in 1972).

Work

Women now constitute 47 per cent of the paid workforce (in 2005), up from 37 per cent in 1976 and 44 per cent in 1990 (Statistics Canada 2006: Table 5.1). The biggest increases came in the 1970s and 1980s. Throughout the second half of the twentieth century, it was only during the 1990s that there was any decline in the participation rate for females. But this began to rebound in the mid-1990s. It should be noted that the decline was largely in manufacturing industries, and this was where the initial effect of free trade had its biggest impact.
- Alberta has the highest employment rate for women, and Newfoundland/Labrador the lowest. The following are employment rates for women by province:
  Alberta, 64%
  Manitoba, 60%
  Ontario, 59%
  Saskatchewan, 59%
  Prince Edward Island, 57%
  British Columbia 56%

Quebec, 56%
New Brunswick, 55%
Nova Scotia, 54%
Newfoundland and Labrador, 47%

- 27 per cent of the female workforce works part-time (< 30 hours per wk). This is lower than in the 1990s when the figure was 29 per cent (Statistics Canada 2006: 109).
- 14 per cent of women have temporary work arrangements.
- The rate of unionization among female workers increased considerably: 32 per cent in 2004 (compared with 16 per cent in 1966) (Statistics Canada 2006: 111). Male and female unionization rates are now identical.
- The labour force participation of women with children increased dramatically – the vast majority have full-time jobs (Statistics Canada 2006: Chart 5.1):
  - In 2004, 73 per cent of women with children under age 16 were in the labour force (39% in 1976);
  - 65 per cent of women with children under age 3 years were employed (28% in 1976).
- Female lone-parents are more likely to be employed:
  - In 2004, 68 per cent of female lone parents were employed (<50% in 1990).
- This period also witnessed an increase in the number of licensed child care spaces:
  - 750,000 in 2003 (twice that of the early 1990s).
- There has been virtually no change in the major occupational categories for women in the past ten years:
  - 67 per cent of employed women work in teaching, nursing and related health occupations, clerical or other administrative position, and sales and services occupations (30% of males are in these occupations); The proportion of females working in these occupations had declined in the previous decade from 72 per cent in 1976 to 67 per cent in 1996.
- Women have substantially increased their proportion of some professions:
  - 55 per cent of all physicians and dentists in Canada were female in 2004 (43% in 1987).
  - Women make up about one-half of professionals in business and finance (37% in 1987).
  - There has been an increase in the proportion of women in

managerial positions. In 2004, 37 per cent of these positions were held by women (30% in 1987). Most of this growth occurred in late 1980s, while the proportion dropped in the period 1995–2004.

- In 2004, women made up 22 per cent of senior managers (27% in 1996).

Earnings and Income

- Women's earnings are generally lower than men's, and the wage gap between female and male earnings has been relatively stable during the 1990s and early 2000s:
  - In 2003, the average pre-tax income of women for all work was 63.6 percent of that received by men.
  - For women working full-time, full-year, average earnings were 70.5 percent of similarly employed males.
  - Lone-parent female headed families have the lowest incomes of all family types, at 60 per cent of those of male lone-parent headed families.

Aboriginal Women

- Aboriginal women were 3 per cent of the total female population in 2000.
- Life expectancy for Aboriginal women is five years below non-Aboriginal counterparts, although about six years above that for Aboriginal men.
- 7 per cent of Aboriginal women over age 25 have a university degree (compared with 17% of non-Aboriginal women).
- 40 per cent of Aboriginal women over age 25 year have not finished high school (compared with 29% percent of non-Aboriginal women and 44% for Aboriginal men).
- 47 per cent of Aboriginal women are employed (compared with 56% of non-Aboriginal women and 53% of Aboriginal men).
- Aboriginal women are heavily concentrated in low-paying occupations such as in sales, service, business, finance, or administration jobs.
- 17 per cent of Aboriginal women were unemployed in 2001 (compared with 7% for non-Aboriginal women and 21% for Aboriginal males).

Immigrant Women

- Foreign-born females are 19 per cent of the total female population in 2001 (up from 16% in 1991).
- Almost half of foreign-born females are a part of a visible minority.
- 62 per cent live in Toronto, Vancouver, or Montreal (compared with 27% of Canadian-born counterparts).
- The foreign-born female population is more likely to be of working age (67%) than their Canadian-born counterparts (52%) and a higher proportion are seniors (20%) compared with their Canadian-born counterparts (12%).
- Foreign-born females are more likely to have a university education (18%) than Canadian-born women (14%).
- 64 per cent of foreign-born females were in the labour force (compared with 70% of non-immigrant women).
- Foreign-born women who immigrated since 1991 have higher unemployment rates (12.1% in 2001) than women born in Canada (7%).
- Earnings relative to males were about the same for foreign-born females (70% of male earnings) as for women born in Canada (71%).

Visible Minorities

- 14 per cent of women living in Canada in 2001 identified themselves as a visible minority. This is up from 11 per cent in 1996 and only 6 per cent in 1986:
  - 75 per cent of visible minority females live in either Ontario or British Columbia.
  - Most (69%) visible minority women were born outside Canada.
  - The largest group of visible minority women identify as: Chinese (26%); South Asian (22%); Black (17%).
- Visible minority females are relatively well educated: 21 per cent have a university degree (compared with 14% of other women).
- Visible minority females are less likely to be in the labour force (63%) than other women (70%), and have higher unemployment rates (8.9% in 2001) than other women (5.6%).
- The occupational distribution for visible minority women is similar to that for other women in Canada.
- Visible minority women employed full-time, full-year earn on average about 10 per cent less than other women.

- Visible minority women are nearly twice as likely as other women to have low incomes: 29 per cent had incomes below the poverty line in 2000 (compared with 16 per cent for other women; 21 per cent of visible minority women reported experiencing discrimination or unfair treatment (compared with 4% of other women).

Senior Women

- Women over age 65 now account for 15 per cent of the population, up from 13 per cent in 1991 and 9 per cent in 1971.
- Women make up 57 per cent of all people over age 65 in Canada.
- 38 per cent of all senior women live alone.
- 9 per cent of all senior women live in an institution (compared with 5% of males).
- Only 4 per cent of women over age 65 have jobs (compared with 9% in 2001 and 15% in the mid-1970s; senior women have low incomes: their average income from all sources is $20,000 (compared with $30,000 for senior males).
- Senior women are highly dependent on government programs: 55 per cent of all income of woman over age 65 comes from Old Age Security, Guaranteed Income Supplements, and spouses allowances, and the Canada and Quebec pension Plans (the comparable rate for senior males is 41%).
- 26 per cent of senior women's income comes from employment-related retirement plans (compared with 41% of senior men's income).

Women with Disabilities

- 13 per cent of the total female population has a disability (compared with 1 1% for males) and 54 per cent of those with a disability in Canada are female:
  - 32 per cent of women with a disability have a mild disability.
  - 42 per cent of women over age 65 have a disability.
  - Women with a disability have lower levels of education than other women: 10 per cent of women with disabilities have a university degree (compared with 19% without a disability).
- Fewer women with disabilities find employment compared with the general female population: 40 per cent of women with disabilities are in the labour force (compared with 69% of women without disabilities):

- Women with disabilities have higher unemployment rates in 2001 (10%) than other women who were unemployed (5%).
- Women with disabilities have low incomes generally. In 2000, the average income for this group was $17,200 (compared with $26,900 for disabled males). This income is about $5,000 less than the average income of women without disabilities.
- 26 per cent of all women with disabilities live on incomes below the poverty line (compared with 20% of disabled males and 16% of non-disabled women).

Notes

1 This was done through Bill 29, the Health and Social Services Delivery Improvement Act, in January 2002. The bill set aside negotiated settlements dealing with contracting out, job security, and layoffs and seniority, paving the way for the privatization of the work.

2 Other governments have changed specific aspects of public sector collective agreements. For example, in 1993 in Ontario the Bob Rae NDP government, through its 'social contract,' rolled back public sector wages (Wolkom, 130-1).

3 Five years later, the Supreme Court of Canada did find the actions of the B.C. government illegal because the government had not consulted the union, the Hospital Employees Union, before making the changes. The Court ruled that this action infringed on the right to bargain collectively (Makin 2007). The Court gave the government one year to rectify the situation, although by this time most of the work had been privatized and it is not expected that putting it back in the public sector will occur as part of the rectification process.

4 The workers made, on average, $17 per hour. Those who remained in the public sector had their wages rolled back by 15%, and those whose work was privatized had their wages reduced to as low as $10 per hour. Many lost work altogether.

5 Unlike most other provinces, British Columbia had no pay equity legislation. This meant it was up to trade unions to negotiate pay equity with employers.

6 Sylvia Bashevkin (1998) says women were on the defensive in Britain from 1979, the U.S from 1980, and Canada from 1984. These mark the years of conservative government when Margaret Thatcher, Ronald Reagan, and Brian Mulroney, respectively, assumed power.

7 The power of the feminist movement in the 1984 election was clear when candidates for prime minister publicly, on television, reserved one entire debate for issues related to women. A televised debate on women was also part of the 1988 election, but there were no reserved televised debates on women's issues in subsequent elections.

8 The National Action Committee on the Status of Women was organized originally to work for the implementation of the Royal Commission on the Status of Women. Its founding convention was in Toronto in 1972 (Cohen 1993).

9 For a description of the various government agencies that deal with women's issues, see Rankin and Vickers (2001) and Brodie (2007).

10 Canada's government was behind the U.S. on women's issues at this point, but Canada's feminist movement was not. For example, Doris Anderson, who was then editor of *Chatelaine*, famously tells of how she rejected chapters of Betty Friedan's *The Feminine Mystique* because Canadian women had already been writing on this for years, and she did not feel Friedan said it more strongly or added anything new (Pierson et al. 1993: 4).

11 Nellie McClung and Helen MacMurchy were both prominent feminists who were active in the eugenics movement. Tommy Douglas, the first CCF premier of Saskatchewan, wrote his MA thesis (1933) on 'The Problems of the Subnormal Family.'

12 Janet Siltanen (2007) makes the important point that the commitment to social rights of citizenship was always fairly weak in Canada, even in the best days of the welfare state.

13 The 'federal family allowance' was distinct from 'provincial mothers' allowances for widows with children.' Mothers' allowances were available in seven provinces only for destitute women, and there were considerable differences in their benefits and the way they were administered across the provinces (Rice and Prince 2000: 258.).

14 The universality of the Family Allowance, after a period of time with no special child measures, was replaced by a means-tested Canada Child Tax Benefit (Bashevkin 1998: 121).

15 For a discussion of social citizenship, see Young et al. (2007) and Siltanen (2007).

16 This two-person unit approach to social insurance was articulated in the *Final Report* of the federal government's Subcommittee on Post-War Problems of Women in 1943. This approach "treats a man's contribution as made on behalf of himself and his wife as for a team, each of whose partners is equally essential and it gives benefits as for the team" (quoted in Cameron 2006: 61).

17 Equal pay laws were passed in most provinces in the 1950s. These required that males and females be paid the same for doing exactly the same work. In the 1980s and early 1990s the notion of 'equal pay for work of equal value' was introduced in federal and some provincial legislation as a way to compare jobs that were not identical, but which took the same skill, effort, and responsibility.

18 By 1984 more than half of Canadian mothers of young children were in the labour force, a figure that increased to 70% by 1990.

19 We are grateful to Constance Backhouse for pointing out that individual discrimination itself is equally hard to prove in law. This is because findings of discrimination often revolve around elusive evidence of intention.

20 Globalization usually refers to the creation of global production processes and markets. In contrast, globalism refers to the ascendancy of a common transnational world view and philosophy of governance that priorizes economic growth and the creation of markets over all other goals and institutions of government. It is sometimes referred to as the "Washington Consensus" (Cohen and Brodie 2007: 1–2).

21 It should be noted that many analysts of public policy opposed the neoliberal economic programs precisely because of the impact they were likely to have on women. Women's groups, e.g., were in the forefront of the popular sector organized against the Canada-U.S. Free Trade Agreement and NAFTA (Bashevkin 1991).

22 The rise in the debt was largely related to a very high interest rate policy during the early 1980s. This had the effect of making government borrowing extremely expensive (Cohen 1997).

23 This deep integration initiative is formally known as the Security and Prosperity Partnership of North America (SPP). It was termed 'deep integration' when first proposed by business interests supporters.

24 First Nations groups also had their communications ability curtailed through cuts to Aboriginal languages funding, cuts to Native communications programs, and the severe reduction in core funding for all twelve First Nations newspapers.

25 Federal program cuts were partially offset by allowing the provinces greater taxing ability. Even so, the CHST (funded both through tax points transferred from the federal government to the provinces and a cash transfer) is estimated to have cost provinces $16.6 billion between 1996 and 2000 in lost revenues (Pulkingham and Ternowetsky 2006). Subsequently, in 2004, the CHST was divided into two components, one for health, and the other (the CST) for transfers for post-secondary education (PSE), social assistance, and social services. In the interim, while some of the lost revenues

were restored through a number of federal budget 'deals' giving provinces additional cash transfers and guarantees of a minimum cash floor transfer, the majority of these additional transfers were earmarked for health care (Day and Brodsky 2007). The Council of the Federation (2006) estimates that the federal government's support for PSE, social assistance, and social services has not been restored to mid-1990s' levels, and in inflation-adjusted dollars it falls short by about $4.9 billion compared with 1994–95 transfers.

26 Youth also became a target for social assistance cutbacks in some provinces.

27 Klein and Long (2003) make the important point, however, that when governments in Canada instituted the workfare and time limits, they did not also do what the U.S. did with regard to increased funding for other social initiatives for those being removed from the welfare rolls; in this way the actions in Canada were much more punitive than those in the U.S.

28 'Workfare' is the term used for the condition applied to social assistance recipients that requires participation in employment. This condition had not been permissible under the Canada Assistance Plan (CAP), but with the Social Union and greater provincial power, it has re-emerged as a practice in Canada.

29 Welfare state regimes are usually categorized based on Esping-Andersen's (1990) typology, according to their social policy frameworks: Canada, Australia, the U.K., and the U.S. are usually described as liberal welfare states.

30 Jane Jenson, Chapter 1, in this volume.

31 Olena Hankivsky, Chapter 4, in this volume.

32 Ibid.

33 Lee Lakeman, Chapter 5, in this volume.

34 Ibid.

35 Lea Caragata, Chapter 6, in this volume.

36 Shauna Butterwick, Chapter 7, in this volume.

37 Margot Young, Chapter 8, in this volume.

38 Ibid.

39 Penny Gurstein and Silvia Vilches, Chapter 9, in this volume.

40 Martha MacDonald, Chapter 10, in this volume.

41 Diane-Gabrielle Tremblay, Chapter 11, in this volume.

42 Andrew Jackson, Chapter 12, in this volume.

43 Ibid.

44 Margaret Menton Manery and Arlene Tigar McLaren, Chapter 13, in this volume.

45 This is one policy issue where very different types of solutions are envisioned, depending on an analysis of the root problem. See also Lakeman, Chapter 5, in this volume.

46 Emily van der Meulen, Chapter 14, in this volume.
47 Jill Hanley and Eric Shragge, Chapter 15, in this volume.
48 Leah F. Vosko, Chapter 16, in this volume.
49 Ibid.
50 Martha MacDonald, Chapter 10, in this volume.

References

Armstrong, Hugh. and Pat Armstrong. (1994) *The Double Ghetto: Canadian Women and Their Segregated Work*, 3rd ed. Toronto: McClelland and Stewart.

Arat-Koc, Sedef. (2002). From 'Mothers of the Nation' to Migrant Workers: Immigration Policies and Domestic Workers in Canadian History. In Veronica Strong-Boag, Mona Gleason, Adele and Perry (eds.), *Rethinking Canada: The Promise of Women's History*. Toronto: Oxford University Press.

Bakker, Isabella (ed.). (1996). *Rethinking Restructuring: Gender and Change in Canada*. Toronto: University of Toronto Press.

Bashevkin, Sylvia. (1991). *True Patriot Love: The Politics of Canadian Nationalism*. Toronto: Oxford University Press.

– (1998). *Women on the Defensive: Living through Conservative Times*. Chicago: University of Chicago Press.

– (2002). *Welfare Hot Buttons: Women, Work and Social Policy Reform*. Toronto: Toronto University Press.

Benería, Lourdes. (2003). *Gender, Development, and Globalization: Economics as if All People Mattered*. New York and London: Routledge.

Bezanson, Kate. (2006). *Gender, the State, and Social Reproduction: Household Insecurity in Neoliberal Times*. Toronto: University of Toronto Press.

Bezanson, Kate, and Meg Luxton (eds.). (2006). *Social Reproduction: Feminist Political Economy Challenges Neoliberalism*. Montreal and Kingston: McGill-Queen's University Press.

Brodie, Janine (ed.). (1996). *Women and Canadian Public Policy*. Toronto: Harcourt Brace.

– (2002). The Great Undoing: State Formation, Gender Politics, and Social Policy in Canada. In Catherine Kingfisher (ed.), *Western Welfare in Decline: Globalization and Women's Poverty*, 90–110. Philadelphia: University of Pennsylvania Press.

– (2007). Canada's Three Ds: The Rise and Decline of the Gender-Based Policy Capacity. In Marjorie Cohen and Janine Brodie (eds.), *Remapping Gender in the New Global Order*, 166–84. London: Routledge.

Buckley, Melina. (2007). The Challenge of Litigating the Rights of Poor People: The right to Legal Aid as a Test Case. In Margot Young, Susan B. Boyd,

Gwen Brodsky, and Shelagh Day (eds.), *Poverty: Rights, Social Citizenship and Legal Activism*, 337–54. Vancouver: UBC Press.

Burt, Sandra. (1995). Gender and Public Policy: Making Some Difference in Ottawa. In Françoise-Pierre Gingras (ed.), *Gender Politics in Contemporary Canada*, 86–105. Toronto: Oxford University Press.

Bussemaker, Jet, and Kees van Kersbergen. (1999). Contemporary Social-Capitalist Welfare States and Gender Inequality. In Diane Sainsbury (ed.), *Gender and Welfare State Regimes*. Oxford: Oxford University Press.

Cameron, Barbara. (2006). Social Reproduction and Canadian Federalism. In Kate Bezanson and Meg Luxton (eds.), *Social Reproduction: Feminist Political Economy Challenges Neoliberalism*, 43–74. Montreal and Kingston: McGill-Queen's University Press.

– (2007). Accounting for Rights and Money in the Canadian Social Union. In Margot Young, Susan B. Boyd, Gwen Brodsky, and Shelagh Day (eds.), *Poverty: Rights, Social Citizenship and Legal Activism*, 162–80. Vancouver: UBC Press.

Canada. (1970). *Report of the Royal Commission on the Status of Women*. Ottawa: Information Canada.

Chappell, Louise A. (2002). *Gendering Government: Feminist Engagement with the State in Australia and Canada*. Vancouver: UBC Press.

Cohen, Marjorie Griffin. (1993). The Canadian Women's Movement. In Ruth Roach Pierson, Marjorie Griffin Cohen, Paula Bourne, and Philinda Masters, *Canadian Women's Issues*, vol. 1, *Strong Voices*, 1–97. Toronto: James Lorimer.

– (1997). From the Welfare State to Vampire Capitalism. In Patricia M. Evans and Gerda R. Wekerle (eds.), *Women and the Canadian Welfare State: Challenges and Change*, 28–67. Toronto: University of Toronto Press.

Cohen, Marjorie Griffin, and Marcy Cohen. (2004). *A Return to Wage Discrimination: Pay Equity Losses through Privatization of Health Care*. Vancouver: Canadian Centre for Policy Alternatives.

Cohen, Marjorie Griffin, and Stephen Clarkson (eds.). (2004). *Governing under Stress: Middle Powers and the Challenge of Globalization*. London: Zed Books.

Cohen, Marjorie Griffin, and Janine Brodie (eds.). (2007). *Remapping Gender in the New Global Order*. London and New York: Routledge.

Corman, June, and Meg Luxton. (2007). Social Reproduction and the Changing Dynamics of Unpaid Household and Caregiving Work. In Vivian Shalla and Wallace Clement (eds.), *Work in Tumultuous Times: Critical Perspectives*, 262–88. Montreal and Kingston: McGill-Queen's University Press.

Council of the Federation. (2006). Reconciling the Irreconcilable: Addressing Canada's Fiscal Imbalance. Electronic version retrieved 27 Sept. 2007 from http://www.councilofthefederation.ca/pdfs/Report_Fiscalim_Mar3106.pdf.

Crossman, Brenda, and Judy Fudge (eds.). (2002). *Privatization, Law, and the Challenge to Feminism.* Toronto: University of Toronto Press.

Day, Shelagh, and Gwen Brodsky. (1998). *Women and the Equality Deficit: The Impact of Restructuring Canada's Social Programs.* Ottawa: Status of Women Canada.

– (2007). *Women and the Canada Social Transfer: Securing the Social Union.* Ottawa: Status of Women Canada.

Dobson, Wendy. (2002). *Shaping the Future of the North American Economic Space: A Framework for Action.* C.D. Howe Commentary, The Border Papers, No. 162. Toronto: C.D. Howe Institute.

Dye, Thomas. (1978). *Understanding Public Policy,* 3rd ed. Englewood Cliffs, NJ: Prentice-Hall.

Esping-Andersen, Gøsta. (1990). *The Three Worlds of Welfare Capitalism.* Cambridge: Cambridge University Press.

Evans, Patricia M. (1997). Divided Citizenship? Gender, Income Security, and the Welfare State. In Patricia M. Evans and Gerda R. Wekerle (eds.), *Women and the Canadian Welfare State: Challenges and Change,* 91–116. Toronto: University of Toronto Press.

Evans, Patricia M., and Gerda R. Wekerle (eds.). (1997). *Women and the Canadian Welfare State: Challenges and Change.* Toronto: University of Toronto Press.

Fairey, David. (2005). *Eroding Worker Protections: British Columbia's New 'Flexible' Employment Standards.* Vancouver: Canadian Centre for Policy Alternatives, B.C.

Fairey, David, and Simone McCallum. (2007). *Negotiating without a Floor: Unionized Worker Exclusion from B.C. Employment Standards* Vancouver: Canadian Centre for Policy Alternatives, B.C.

Grinspun, Ricardo, and Yasmine Shamsie (eds.). (2007). *Whose Canada? Continental Integration, Fortress North America, and the Corporate Agenda.* Montreal and Kingston: McGill-Queen's University Press.

Guest, Dennis. (1980). *The Emergence of Social Security in Canada.* Vancouver: University of British Columbia Press.

Harvey, David. (2005). *A Brief History of Neoliberalism.* Oxford: Oxford University Press.

Klein, Seth, and Andrea Long. (2003). *A Bad Time to Be Poor: An Analysis of B.C.'s New Welfare Policies.* Vancouver: Canadian Centre for Policy Alternatives, B.C.

Kingfisher, Catherine. (2002). Neoliberalism I. Discourses of Personhood and Welfare Reform. In Catherine Kingfisher (ed.), *Western Welfare in Decline. Globalization and Women's Poverty.* Philadelphia: University of Pennsylvania Press.

Larner, Wendy. (2000). Neo-liberalism: Policy, Ideology, Governmentality. *Studies in Political Economy* 63: 5–25.

Little, Margaret. (1998). *'No Car, No Radio, No Liquor Permit': The Moral Regulation of Single Mothers in Ontario 1920–1997.* Toronto: Oxford University Press.

Luxton, Meg. (1980). *More Than a Labour of Love: Three Generations of Women's Work in the Home.* Toronto: Women's Press.

Makin, Kirk. (2007). Collective Bargaining Is a Right, Top Court Rules. *Globe and Mail,* 9 June: A4.

Marsh, Leonard. (1943) [1975]. *Report on Social Security for Canada.* Toronto: University of Toronto Press.

McLaren, Angus. (1990). *Our Own Master Race: Eugenics in Canada, 1885–1945.* Toronto: McClelland and Stewart.

McIntyre, Sheila. (2000). Studied Ignorance and Privileged Innocence: Keeping Equity Academic. *Canadian Journal of Women and the Law* 12(1): 147–96.

Mishra, Ramesh. (1990). *The Welfare State in Capitalist Society.* Toronto: University of Toronto Press.

Mosher, Janet E. (2007) Welfare Reform and the Re-making of the Model Citizen. In Margot Young, Susan B. Boyd, Gwen Brodsky, and Shelagh Day (eds.), *Poverty: Rights, Social Citizenship and Legal Activism,* 119–38. Vancouver: UBC Press.

Myles, John. (1988). Decline or Impasse? The Current State of the Welfare State. *Studies in Political Economy* 26: 73–99.

Newman, Christina. (1969). What's So Funny about the Royal Commission on the Status of Women? *Saturday Night,* Jan.: 21–4.

O'Connor, Julia S. (1996). From Women in the Welfare State to Gendering Welfare State Regimes. *Current Sociology* 44(2): 1–130.

Pierson, Ruth Roach. (1986). *'They're Still Women after All': The Second World War and Canadian Womanhood.* Toronto: McClelland and Stewart.

Pierson, Ruth Roach, Marjorie Griffin Cohen, Paula Bourne, and Philinda Masters. (1993). *Canadian Women's Issues,* vol. 1, *Strong Voices.* Toronto: James Lorimer.

Porter, Ann. (2003). *Gendered States: Women, Unemployment Insurance and the Political Economy of the Welfare State in Canada, 1945–1997.* Toronto: University of Toronto Press.

Pulkingham, Jane, and Gordon Ternowetsky. (1996). The Changing Landscape of Social Policy and the Canadian State. In Jane Pulkingham and Gordon Ternowetsky (eds.), *Remaking Canadian Social Policy: Social Security in the late 1990s.* Halifax: Fernwood.

– (2006). Neoliberalism and Retrenchment: Employment, Universality, Safety-Net Provisions and a Collapsing Canadian Welfare State. In Vivian Shalla (ed.), *Working in a Global Era: Canadian Perspectives,* 278–92. Toronto: Canadian Scholars' Press.

Pulkingham, Jane, and Tanya van der Gaag. (2004). Maternity/Parental Leave Provisions in Canada: We've Come a Long Way, but There's Further to Go. *Canadian Women's Studies/les cahiers de la femme* 24(3,4): 116–25.

Radbord, Joanna L. (2004). Equality and the Law of Custody and Access. *Mothering, Law, Politics and Public Policy* 6(1): 28–51.

Ramkhalawansingh, Ceta. (1974). Women during the Great War. In Janice Acton, Penny Goldsmith, and Bonnie Sheppard (eds.), *Women at Work: Ontario 1850–1930*, 261–307. Toronto: Canadian Women's Educational Press.

Rankin, Pauline L., and Jill Vickers. (2001). *Women's Movements and State Feminism: Integrating Diversity into Public Policy.* Ottawa: Status of Women Canada.

Rebick, Judy. (2005). *Ten Thousand Roses: The Making of a Feminist Revolution.* Toronto: Penguin.

Rice, James J., and Michael J. Prince. (2000). *Changing Politics of Canadian Social Policy.* Toronto: University of Toronto Press.

Sainsbury, Diane (ed.). (1999). *Gender and Welfare State Regimes.* Oxford: Oxford University Press.

Sharp, Rhonda, and Ray Broomhill. (2007). The Problem of Social Reproduction under Neoliberalism: Reconfiguring the Male-Breadwinner model in Australia. In Marjorie Griffin Cohen and Janine Brodie (eds.), *Remapping Gender in the New Global Order*, 85–108. London and New York: Routledge.

Siltanen, Janet. (2007). Social Citizenship and the Transformation of Paid Work. In Vivian Shalla and Wallace Clement (ed.), *Work in Tumultuous Times: Critical Perspectives*, 249–79. Montreal and Kingston: McGill-Queen's University Press.

Stasiulis, Daiva K., and Abigail B. Bakan. (2005). *Negotiating Citizenship: Migrant Women in Canada and the Global System.* Toronto: University of Toronto Press.

Statistics Canada. (2006). *Women in Canada: A Gender-Based Statistical Report*, 5th ed. Ottawa: Minister of Industry.

Stephen, Jennifer A. (2007). *Pick One Intelligent Girl: Employability, Domesticity, and the Gendering of Canada's Welfare State 1939–1947.* Toronto: University of Toronto Press.

Vickers, Jill, Pauline Rankin, and Christine Appelle. (1993). *Politics as if Women Mattered: A Political Analysis of the National Action Committee on the Status of Women.* Toronto: University of Toronto Press.

Vosko, Leah (ed.). (2006). *Precarious Employment: Understanding Labour Market*

Insecurity in Canada. Montreal and Kingston: McGill-Queen's University Press

Young, Margot, Susan B. Boyd, Gwen Brodsky, and Shelagh Day (eds.). (2007). *Poverty: Rights, Social Citizenship and Legal Activism*. Vancouver: UBC Press.

Wilson, Elizabeth. (1977). *Women and the Welfare State*. London: Tavistock.

Wolkom, Thomas (1994). *Rae Days: The Rise and Follies of the NDP*. Toronto: Key Porter Books.

1 Rolling Out or Backtracking on Quebec's Child Care System? Ideology Matters

JANE JENSON

In 1997 Quebec launched a child care program that pushed against the current in which other North American jurisdictions were swimming. Quebec's family policy reform was a precocious example of post-neoliberal public policy, one that explicitly recognized the multidimensionality of the challenges. As then-leader of the Parti Québécois government, Premier Lucien Bouchard put it: 'Quebec's new family policy measures resonate with several of the state's key objectives – the struggle against poverty, equal opportunities, development of the social economy, integration of social assistance recipients into the labour force, and greater support for parents already employed' (MEQ 1997: 1, my translation).

The 1997 initiatives were successful in supporting women's employment, with clear evidence of the effects of better access to quality services: 'The participation rate of Quebec women with young children has completely eliminated its traditional lag behind the rest of the country. In 1976 their participation rate was well below the Canadian average (30.0 percent versus 35.6 percent), before catching up to the national average by 1999. Equally important was the speed of this increase, especially this decade. Since 2000, it accelerated further, and surpassed the national average by 4.2 points (76.0 percent versus 71.8 percent) in 2005' (Roy 2006: 3.1, 3.3).

Yet, even as experts from the Organisation for Economic Cooperation and Development (OECD 2005) were touring Canada and developing their high praise for the Quebec model, the newly elected Liberal government of Jean Charest was trying, by stealth as well as by policy pronouncements, to undermine it. In summer 2003 the Quebec government tried to redesign the child care system, but in the face of widespread opposition it only was able to increase fees from $5 to $7 per day. Since then, however, the government has successfully provided new access and greater encouragement to for-profit providers while dragging its feet on meeting the demands of the child care workers – most of whom are women – for wage increases and pay equity and while threatening the quality of services. For its part, at its 30th Members' Congress in March 2008, the Liberal Party promised to go to the next election with a platform that would provide 'more choice' for parents about the kind of child care they would use (including informal but receipted) as well as to raise the daily cost to $8 per child.[1]

How might we understand this government strategy, whose consequences will weaken support for employed mothers and workers in the child care sector? The question is of both theoretical and political interest. In 2006 the Conservative government of Prime Minister Stephen Harper dismantled the policies that had been constructed in the first half of the decade by the federal Liberals working with the multiple advocates for improved early childhood education and care (ECEC) and social reform. This dismantling was done in the name of that classic neoliberal principal : 'choice.' It is important to assess, then, whether the Quebec story is simply one of *rolling out* neoliberalism, in which the Liberals are designing a better form of neoliberalism than the Parti Québécois government could achieve because it was under pressure from women's groups and other progressive forces. To pose the question counterfactually, would the PQ have done the same? Or, is the story better understood as efforts inspired by the ideology of classic neoliberalism to which the Charest government subscribes and which therefore finds the Quebec model a weight to be cast off, bit by bit if one heave is politically impossible? In other words, are these efforts to *backtrack* on what in 1997 was a significant innovation in the direction of a progressive post-neoliberal social politics supporting, among other goals, the conditions for women's economic autonomy?

Via a detailed examination of Quebec's ECEC system, this chapter will argue that the policy story is best told as one of an ideological frontal assault by particular interests within the political institutions of Quebec, and therefore as backtracking. To translate its neoliberal ideology into practice, the Charest government is prepared to weaken substantially an essential support for parents (and always this means mothers) as well as the working conditions of those (again, overwhelmingly women) employed in the child care sector.

Thinking about Neoliberalism

There is now consensus that neoliberalism profoundly challenged and destabilized post-1945 political projects, policy arrangements, and practices of governing. Agreement breaks down, however, about whether 'after neoliberalism' is a meaningful category (Larner and Craig 2005; Graefe 2005). Two principal positions exist.

One stance is that neoliberalism is still hegemonic, reflecting major structural shifts in global capitalism. Political projects that claim to offer post-neoliberalism are little more than a 'roll-out phase,' a slightly adjusted version of the basic form. This stance treats neoliberalism as an overarching set of power relations still shaping everything from international financial markets to gender relations, social citizenship, and public administrations, in the global South as well as in the OECD world. Jamie Peck and Adam Tickell summarize the situation this way: 'Neoliberalism seems to be everywhere. This mode of free-market economic theory, manufactured in Chicago and vigorously marketed through principal sales offices in Washington, DC, New York, and London, has become the dominant ideological rationalization for globalization and contemporary state "reform"'(2002: 380).

Much contemporary policy analysis claims that Canada is living through a classically neoliberal moment, and therefore many policies are still being straightforwardly designed in accordance with that ideology (Smith 2005). For example, Stephen McBride wrote recently: 'The Keynesian post-war consensus was in its heyday from 1945 until about 1975 ... Since then, neoliberalism has been the dominant policy paradigm' (2005: 95). For her part, Janine Brodie writes: 'throughout the 1980s and beyond, the welfare states of most advanced capitalist countries and the politics they inspired were systematically eroded by retrenchment and restructuring. The assault on the logics and institutions of the postwar welfare state was most intense in liberal welfare regimes that embraced the imperatives of neoliberal governance as an alternative to postwar welfare liberalism (2008: 169).

Policy analysis within this framework seeks to document *similarities* across various policies and programs. In many ways, such formulations take us back to the all-encompassing structuralism of earlier decades. In the case of ECEC in Quebec, such analyses would see the parts of the 1997 reform that appeared to break with neoliberalism as little more than a version of the hegemonic project, while adjustments since the Liberals came to office would be described as simply a clearer expression of neoliberalism. For these writers, there would be little analytical interest in accounting for the differences between the Liberals and the PQ in government.

A second stance is that neoliberalism hit an impasse in the mid-1990s, as social problems multiplied across OECD countries, as well in countries subjected to the structural adjustment imperatives of the Washington consensus (Larner 2003). Therefore, after two decades of hegemony, enthusiasm for neoliberalism waned and policy communities began to search for alternatives, albeit without a return to past practices of Keynesianism and post-1945 ideas and policies. The detailed policy analysis that such studies carry out reveal that this notion of a single neoliberal moment is too blunt an instrument for understanding what is actually happening in social and employment policy, and for appreciating the variations across policy designs that may provide more or less progressive responses to gender, social class, and other structural inequalities.

Sharing this second analytical stance, this chapter examines three indicators of the positions of Quebec governments from the mid-1990s to the present. Ideas, including discursive reconstructions of the role of the state, are a first indicator of the position of each government. Simply documenting the discourse of various actors is not sufficient, however. A second indicator involves demonstrating coherence in thinking, such that there is a different modelling of state-society relations, and in particular there must be an observable shift in the elements of the citizenship regime.[2] Third, there must be concrete policy consequences.

Quebec's story of ECEC will be read through these three indicators in order to demonstrate that (1) the 1997 reform was a precocious move towards a post-neoliberal policy stance, and (2) since the election of the Liberals in 2003 there has been a concerted effort to return to the basic principles of classical neoliberalism, including re-legitimating market regulation and reducing the legitimacy of the community sector and the social economy. The Charest government is in line with standard neoliberal positions such as those of the Harper government (which is providing parents $1,200 so they can 'choose' the kind of child care arrangements they want) and of Alberta's government under Ralph Klein (which systematically refused to adequately support child care, despite the consequences for the province's economic conditions and the autonomy of women).[3]

Precocious 'Post-neoliberalism'

Ironically, Quebec led Canada in bringing neoliberalism into the country. Beginning in the mid-1980s, the Liberal government injected principles of compulsory 'workfare' into its reform of social assistance, even before the word was well known in English (Bouchard et al. 1996: 94).

In addition, market-performance features rewarded efforts to enter and stay in the labour force (Boychuk 1998: 88). The combination generated a social assistance regime that included both sticks and carrots. One of the earliest manifestations of this was the Parental Wage Assistance program instituted in 1988. It provided a wage supplement and extra support for child care expenses to families with a small amount ($100 per month) of earned income in order to encourage them to stay in the labour force. Within a decade, neoliberalism created a transformed social assistance regime, one based on both income support and 'employability' (Noël 1996).

Then, however, because of the limited results obtained by training and other programs, and because of rising rates of unemployment and social assistance, there was mounting dissatisfaction within policy communities as well as among citizens about the high levels of poverty and joblessness. The debate about social solidarity was reopened in the mid-1990s, focusing on children and families, as well as on women and poverty.

The difficulties of lone mothers and other poor families were clearly in Quebec policy-makers' sights. In 1995 the PQ government asked a group of experts to make proposals for redesigning the social assistance regime. They returned majority (Bouchard Report) and minority (Noël 1996) reports. Despite their disagreements on a range of other matters, both groups agreed that 'children should be removed from social assistance,' and both recommended the creation of an integrated family allowance as well as new services (Lefebvre 1998: 215–16). Experts speaking for the education sector also recommended extending pre-school education services, to combat high school dropout rates and school failure in general (Jenson 2002: 318).

Ideas about post-neoliberalism – or what was described by progressives as reforms in the name of social justice – were constructed from several elements. One element was the ideas about social citizenship and social risk that informed the Bouchard Report. It included a focus on poverty that called not only for redistribution of income but also redistribution of political power (Noël 1996). A strengthened social economy was identified as the mechanism to empower the poor, as well as to provide income.

A second important discursive element came from the women's movement and especially the Fédération des femmes du Québec (FFQ), which reoriented its strategic focus in the mid-1990s, putting the accent on antipoverty struggles. Quebec's dramatic 2002 Anti-Poverty Law

(Bill 112) was an expression of this critical post-neoliberalism perspective, promoted by both social policy experts and social movements, including the women's movement (Dufour 2005: 173–4). Support for families and for child care were described as good tools for fighting poverty.

Added to this understanding of social solidarity was the expertise of child development experts. Again, Camil Bouchard played a key role, publishing *Un Québec fou de ses enfants* (*Quebec, crazy about its children;* MSSS 1991). This analysis made the case that early childhood education was crucial to proper child development and that poverty and disadvantage were the factors most likely to place children at risk for negative developmental outcomes. In the preparations of the 1997 White Paper on Family Policy, Camil Bouchard helped to make the links across domains such as social assistance, early childhood education, women's poverty, and employment strategies.

These ideas influenced the policy community in large part because of Quebec's structures of representation that had long included a role for the social partners (labour and business) and that by the mid-1990s had been forced to include other social movements, such as women, students, and the antipoverty movement. Quebec's 1996 Summit on the Economy and Employment brought together employers, unions, and a broad selection of popular sector groups for what developed into a tumultuous discussion of plans for the medium-term future of the province. At the end of the summit, Lucien Bouchard announced a fundamental revision of family policy. Maligned by students over tuition fees and under pressure from antipoverty activists to embrace the goal of 'zero poverty' rather than striving only for a 'zero deficit,' Bouchard might be accused of searching for a theme that would unite rather than divide. But the decision to announce a major reform of family policy was much more than an effort to get out of a sticky political situation. It represented the victory of a coalition of activists and officials seeking to address the needs of women, families, and children within a progressive societal strategy. The FFQ and its president Françoise David played a key role at the summit, as did 'femocrats' within the government when the new family policy was being written into law.

These ideas helped to underpin struggles within Quebec's citizenship regime over democracy and participation, as well as against poverty. The FFQ, which organized the first World March of Women, also promoted a new vision of social citizenship, global as well as local, with a clear emphasis on democracy. In addition, the FFQ's critiques of the government's plans for reforming social assistance called for a multidimensional strategy for fighting poverty and advancing gender equality, one focused, among other things on activation (i.e., emphasizing job creation as well as labour force participation) and on access to services, including good quality child care and pay equity (FFQ 1997).

Such notions of citizenship were echoed in the 1997 reform, always presented as part of a recommitment to universality in social programs. For example, the highest-ranking civil servant responsible for Quebec's family policy listed its first goal 'to ensure fairness by offering universal support to families' (Jenson 2002: 320). Affordable child care services, as well as a range of universal tax credits and the implementation of full-day kindergarten for 5-year-olds, all expressed this commitment to maintaining solidarity via universality. By promising that middle-class families could, at a reasonable price, have access to quality services, the province was rejecting the liberal welfare state's long-standing form of targeting, which subsidized licensed care for poor families, while in the name of 'choice,' sent middle-income families into a market in which they confronted hard decisions about trading off quality and dependability against affordability.[4]

At the same time, however, the reform was presented as a form of social citizenship. As the same high-ranking civil servant said: 'We decided that we had to increase our support to families ... As a result we put in place a number of structural measures for the society of the year 2000, the harmonious functioning of which centres on employment' (Jenson 2002: 311). And, as the Ministry of Child and Family Welfare straightforwardly said: 'Poverty is less present in families with full-time jobs. This is why the government has chosen to fight against it not only through providing financial support to the poorest families but also in the field of employment by offering parents conditions making it easier to balance family and job responsibilities' (ibid.). Even the educational emphasis on child care and the extension of school to younger children is justified as much in terms of avoiding costly school failures by promoting school readiness as it is in terms of the development of the child.

We see, then, that the design of the 1997 policy reform reflects specific ideas for post-neoliberalism. First, family policy was meant to support parental employment and children's development. Second, both goals required the provision of affordable public services (delivered by non-profit providers). Markets were providing neither sufficient quality child care nor a breadwinner salary to couple families, while lone-parent families clearly needed child care in order to maintain employment. Third, ECEC was seen as good in and of itself for children's development; it was not simply day care to allow parents to balance work and family. Concretely, the policy provided affordable access to parents ($5 per day per child) to a child care centre or to family daycare. Kindergarten became full-day. After-school and holiday child care was integrated into the system, provided by school boards also at $5 per day. An age-appropriate educational program was developed for use by centres and family daycare providers (who were to be supervised by a local early childhood centre's trained staff).

Despite its coherence, with design matching goals, there were a number of pressure points in the system. These helped the Liberals' case for 'redesign' when they decided to push back. First, there were never enough child care spaces. While the 1997 plan promised, and produced, a massive increase in spaces, there was never an intention to provide a space for every child. Therefore, parents still had to scramble. There were major differences across regions, moreover, with rural and peripheral regions actually benefiting the most and large urban areas still lacking spaces. Especially parents with 'atypical needs,' such as those who worked weekends and evenings, still had difficulty finding a space. There was, therefore, constant pressure to do something about waiting lists.

Second, there were many critics of the 1997 program of reform both inside and outside the state. The auditor-general issued a damning report in 1999, criticizing the ministry for mismanagement of the child care system, as well as for a lack of evaluation criteria. Beyond these somewhat accountantlike criticisms the report went to the heart of the matter. The auditor-general found an increased use of family daycare, from 26 per cent of spaces in 1996 to 34 per cent in 1999, but with only minimal oversight by early childhood centres (Québec 1999). The report also pointed out that Quebec still lacked the administrative capacity to license drop-in centres and private kindergartens, although these were providing a significant amount of child care.

Three main groups pressured the government for change. One group was the parents who were losers under the new program. Large families had lost their generous baby bonuses with the 1997 reform. Parents employing nannies and in-home babysitters or using unregulated but receipted care sometimes could no longer deduct those expenses from their Quebec taxes (they did retain the federal deduction). Parents also complained that, in this competitive market for spaces, providers were charging additional fees, for registration, for example, or hiding higher costs in 'program fees.' Therefore, the promise of affordability was in some cases illusory.

A second vociferous group of critics were for-profit providers of child care, and the PQ minister made no bones about preferring to see them eliminated from the system. The original White Paper had said that commercial provision of child care would be phased out, but commercial operators refused to go quietly. After a major mobilization and rising recognition that there would not be enough spaces available, a compromise was eventually struck and commercial operators were permitted to receive some public subsidies.

A third type of criticism came from the family movement, whose positions meshed with those of neoliberals. The movement supports state spending on children and families, but would prefer to see the generosity that Quebec directs towards child care diverted to a universal family allowance. For example, the Institute for Research on Public Policy (2000) reissued a report written by researchers close to the family movement. The authors were critical of targeting low-income parents, instead recommending a generous and universal family allowance. However, their recommendation with respect to child care was that it be market driven, allowing parents to choose whether to pay for care or provide it themselves, as well as to select the type of care they prefer. The report was virtually silent on matters of gender equality – never the strong suit of the family movement.

In the rest of this chapter, I will follow the story only of the child care system, leaving aside the equally important matters of income supports and parental leaves.

Backtracking : The Charest Liberals Come to Power

The new child care system was immediately popular with parents. Statistics Canada reported a significant increase in Quebec children using some form of child care, with a big jump in the number attending a child care centre (Canada 2005). Quebec accounted for only about one in five Canadian children but over two of every five child care spaces.

The greatest increase in the new system was actually in family daycare. The goal set in 1997 was to create 100,000 child care spaces, half in family daycare (supervised by the staff of a centre) and half in an early childhood centre (usually called a CPE after its name in French, *Centre de la petite enfance*; Grégoire 2002: 32). But as Figure 1.1 shows,

Figure 1.1 Increase in type of services, Quebec 1997–2004.

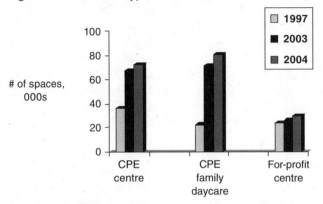

Sources: for the 1997 and 2003 data, see Japel et al. (2005: 9); for 2004, see Québec (2004a).

the increase in family daycare spaces has been both faster and larger. The other pattern of note is the increase, especially recently, in reliance on for-profit centres, an increase that took off after a moratorium on creation of new child care spaces in the commercial sector was lifted in 2002; once the Liberals entered government, the rise was faster, going up almost 30 per cent between 2003 and 2005 (Chouinard 2005b).

Despite the popularity of the new program, both opposition parties targeted child care for significant reforms in the run-up to the 2003 election. The right-wing Action démocratique du Québec (ADQ) promised to give parents vouchers, good for either non-parental child care (of any type, including informal care) or parental care. The Liberals focused on increasing family income and greater 'access.'

The for-profit providers of child care were a major influence on the opposition. From 1997 on, the powerful Association des garderies privées du Québec (AGPQ) continued to push for further concessions. The Parti Québécois government held the line, defending the original vision of the system despite complaints about the waiting lists. For example, PQ Minister Linda Goupil defended the notion that ECEC is not just about balancing work and family but that all children need access to ECEC. Therefore, child care spaces should not be reserved only for those whose parents are working or studying. Goupil also defended the clear preference for non-profit forms of child care. Despite the moratorium on opening for-profit centres being lifted in 2002, such new centres were not eligible for subsidies, and therefore their fees were $35 per child per day on average, putting them *above* the Canadian average (Grégoire 2002: 34). In addition, the government raised the wages of early childhood workers by 38 per cent in 1999, partly to improve quality, and partly because of the threat of a strike.

Liberals, however, were supportive of the AGPQ's position, claiming that for-profit child care centres could create new spaces more quickly, in large part because they did not have to take into account the democratic boards of directors that all non-profit early childhood centres had. The Liberal critic for family policy in opposition, Russell Copeman, is worth quoting because the position he articulated prevailed throughout the Liberals' years in office: 'The private sector is able to create spaces much more quickly. It takes two years to open a CPE [early childhood centre] because the board of directors, made up of parents and volunteers, is slow. It only takes a year to open a private centre' (Grégoire 2002: 34, my translation).

The lines of battle were drawn. The PQ argued in terms of social justice, gender equality, child development, and increasing employment rates while both neoliberal opposition parties continued to argue for 'choice,' by which they meant both parental care and access to for-profit services. In addition, the neoliberals argued for enhancement of the market's role and limits on the role of both the state and the community.

As we will see below, the only promise actually kept was for more 'access' to for-profit child care services. The net result has been a significant reduction in the notion that Quebec's citizenship regime involves a shared responsibility for children, in which communities, the state, and families are involved in both education and financing. Now, the state still shares some of the costs of child care, even with those who make a profit, but the commercial sector is enlarging its space and squeezing down that of public services.

The Liberal government's backtracking came in two steps: the first, in 2003, which brought favouritism for for-profit child care, and the second, in 2005, which reduced the emphasis on ECEC for all children and marked a return to a day care philosophy, as well as an even greater emphasis on for-profit provision of child care.

Such backtracking to a classic neoliberal position was not easy to achieve, however. Resistance came not only from parents and progressive forces, but within the Liberal Party itself, where ministers responsible for family policy were sometimes simply bypassed by hard-line neoliberals such Premier Charest, President of the Treasury Board Monique Jérôme-Forget, and the minister of finance.[5] However, the Quebec Liberals could not, as the Harper government did in 2006, announce that they would go back on existing commitments and dismantle the child care system completely. The Quebec government had to proceed in less transparent steps. Each time there was one 'big issue' on which compromise was possible and less visible ones that actually altered the principles of the system.

Backtracking: Step 1 – More than a Price Hike

The 2003 change in child care policy is usually remembered for the efforts to increase the share of costs paid by parents. Although the Liberals had promised in the election campaign not to increase fees, in the first six months of coming to power they announced that fees for child care 'must' and, therefore, would increase. A major debate broke out pitting parents and non-profit providers of child care against the government. Eventually, between the hard-line position of sliding scales as well as a higher base rate and those wanting to hold the line, the compromise was $7 per day per child for both pre-school and out-of-school care (Breton and Bérubé 2003).

Behind this much-publicized increase in child care fees, however, was another issue, which received much less public attention and yet was also important: the decision to support for-profit day care centres.[6] Elected in March 2003, by May the Charest government had already announced that the future of spaces in CPE was in danger: spaces that had been approved by the previous government but had not yet been implemented (land or buildings had not yet been acquired) might not be developed. This announcement caused consternation among non-profit providers, mobilized parents, and eventually resulted in a 'compromise' (Pontoreau 2003). Always insisting on the need to create the promised child care spaces 'quickly,' so as to reduce waiting lists, in June the minister finally announced that of the 13,900 spaces to be created in 2003–04, 6,500 would be in CPE centres, 4,400 in family daycare arrangements, and fully 3,000 in for-profit child care centres (MFACF 2003a).

Then, after consultations in summer 2003, when most of the focus was on the proposals to alter parental fees for child care, the government announced that the rules would be changed so that new for-profit centres would be permitted to receive subsidies for the $7 per day spaces, something that the previous government had refused to do (MFACF 2003b).

These were, in other words, clear policy changes underpinning the reassertion of neoliberal principles. Within the first few months of being elected, the Liberal government of Quebec was using a set of ideas to justify its return to a neoliberal vision, maintaining that the two most important factors to consider with respect to child care were costs to government and flexibility, with the latter supposedly necessitating a 'rapid' creation of spaces. As the AGPQ constantly reminded the Quebec public (and echoed in the quote from Copeman above), child care spaces could be created more cheaply in the private sector. The AGPQ president explained, for example, that pretty much 25 per cent of costs could be saved by economizing on salaries: 'The private sector succeeds in giving the same service at less cost all the while making a profit, essentially by paring costs for management and salaries' (Pontoreau 2003, my translation).

Was it really 'the same service'? Gone from this discourse was the idea of quality. During the consultations of the parliamentary committee, the highly respected child development expert Richard Tremblay and his team reported on the real differences in the quality of care that existed in Quebec between CPE centres, family daycare, and for-profit child care centres. In more than one-third (34%) of the for-profit centres the quality was judged to be inadequate, compared with 7 per cent of CPE centres and only 8 per cent of family daycares supervised by a CPE. Even licensed family daycare not supervised by a CPE did better (27%) than did the for-profit centres.[7]

The Liberals were determined to alter the responsibility mix of the citizenship regime, however, no matter the research evidence. While the state retained a significant responsibility for financing child care, families would also have to pick up a greater share of the costs. Alterations in the responsibility mix were perhaps even more important for the longer term. The 2003 reforms opened significant new space to the market and limited, even if they did not yet reduce, the role of the community sector. Sidelining the community sector would come next, as child care jobs (mostly held by women) were eliminated from the system in the name of 'cost-saving.'

Backtracking: Step 2 – Pushing Back the Community Sector

The next set of policy changes involved a frontal assault on one of the most cherished elements of Quebec's citizenship regime, the role of the community sector. Early childhood centres in Quebec were, in part, as we have mentioned, based on the idea that the social economy would play a major role in post-neoliberalism, providing work for those (often women) marginalized in the market economy and empowering them not only with respect to the labour market (by providing earned income) but also politically by means of the organization of workplace relations and political participation more generally. Child care is one of the major areas in which experiments in the social economy have occurred (Graefe 2005). The 2005 reform reduced the role of the community sector in the citizenship regime, at the same time as it again reinforced the position of for-profit providers of child care and de-emphasized the educational and developmental content of child care. All of this was justified in classic neoliberal terms: there would supposedly be $50 million in savings, less administration, and greater flexibility because there would be fewer workers.

This rebalancing of the responsibility mix in favour of the market and away from the community involved several significant dimensions of the law rammed through at the end of the 2005 legislative session, including the following:

- The new law promised only educational child care rather than educational services for children. For many this shift in terminology marked a return to family daycare and a reduction of the emphasis on ECEC (AQCPE 2005; Neamtan 2005).
- The legislation's name was changed, thereby signalling that for-profit child care was now a full participant in the system. The *Loi sur les centres de la petite enfance et autres services de garde à l'enfance* (Bill on Early Childhood Centres and Other Child Care Services) became the *Loi sur les services de garde éducatifs à l'enfance* (Bill on Educational Child Care Services). As the AQGP said happily in its brief to the parliamentary commission, this name change marked the 'elimination of the ideological bias in favour of CPE' (AQGP 2005: 1, my translation). Since then, for-profit child care centres have been always described by the ministry as equal participants.
- A new mechanism for overseeing family daycare providers was created. Instead of being under the purview of a local CPE, family daycare providers would now be overseen by one of 163 coordinating agencies, each covering a territory substantially larger than any of the 884 CPEs that previously had supervised family daycare providers.[8] The agencies' task is primarily to enforce the regulations and serve as a clearing house for information about available spaces. Educational programming is much further down the task list.[9]

- More flexibility was introduced in the programming, which would allow drop-in centres and for-profit child care centres to develop programming for part-day, evening, and weekend clients. By the time the 2006 budget was announced, the only increase in funding for the system went to drop-in centres, whose development was to be encouraged.

When proposed in October 2005, when debated in parliamentary committee, and when suddenly pushed through in December 2005 (to the surprise of Minister Carole Thébarge, who was involved in negotiating with the stakeholders at the time), the legislation was tremendously controversial. It received the full support of business representatives, as well as the AQGP and a small breakaway group representing about 100 CPEs. It was opposed, however, by the main organization representing CPEs (the Association québécoise des centres de la petite enfance, AQCPE), trade unions, the PQ, and the social economy sector. The coordinating agencies were the main focus of criticism, although there was also concern about proposals to alter the composition of the board of directors of CPEs.[10]

Again, as in 2003, the Liberal government had to make some concessions to its opponents, in particular by agreeing that CPEs could become coordinating agencies and reaffirming the community nature of their boards of directors. However, the Quebec government made no concessions on the key point, which was to diminish the emphasis on ECEC in the family daycare part of the system and to strip jobs from the system. Nor was much attention in the controversy focused on an aspect of the law that could have long-term consequences, especially when coupled with the Liberals' enthusiasm for commercial provision: The legislation allows several child care centres to be established under a single licence, which some commentators saw as opening the way to chains of child care centres (Chouinard 2005a; 2005b).

The consequences of the Liberals' preference for the for-profit child care sector are a levelling off of spaces available in the educational and non-profit portion of the system and a significant increase in the private sector, which both academic studies and the ministry's own research describe as low quality.[11] As Table 1.1 shows, the ministry's research found for-profit child care to be of the lowest quality, just as the study released by the IRPP (Japel et al. 2005) had found. The failing grade on educational programming in the private child care centres was due both to an absence of physical infrastructure supporting educational programming and the programming itself.

Table 1.1 Quality Scores (%) for Types of Child Care, Quebec 2003

	Unsatisfactory	Fair	Good/Very good	Mean (Range, 0–4)
Early childhood centre (CPE)	3.4	36.0	60.6	3.05
Family day care, affiliated with a CPE	20.9	60.0	19.1	2.75
Private day care centre	28.5	62.1	9.5	2.62

Source: Québec (2004b).

Conclusion

The complete lack of attention to the findings of evidence-based policy research provides yet another indicator that the Quebec Liberals are committed to a return to classic neoliberalism and are engaged in steady backtracking on the vision of a progressive post-neoliberalism that was begun in 1997. The government exhibited a classic neoliberal trait: it claimed that having won the election was a sufficient mandate, and it did not have to consider opposition to its proposals from stakeholders or civil society more generally. When its proposals for child care reform in both 2003 and 2005 provoked large and mobilized opposition, some concessions were made, but compromise on the essentials – which would remake the system as a whole – was not entertained. Thus, the new legislation was forced through at the end of the 2005 session, despite representatives of the ministry being engaged in negotiations with representatives of the child care sector, including representatives of both the women working in the sector and those using the services. Such negotiations respected Quebec's long-standing structure of representation. The government high-handedly ignored those democratic forms, as well as the National Assembly's right to consider the legislation clause by clause.

It is also in the content of its reforms that we recognize the fundamentally different vision of the Liberals, one that pays no heed either to the negative consequences of neoliberal strategies or gender equality. Gone is any emphasis on the needs of all children for ECEC and the needs of their mothers for affordable and quality child care services. The principal goals are to keep costs down, to ensure a supply of spaces, to level the playing field for commercial providers, and to provide parents with flexible forms of services. This is, in other words, a publicly funded child care system emptied of much of its ECEC content and of its goals for equality, one meant to be increasingly responsive to market signals rather than social justice concerns.

This backtracking is not, of course, surprising. The Liberals have not hidden their sources of inspiration for a neoliberal citizenship regime, whether it is the Thatcherist view of TINA (there is no alternative; Bois-menu et al. 2004) or Monique Jérôme-Forget's fondness for the Milton Friedman quotation, 'less government is better government' (Cornel-lier 2004). Nor have the Liberals concealed their vision of Quebec: Pre-mier Charest lauds a 'Québec of 7 million ambitions,' that is a collection of individuals rather than a society.[12] Nothing in their platform or their recent history, including that of their leader, would have led to an ex-pectation of anything but neoliberalism.

The broader lesson of this experience is that ideology does matter. First, the recent past has not been one of undifferentiated neoliberal-ism, as many analysts focusing only on big structures and ignoring policy details often suggest. Rather, there have been significant exam-ples of strategies for progressive post-neoliberalism both in Canada and elsewhere. Yet, these post-neoliberal positions by no means have achieved hegemony, and electoral wins altered the balance of forces in major ways. Just as Stephen Harper's Conservatives could imme-diately begin to institute a return to many of the policy stances of the late 1980s and early 1990s (hollowing out Status of Women Canada and attacking feminists as 'special interests,' as well as bowing to the notion that parents 'choosing' to provide their own child care should receive public support), so too did the Liberal government of Quebec move to backtrack on the family policy of its predecessor. Thus, political parties strongly pushing an ideological position can threaten policies designed to advance, among others, gender goals.

The second lesson from Quebec's story is, however, that even such determination can be limited. When social movements, including the women's movement, mobilize, the government can be forced to back down. All the backtracking has not been halted, but there is less than there might have been if the mothers, fathers, and child care workers had not banded together to protest.

Notes

1 See the report of this congress (electronic version retrieved 14 March 2008 from http://www.plq.org/fr/documents/) as well as the working docu-

ment on the family that was presented to it (http://www.plq.org/fr/actu-alites_au_plq/communiques/04_03_2008_02.php).

2 On the concept of citizenship and a description of Quebec's citizenship regime, see Jenson (1997).

3 In 2005 Alberta had the *lowest* labour force participation rate for mothers of children under age 6, despite severe labour shortages in its booming economy. In 1999 it was at the provincial midpoint. It has lost ground because other provincial rates increased, and Alberta's fell from 67.9% to 64.9% (Roy 2006: 3.3–3.4). A *decline* is completely unexpected. Women's labour force participation generally has been rising in the OECD world since the 1960s (OECD 2005).

4 This is the Head Start model used in the United States and in Aboriginal communities in Canada, as well as the practice in nine Canadian provinces as a legacy of the Canada Assistance Plan (CAP).

5 See Breton and Bérubé (2003) for an analysis of the internal situation during the first reform, and Dutrisac and Robitaille (2005) for the second.

6 In 2005, and in line with family movement positions as well as neoliberal promises of administrative rationalization, the Liberals reorganized universal tax credits for families. Favouring low-income and lone-parent families, the universal reimbursable credit was praised not only by the for-profit child care providers but even by policy experts. See, e.g., Rose (2007).

7 This important study was eventually published as Japel et al. (2005).

8 In the interest of saving money by cutting jobs from the system, the Charest Liberal government proposed creating 126 coordinating agencies, but under pressure from the association of early childhood centre providers, the Association québécoise des centres de la petite enfance (AQCPE), the number was slightly increased, but not to the 253 the association had wanted.

9 Of the eight responsibilities of such an agency, providing training to family day care providers and supporting them in programming is number six.

10 In spring 2005 the Quebec government floated the idea of putting a civil servant on the board of CPEs, an idea that was vehemently opposed by the milieu (see Chouinard 2005a). The idea was shelved.

11 The key academic study is Japel et al. (2005). The ministry began its own study when the PQ was in office, but the final report was not available until after the elections. The new minister did not hurry to make it public, and it was only under pressure that the $3 million study, *Grandir en qualité,* was leaked and then finally released in June 2004 (Richer 2004).

12 See Premier Jean Charest's message (electronic version retrieved 23

May 2006 from http://www.briller.gouv.qc.ca/messages/message_pm_
en.htm).

References

Association québécoise des centres de la petite enfance (AQCPE). (2005).
Les véritables enjeux de la réforme Théberge. Electronic version retrieved
4 Feb. 2006 from http://www.childcareadvocacy.ca/resources/pdf/cpe_
veritables.pdf.

Association québécoise des garderies privées (AQGP). (2005). Les véritables
enjeux du projet de loi 124. Press release, 22 Nov. Electronic version retrieved 25 May 2006 from http://www.agpq.ca/communiques.htm.

Boismenu, Gérard, Pascale Dufour, and Denis Saint-Martin. (2004). *La décon-
struction libérale du Québec: Réalisations et promesses du gouvernement Charest*.
Outremont: Athéna.

Bouchard, Camil, Vivienne Labrie, and Alain Noël. (1996). *Chacun sa part: Rapport de trois membres du comité externe de réforme de la sécurité du revenu*. Montreal: Gouvernement du Québec, Ministère de l'Emploi et de la Solidarité
sociale.

Boychuk, Gerard. (1998). *Patchworks of Purpose: The development of provincial social assistance regimes in Canada*. Montreal: McGill-Queen's University Press.

Breton, Pascale, and Nicolas Bérubé. (2003). Des garderies à 7$ dès janvier. *La
Presse.com*, 14 Nov. Electronic version retrieved 25 Jan. 2006 from http://
www.cyberpresse.ca/section/CPPRESSE.

Brodie, Janine. (2008). Putting Gender Back In: Women and Social Policy
Reform in Canada. In Yasmeen Abu-Laban (ed.), *Gendering the Nation-State:
Canadian and Comparative Perspectives*, 165–84. Vancouver: UBC Press.

Canada. (2005). Child Care 1994/95 and 2000/01. *The Daily*, Ottawa: Statistics
Canada, 7 Feb.

Chouinard, Tommy. (2005a). Les CPE accusent Québec d'ingérence. *La Presse.
com*, 31 May. Electronic version retrieved 25 Jan. 2006 from http://www.
cyberpresse.ca/section/CPPRESSE.

– (2005b). Des garderies à la chaine. *La Presse.com*, 24 Nov. Electronic version
retrieved 30 May 2006 from http://www.cyberpresse.ca/section/
CPPRESSE.

Cornellier, Louis. (2004). Un terrible constat d'échec du gouvernement actuel.
Le Devoir.com. Electronic version retrieved 11 Sept. 2006 from http://www.
ledevoir.com/index.html.

Dufour, Pascale. (2005). L'adoption du projet de loi 112 au Québec : Le produit d'une mobilisation ou une simple question de conjoncture politique? *Politique et Sociétés* 1–2: 159–82.

Dutrisac, Robert, and Robitaille, Antoine, (2005), Le gouvernement Charest impose sa loi sur les CPE et ses conditions de travail aux quelque 500,000 employés au secteur public. *Le Devoir.com,* 15 Dec. Electronic version retrieved 25 Jan. 2006 from http://www.ledevoir.com/index.html.

Fédération des femmes du Québec (FFQ). (1997). *De l'insécurité du revenu à un parcours vers l'inconnu: Une réforme qui continue d'appauvrir les femmes assistées sociales.* Mémoire présenté à la Commission des affaires sociales, Jan.

Graefe, Peter. (2005). Roll-Out Neoliberalism and the Social Economy. Paper presented at the Annual General Meeting of the Canadian Political Science Association, Toronto, 3 June.

Grégoire, Isabelle. (2002). Les garderies de la discorde. *L'Actualité,* 1 Nov.: 30–9.

Institute for Research in Public Policy (IRPP). (2000). Quebec Family Policy: Impact and Option. *IRPP Choices* 6(1): 52 pp.

Japel, Christa, Richard E. Tremblay, and Sylvana Côté. (2005). Quality Counts: Assessing the Quality of Daycare Services Based on the Quebec Longitudinal Study of Child Development. *IRPP Choices* 11(5): 46 pp.

Jenson, Jane. (1997) Fated to Live in Interesting Times: Canada's Changing Citizenship Regimes. *Canadian Journal of Political Science* 30(4): 627–44.

– (2002). Against the Current. In Sonya Michel and Rianne Mahon (eds.), *Child Care Policy at the Crossroads: Gender and Welfare State Restructuring,* 309–32. London: Routledge.

Larner, Wendy. (2003) Neoliberalism? *Environment and Planning D: Society and Space* 21: 509–12.

Larner, Wendy, and David Craig. (2005). After Neoliberalism? Community Activism and Local Partnerships in Aotearoa New Zealand. *Antipode* 37(3): 402–24.

Lefebvre, Pierre. (1998). Les nouvelles orientations de la politique familiale du Québec: Une critique de l'allocation unifiée. In J.-Pierre Lamoureux, Renée B. Dandurand, Pierre Lefebvre (eds.), *Quelle politique familiale à l'aube de l'an 2000?* 215–45. Paris: L'Harmattan.

McBride, Stephen. (2005). *Paradigm Shift: Globalization and the Canadian State,* 2nd ed. Halifax: Fernwood.

MFACF. (2003a). Création de nouvelles places en services de garde et consultation sur les scénarios de financement et développement. Press release, 18 June. Electronic version retrieved 25 May 2006 from http://www.mfacf.gouv.qc.ca/thematiques/famille/services-garde/consultation/communiques/comm5.asp.

– (2003b). Développement et financement des services de garde – des choix qui assureront la pérennité du système. Press release 13 Nov. Electronic version retrieved 10 July 2008 from http://communiques.gouv.qc.ca/gouvqc/communiques/GPQF/Novembre2003/13/c2049.html.

Ministère d'Éducation du Québec (MEQ). (1997). La politique familiale: Les enfants au cœur des choix du gouvernement. Press release, 23 Jan. Electronic version retrieved 22 May 2006 from http://www.meq.gouv.qc.ca/cpress/CPRSS97/c970123.htm.

Ministère de la Santé et des Services sociaux (MSSS). (1991). *Un Québec fou de ses enfants*. Quebec: MSSS.

Neamtan, Nancy. (2005). Projet de loi sur la reforme des services de garde: Un recul, un affront, une geste politique inacceptable. Presentation to the Parliamentary Committee examining Bill 124. *Le Devoir.com*, 24 Nov. Electronic version retrieved 30 May 2006 from http://www.ledevoir.com/index.html.

Noël, Alain. (1996). La contrepartie dans l'aide sociale au Québec. *Revue française des Affaires sociales* 50(4): 99–122.

Organisation for Economic Cooperation and Development. (2005). *Babies and Bosses: Reconciling Work and Family Life: Canada, Finland, Sweden and the United Kingdom*, vol 4. Paris: OECD.

Peck, Jamie, and Adam Tickell. (2002). Neoliberalizing Space. *Antipode* 34(3): 380–404.

Pontoreau, Pascale. (2003). La fin des garderies à 5$? *PetitMonde.com, le Magazine Web des parents*, 4 June. Electronic version retrieved 25 May 2006 from http://www.petitmonde.com.

Québec. (1999). *Rapport à l'Assemblée nationale pour l'année 1998–1999*. Québec: Vérificateur général du Québec.

– (2004a). Profil des utilisateurs des services de garde, Québec: Famille et Aînés Québec. Electronic version retrieved 26 March 2006 from http://www.mfacf.gouv.qc.ca/statistiques/services-de-garde/profil-utilisateurs.asp.

– (2004b). Enquête québécoise sur la qualité des services de garde éducatifs, Québec: Institut de la statistique. Electronic version retrieved 18 June 2007 from http://www.grandirenqualite.gouv.qc.ca/publications_an.htm.

Richer, Jocelyne. (2004). Une étude décerne la mention 'passable' au réseau des garderies. *La Presse.com*, 2 June. Electronic version retrieved 25 Jan. 2006 from http://www.cyberpresse.ca/section/CPPRESSE.

Rose, Ruth. (2007). *L'universalité des subventions aux frais de garde répond à un souci d'équité horizontale. Etude préparé pour l' Association québécoise des centres de la petite enfance*. Electronic version retrieved 21 June 2007 from http://www.rcpem.com/communication/RRose-EquiteHorizontale.pdf.

Roy, Francine. (2006). From She to She: Changing Patterns of Women in the
    Canadian Labour Force. *Canadian Economic Observer.* Ottawa: Statistics
    Canada, Cat. No. 11-010 (June): 3.1–3.10.
Smith, Miriam. (2005). *A Civil Society? Collective Actors in Canadian Political Life.*
    Peterborough: Broadview Press.

2 The Politics of the National Children's Agenda: A Critical Analysis of Contemporary Neoliberal Social Policy Change

WENDY McKEEN

The federal government has long played an important role in providing national 'child benefits' programs that serve to transfer income to families with children. Through the 1980s these measures included a tax exemption, a tax credit, and a direct payment known as the Family Allowance. Through such measures the federal government redistributed income from wealthier to poorer families and citizens and from those without children to those with children. One of the important premises of this system was the notion that as a society we should take collective responsibility for ensuring the welfare of families with children. The idea of collective responsibility still has some resonance today, and this is still reflected (albeit, in a modified way) through the targeted Canada Child Tax Benefit/National Child Benefit program (CCTB/NCB), which is the contemporary counterpart to the Family Allowance. Nevertheless, the nature and extent of what it means for society to provide collectively has shifted considerably, as is reflected in a number of fundamental changes to the child benefits system since the 1980s.

This chapter focuses on an initiative that was adopted by the federal government in the late 1990s: the National Children's Agenda (NCA). The NCA came to encompass the CCTB/NCB program, but it also has been a vehicle for the development and promotion of early childhood development (ECD) programs, many of which are geared specifically to helping families designated as being 'at risk.' The income transfer portion of the NCA (i.e., the CCTB/NCB) has received considerable commentary, but relatively little attention has been paid to the new ECD/at risk aspect of this agenda. Moreover, while most of the existing analyses in the field examine the more immediate impact of policy change, they tend not to delve very deeply into possible long-term effects on the ways in which policy reforms may transform social relations, reconfigure power relations, and recast social identities.

This chapter seeks to rectify these gaps and weaknesses by critically examining the National Children's Agenda, and specifically, the ECD/ at risk aspect of it. The purpose of the analysis is to clarify the potential ways that these policies and practices affect women's social relations and, specifically, how they may be affecting gender relations and the prospects for gender equality. The analysis considers both politics and policy involved in the area. With respect to politics, the focus here is on the transformation of ideas at the level of the federal social policy community in the context of debates on the NCA. It shows the degree to which individualized, casework-style programs began to be embraced by this community as a central approach to supporting families with children. To be clear, the ideas embraced are not particularly novel in the history of Canada's social policy. 'Casework' has long been a standard approach under provincial and municipal social assistance and child welfare programs, and earlier, under mothers' allowance programs. Indeed, the design and implementation of ECD/at risk programs have been left to the provincial or territorial level and to local voluntary or non-profit sectors. Yet, the sudden renewed embrace of this thinking and approach by federal actors appears to break with the historical role that this policy community has played in upholding more collectivist or universalistic values and principles for this policy area.

This chapter examines ECD/at risk policy through two critical lenses. The first is that of feminist political economy. From this vantage point, ECD/at risk policy can be seen as grounded in ideologies of individualism, familialism, and privatization – one consequence of which has been that women and those belonging to marginalized groups have been unduly targeted for intervention. The second critical lens adopted here is that of governance and subjectivity. This is a relatively underacknowledged and underutilized tool in the critical social policy literature in Canada, and yet, as this chapter shows, it offers crucial insight into the ways ECD/at risk programming often works on the very subjectivities and identities of their clients, and does so in ways that harmonize with, rather than challenge the inequitable status quo. The view presented in this chapter is that to the extent that there is a renewed emphasis on 'at risk' approaches as a response by governments to social distress, it marks further movement down a 'low road' social vision and strategy – one that is detrimental for women and other marginalized and disadvantaged groups.

The remainder of this chapter unfolds as follows. The first section provides a brief overview of the past three decades of shifts in Canadian social policy and child benefits policy. The next section discusses the critical literature on Canadian child benefits policy and explores the question of what 'critical analysis' means in this policy context. The third section focuses on the ideological shifts that took place in and around the federal debates on the NCA. The final section provides a detailed, critical view of how a typical ECD/at risk program operates, with a particular focus on how it impacts poor women. It uses Nova Scotia's home visiting program, Healthy Beginnings, as a case study. The concluding section summarizes the analysis and ends with a brief discussion of future action that could be taken by progressive actors.

Changes in the Canadian Welfare State and the Federal Child Benefits System

In the past three decades or more, the Canadian welfare state has undergone a profound transformation. The past two decades, in particular, saw large-scale reductions in social programs and social security benefits (e.g., unemployment insurance benefits), the closing of schools, the reduction of health and hospital services, and an end to the ideal of national standards – as the balance of power over social policy was shifted from the federal to the provincial and territorial governments. The 1995 federal budget, in particular, was instrumental in implementing this shift and in reducing the amount of support available for health care and social programs overall. These changes were implemented through the elimination of the Canada Assistance Plan (CAP) and the institution of the Canada Health and Social Transfer (CHST), as well as through extensive reductions to federal social transfers to the provinces, which in turn precipitated further provincial slashes to social assistance benefits and social services, including services such as legal aid, shelters and transition housing, day care subsidies, counselling, hot lunch programs to schools, and so on (Pulkingham and Ternowetsky 1999). Federal child benefits programs, as well, were significantly altered over this period. Up until the late 1980s, the system provided a monthly payment (the Family Allowance) to all families with children. It also included tax deductions for families with dependent children and a refundable tax credit for low-income families.[1] In 1992 the entire system was rolled into a single income transfer program (then called the Child Tax Benefit, the CTB, and now called the CCTB/NCB) that provides benefits, not on a universal basis to all families, but on an income-tested basis (calculated on the basis of total 'family' income), and on a sliding scale, to families with children who qualify. This change altered the meaning of the program: it was no longer a 'safety net' for all families, but a means of addressing 'child poverty' and reinforcing work incentives for parents. The latter idea was reflected, in particular, in the introduction of an 'earned income supplement' portion and the rule allowing provinces to 'claw back' the benefits from families who did not have earned income. These changes were part of a more general reorientation of social policy over the 1990s towards the embrace of a 'human resources' rationale for social policy that included identifying 'the child' as opposed to adults, as the optimal subject in which to 'invest.'

In the 1990s the NCB was further expanded, and in the late 1990s (under conditions of a federal budgetary surplus and a new climate of cooperative federalism), the National Children's Agenda came into being. Under this agreement, federal and provincial and territorial governments pledged to work together to achieve four goals relating to child health and development: (1) ensure that children achieve good physical and emotional health and (2) are safe and secure, (3) become successful learners, and (4) become socially engaged and responsible citizens (Canada 1999b). The tools for achieving these goals included the existing NCB program (which ostensibly became the 'flagship' program of the NCA), as well as early childhood development initiatives. The latter initiatives received funding under both the Early Childhood Development Agreement (ECDA), announced in 2000, and the Early Learning and Childhood Framework, announced in 2003. Under the agreements, the federal government transfers funds to the provinces and territories on condition that they invest in, mount, and run ECD and child care programs to serve families with young children.[2] Many of the goals of these agreements (e.g., encouraging healthy pregnancy, birth, and infancy, as well as parenting and family supports), follow those set out in earlier programs mostly established under the auspices of the federal health department, including, 'Brighter Futures,' the Community Action Program for Children (CAPC), the Canada Prenatal Nutrition Program (CPNP), and Aboriginal Head Start.[3] The 1998 NCB agreement also indirectly contributed funds to ECD policy by freeing up resources that provinces and territories would otherwise have spent on social assistance payments to families with children.[4] Provinces and territories are required to reinvest these monies in 'complementary' benefits (i.e., child benefits, earned income supplements, child care, and early childhood services and/or children-at-risk services, supplementary health benefits, and other initiatives; Canada 2005b: 9, 10). Indeed, to be clear, while the NCA was federally initiated and orchestrated, the programs actually fall under provincial or territorial and local jurisdictions. Moreover, the goals of the agreements are framed to ensure that these governments have considerable leeway and flexibility in choosing which programs to provide. A key issue, however, is that large portions of the money have been funnelled into early childhood development and 'children at risk' services (as opposed to child care), and much of it provides services in 'direct intervention' to families 'at risk' (McKeen 2006b; Vosko 2006; Child Care Advocacy Forum 2004).[5] While these services might be viewed as compensating in some way for the loss of community social services of the past decades, this view overlooks the significance and impact of the new policy thrust. It is important that we examine this program area and its implications more closely and critically.

Approaches to the Critical Analysis of Contemporary Social Policy Change

Before turning to a detailed analysis of the NCA, it is important to ask what we mean by 'critical analysis' in this field. Wendy Larner (2000) provides a useful framework for characterizing the range of critical approaches to neoliberalism that can serve as a road map for interpreting the critical literature in this field.[6] Larner divides interpretations of neoliberalism into three groupings according to whether it is viewed primarily as a set of policies, as an ideology, or as a practice of governance. Under the first frame, neoliberalism is treated simply as an assemblage of policies that reflects a coherent theoretical and ideological package of ideas (i.e., one that advances the market, privatization, and deregulation). This work tends to assume that the policies in question are basically worthwhile, if 'flawed.' Indeed, most commentaries on the NCB, NCA, and related topics (e.g., child poverty) by the academic community and the progressive social policy sector, fall under this category.[7] These approaches often raise questions regarding the efficacy and effectiveness of the policies (e.g., in addressing poverty, gender inequality, and meeting the needs of the poorest), and generally make recommendations on how to improve the policy (e.g., enhance the child benefit, eliminate the claw-back of the NCB for welfare recipients, introduce tighter requirements for how provinces spend their child care money, and so on).

There is also an important body of more critical work that falls under the 'policy as ideology' interpretive frame, and it is mainly concerned with revealing how the changes taking place in this policy area are a manifestation of neoliberal ideology. One example is research that argues that the introduction of the CCTB/NCB reflects a moment in the devolution of responsibility for social programs from federal to provincial governments and from governments to parents (Bach and Phillips 1997). Another example is work that views the shifts in child benefits and other changes brought about under the CHST as an unfolding of the neoliberal agenda that has led to the near collapse of the Canadian welfare state (Pulkingham and Ternowetsky1999). Although assumptions are still often made that the neoliberal agenda is a coherent package simply bought into by key actors and politicians, there also is growing interest in explaining the changes, for example, through interrogation of policy discourses. For example, Wanda Wiegers (2002) has deconstructed the policy discourse on 'child poverty' from a feminist perspective as a factor impeding a focus on gender inequality. Analysts also increasingly embrace the position that new regimes come into being in complex and contradictory ways, and are achieved through an ongoing process of contestation and struggle involving a wide range of actors and organizations. Susan McGrath's (1997) analysis of the limited influence that child poverty advocates had on shaping policies meant to address child poverty reflects this emphasis. McGrath argues that the discourse on 'child poverty' was co-opted by the neoliberal agenda such that child poverty was reframed as child neglect, with the result that families (women) were blamed, and addressing families 'at risk' was seen as the solution. My own work has focused on the ways that the choices of oppositional actors have mattered over the longer term in shaping debate on child and family benefits, for example, in exploring the impact that the discursive turn towards 'child poverty' had on women's voice in poverty and social policy debate (McKeen 2004; Dobrowolsky and Jenson 2004).

A third framework for understanding neoliberalism ('policy as governance') draws from the poststructuralist, neo-Foucauldian literature on governmentality (Larner 2000). This body of work sees government as sets of practices, techniques, discourses, and forms of expertise and knowledge that are concerned with 'the conduct of conduct,' or as defining the proper and legitimate orientation and conduct of citizens (Dean 1995: 561). Work from this perspective tends to focus on how policies and practices operate to mould and shape the identities and subjectivities of individuals, including their conduct, aspirations, needs, desires, choices, capacities, wants, and lifestyles, in order to support certain modes of existence (Dean 1995; Grundy 2005). Janine Brodie's (1995; 1996) work stands out as an important Canadian contribution in this respect. Brodie examines 'restructuring discourse' generally in Canada by focusing on how this discourse makes impositional claims that serve to encode, construct, and regulate categories of people, institutions, and services, and concepts such as citizenship and state responsibility, to bring them into alignment with neoliberal priorities. What is particularly valuable about her analyses, and those of others working within this framework (e.g., Kingfisher 2002) is that they show that new policies are rarely simply a return to an earlier model (e.g., the residual model), as a purely ideological interpretation might suggest, but reflect a transformation to something qualitatively different, more subtle and complex, and laden with significance and social implications that are specific to our time and place.

The point made by Larner and underlined here is that both the 'policy as ideology' and 'policy as governance' frameworks are critical tools for policy analysis, that the insights of each can inform the other and lead to more adequate understandings of the changes taking place. This is an important issue because our readings of social change ultimately inform our decisions and choices concerning whether and how to respond politically. It is with these ideas in mind that this chapter turns to study the new line of ECD/at risk programming under the National Children's Agenda and begins by focusing on the discursive politics that the NCA entails.

The Politics of the NCA: Shifting Discourses, Actors, and Norms for Social Policy

Before turning to the specifics of the NCA debate, we need to clarify certain assumptions concerning the change process itself within the social policy field. First, while changes in the social policy system reflect macrolevel influences, ideas, and structures, to be sure, they also reflect processes of struggle over ideas at the level of the 'social policy community.' Second, issues and discourses emerge from a process of deliberation and debate in which the voices of a range of political actors intermingle and mutually influence each other. In this regard, the strategic and discursive choices of even marginalized, oppositional actors can have an impact in shaping the ideas and discourses that frame policy debates. In fact, these actors can sometimes inadvertently play into the debates in ways that can facilitate the dominant model (McKeen and Porter 2003; McGrath 1997).

Turning to the struggle over the National Children's Agenda, it is clear that, from the outset, this project advanced a specific knowledge set about and philosophical approach to social problems. The terms of the NCA were largely defined by specific established professional bodies and research sectors. Discourses on early childhood development were introduced by coalitions of child health and child welfare professionals and by researchers working from a human capital perspective (Dobrowolsky and Jenson 2004; Dobrowolsky and Saint-Martin 2001). Within this knowledge base, child development was framed as a public health issue and, indeed, as a 'social determinant' of health. The NCA vision statement captured these ideas in calling on all communities, families, parents, and businesses to work together to ensure that all children have the opportunity to develop their capacities to the fullest (Canada 1999b). The broader vessel for these ideas, however, was the neoliberal, 'third way,' or human capital approach to social policy, which views social policy primarily as an instrument for 'activating' citizens (i.e., giving them a 'hand up,' as opposed to a 'hand out') in order to facilitate their entry into paid work. Beneath the rhetoric of the NCA, the onus was on individuals to transform themselves (or their children) into healthy, successful, independent, autonomous people who are fully integrated into the labour market and adaptable to shifting market conditions.

Second, the debate on the NCA, itself, was a further moment in transforming the ideas of the social policy community (McKeen 2005; 2006a). One of the key venues for discussing the NCA in the late 1990s was the Human Resources and Development Canada (HRDC), Subcommittee on Children and Youth at Risk.[8] The narrow focus on families and children, however, meant that 'new' participants and sectors were suddenly perceived as credible actors in the debate. Committee members viewed health and social service professionals as having especially relevant and worthwhile solutions to social problems – that is, solutions based on 'what works' for families in addressing the problem of 'activation' – and these actors were able to have undue influence on policy-makers in this area. The preferred solutions of the committee thus gravitated towards that of therapy for vulnerable populations and providing them with services such as counselling, training in parenting, skills upgrading, and the like. These ideas were supported by the voices of neoconservative actors who viewed the problems of poverty, homelessness, family breakdown, and wayward children as rooted in and caused by the prevalence of dysfunctional families and bad parenting practices (McKeen 2006a).

While the progressive social policy sector (e.g., Canadian Council on Social Development, the National Council of Welfare, the National Anti-poverty Organization, and Campaign 2000) sought to assert more structural analyses of the issues and to raise concerns regarding issues of inequality and social justice, the sector (once again) experienced pressure to curtail this more critical orientation. These long-standing social policy organizations found themselves with limited room to manoeuvre; they were put on the defensive as never before in fielding attacks on basic concepts and premises of social justice (i.e., the rights of welfare recipients to live in dignity, the legitimacy of the welfare system, the universal need for child care and therefore the importance of child care programs generally), and they were often drawn into discussions 'not of their own choosing' (McKeen 2006a). Also missing from this discussion were the voices and critical proposals of the broader social justice sector (i.e., social justice organizations).

The result of this process of debate was a new 'lowest common denominator' view of social problems that affected the federal social policy community as a whole. The new 'normal' thinking of this community marked a lowering of the bar with respect to focusing on issues of inequality and injustice, and in understanding social policy's role in upholding these important values and encouraging a general belief in them. It further consolidated and entrenched health and psychological perspectives (as opposed to sociological perspectives) as reference points for understanding social problems, and augmented a preoccupation with issues of family and individual shortcomings and incapacities, and the goal of finding specific remedies to these (McKeen 2006a). To be sure, these ideas did not represent a straightforward return to the old residual notion of blaming individuals (as reflected, e.g., in Ontario's punitive welfare model under Premier Mike Harris) but offered a more positive and compassionate approach guided by a belief in giving a 'hand up' to disadvantaged and isolated families through 'tailor-made,' community-based services. To gain further insight into the meaning and consequences of these shifting ideas, we must turn to examine the programs and the practices operating within them.

Policy, Programs, and Practices under the NCA: ECD/at Risk Programs and Women

The goals of these programs are often framed in terms of 'healthy child development,' for example, to promote 'healthy birth outcomes and the healthy development of children' (Canada 2005a), to improve the 'physical, cognitive, emotional and social development' of children (Lilley and Price 2004: 6), or, in the case of Nova Scotia's family resource centres, to 'reduce the risk factors for child abuse and promote healthy child development' (Nova Scotia 2004: 18). Indeed, much of the program emphasis and discourse in this policy area is grounded in the idea of helping parents to be the best they can be as parents, with the priority on helping particularly vulnerable families.[9] The focus is not, however, on ensuring that parents have the material means or time resources to provide for a stable family life but rather on equipping parents with skills and knowledge in parenting. The interest in parenting partly reflected the 'scientific' discovery that parenting style is an important factor influencing child well-being and behaviour and has a stronger influence than income on a child's behaviour (Canada 2003). As one program document puts it, 'parenting style has a stronger influence than income and parenting style influences a child's behaviour more than several other factors combined' (Nova Scotia 2004: 19). The services in question are generally housed in family or community resource centres (e.g., the Ontario Early Years Centres; family resource centres in Nova Scotia) or delivered through home visiting programs, and they have usually been integrated into, or linked with, the existing local non-profit and/or public health infrastructure (Vosko 2006; White 2003a). The programs usually include such areas as counselling and referral services, and programs to educate and train parents in such areas as literacy, nutrition, parenting practices, and knowledge and skills relating to the birth and care of babies. Some of the programs address specific issues such as fetal alcohol syndrome, emotional and behavioural disorders, developmental delays and autism, and so on. One of the key features of this program area is the common use of a relatively humanistic and compassionate helping ethic, termed 'empowerment theory,' or 'strengths-based theory.' This ethic aspires to steer away from judging or blaming clients; it favours working 'with' clients as opposed to working 'on' them, as is seen to be the case under more traditional casework models. These ideas are implied in the language that describes program activities – for example, to 'reach and support,' to 'build family confidence, knowledge and awareness,' to teach 'problem-solving in respectful and non-judgmental ways,' to encourage 'social connectedness,' to 'enable parents to build on their strengths,' and to 'support [them] in their role of nurturing their children' and so on.[10] Other principles that are valued include being 'flexible,' 'holistic,' 'attentive to the unique and changing needs of each family,' being 'family-driven' or 'mother-driven,' going at the family's own speed, and ensuring the process is completely voluntary, and providing the services that will 'make a difference' to families (Lilley and Price 2003). Under the Nova Scotia's Healthy Beginnings program, for example, 'the services vary according to the changing needs of the family. The service must be of a sufficient intensity to make a difference in families that need that level of assistance … Unique characteristics and circumstances of the family are identified and responded to creatively and non-judgmentally' (Lilley and Price 2003: 45).

Examining these programs and practices through the lenses of both 'ideology' and 'governance/subjectivity,' however, provides important insights into the limitations and contradictions that these services entail. According to Janine Brodie (1995), the defining feature of the neoliberal paradigm is the subordination of social policy to the demands of labour market flexibility and structural competitiveness, in which social problems are located in individual failure, and change is understood to rest on the ability of individuals to 'maximize their personal self-interest' (Fiona Williams, cited in Brodie 1995: 58). The role of government is to alter public expectations away from the notion of entitlements and collective provision for social needs (Brodie 1995). Under this world view, 'there is little tolerance for making "special" claims on the basis of difference or systemic discrimination' (Brodie 1995: 57), and so, for example, women are necessarily recast as 'bad individuals – the ones who are different, dependent, and blameworthy' and needing the kind of therapy provided by policy offering micro-individual self-help solutions (Brodie 1995: 61).

To be sure, 'at risk' programming, with its individualized terms and its strategy of identifying and treating those at risk, in many ways puts this philosophy into action. The concept of 'risk' is a crucial pillar for these programs, and they usually rely directly on research that has been done on tools for identifying the families or individuals 'at risk.' These tools have been developed based upon statistical correlatives, and they invariably identify as at risk the groups that least fit into standard, white, middle-class norms of family and family life and who are the most disadvantaged under the existing social structures. As such, these programs effectively intervene in ways that are highly classed, gendered, and raced – targeting the poor, lone-mother families, families of racially marginalized communities, and so on. Leah Vosko has made a similar observation with respect to Ontario's Early Years Centres: 'their hallmark was standardization, where the norm of the service recipient was narrowly conceived around the white, English-speaking male breadwinner-female caregiver household' (2006: 157). Moreover, while much of the language of the programs and the related research material is carefully framed in gender-neutral terms, women are a central focus – and they are the main clientele. For example, the programs' operational material clearly reveals the expectation that their main clients are women.[11] Mothers are also central figures in the most frequently named target groups, or 'priority' populations, for these programs (i.e., low-income mothers, lone mothers, pregnant women, new mothers, adolescent mothers, isolated mothers, First Nations mothers, mothers who are new immigrants or refugees, and so on). These mothers (and their young children) are most often profiled in the promotional material for these programs.

Again and again, the language of these programs puts the emphasis on individual responsibility for change. This is seen, for example, in the preoccupation in the Healthy Beginnings program with ensuring that home visitors are able to distinguish appropriate boundaries between themselves and their clients, so that workers can avoid being overly drawn into their client's 'stuff': 'The worker needs to know how to recognize dangers, how to handle themselves in home visiting – it's really easy to be pulled into someone's stuff, and to give advice that you really shouldn't be giving – it's critical that the person can establish boundaries and can understand what the boundaries should be' (Lilley and Price 2003: 31).

An individualized frame of reference is reinforced through other program constructs as well. For example, issues such as poverty and violence are treated as 'symptoms' or as 'warning signs' that alert home visitors to a family's vulnerability (Lilley and Price 2003: 21, 22), and healthy eating or smoking cessation are considered to be merely matters of personal lifestyle choice. Although there is an intention to avoid stigmatizing and blaming individual clients, the terms and practices of these programs help create the very conditions for this to occur. For example, under the home visiting program, clients become the objects of discussion among a range of program staff and community-services–based professionals, including discussion of child protection issues, and so they are easily subjected to scrutiny, intrusiveness, and discretionary judgments concerning their deservingness:

> In some programs, home visitors collaborate and follow-up regularly with workers from other agencies. They participate in case conferencing and provide reports back to referring agencies ...
>
> Home visitors interact with a long list of other service providers, including public health nurses, social workers, psychologists, physicians and lawyers. Interaction is often regarding referrals, either referrals to the home visiting service or to other services in the community. (Lilley and Price 2003: 24, 26)

Viewing these programs through the 'ideology' frame alone, however, does not capture all of the ways that they impact 'the social.' One of the important aspects of these programs is the way that they also operate directly 'on' clients to shape their identities and subjectivity. Programs such as CAPC, CPNP, and others, participate in *constructing* the very 'at risk' populations that they seek to help. They do this through repeated claims about the existence of these populations and the extent and nature of their vulnerability. Moreover, the constructions are inflected with classed, raced, and gendered characteristics. For example, program discourses tend to define particular categories of mothers as being vulnerable or having particular weaknesses and challenges. Typically, their weaknesses are thought to be low self-esteem; lack of competence, judgment, and information; having fears and insecurities; and being isolated and 'struggling.' The programs publicize themselves as offering vital solutions for these populations – providing mothers with emotional support and reassurance, helping them to gain more self-esteem and confidence, and allowing them to acquire the right knowledge to enable them to 'grow' and to be the best they can be for their children. Moreover, much of the activity of the programs is dedicated to convincing clients of their need for the services and of securing their cooperation. For example, the design and operations of Healthy Beginnings are geared to handling clients in a manner that will achieve 'family buy in' or 'win family trust.' This would appear to be a key rationale for the use of 'peers' as home visitors. As the program's front-line workers, peer home visitors are usually local women who are chosen partly because of the similarity of their life experiences with those of their clients, for example, as mothers who may have breastfed, raised a child on their own, lived on social assistance, and so on (Lilley and Price 2003). Peer home visitors are also seen by clients as credible in representing 'the community.' The central modus operandi of the home visitor is to 'overcome resistance,' gain 'family trust,' and undertake 'positive, persistent outreach with clients' (ibid.: 54). The trusting relationship between client and home visitor is viewed as the key that 'will enable the family to grow and be open to learning' (ibid.: 23) and 'increase a family's willingness to access other supportive services' (ibid.: 45). A constant emphasis in the role of the home visitor is providing emotional encouragement and working on mothers' self-esteem, while also helping with practical issues: 'Just setting up, for example, a budgeting program and a parenting program isn't enough. Such things can sometimes do more damage than good because people go away feeling like they can never measure up. You need to work on self-esteem at the same time' (ibid.: 24, quoting an administrator).

Other program activities direct clients to reflect on their inadequacies and weaknesses and to recognize that these deficiencies need constant work. For example, under Healthy Beginnings, the assessment process steers clients to identify their strengths and challenges and to formulate family goals in accordance with them: 'Family goal-setting' is supposedly a central part of the family-centred, strengths-based model and is one area in which home visitors are trained (Nova Scotia 2005: 11). The process is set in motion when the family (i.e., most often, the mother) is administered a series of standardized assessment tools.[12] The answers given are translated into family 'strengths and challenges,' from which 'family goals' are then drawn (ibid.: 34). Workers are instructed to ensure that these goals are expressed in the family's 'own words' (ibid.: 37). These ideas are also promoted through program evaluation tools and processes. For example, as part of the ongoing evaluation of the Healthy Beginnings program, clients are asked to complete a family outcomes survey in which they list three goals that they have 'identified and worked on with [their] home visitor' and to rate their own success in achieving their goals (Lilley and Price 2004: 43). The survey also asks clients to evaluate themselves on their parenting ability by rating themselves on the 'parenting ladder' (ibid.). The ladder interrogates parents on their level of confidence in their ability to parent – in knowing how children grow and develop, in helping their children to learn, in knowing positive ways of helping their children behave, in coping with the stress in their life, in knowing how to find the right people for advice and emotional support, and in knowing where to go for help if they need it (ibid.).

In this regard, the specific qualities valued in the client-mother appear to be the same ones that are sought when recruiting the peer home visitors (who are also valued for their relationship-building capacities). Ironically, but perhaps, not surprisingly, the traits have a somewhat traditional gender twist: client-mothers are to be empathetic, warm and caring, non-judgmental, flexible, supportive of others, well organized, able to multitask, good communicators, good listeners, self-directed, not easily stressed, not afraid to ask for help, and willing to do the mundane (Lilley and Price 2003). Other characteristics that are evidently valued in clients include being grateful for the assistance received and, when they do finally 'make it,' being willing to 'give back' to the community as a volunteer (Canada: n.d.).

Conclusions and Future Strategies and Directions

We can see that subtle changes have been taking place over the past several years in the nature and orientation of federal program support for children. These changes are especially evident in the advent of the National Children's Agenda, with its turn to a policy of intervening with people deemed to be 'at risk.' This chapter presents a critical analysis focusing on how the NCA, and the turn to 'at risk' programming, is affecting our ideas about social problems and solutions, who we are, and what we can expect as citizens. The main argument put forward is that this realm of programming is not simply 'flawed policy.' It is policy that 'facilitates governing of individuals from a distance' (Larner 2000: 6), and it is in many ways a further unfolding of neoliberal 'restructuring' discourse and ideology, as described by Janine Brodie (1995). This programming is not primarily directed towards meeting the material needs of vulnerable citizens. It is primarily concerned with enjoining clients to adopt a mode of self-governance and identity based on self-investment and self-reliance. Indeed, the entailed practices help construct the act of turning to the state for support as a mark of personal failure and/or immorality (Korteweg 2003). Such effects are endemic to the basic techniques and practices of the programs in determining who is, and is not, 'at risk,' and to the ongoing silence that these programs maintain about the structural and material realities that shape people's lives (e.g., the lack of decent paying jobs, gender inequality in pay, women's disproportionate burden for child care). The individuals caught up in these programs are allowed such partial and strategic 'at risk' identities as vulnerable parents, lone and teen parents, and so on, but are denied subjectivity as belonging to a particular collective group, for example, as having a racial, ethnic, class, or gender belonging. While this programming is formally gender-neutral, poor women (and often, racialized and marginalized women and men) are among those most targeted, and by implication, are defined as 'the problem' group. One of the implied messages of the policy is that women, or mothers, are the sector of society most responsible for the goal of 'healthy child development.' The programs' implied prescription to clients is to acquire the right interpersonal skills for being successful in building and maintaining the right community connections and linkages. The implied ideal subject is the maternal citizen who is self-sacrificing, resourceful, resilient, and flexible – a mother who uses her own inner will power, determination, and perseverance to face difficult life challenges. This 'activation,' however, takes place within social conditions that provide poor or limited life options, including poverty-level jobs and pay, poor access to quality child care, few meaningful training and education opportunities, and minimal public social services and supports.

The promotional material for these programs often claims that these services empower 'communities' by empowering families, one family at a time. This is a very persuasive message, and one that resonates strongly with the long-held belief that the proper role of the community is to informally reach out to its members, to take care of its own (Valverde 1995). This idea is reflected in the view put forward by an administrator within the Healthy Beginnings program: 'Don't complicate it – if you could go back in time 100 years, that's all it needs to be. A person comes by, has a cup of tea, reaches out to you, but with a little more structure. But don't make it more structured than it has to be' (Lilley and Price 2003: 17).

There appears to be a strong sentiment within local voluntary and public health sectors concerning the 'rightness' of this realm of programming. As Lilley and Price express at the conclusion of their 'scan' of the home visiting program in Nova Scotia: 'Our experience over the past few months has provided us with a very visceral sense of the importance and absolute "rightness" of these goals and of using a peer home visitor model to achieve them. As we spoke with people about their programs, we became increasingly convinced of the strong lifeline that home visitors provide for struggling young mothers and the long-term benefits for children, parents and society as a whole' (2003: 55).[13]

Yet, clearly, the important question that remains is whether such an approach can ever lead the way forward to ensuring social cohesion, equality, and social justice. The answer is that it very likely cannot. Deena White has argued that this approach to social policy represents 'a micro level vision of social cohesion,' in which responsibility for the organization of social cooperation has been left to the institutions of the market, family, and community (2003b: 65). The problem is that these institutions can only ever foster limited social cohesion, and the likely consequences of assigning this responsibility in this way are a society marked by 'individualism, exclusion and fragmentation' (ibid.: 67).

It is important that the progressive community respond to these policy developments. There is urgent need to refocus social policy debate around a discourse of social responsibility, social citizenship, equality, and social justice. A large part of this struggle would surely be to rebuild the belief in the value and importance of conserving and building social rights and social citizenship, or a sense of social responsibility. It is important that ways be found to do this that also provide for the immediate, practical needs of families and citizens. It would seem important in the immediate term to not abandon the 'at risk' program area to others who are not particularly convinced of the importance of social rights and equality but rather to raise critical questions within the context of these programs and practices. Many have asked, for example, how an agenda of healthy childhood development is at all comprehensible or viable without also advancing a strong agenda of equality for women (Wiegers 2002). As many commentators have noted, policies to ensure the availability of good jobs with decent pay, and a universal, accessible, quality child care system are necessary conditions for achieving the goal of healthy childhood development (Vosko 2006; White 2003b). A more general strategy for those working from within this field is to help find ways of opening space for collective discussion that allow clients and others to build awareness of the structural realities that shape people's lives and the need to address them.

Second, in relation to both the immediate and long term, it is important to challenge and resist the 'at risk' policy as a general direction for social policy for families. Parenting is obviously important, but the solutions should not simply focus on so-called risky families, but on the risk to parents living within increasingly deteriorating social and economic conditions, including the current serious inadequacies of social benefits and supports. Policies that would help build such a system have been well articulated by progressive advocates, and include such measures as universal child care, effective job creation, increased child benefits, increases to minimum wages, the creation of affordable housing, and meaningful strategies for addressing racial and other forms of discrimination. Moreover, without these more universal measures, the role and work of parenting will continue to remain the largely devalued, personalized, invisible, and isolating responsibility that it is at present, and it will continue to exact high personal costs from parents, and especially, from women.

Finally, recognizing that the 'universal' social policy system of the Keynesian welfare state never adequately addressed social needs or advanced the causes of equality and social justice, it is important to work to develop and advance alternative models for social policy that recognize peoples' real needs and advance a strong, socially just, version of 'the social.' Such a model might, for example, give women the ability to form autonomous households. It might also be built on recognition of the everyday, interrelated needs and tasks of all families to secure sufficient material resources to allow for day-to-day and generational survival, to give and receive care, and to participate as citizens with value and dignity in the decision-making that affects their lives (Orloff 1993; Winkler 1998). Such a model might also value and build on a sense of solidarity and community, and of shared concern for the welfare of others – all things that are missing in the new so-called child-centred social policy.

Notes

1 The child tax exemption was introduced in 1918, the family allowance in 1944, and the child tax credit in 1978.
2 The ECDA involved transferring $300 to $500 million from the federal government to the provinces over the period 2001–06. Under the early learning and childhood framework agreement, $935 million was pledged over a five-year period as matching federal funds to the provinces (White 2003a: 21).
3 The objective of CAPC, e.g., is 'to assist parents in raising happy, healthy children, promote healthy pregnancies, improve parenting and family supports, and to strengthen early childhood development, learning and care' (Murray 2004: 60).
4 As originally designed, the long-term goal of the NCB is to eventually

fully replace the income support allowance for children provided under provincial social assistance benefits.

5 Data presented by the Canadian Day Care Advocacy Association suggest that a very high proportion, in some cases more than half, of all new ECD funding has been spent on programs that are non-child care (Tammy Findlay, personal communication, May 2006). Funding for child care, specifically, was provided under the bilateral agreements negotiated between the federal Liberal government and the ten provinces in 2005, although the agreements were cancelled by the incoming federal government, under Steven Harper in 2006.

6 I am indebted to John Grundy for the idea of using Wendy Larner's framework; see Grundy.

7 Some examples (on the NCB) include: Myles and Pierson (1997); selections in Durst (1999); Paterson, Levasseur, and Teplova (2004); Wiegers (2002); and on ECD initiatives Friendly (2001); Rothman (2001); and Wiegers (2002).

8 For the transcripts, see Canada (1999a).

9 The specific goals of parent-education programs in Nova Scotia are to reduce parental stress, improve coping skills, reduce feelings of isolation, improve awareness of and ability to access community supports, decrease family conflict, improve self-esteem and self-confidence, and reduce the likelihood that families with young children will require longer, more intrusive services in the future (Nova Scotia 2004).

10 The terms were found in Manitoba (2003).

11 The Healthy Beginnings program makes this assumption throughout its operational manuals.

12 Standardized assessment tools used as part of the initial assessment process under Healthy Beginnings include 'NCAST Feeding/Teaching Scale, Difficult Life Circumstances, Community Life Skills Scale, and Network Survey or My Family and Friends' (Nova Scotia 2005: 33).

13 Lilley and Price also stand back from the program and recognize some limitations, although, ultimately, they frame it as an issue of 'flawed policy': 'These programs provide this critical support as best they can, with limited coverage, to limited populations and with very limited resources' (2003: 55).

References

Bach, Sandra, and Susan Phillips. (1997). Constructing a New Social Union: Child Care beyond Infancy? In Gene Swimmer (ed.), *How Ottawa Spends,*

1997-98 – Seeing Red: A Liberal Report Card, 235–58. Ottawa: Carleton University Press.

Brodie, Janine. (1995). *Politics on the Margins: Restructuring and the Canadian Women's Movement*. Halifax: Fernwood.

– (1996). Restructuring and the New Citizenship. In Isabella Bakker (ed.), *Rethinking Restructuring: Gender and Change in Canada*, 126–40. Toronto: University of Toronto Press.

Canada. (n.d.). *The National Child Benefit: Featured Success Story*. Human Resources Social Development Canada. Electronic version retrieved 20 Sept. from http://www.nationalchildbenefit.ca/ncb/success1.shtml.

– (1999a). Minutes of Proceedings: Sub-Committee on Children and Youth at Risk, Standing Committee on Human Resources Development and the Status of Persons with Disabilities, 36th Parliament, 1st Session, 22 Sept. 1997 – 18 Sept. 1999. Electronic version retrieved 17 Dec. from http://www.parl. gc.ca/InfoComDoc/36/1/SCYR/Meetings/Evidence/scyrev07-e.htm.

– (1999b). National Children's Agenda 'Backgrounder.' Ottawa: Ministerial Council on Social Policy Renewal. Electronic version retrieved 25 Feb. from http://www.scics.gc.ca/cinfo99/83064905_e.html.

– (2003). *The Well-Being of Canada's Young Children: Government of Canada Report 2003*. Federal/Provincial/Territorial Early Childhood Development Agreement. Ottawa: Human Resources Development Canada and Health Canada.

– (2005a). *Canada Prenatal Nutrition Program/Community Action Program for Children – Tracking Our Progress – Renewal 2003*. Ottawa: Public Health Agency of Canada, Minister of Public Works and Government Services Canada.

– (2005b). *Evaluation of the National Child Benefit Initiative: Synthesis Report*. Federal, Provincial and Territorial Ministers Responsible for Social Services. Retrieved on 2 October 2005, from http://www.nationalchildbenefit. ca/ncb/SP-Att215/english/page00.shtml.Child Care Advocacy Forum. (2004*). B.C.'s Annual Reporting on Early Childhood Development (ECD: Analysis of Impacts on Child Care*. Prepared by Lynell Anderson. Vancouver: CCAF.

Dean, Michell. (1995). Governing the Unemployed Self in an Active Society. *Economy and Society* 24(4): 559–83.

Dobrowolsky, Alexandra, and Denis Saint-Martin. (2001). Re-thinking Retrenchment: Ideas, Actors and the Politics of 'Investing in Children' in Britain and Canada. Paper prepared for the American Political Science Association Annual Meeting, San Francisco, 30 Aug. – 2 Sept.

Dobrowolsky, Alexandra, and Jenson, Jane. (2004). Shifting Representations of Citizenship: Canadian Politics of 'Women' and 'Children.' *Social Politics* 11(2): 154–80.

Durst, Douglas. (1999). *Canada's National Child Benefit: Phoenix or Fizzle?* Halifax: Fernwood.

Friendly, Martha. (2001). Is This as Good as It Gets? Child Care as a Test Case for Assessing the Social Union Framework Agreement. *Canadian Review of Social Policy* 47: 77–82.

Grundy, John. (2005). The Contested Terrain of Lifelong Learning in Canada: Policy, Ideology and Governmentality. Unpublished paper, n.d.

Kingfisher, Catherine (ed.). (2002). *Western Welfare in Decline: Globalization and Women's Poverty.* Philadelphia: University of Pennsylvania Press.

Korteweg, Anna C. (3003). Welfare Reform and the Subject of the Working Mother: 'Get a Job, a Better Job, then a Career.' *Theory and Society* 32(4): 445–80.

Larner, Wendy. (2000). Neo-liberalism: Policy, Ideology, Governmentality. *Studies in Political Economy* 63: 5–25.

Lilley, Susan, and Phyllis Price. (2003). *Home Visiting to Support Young Families in Nova Scotia: Report of a Province-wide Program Scan.* Prepared for the Nova Scotia Department of Health and the Healthy Beginnings: Enhanced Home Visiting Initiative, Provincial Steering Committee, Halifax.

– (2004). *Healthy Beginnings: Enhanced Home Visiting Initiative – Evaluation Framework.* Prepared for the Nova Scotia Department of Health and the Healthy Beginnings: Enhanced Home Visiting Initiative, Provincial Steering Committee, Halifax.

Manitoba. (2003). *Investing in Early Childhood Development Programs: 2003 Progress Report to Manitobans.* Electronic version retrieved 12 Sept. from http://www.gov.mb.ca/healthychild/ecd/ecd_2003_progress_report.pdf .

McGrath, Susan. (1997). Child Poverty Advocacy and the Politics of Influence. In Jane Pulkingham and Gordon Ternowetsky (eds.), *Child and Family Policies: Struggles, Strategies, and Options*, 172–87. Halifax: Fernwood.

McKeen, Wendy. (2004). *Money in Their Own Name: The Feminist Voice in Poverty Debate in Canada, 1970–1995.* Toronto: University of Toronto Press.

– (2005). The Discourse on Children and the Shrinking Politics of Social Policy in Canada. Paper presented at the Canadian Political Science Association Meetings, University of Western Ontario, London, 2 June.

– (2006a). Diminishing the Concept of Social Policy: The Shifting Conceptual Ground of Social Policy Debate in Canada. *Critical Social Policy* 27(1): 865–87.

– (2006b). Neo-Liberalism in Canadian Child Policy: The Case of the 'National Children's Agenda.' Paper presented at the Canadian Political Science Association Meetings, York University, Toronto, Workshop: Women and Public Policy, Post Neo-Liberalism? A Study of Continuity and Change, 1 June.

McKeen, Wendy, and Ann Porter. (2003). Politics and Transformation: Welfare State Restructuring in Canada. In Wallace Clement and Leah Vosko (eds.), *Changing Canada: Political Economy as Transformation*, 109–34. Montreal and Kingston: McGill-Queens University Press.

Murray, Karen. (2004). Do Not Disturb: 'Vulnerable Populations' in Federal Government Policy Discourses and Practices. *Canadian Journal of Urban Research* 13(1): 50–69.

Myles, John, and Paul Pierson. (1997). Friedman's Revenge: The Reform of 'Liberal' Welfare States in Canada and the United States. *Politics and Society* 25(4): 443–72.

Nova Scotia. (2004). *Nova Scotia's Early Childhood Development Initiative: Evaluation Framework*. Halifax: Nova Scotia Department of Community Services.

– (2005). *Healthy Beginnings:Enhanced Home Visiting Initiative – Support Manual*. Halifax: Nova Scotia Department of Health.

Orloff, Ann Shola. (1993). Gender and the Social Rights of Citizenship: The Comparative Analysis of Gender Relations and Welfare States. *American Sociological Review* 53(3): 303–28.

Paterson, Stephanie, Karine Levasseur, and Tatyana Teplova. (2004). I Spy with My Little Eye … Canada's National Child Benefit. In G. Bruce Doern (ed.), *How Ottawa Spends, 2004-2005: Mandate Change in the Paul Martin Era*, 131–50. Montreal and Kingston: McGill-Queen's University Press.

Pulkingham, Jane, and Gordon Ternowetsky. (1999). Neo-Liberalism and Retrenchment: Employment, Universality, Safety-Net Provisions and a Collapsing Canadian Welfare State. In Dave Broad and Wayne Antony (eds.), *Citizens or Consumers: Social Policy in a Market Society*, 84–98. Halifax: Fernwood.

Rothman, Laurel. (2001). Reflections on the Social Union Framework Agreement and the Early Childhood Development Services Agreement: Are We Moving in the Right Direction for Young Children? *Canadian Review of Social Policy* 47: 89–93.

Valverde, Mariana. (1995). The Mixed Social Economy as a Canadian Tradition. *Studies in Political Economy* 47: 33–60.

Vosko, Leah. (2006). Crisis Tendencies in Social Reproduction: The Case of Ontario's Early Years Plan. In Kate Bezanson and Meg Luxton (eds.), *Social Reproduction: Feminist Political Economy Challenges Neo-Liberalism*, 145–72. Montreal and Kingston: McGill-Queen's University Press.

White, Deena. (2003a). The Children's Agenda: How New Is it, and How Is It New? Draft manuscript, retrieved from author.

– (2003b). Social Policy and Solidarity, Orphans of the New Model of Social Cohesion. *Canadian Journal of Sociology* 28(1): 51–75.

Wiegers, Wanda. (2002). *The Framing of Poverty as 'Child Poverty' and Its Implications for Women*. Ottawa: Status of Women Canada.

Williams, Fiona. (1989). *Social Policy: A Critical Introduction*, London: Polity Press.

Winkler, Celia. (1998). Mothering, Equality and the Individual: Feminist Debates and Welfare Policies in the USA and Sweden. *Community, Work and Family* 1(2): 149–66.

3 A Study of Women's Provisioning: Implications for Social Provisions

SHEILA M. NEYSMITH, MARGE REITSMA-STREET,
STEPHANIE BAKER-COLLINS, AND ELAINE PORTER

Disappearing Social Provisions – Fading Entitlements?

After the Second World War many Western countries, including Canada, developed and supported a variety of publicly funded health, social, and employment services (Esping-Andersen 1996). These services were seen to embody a commitment to collective responsibility for the welfare of a nation's citizens. However, this postwar welfare state, even in its heyday, often only provided a tattered social safety net, with its many gaps filled by the voluntary sector and the informal helping networks of family and friends. Much of the work in these latter arenas was done by women, because in Canada, women enjoyed few entitlements to child and elder care. At the same time, women's labour force patterns limited the benefits that they could derive from programs such as Employment Insurance (EI) and pension plans that relied on eligibility criteria related to paid work (employment). During this period welfare state discussions did not recognize the types, amount, and range of work that women often undertake to provide for those people for whom they assume and carry responsibility; nor did these discussions acknowledge the complex social relations involved in such provisioning activities (Taylor 2004).

Since the mid-1990s in particular, the context of women's provisioning role has shifted because of cuts to services to women on low or insecure incomes, the destruction of local non-profit women-centred groups and organizations, and the shrinking of spaces where women collect to talk and imagine other ways to survive and prosper. The analysis presented here emerges from a cross-site research project that examines the question: 'What supports and constrains how women and groups provision for themselves and others for whom they have relationships of responsibility?' This question is an important one to address, given the magnitude of the more recent changes in welfare state services, benefits, and supports available to women.

A Study of Women's Provisioning

Provisioning, a term used by feminist economists, is the daily work performed to acquire material and intangible resources for meeting the responsibilities that ensure the survival and well-being of people. The concept allows for a much more inclusive starting place for understanding and shaping social policy than does market work, with its associated dualisms of public/private, economic/caring, or productive/reproductive labour. The central concern of the provisioning literature is explicating how people living in varied circumstances interact with each other and with social institutions to sustain human life (Beneria 1995; Donath 2000; Nelson 1993; Power 2004). The concept of provisioning enables an exploration of the range of responsibilities that women carry as individuals embedded in meaningful familial, market, and community relationships.

In this chapter women's provisioning activities, and the implications of recent welfare state restructuring on women's provisioning role, are considered in terms of two key concepts: civil society and work-life balance. Although these terms and the debates in which they are situated are important ones, the terms are often deployed in political and policy discourses in a problematic way insofar as they are used to deflect attention from the fact that women, especially marginalized women, are having to take on more provisioning activities in the face of reductions in public/state responsibility for social provisioning. Even though debates about civil society and the ramifications of the new economy on work-life balance tend to take place in different disciplinary arenas, this chapter brings them together to reveal how, in practice, they mutually reinforce each other to exclude possibilities for expanding social provisions.

The analysis presented here is based on a multisite study of the provisioning responsibilities of women who are members of different types of community groups. Six sites were selected purposefully to ensure diversity among study participants and organizations.[1] The six sites in the study are: (1) a network of feminist older women; (2) a food cooperative program within a multiresource centre; (3) a women's

society offering employability training to women who have left abusive relationships; (4) a community resource centre for families in two
poor, multicultural neighbourhoods; (5) a program focusing on young
immigrant women that was part of a large, multiservice organization;
and (6) a tenant group in a large urban social housing complex.[2] Interviews with participants are used to anchor this discussion about how
discourses concerning civil society and work-life balance are reflected
in policies that differentially affect women's capacity to provide.

Enter Civil Society, Exit State Responsibility?

Today, in Europe and North America, policy analysts and activists are
highlighting the importance of new social movements and networks as
spaces for developing alternative democratic practices. The term 'civil
society' is typically used to refer to the arena in which these activities
occur. Ideally, civil society can be a space for articulating alternatives;
for organizing across divisions such as those of gender, race, and social class; and a space for developing skills and leadership. In theory,
its institutional forms are distinct from those of the state, family, and
market; in practice, the boundaries between state, civil society, family,
and market are often complex, blurred, and negotiated (Centre for Civil
Society 2004). However, it is important to examine issues of accountability across institutions and actors because public policy encourages
non-government organizations (NGOs) and corporations to partner in
delivering health care and social services in North America and Europe,
as well as in Third World countries. Canadians and their governments
make significant and consequential choices about responsibilities and
rights in their everyday actions, and as Jenson (2001) points out, the
location of these choices is sometimes democratic associations, sometimes families, sometimes markets, and sometimes communities. The
actors in some of these social institutions are more powerful than in
others, and thus it is important to pay attention to the spaces where
choice is exercised and where responsibilities fall. In recent decades
markets have once again become significant players in service models.
Families and voluntary organizations have acquired greater responsibility for delivering social services, while a market language of choice
now inhabits voluntary, state, and familial spaces.

For the women in our research sites the demands of their provisioning responsibilities curbed possibilities for them to engage in civil society associations. Literature on deliberative democracy has focused on
the importance of an active civil society and the integration of different

participatory modes to facilitate citizen engagement in the public sphere (Newman et al. 2004); however, most suggested avenues for inclusion, such as mediation, citizen forums, and citizen initiatives assume that persons are able to participate in these public spaces. This is a questionable assumption for women, given the types and amount of responsibilities that they carry. For instance, 'Rose' is a widow and member of an association of older women. Rose was employed throughout her life, but now in her seventies, she is carrying major family responsibilities that affect the time and energy that she has available to participate in community activities that assume that such family responsibilities are a thing of the past. Rose said, in an interview:

> My granddaughter is #1 [responsibility]. I'm completely responsible for her financially. She lives with me. I support her financially, emotionally; she's living with me on a permanent basis ... And #2 [responsibility] would be my daughter. When she's working, when she can find work, she makes $10.00 an hour, which is not a living wage. She has three children, two with special needs. My son-in-law doesn't make much money. Therefore I am, to an enormous extent, still and will remain responsible for my daughter.

What this interview material demonstrates is that women's patterns of civil participation are tied to relationships that reflect their responsibilities within families, neighbourhoods, and jobs (Misztal 2005; Adkins 2005). Lynn Staeheli and Susan Clarke (2003), using a telephone survey, identified several clusters of participatory patterns among respondents. They concluded that ideas of participation that are limited to traditional patterns of organizational involvement both negate other forms of participation and miss new possibilities. Networking and sharing information are some of the pathways of engagement used by women but their format and process are unique. Irene, another member of the same older women's group articulates how this happens:

> People know me. They will stop me on the street. They will have a problem. They will, you know, I become their resource for the day. My boundaries allow, sort of dictate who I'll stop for and for how long ... I've always just shared information. I don't expect anything from anybody else but because I don't expect I get all sorts of wonderful surprises and invitations and gifts. And I don't mean gifts in the sense of gifts but just gifts of people saying, you know, 'I thought of you the other day and thought this might be of interest to you. I know you're dealing with this, or whatever.'

An increased focus on civil society can reduce pressure for the state to assume responsibility for social provisioning. This is clearly evident in the area of in-home supportive services for elderly persons, an arena that is especially well documented (Aronson and Neysmith 2001; 2006; Light 2001; Scourfield 2005; Ungerson 2004). Developments in this sector demonstrate that the spotlight is taken off the power exerted by the state as it regulates, for instance, the mixed economy of care, even as it withdraws from supplying supportive programs for women's provisioning work. But this shift is not limited to in-home supportive services; rather, it is happening across program types, as the following statement from a person on the staff of an employability program illustrates:

> The new [B.C. Liberal] government wants programs with objective measures, they want people to be self-reliant, they are really big on free enterprise. In my opinion, our women's organization fits every single one of those criteria – especially with the measurable outcomes. And yet, in the political arena, that obviously meant nothing when the ministry decided that our organization would be cut. All employability programs bridging women leaving abuse to enter the job market were cut in the second year of the new regime – and I use the word 'regime' on purpose!

Developing funding strategies and writing proposals are not activities easily undertaken by poor and already overworked women who may well have limited literacy skills; however, to win grants and demonstrate their accountability, women's groups are forced to develop formal organizational structures, seek out matching grants, and hire professional staff (Jaggar 2005). In all the sites we studied, women spent many hours getting and keeping funding in the face of public funding cutbacks.

   In sum, the argument presented here is that the discourse around civil society needs to be imbued more strongly with an analysis of how the changing presence of the state and the subsequent increase in the space occupied by family, formal not-for-profit agencies, and the market have reduced the options available to women. Not all civil actors are equally positioned. Disparities in income, time, and caring responsibilities are not denied so much as they are not even considered in discussions of civil society as an arena for democratic practices. Without this recognition, civil society models of democratic arenas can pose new threats by adding another layer of political exclusion for women, even as they counter some of the well-documented limitations of paternalistic welfare states. What still needs to be addressed are questions such as: What kinds of activities are deemed to be contributions to society? What are the linkages between civil society institutional forums and the provisioning of individuals? What are the responsibilities of the state to its citizens who carry relationship-based provisioning responsibilities? The lack of an active state presence in visions of civil society does not bode well for women such as those in our research sites. The policy alternatives presented later in this chapter are influenced by these questions. The power of state actors to negotiate dramatic policy initiatives has not diminished; instead, the state often uses its power to support market or familial rather than social provisioning. This reality is amply illustrated by recent federal-provincial negotiations over a national child care policy: in an unsuccessful attempt to avert defeat in the 2004 election, the Liberal federal government managed to overcome long-standing provincial differences on child care policy matters to negotiate a national child care policy.

Work-Life Balance: Just What Is Teetering?

Women's struggles to meet the needs of family members reflect the effects of an economic citizenship policy premise that equates independence and social contribution with employment. Assumptions about what types of work are valued underpin 'welfare to work' or activation policies, as well as tax credit schemes for low-income families (Skevik 2005). On the surface these policies may appear quite different, but they all share the assumption that employment, not unpaid caring labour or community engagement, is the route to full citizenship. Increasing women's participation in paid work has become the certified route to economic and gender equality. If following this path results in low income, then, it is argued, it is women's lower earnings in the labour force that need to be addressed, not whether or how to reward other types of work. Within such an employment-worker framework, progressive policy focuses on programs such as promoting employment equity through mainstreaming initiatives, developing incentives to attract women into traditionally male occupations, and expanding the knowledge economy (Perrons 2005; Skevik 2005; Squires 2005). Flexible scheduling to promote 'work-life balance' becomes an important strategy for implementing such programs.

The language of work-life balance is used to refer to policies targeting factors that constrain the work and care timetables that families are able to construct. Resolving work and family conflicts are presented to employees as individual choices to be exercised through flexibility options. Work-life policies and practices are seen as empowering women to exercise autonomy as they negotiate trade-offs in order to accommodate family life. Supportive policies include generous care services, instituting flexible working hours, respecting women's own work-life preferences, and recognizing family type and cultural differences. The language of these programs sounds quite inclusive. On closer inspection, however, such policies reflect an assumption of employee autonomy about where and when to work, and problems tend to be portrayed in terms of a simple dualism of work-family obligations. Recent studies suggest that these policies do not seem to have the type of impact one would expect. Time pressures and what some authors call 'scheduling problems' still abound. Juggling multiple demands occupies a large part of the accounts of women's lives (Baldock and Hadlow 2004). Creating a work-life balance is seldom simply a technical matter requiring the right policy tools. Contradictions and tensions between employment demands and family life arise from different ethical principles that value work and care differently. These ethical dilemmas are not easily resolved by women who struggle to subscribe to both (Brannen 2005; Williams 2001).

These policies to deal with work-life balance are limited to paid employment, reflecting once again a model of citizenship that is restricted to the employed adult, excluding all who are not part of the paid labour force. Thus, when work is done in the home, working conditions and balancing demands are unavailable discourses to invoke in situations that are clearly oppressive. In the following quote a woman who belongs to a food co-op is describing the conditions under which she is caring for her incapacitated husband in a household within which her son, young grandson, and daughter-in-law also live:

> He [grandson] plays hockey. So my son took him to the game. Everybody was gone so I went for a walk too. Before going I checked and he [husband] was sleeping. Then when I came back my son told me 'grandpa fell down.' I didn't say anything. Next morning, before leaving, my son said: 'Make sure you don't leave him alone because he was half an hour on the floor.' So, you know, I can't go for walks. I don't have time for me at all, since he's – no time.

The following further contextualizes the quote above and suggests the precarious conditions in which the woman is living, despite the work that she has contributed to her husband's care:

> On Father's Day he was ready to leave me. He said, he said to my daughter, 'I don't need you, I don't need your brother, I don't need your mother. I can take care of myself.' All he's getting is $800 pension. I don't mind if somebody takes him – his pension can go there and he can live there. At least I would be stress-free.

Work-life balance is not the type of concept that can bring about the changes needed to improve the quality of life of this participant. The term 'work-life balance' obfuscates the fact that work permeates all aspects of life – not just employment situations. Furthermore, the concept promotes an individual response to a systemic problem. Policies such as flexible work schedules or the use of mobile technologies address the work needs of a very limited segment of the population. They do not challenge the assumption that paid work is the only type of work (Hoskyns and Rai 2007). The working conditions of Maria, the woman quoted above, would be considered intolerable in an institutional setting. Regulations defining when she is entitled to take a break do not exist in informal work settings; when she does take a break she is threatened with insinuations that she is neglecting her responsibilities. This woman does not have the option to go on strike or quit, even though the emotional, physical, and mental stress of the situation negatively affect a range of family relationships. Although giving pause for thought, these types of comparisons ultimately ring false because market and family relationship differences, which underpin the work, are ignored. That is, the demands of familial caring work are taxing, but the associated relationships are not those of the marketplace. The dynamics of these relationships need to be part of policies developed to address situations such as that in the example. One important thread in feminist policy discussions, which we return to later, centres on how differences between the male breadwinner, the adult worker, and the universal caregiver models would lead to very different employment, social assistance, and pension policies (Fraser 1997; Lewis and Giullari 2005; Pascall and Lewis 2004).

Imagining Policy with Social Provisions that Support Women

As the interview material suggests, women can be so focused on day-to-day work and life demands that they have little time or energy for making plans for the future or developing collective social spaces where alternatives might be considered and shared activities promoted. These women show that practices in, as well as discourses on, civil society and work-life balance can mesh in ways that reinforce the social exclusion of certain groups of women. In virtually all areas of life there is a possibility for alternate provisioning. In what follows, one specific policy arena – supportive services for elderly persons – will be used to demonstrate how an alternative approach might develop. This new type of provisioning would require changes to current assumptions about the value of different types of work, and it would focus both on imagining how state provisions can support the work done by women and what the nature of the care would look like.

Since the 1980s social policy in North America, and in many European countries, has focused on developing mixed economies of care. In such models, for-profit and not-for-profit agencies partner with government for service delivery. The process is typically one wherein agencies, such as those delivering home care, are asked to compete in developing service packages that are then submitted as contract bids for public funding. The winning contractor is assured that the government will purchase an agreed-upon amount of service from it for the length of the contract. Couched in the language of consumer choice, on the one hand, and respect for local diversity, on the other, the state can then step back, delimiting its role to that of proposal arbitrator within a fixed budget. As in other jurisdictions, this policy approach in most Canadian provinces has resulted in decreasing service hours covered by public funds (Penning et al. 2006), the promotion of caring allowances for kin (Keefe et al. 2005; Ungerson 2004), and the marked growth over the past decade of home care service businesses (Williams et al. 1999). Not quite so visible in this policy debate is that home care budgets have prioritized the care needs of most acute care patients (Ontario 2004) and thus supportive services to frail elderly persons, who are primarily women, have virtually disappeared – leaving a caring gap to be filled by family (Burr et al. 2005; Hollander et al. 2007). These developments have significant gender and social class impacts.

The failure of the model of the mixed economy of care has been well documented (Lewis and Giullari 2005; Light 2001), but of particular interest in this chapter is how such a model reproduces the very conditions that perpetuate problematic assumptions about citizenship. Specifically, in these policies adults are assumed to be employed, and thus in a position to access or purchase care services. The unpaid labour performed at home or in the community is erased (Skevik 2005) or minimized through allowance schemes. In policy discussions and implementation it is quite evident that the term 'worker' is limited to adults' activities in the paid labour force. A good deal has been written about the issues, services, and dilemmas of caring for children and adults who need it. Although this now vast literature has various emphases, in the field of elder care, debates have focused either on the needs of the person being cared for and/or the emotional, mental, and physical (as well as financial) costs borne by female kin. This focus stems from the fact that many of the persons writing in the area are policy analysts or service providers. Entitlements to social provisions in the form of service guarantees are not a feature of Canadian social policy as they are, for example, in a number of Scandinavian countries. In these countries, although the translation of such entitlements into services may have decreased (Johanssen et al. 2003; Szabehely 2005), a person's right to them as a citizen has not. Such an orientation in Canada would force us to figure out how to ensure that neither providers nor receivers are in care roles against their wishes (see, e.g., Armstrong 2002).

Given the failure of worker-citizen assumptions to meet the needs of women who continue to carry the lion's share of caring responsibilities, it seems that another route is worthy of consideration. In the study that informs the analysis presented in the preceding pages, the concept of provisioning was used to capture the range of relationship-based responsibilities that women carry. Our argument is that under current conditions these realities impede women's capacity to engage in civil society. Women need policies that support their work-life balance, but these will discriminate against women unless the unpaid work that they do is factored into 'work' policies. Some feminist policy analysts have countered this worker-citizen model with that of a universal caregiver model. This has been informed by understandings of care developed in feminist philosophy (Nelson and England 2002; Tronto 1993), political science (Fraser 1997), and economics (Nelson 1993).

The universal caregiver model opens up other possibilities by assuming interdependence as characterizing relationships among people rather than states of independence or dependency. One impasse that this circumvents is reconciling demands for autonomy by both the carer and the person cared for. A person's agential freedom to be and to do, that is, her autonomy, is not simply dependent on the existence of social entitlements or guarantees of procedural justice; it also depends on the needs and actions of others. Such interdependence is particularly acute at the household level (Lewis and Guilleri 2005). Both women's and men's capability to choose to engage in paid work or political activism are dependent on each other's choices to care or not to care for their children and others needing care – such as the elderly man in the earlier quote. Agency is unequally restricted along gender lines: men are not constrained by caring expectations as women are. For instance, it is difficult to even conceive of a scenario where the grandmother mentioned above could assume that norms of filial obligation dictated that her son care for his father while she exercised intergenerational rights to spend time with her grandson in a leisure activity – which may well be at hockey practice. The point here is that very likely the older woman, her son, service providers, and hockey coaches *all* share assumptions about who takes on what caring responsibilities within the family. Changing these assumptions will not happen within the isolation of either nuclear or extended families. The dynamics of negotiations within households are shaped by the broader sociopolitical context, not just by individual actors. Although access to regular services that took the grandfather out of the house (respite day programs) would provide some breathing space for the grandmother, such day programs do not promote women's agency by making men more accountable for their responsibility to care for others. To do this, policies would need to institutionalize (normalize) all citizens as having caring as well as income-generating responsibilities.

We put forward three policy suggestions in the area of supportive care for elderly persons that are consistent with the vision of state social provisions that support citizens situated as caregivers: the first focuses on services, the second on tax possibilities, and the third on employment practices. These may seem unlikely at this historical moment; however, the intent is to imagine alternatives. The challenge is to sketch policy directions that promote both class and gender equity.

It is telling that the one policy that all women's groups have supported as essential to the autonomy of women is a viable national child care policy. Yet multiple campaigns by day care advocates have been met with what can only be described as stonewalling over the decades, as a patchwork of tax benefits and subsidies keeps reappearing under different names. Likewise, advocates of supportive home care and respite programs have presented sophisticated statistical analyses documenting their cost effectiveness (Hollander 2003). Although each province has some form of community-based care legislation, Canada does not have a national home and community care program like, for example, what exists in Australia – a country with state structures quite similar to those found in Canada (Neysmith 1995). As in child care, there have been numerous attempts to create such a mechanism, but to date they have failed to garner the political support that undergirds the Canada Health Act (CHA). The most recent were the National Forum on Health in the mid-1990s (see NFH 1997). In 2002 the agenda of the Romanow Commission, and similar inquiries, was silenced on the issue by threats of a move to market-based approaches to services now covered by the CHA.

A feature of many social care services is the social class and gender contradiction, wherein caregiving services are usually provided by low-income, frequently newcomer, women of colour. In the Canadian context policies such as the Live-In Caregiver Program (Citizenship and Immigration Canada) have been criticized for reproducing inequities locally while exacerbating imbalances in the international flow of women's labour between North and South (Bakan and Stasiulis 1997; Isaken 2007; McWatt and Neysmith 1998). However, one reason the policy continues is that it supplies child and elder care workers. Despite its well-documented shortcomings, this policy meets the labour needs of those women who are able to purchase some help with their caring responsibilities. It thereby gives these women options for participating in the labour market and/or engaging in a range of civil society institutions. If it were abolished, at a minimum there would be pressure to expand home care services, and a market response to this pressure would not suffice. Many families do purchase hours of home care support from both profit and not-for-profit agencies. Not only is this expensive, but there is limited quality control, and, most importantly, what is purchased is care hours, not a particular person to provide the care. However, caring labour by definition is often relationship-based. One appeal of the Live-In Caregiver program is that the same person is there to monitor the situation as well as provide daily care. 'Being there' and establishing relationship pathways for getting the work done are both features of caring labour. In most Canadian provinces home care services are defined and paid in terms of tasks; service personnel-client relationships and the work of monitoring are excluded from job descriptions and service-funding calculations. Building service models where relationships rather than tasks are central in the organization of the work is possible, but it requires changing what is valued in the job and thus what is paid for. Alternative models do exist. For example, in

Australia, as in Canada, funding formulas are based on assessments of an older person's functional capacity. However, how service packages are organized and delivered is different in the two countries; in Australia, this is determined by the local responsible agency. In one model, each elderly client is assigned a home care worker who then determines what to do and when (Benevolent Society 2008). The client knows she has one worker (and a back-up). Thus, the relationship part of the work is part of the structure; maintaining it is seen by case managers as an important pathway to getting the work done.

The tax system is an important policy route for promoting equity, but in Canada this will require a change from its present emphasis on child or old age tax credits. The state will need to put in place policies that direct money to services that support the care needs of older persons and their families. The temptation here is to make the suggestion that designated funds come out of general tax revenue. However, it is anticipated that such a recommendation would be immediately translated into a need to increase personal income taxes. Raising tax levels seems quite improbable at this political historical moment. In addition, the income tax system in Canada is not progressive, in the sense that higher-income households have more avenues for decreasing their tax burden than middle-income earners do. Instead, there is an alternative approach that seems politically feasible, if not popular. This is to introduce a graduated care tax, called Care Insurance, on the earnings of employed individuals. A parallel employer tax would be initiated simultaneously. If the assumption were that all adults carry caring responsibilities (not just certain groups of women), this model would be as logical as Employment Insurance and other social benefits now associated with employment. The latter assume that all adults are workers. Put differently, the assumption of the universal carer is no more illogical than the universal worker assumptions that underpin policies directed at moving sole support mothers on social assistance into low-income jobs. Another tax approach would be to model a carer insurance premium on existing health insurance premiums like those of the Ontario Health Insurance Plan (OHIP) – despite the many criticisms of such schemes. What such policy approaches do demonstrate is that program-specific tax schemes covering the population are politically viable, even when raising general tax revenues seems to be out of the question. Advocacy groups would need to monitor the process closely to ensure that revenues from specific insurance premiums are red-circled, to be used only for their intended purpose. Such a policy would give women of all ages, whether elderly users, caring family members, or care workers, options for services and jobs, addressing class as well as gender inequities.

A reader might well point out that by itself, the foregoing will not change the assumption underpinning labour market dynamics that adults are workers/breadwinners, even while it opens up options for women. The conundrum facing advocates of generous care leave policies is that these policies may ameliorate the care and time crunch facing some families in the short term, but in the long run, these policies may reinforce women's traditional caring role without challenging the relative invisibility or lack of respect afforded these activities more generally. This is because it is women who will likely continue to make use of leave provisions – because of women's lower earnings. Thus, while we support care leave as a policy direction, we predict that its impact will be limited. Research done in countries that have such leave policies shows that it is women who take such leave up far more than men (Olson 2002). This behaviour has been linked to career costs, namely, that taking time out results in lost promotion opportunities and thus a decrease in overall life-time earnings. Changing this labour force dynamic will need something more than leave incentives. In addition, policies directed at local labour market practices will probably become less relevant as the economic realities of worldwide markets change patterns of job retention, mobility, and ideas about career paths. Although recognizing that national policies will have a limited impact on changing the many inequities of a globalized economy, an active state, rather than one that assumes the passive stance of arbitrator, is necessary as citizens cope with the effects of economic forces well beyond their control. Such a state would promote services that care users, both receivers and providers, in different social locations can access as they weigh their options.

Thus, our third policy suggestion is that employment practices build in caring as a normal and expected responsibility of adults, a responsibility that requires work schedules that accommodate the demands of caring. Most jobs are regulated by employment standards and minimum wage schedules; many also have pension benefits and supplementary health insurance. In recent years some unions and progressive employers have even brought in family care benefits, but these are concessions from the 'normality' of paid employment. They are defined as fringe benefits, suggesting that they are not central to paid employment, even though the demands made on the employee may be anything but fringelike in their impact. A universal caregiver model would assume that all adults carry caring responsibilities; the ebb and flow of these responsibilities may change over the life cycle of individuals, but caring responsibilities are a social given. Under such a model employment policies and job descriptions would have caring-related rights and benefits that complement the health and pension benefits today. Promotion ladders that do not allow for caring responsibilities could be challenged as discriminatory. Implementing such a model is pivotal if women's citizenship claims are to be realized. This will happen only if caring for others is seen to be central to the lives of all citizens, as central as holding down a paid job, participating in community affairs, paying taxes, and being a consumer.

Conclusion

The scenario imagined above reveals how critical it is that policy debates be preoccupied with a different set of issues than they now are. Such debates are important because they will affect the hard choices all of us have to make regarding what to support, what to steer away from, and what coalitions to participate in. Policies that position men as well as women as citizens who carry caring responsibilities even as they are employed would increase the capacity of women to choose to engage in various forms of participation, including politics. From such spaces, other possibilities can develop. Thus, maintaining these spaces is important. As noted in our opening remarks in this chapter, one impetus for sampling women who are members of civil society groups was our alarm over how rapidly these spaces for participation are disappearing.

Political imagining is important because it allows us to think of alternative ways of constructing and organizing society according to different models of administration and economics. It is the location between the ideal and the material that makes political imagination such a potentially powerful tool in shaping experience. Its potential is realized when it can maintain a dynamic relationship between idealism and material conditions or, in more common parlance, when it negotiates between theory and practice. Importantly, imagination is not controlled entirely by the individual. It may be felt to be individual, but the individual is influenced by the collective (McBride 2005). The state, as well as the market and family, will continue to be very present in the lives of women and in twenty-first century social policy-making – the question is how it will affect different groups of women. The concept of provisioning helps us to explore the scope and diversity of the responsibilities that women carry: It allows for a relationship to be articulated between women and the state, ensuring that the interdependencies that support well-being are recognized and supported. It forces recognition of the fact that the state and what it does matter in the lives of citizens who do not fit neatly into market, family, or community stereotypes, yet are expected to assume increasing responsibility for the people around them.

Notes

1 The sites were also selected for feasibility and mutual interest. There were six researchers, each responsible for a site geographically, historically, and culturally close to them. The focus, governance, membership, and activities of each site were quite different. The researchers already had established relationships with the sites, and with the help of community advisory panels, successfully approached the members and decision-makers of each site to invite participation in the study.

2 Data were collected on 100 women in these six sites, selected purposively, and varying by race, age, income, and family size. They were asked about their own provisioning responsibilities, and those of the site they were associated with. At several points during the four-year study, additional persons participated in focus groups and key informant interviews to better understand the context of site activities and the constraints the participants faced. Before starting the interview, an information and consent form was signed by all participants. This process included an oral and written explanation of the concept of provisioning, as well as why we were using it rather than 'work' or 'care' in the interview. Interviews were taped and later transcribed for analysis using NVIVO software package for qualitative data. The questions that guided the interviews are: *Who* are you responsible for? What *activities* do you do to provide for the persons you are responsible for? (Interviewer would point to the persons indicated on the map.) *How* do you carry out this work? What *helps* you and what makes it *difficult*? What *changes* do you foresee in these provisioning responsibilities in the next three to five years? What do you see *affecting* this work in the future? Twenty-one types of work were identified, allowing us to create six categories of activities and six strategies used by women to meet their provisioning responsibilities as they went about their daily lives.

References

Adkins, Lisa. (2005). Social Capital: The Anatomy of a Troubled Concept. *Feminist Theory* 6(2): 195–211.

Armstrong, Pat. (2002). The Evidence Is in … It's Time to Act on Home Care. *Network* 2/3. Electronic version retrieved from Canadian Women's Health Network, http://www.cwhn.ca.

Aronson, Jane, and Sheila Neysmith. (2001). Manufacturing Social Exclusion in the Home Care Market. *Canadian Public Policy* 27(2): 151–65.

– (2006). Obscuring the Costs of Home Care: Restructuring at Work. *Work Employment and Society* 20: 27–45.

Bakan, Abigail, and Daiva Stasiulis (eds.). (1997). *Not One of the Family: Foreign Domestic Workers in Canada*, 53–79. Toronto: University of Toronto Press.

Baldock, John, and Jan Hadlow. (2004). Managing the Family: Productivity, Scheduling and the Male Veto. *Social Policy and Administration* 38(6): 706–20.

Benevolent Society. (2008). Site Visits to Live at Home Programs, February 20, 21, 2008, Sydney, Australia.

Beneria, Lourdes. (1995). Toward a Greater Integration of Gender in Economies. *World Development* 23(11): 1839–50.

Brannen, Julia. (2005). Time and the Negotiation of Work-Family Boundaries: Autonomy or Illusion? *Time and Society* 14(1): 113–31.

Burr, Jeffrey, Ian Mutchler, and Jennifer Pitcher Warren. (2005). State Commitment to Home-Based Services: Effects on Independently Living Older Women. *Journal of Aging and Social Policy* 17(11): 1–18.

Centre for Civil Society. (2004). What is Civil Society? Electronic version retrieved 13 Feb. 2007 from http://www.lse.ac.uk/collections/CCS/what_is_civil_society.htm.

Citizenship and Immigration Canada. (N.d.) Working Temporarily in Canada: The Live-In Caregiver Program. Electronic version retrieved 16 March 2008 from http://www.cic.gc.ca/ENGLISH/work/caregiver/index.asp.

Donath, Susan. (2000). The Other Economy: A Suggestion for a Distinctively Feminist Economy. *Feminist Economics* 6(1): 115–23.

Esping-Andersen, Gøsta (ed.). (1996). *Welfare States in Transition: National Adaptations of Global Economies*. London: Sage.

Fraser, Nancy. (1997) *Justice Interruptus: Critical Reflections on the 'Postsocialist' Condition*. New York and London: Routledge.

Hollander, Marcus J. (2003). Unfinished Business: The Case for Chronic Home Care Services. Policy paper updated October 2004. Victoria, B.C.: Hollander Analytical Services.

Hollander, Marcus, Neena Chappell, Michael Prince, and Evelyn Shapiro.

(2007). Providing Care and Support for an Aging Population: Briefing Notes on Key policy issues. *Healthcare Quarterly* 10(3): 34–45.

Hoskyns, Catherine, and Shirin Rai. (2007). Recasting the Global Political Economy: Counting Women's Unpaid Work. *New Political Economy* 12(3): 297–317.

Isaken, Lise. (2007). Gender, Care work and Globalization: Local Problems and Transnational Solutions in the Norwegian Welfare State. In Marjorie Griffin Cohen and Janine Brodie (eds.), *Remapping Gender in the New Global Order*, 44–58. London and New York: Routledge.

Jaggar, Alison M. (2005). Civil Society, State and the Global Order. *International Feminist Journal of Politics* 7(1): 3–25.

Jenson, Jane. (2001). *Social Citizenship in 21st Century Canada: Challenges and Options.* The Timlin Lecture, University of Saskatchewan, Saskatoon, Saskatchewan, 5 Feb.

Johansson, Lennarth, Gerdt Sundström, and Linda Hassing. (2003). State Provision Down, Offspring's Up: The Reversed Substitution of Old-Age care in Sweden. *Ageing and Society* 23(3): 269–80.

Keefe, Janice, Pamela Fancey, and Sheri White. (2005). *Consultation on Financial Compensation Initiatives for Family Caregivers of Dependent Adults: Final Report.* Halifax: Maritime Data Centre for Aging Research and Policy Analysis, Mount Saint Vincent University.

Lewis, Jane, and Susy Giullari. (2005) The Adult Worker Model Family, Gender Equality and Care: The Search for New Policy Principles and the Possibilities and Problems of a Capabilities Approach. *Economy and Society* 34(1): 76–104.

Light, David W. (2001) Managed Competition, Governmentality and Institutional Response in the United Kingdom. *Social Science and Medicine* 52: 1167–81.

McBride, Keally D. (2005). *Collective Dreams: Political Imagination and Community.* University Park: Pennsylvania State University Press.

McWatt, Sue, and Sheila Neysmith. (1998). Enter the Filipina Nanny: An Examination of Canada's Live-In Caregiver Policy. In C. Baines, P. Evans, and S. Neysmith (eds.), *Women's Caring: Feminist Perspectives on Social Welfare*, 2nd ed., 218–32. Toronto: Oxford University Press.

Misztal, Barbara A. (2005). The New Importance of the Relationship between Formality and Informality. *Feminist Theory* 6(2): 173–94.

National Forum on Health. (1997). *Canada Health Action: Building on the Legacy.* Final report of the National Forum on Health. Ottawa: Health Canada.

Nelson, Julie A. (1993). The Study of Choice or the Study of Provisioning: Gender and the Definition of Economics. In M.A. Ferber and J.A. Nelson (eds.), *Beyond Economic Man*, 23–36. Chicago: University of Chicago Press.

Nelson, Julie A., and Paula England. (2002). Feminist Philosophies of Love and Work. *Hypatia* 17(1): 1–18.

Newman, Janet, Marian Barnes, Helen Sullivan, and Andrew Knops. (2004). Public Participation and Collaborative Governance. *Journal of Social Policy* 33(2): 203–23.

Neysmith, Sheila. (1995). Would a National Information System Promote the Development of Canadian Home and Community Care Policy? An examination of the Australian experience. *Canadian Public Policy* 21(2): 159–73.

Olson, Kevin. (2002). Recognizing Gender, Redistributing Labour. *Social Politics: International Studies in Gender, State and Society* 9(1): 380–410.

Ontario. (2004). *Commitment to Care: A Plan for Long-Term Care in Ontario.* Prepared by Monique Smith, Parliamentary Assistant, Ministry of Health and Long-Term Care, Toronto.

Pascall, Gillian, and Jane Lewis. (2004). Emerging Gender Regimes and Policies for Gender Equality in a Wider Europe. *Journal of Social Policy* 33(3): 373–94.

Penning, Margaret, Moira Brackley, and Diane Allen. (2006). Home Care and Health Reform: Changes in Home Care Utilization in one Canadian province 1990–2000. *Gerontologist* 46(6): 744—58.

Perrons, Diane. (2005). Gender Mainstreaming and Gender Equality in the New (Market) Economy: An Aalysis of Contradictions. *Social Politics: International Studies in Gender, State and Society* 12(3): 389–411.

Power, Marilyn. (2004). Social Provisioning as a Starting Point for Feminist Economics. *Feminist Economics* 10(3): 3–19.

Scourfield, Peter. (2005). 'What Matters Is What Works'? How discourses of modernization Have Both Silenced and Limited Debate on Domiciliary Care for Older People. *Critical Social Policy* 26(1): 5–30.

Skevik, Anne. (2005). Women's Citizenship in the Time of Activation: The Case of Lone Mothers in 'Needs-Based' Welfare States. *Social Politics: International Studies in Gender, State and Society* 12(1): 42–66.

Squires, Judith. (2005). Is Mainstreaming Transformative? Theorizing Mainstreaming in the Context of Diversity and Deliberation. *Social Politics: International Studies in Gender, State and Society* 12(3): 366–88.

Staeheli, Lynn A., and Susan E. Clarke. (2003). The New Politics of Citizenship: Structuring Participation by Household, Work and Identity. *Urban Geography* 24(2): 103–26.

Szebehely Marta. (2005). Care as Employment and Welfare Provision: Child Care and Elder Care in Sweden at the Dawn of the 21st Century. In Hanne

Marlene Dahl and Tine Rask Eriksen (eds.), *Dilemmas of Care in the Nordic Welfare State*, 89–107. Aldershot: Ashgate.

Taylor, Rebecca F. (2004) Extending Conceptual Boundaries: Work, Voluntary Work and Employment. *Work, Employment and Society* 18(1): 29–49.

Tronto, Joan C. (1993) *Moral Boundaries: A Political Argument for an Ethics of Care*. New York and London: Routledge.

Ungerson, Clare. (2004). Whose Empowerment and Independence? A Cross-National Perspective on 'Cash for Care' Schemes. *Ageing and Society* 24: 189–212.

Williams, Fiona. (2001) In and beyond New Labour: Towards a New Political Ethics of Care. *Critical Social Policy* 21(4): 467–93.

Williams, Paul, Jan Barnsley, Sandra Leggat, Reisa Deber, and Pat Baranek. (1999). Long-Term Care Goes to Market: Managed Competition and Ontario's Reform of Community-Based Services. *Canadian Journal on Aging* 18(2): 126–53.

4 Gender Mainstreaming in Neoliberal Times: The Potential of 'Deep Evaluation'

OLENA HANKIVSKY

Gender mainstreaming (GM) or as it is known in Canada, gender-based analysis (GBA), has become an internationally recognized strategy for promoting gender equality. In Canada, federal and provincial governments alike, including British Columbia, have introduced GBA policies and frameworks. To date, however, GM has not been particularly successful in advancing women's equality, and researchers and policy-makers are seeking to better understand the slow progress with this strategy. While numerous explanations are being offered in the litera- ture, with a few exceptions, such as the work of Teghtsoonian (2003; 2004; 2005), less attention has been paid to the political terrain on which GM is conceptualized and operationalized. Specifically, little research has been dedicated to examining whether GM can be an effective strat- egy for confronting neoliberal political agendas at the global, national, and provincial levels of government, including the political agenda of the Liberal government in the province of British Columbia, which has been singled out internationally for its role in undermining women's social and economic security.

In this chapter I provide a brief introduction to gender mainstream- ing, which includes a discussion of the implementation barriers that have been identified in the literature. I then move on to examine the rela- tionship between neoliberalism and GM, and in so doing, illuminate the current political situation in British Columbia vis-à-vis gender equality, which I argue does not, at first glance, provide much promise for the operationalization of GM. Indeed, such an examination raises a funda- mental question about whether the strategy of GM can ever be effective within neoliberal policy contexts. In tackling this question, I draw on and investigate the potential of an alternative GM strategy proposed by

Carol Bacchi and Joan Eveline (2003) in the Australian context, 'Deep Evaluation' and its related 'Gendering Based Assessment,' which are intended to enable policy analysts to effectively critique neoliberal norms and, in particular, dominant constructions of policy problems and gender relations. Although there are certain shortcomings in their analysis of GM and the conventional policy cycle, their proposal, which calls for producing GM as an ex ante intervention, does improve on conventional GM analysis for neoliberal policy contexts such as British Columbia. In particular, their approach provides an effective tool for policy analysts within government and citizens outside government to critically analyse how policy works, including how policy problems are identified and shaped, which is an essential stage in moving towards setting a policy agenda that enhances rather than undermines equality.

Background

Gender mainstreaming was formally adopted at the Beijing Conference on Women in 1995 and further entrenched with the establishment of the United Nations Convention on the Elimination of All Forms of Discrimination against Women (CEDAW). According to the Beijing Platform: 'governments and other actors should promote an active and visible policy of mainstreaming a gender perspective in all policies and programs so that before decisions are taken, an analysis is made of the effects on women and men respectively' (United Nations 1995: par. 79). While there are variations in definitions, according to the U.N. Office of the Special Adviser on Gender Issues and the Advancement of Women, 'mainstreaming involves ensuring that gender perspectives and attention to the goal of gender equality are central to all activities – policy development, research, advocacy/dialogue, legislation, resource allocation, and planning, implementation and monitoring of programmes and projects' (OSAGI 1997: par. 1). In Canada gender mainstreaming is largely conceptualized in terms of a gender-based analysis. Status of Women Canada, the federal government department responsible for GBA, describes it as, 'a process that assesses the differential impact of proposed and/or existing policies, programs and legislation on women and men (1998: 4). It makes it possible for policy to be undertaken with an appreciation of gender differences, of the nature of relationships between women and men and of their different social realities, life expectations; and economic circumstances; it is a tool for understanding social processes and for responding with informed and equitable options' (ibid.).

The Canadian government has made a series of commitments to GBA, beginning with Setting the Stage for the Next Century: The Federal Plan for Gender Equality (1995–2000), and most recently, with the Agenda for Gender Equality (2000–2005). In essence, GBA is intended to illuminate how and why women and men are affected differently by policy issues. It seeks to disrupt the assumption that policies are gender-neutral and that all groups of women and men experience policy, programs, and legislation similarly. Gender-based analysis prioritizes social justice, and in particular, substantive equality, which requires the accommodation of differences and consideration of how gender burdens and benefits are shaped by policy. According to some analysts, it is also a mechanism through which governments can balance gender considerations with other government priorities (Rankin and Vickers 2001). The goals of GBA are also congruent with equality guarantees found in Section 15 and Section 28 of the Canadian Charter of Rights and Freedoms, as well as numerous other international conventions and agreements to which Canada is a signatory.

With its focus on gender, gender mainstreaming is often referred to as a strategic, agenda-setting approach to gender equality within increasingly hostile policy environments that are not always responsive to the needs of marginalized and vulnerable populations, especially specific and targeted requests from women. Gender mainstreaming is seen to be a mechanism that moves beyond the integration of gender considerations into policy to actually 'challenge and transform policy paradigms in the process of engendering policy' (Hankivsky 2005: 980). Despite its perceived transformational potential, GM has not brought about radical changes in the realm of policy (Hankivsky 2005; Sjoroup 2001). This is especially significant in the Canadian context, where GBA is a cornerstone of Canadian policy mandates both nationally and provincially. In 2005 the House of Commons, Standing Committee on the Status of Women, in its evaluation of GBA concluded that despite ten years of effort, 'GBA is still not being systematically incorporated into policy-making' (2005: 31) and that in fact, program and policy changes in the past decade have had significant and negative impacts on all Canadian women (Hankivsky 2006a).

A number of reasons for this lack of progress have been identified in the literature. These include the relative 'newness' of the GM strategy and its demanding nature (Bretherton 2001), the exclusion of equity-seeking groups from influencing GM, the need for better methodologies and tools and training (Status of Women Canada 2002; Booth and

Bennett 2002; Woodward 2001), and the necessity of enabling political environments and proper resourcing for GM efforts (Squires and Wickham-Jones 2002; Rees 2002). What is becoming especially important is how GM can fare in policy environments that have been transformed in the past decade by significant political, economic, and social restructuring and downsizing resulting from the proliferation of economic globalization and its concomitant policies. Ironically, the formal endorsement and growth of GM internationally has occurred at the same time as the expansion of the political ideology of neoliberalism, a development that is typically seen as not conducive to the promotion of social justice or gender equity. Consequently, as Teghtsoonian correctly observes, 'the simultaneous development of these two trends invites a closer look, since there are noteworthy tensions between them' (2004: 268).

Mainstreaming in the Political Context of Neoliberalism

Neoliberalism 'includes the contraction of government, the roll back/ restructuring of welfare-state programs, deficit fighting and increased influence by the market' (Rankin and Vickers 2001: 20). According to Pierre Bourdieu, in its essence, neoliberalism is "a programme for destroying collective structures which may impede the pure market logic" (1998: n.p.). Certainly, neoliberalism takes on different configurations in different political contexts (Teghtsoonian and Chappell 2005; Larner 2000). In Canada the consequences of neoliberal reforms, including the restructuring of the welfare state, spending reductions for programs and services – especially for social programming aimed at vulnerable populations – have been documented both at the federal and the provincial levels (Ricciutelli et al. 1997; Brodie 1996). Certain generalities emerge in the literature regarding the effects of neoliberalism on women's lives, especially those women who are marginalized and poor (Bakker 2003; Bashevkin 2002; Brodie 2002).

As Morrow et al. explain, 'in Canada, the idea that social entitlements are important components of citizenship and equality is currently being undermined by neoliberal state values, expressed in federal and provincial policy shifts that favour self-sufficiency and economic competitiveness over a strong welfare state' (2004: 358). In this context, social problems are seen as individual failures that require private rather than state-based solutions (Teghtsoonian and Chappell 2005; Bashevkin 2002). Shifts from state responsibility for social justice to market-based individualistic solutions have also established new categories of the deserving and undeserving poor. Gender issues, including gender equality, are increasingly linked to the priorities of special interests, often falling outside the government's mandate, as it continues to reconceptualize and narrow the perimeters of the social welfare state.

This narrowing has deleterious effects on women, who because of inequities in income and the unequal division of labour, have generally been more dependent on the state in terms of public services and income transfers. In addition, the accomplishments of the women's movement have been severely undermined by the rapid spread of neoliberalism. Janine Brodie, for instance, has observed that the 'political muscle and tangible accomplishments of the second wave of Canadian feminism during the 1970s and 1980s have all but disappeared' and that 'in only a few years, gender and the equality agenda generally have been virtually erased from public discourse and public policy' (2002: 91). As one consequence, women's machineries within government have shifted their focus to ensure 'least worst outcomes' (IDRC 2003), rather than thinking about how to progress forward in terms of gender equality.

It may be asserted that neoliberalism's weakening of the state has unequal gender effects. Such generalizations, however, should not detract from nuanced analyses that resist unified understandings of the gendered effects of neoliberalism and that recognize that 'complex and contradictory gender relationships and alliances are being produced under neoliberal economic governance, resulting in both an intensification and erosion of gender difference' (Haraway 1991, cited in Bakker 2003: 66). Importantly, various groups of women experience the effects of neoliberalism very differently, and yet, many assessments do not capture the diversity in these experiences. For instance, not only does neoliberalism create new challenges for women activists, this is especially the case for those women who do not belong to the dominant culture but do strive to influence public policy (Rankin and Vickers 2001).

Although the gendered effects of neoliberalism are varied, the main concerns of neoliberalism – the emphasis on personal duty and responsibility, reduced public spending, work-tested benefits, a fiscalized view of policy, decentralization, and increasing privatization, do not appear particularly conducive to creating an environment in which gender mainstreaming, with its aim of gender equality, can thrive. According to Katherine Teghtsoonian (2000), GM is fundamentally at odds with the neoliberal focus on individuals and suspicion of identity-based politics. Similarly, Janine Brodie (2002) maintains that gender, among other systemic barriers to equality, is explicitly rejected in the neoliberal state. And for others still, in this kind of market-oriented policy environment, 'the low priority accorded to gender issues ... demonstrates that obligations to mainstream gender equality will not be permitted to obstruct the real mainstream' (Bretherton 2001: 75).

It is important to acknowledge that at the same time that neoliberalism has been proliferating, so too has gender mainstreaming and state bureaucracies supporting this policy innovation (True and Mintrom 2001). For Jacqui True and Michael Mintrom 'much of the impetus for gender mainstreaming efforts has come precisely from a desire to resist arguments and pressure faced by nation-states to accept uncritically economic reforms inspired by the neoliberal global governance agenda' (2001: 34). Elsewhere, Emilie Hafner-Burton and Mark Pollack argue that, in reality, 'people, states and organizations can be placed along a continuum in terms of their support for either a neoliberal frame emphasizing the efficiency of market mechanisms, or a more interventionist frame that accepts the intervention of states and international organizations in the marketplace in pursuit of social goals, including the goal of sexual equality' (2002: 287). Thus, the continued, and in some instances increasing, presence of gender mainstreaming strategies suggests that gender as a policy category has not been altogether rejected, and in fact, some level of commitment by governments and other international organizations to gender equality remains.

Even if there has been an international push towards GM, however, the question as to what extent GM has been co-opted by neoliberal agendas requires further investigation. There does appear to be at least some evidence that GM has been ineffective when forced to confront the priorities and values of neoliberal policies. For instance, in her review of the impact of neoliberalism on gender analysis mainstreaming in Aotearoa/New Zealand, Teghtsoonian (2004) illustrates the extent to which the neoliberal policy context undermined the government document, entitled The Full Picture, that was developed in 1996 to assist policy analysts in undertaking gender analysis. Teghtsoonian concludes that, ultimately, the discourse of neoliberalism dominated the feminist discourse that was explicit in The Full Picture, and in the process diluted any GM efforts in the policy realm. Moreover, in their assessment of the Canadian federal Liberal government's neoliberal agenda in the 1990s, Sandra Burt and Sonya Hardman (2001) conclude that, far from making any significant improvements in terms of gender equity, gender-based analysis often masks under the veneer of legitimacy the detrimental consequences of policy developments on the lives of women. This is evident in the case of changes to the Unemployment Insurance system that took place in Canada during this same period. Even though a gender-based analysis of such proposed changes showed detrimental effects on women's economic security, it did not prevent the government from moving forward with their planned reforms (Burt and Hardman 2001; Grace 1998). Again, this raises questions about the overall efficacy of GM strategies in neoliberal policy contexts.

Bacchi and Eveline argue that one of the reasons that GM has 'become so popular and spread so quickly is that dominant models pose no real threat to neoliberal projects' (2003: 101). Largely, this is because they see conventional mainstreaming models to be congruent with the new public management paradigm (NPM), so firmly entrenched in neoliberal political paradigms. For them NPM is 'driven by governments of a neoliberal persuasion, with key principles of user-pays and small government providing the rationale' (2003: 102). This can be explained by government moving from the 'direct production and delivery of public goods and services, to a focus on the policy setting and management aspects of providing public programs' (2003: 103). This entails the downsizing of the public sector, introduction of market-based reforms, public-private partnerships, self-managed accountability, and performance indicators (Teghtsoonian 2005).

It is worth highlighting that, even as they criticize gender mainstreaming, Bacchi and Eveline also seek a different method to this strategy, one that avoids the trappings of conventional approaches that are ineffective in challenging the policies and norms of neoliberalism. In so doing, they offer an alternative, potentially promising way to view and implement GM. Put in a different way, it may be that GM is the ideal strategy for a policy milieu that has limited tolerance for any explicitly feminist approach to gender equity; the key is to identify how to ensure that the gender analysis, which is at the heart of GM, is effectively implemented. As Teghstsoonian so eloquently puts it: 'in a political context in which the government's policy agenda is informed by neoliberal commitments, advocates and practitioners of gender analysis must walk a fine line between framing arguments in terms which can be "heard" and ensuring that the well-being of diverse groups of women remains at the heart of gendered policy analysis and the tools and strategies designed to support it' (2004: 281). Accordingly, exploring alternative gender mainstreaming methods, such as the one proposed by Bacchi and Eveline, provides new ideas for how to shift policy in directions that support equity.

British Columbia: The Political Context

British Columbia provides the ideal case study through which to investigate the transformative potential of gender mainstreaming in an era of neoliberalism in Canada. Much attention has been paid to the changes in policies and programs brought about by the Liberal Party in British Columbia since it came to power in May 2001. In many ways, the direction of the government over the past seven years is similar to past and current trends in provinces such as Alberta and Ontario, but what has transpired in British Columbia is some of the deepest cuts to social spending in Canadian history (Klein and Long 2003). Importantly, previous to the Liberal government coming to power, the province was considered to be a national leader in the area of gender-based analysis. Predating even the Beijing Conference in 1995, where GM was formally endorsed, in 1993 the B.C. government's cabinet submissions guidelines required that each government department conduct a gender impact analysis on new policy options. A year later, in 1994, the Ministry of Women's Equality – the first free-standing gender-based provincial ministry in Canada – developed the first provincial tool for GBA: The Gender Lens: Policy Analysis Version, and in 1997 it revised this tool, producing Gender Lens: A Guide to Gender Inclusive Policy and Program Development. In 1995 the B.C. government also produced a Gender Lens for Program Evaluation. In their 2001 analysis, Rankin and Vickers observed: 'British Columbia has shown a substantive commitment to gender-based analysis through its development of a comprehensive gender lens strategy in conjunction with the establishment of a free-standing Ministry of Women's Equality' (2001: 33).

This attention to gender analysis has not continued with the present B.C. government. To understand the current situation better, it is helpful to review some key changes. First, the Ministry of Women's Equality was dismantled in 2001. Recent changes include the establishment of a Ministry of Community Services, on 16 June 2005. It replaced the Ministry of Community, Aboriginal and Women's Services (in which the successor to the Ministry of Women's Equality – Women's Equality and Social Programs – was housed). The new ministry contains the Seniors', Women's and Community Services Department, which houses a Seniors' and Women's Policy Branch. According to the ministry's 2008/09–2010/11 Service Plan, the ministry is committed to 'working with other ministries, the federal government, and other sectors to address women's … issues through public policy, legislation, programs and services' (British Columbia 2008: 7). And yet, the ministry does not apply this commitment broadly. Instead, it has chosen to limit its focus to two key goals: ensuring that women are safe from domestic violence and that women have the opportunity to reach their economic potential.

It is not clear that in addressing women's issues in public policy and legislation, GBA is being used effectively by policy analysts in the province. According to one senior analyst in the Seniors' and Women's Policy Branch, the way in which this commitment to women's issues is realized is that 'we do policy analysis in a traditional way with an "eye" to women's issues, but not using any particular kind of lens' (personal communication, September 2005). Although current work may still be informed by the Guide to Best Practices in Gender Analysis, a GBA guide that was published by the B.C. government in 2003, it is important to emphasize that this guide is a very watered down, largely ineffectual version of previous comprehensive and detailed B.C. gender-based analysis policies and guides.

Finally, the government has established the Children's, Women's and Seniors' Health Branch, which is responsible for providing subject matter expertise, critical analysis, and advice to the Ministry of Health on issues affecting the health of women and seniors. The branch monitors current planning, policies, and programs, and works with stakeholders to ensure that key women's, children's, and seniors' health issues are reflected within the health care system. One highlight in the area of health policy is A Women's Health Strategy for British Columbia, released in 2004, in which the importance of sex and gender-sensitive health research and policy are emphasized and, in particular, the importance of a gender-based analysis for 'the identification of potential inequalities that arise for belonging to one sex or the other, or from relations between the sexes' (British Columbia 2004: 19). Moreover, in 2005 the province invested $2 million in the support of the Women's Health Research Institute. However, it is not clear how effective these initiatives have been in reshaping health policies and priorities. Significantly, in both the 2006/07–2008/09 and 2007/08–2009/10 Service Plans, the Ministry of Health makes no mention of women's specific or unique health needs, nor does it provide any evidence in the form of sex or gender disaggregated data.

Critiques of B.C. Policies

The change in government, the restructuring of government ministries, the transformation in programs and services, and the elimination of key programs and services in other instances have had devastating consequences for all B.C. women, especially those who are most vulnerable and marginalized. Beginning in 2003, the British Columbia CEDAW Group prepared a submission to the United Nations Committee on the Elimination of Discrimination Against Women. In this report, the group argued that the government of British Columbia 'is failing to fulfill its obligations under the Convention on the Elimination of All Forms of Discrimination Against Women' (B.C. CEDAW Group 2003: 2), and in fact is dismantling the very programs and protections that are essential to advancing women's exercise and enjoyment of their human rights. In turn, the United Nations Committee singled out British Columbia for special criticism after reviewing Canada's compliance with the Convention on the Elimination of Discrimination Against Women, highlighting its concern about 'changes in British Columbia which have a disproportionately negative impact on women, in particular, Aboriginal women' (cited in Archibald and Goldney 2005: 5).

Joining a growing body of literature, Gillian Creese and Veronica Strong-Boag (2005) have reported on the wide-ranging impacts that government legislation and policy decisions are having on women in British Columbia, in particular elderly women, and women and girls who are Aboriginal, of colour, disabled, lesbian, recent immigrants, refugee claimants, single mothers, living on low incomes, or living in rural areas. They discuss the effects on caring work, health care services, women's safety, recreational and leisure programs, food security, income assistance, education, training, legal services, women's advocacy services, and employment conditions. Creese and Strong-Boag conclude that the Campbell government 'likes to pretend that gender equality has already been achieved and that policy formation can be indifferent to women' (2005: 32).

Other critiques include the analysis of the B.C. Coalition of Women's Centres regarding the effects of having thirty-seven women's centres in the province lose their core funding, resulting in the lack of advocacy services in many communities (Archibald and Goldney 2005). Moreover, Vancouver Status of Women has provided a critical review of the B.C. welfare system and other provincial legislation that dispossesses and criminalizes marginalized women (VSW 2004). Morrow et al. (2004)

have documented the extent to which cuts and changes related to social assistance, legal aid, and women's services have seriously eroded
women's organizations and the necessary supports to ensure a coordinated intersectoral response to violence. Teghtsoonian has analysed
the gendered consequences of dismantling the Ministry of Women's
Equality (2005) arguing with Chappell in 2008 that in British Columbia,
gender mainstreaming has been erased rather than profiled, as part of
the downsizing of women's policy machineries (see Teghtsoonian and
Chappell 2008: 36). Most recently, Creese and Strong-Boag have provided an updated assessment on provincial polices and gender equality in
the province, concluding that 'neoliberal policies adopted since 2001,
buttressed by federal policies enacted since the election of the Harper
government in 2007, have left many women – and disproportionately
those who are aboriginal, immigrant, of colour, elderly, unemployed,
low wage workers, single mothers, or with disabilities – in an increasingly precarious position' (2008: 8).

Given what has transpired, and the fact that it seems that no type
of gender talk is on the agenda, it is fair to question whether there is
a future for gender mainstreaming in the current neoliberal political
climate of British Columbia, among other provinces in Canada following the same policy trajectory. Clearly, there is a tension between
the general policy direction of the B.C. government and the statement
made by its Minister of State for Women's Health in 2003 that the B.C.
Guide to Best Practices in Gender Analysis will 'help government meet
its New Era commitments to accountability, sound fiscal management
and openness and transparency in the public policy process' (British
Columbia 2003: 1). As a first step in dealing with this apparent contradiction in policy objectives, it is important to emphasize that neoliberalism is neither monolithic nor uncontested (Teghtsoonian 2004:
270). And GM, as evidenced by the proposal put forward by Bacchi and
Eveline (2003), does not necessarily have to be a smokescreen for doing "business as usual" (Casqueria Cardoso 2000). Arguably, GM is not
necessarily congruent with neoliberalism; nor is neoliberalism, with its
fractures (Larner 2000), necessarily antithetical to GM.

Deep Evaluation and Gendering-Based Assessment

In putting forward their alternative, Bacchi and Eveline explain that
they locate their initiative 'alongside those of other feminists who wish
to overcome the limitations of current gender analysis frameworks and

to make mainstreaming more effective" (2003: 112). Their goal is "to identify ways to strengthen the potential of mainstreaming initiatives to step outside of and critique neoliberalism's strategic norms' (2003: 98). They are interested in exploring whether gender mainstreaming can question the framing principles and objectives of a policy under examination, and moreover, to examine how policies produce social relations and particular kinds of subjects. Bacchi and Eveline argue that the problem with most versions of mainstreaming is that they are shaped by neoliberal agendas driving globalized economies and, as such, produce women as individuals, undermining substantive equality goals. Specifically, they maintain that typical approaches consider the differential impact of policy at each stage and that difference is found in women (2003: 108) rather than in politics and/or relationships of power. They argue that what is needed is more attention on the practices that render women different and disadvantaged (2003: 109). To this end, they focus on developing an approach to gender analysis that intervenes ex ante instead of ex post.

Accordingly, they introduce the mechanism of 'Deep Evaluation,' which they argue puts into question the grounding premises of any proposed or existing policies. This framework is intended to create a space at the beginning of a policy development process to allow policy analysts to reflect on the full implications of pursuing a particular policy objective. The steps in such an analysis include: examining the way(s) in which the 'problem' under consideration is represented and with what effects; noting how particular assumptions about contexts underpin the policy; and paying heed to the particular interpretations of key concepts and how these impose certain understandings of the issue(s). Of course, they do concede that there are operational considerations to take into account, such as: location of responsibility for implementation, method of analysis, resource allocation, terms of evaluation, and training. Nevertheless, they are confident that 'the insights generated through Deep Evaluation would lead to the development of a different form of gender analysis' (2003: 112). They refer to this different form as 'Gendering Based Assessment,' which 'would encourage reflection on the ways in which "problems" and "contexts" are represented in specific policy projects, encouraging scrutiny of important developments in trade and commerce, instead of accepting these as inevitable' (2003: 112). For them, it would lead to an understanding of policy as both a creative process and one that produces gender.

Shortcomings and Promises of Deep Evaluation/Gendering-Based Assessment

As evidenced by the observations of other gender-mainstreaming scholars, Bacchi and Eveline are not putting forward an altogether novel proposal for transforming GM. For instance, Fiona Beveridge and Sue Nott have argued that 'there is a connection which must be recognized between the day-to-day "routine" of gender politics and the wider ideological frame within which they are pursued' (2002: 304). Similarly, Mieke Verloo (1999) has asserted that the pursuit of GM can be interpreted as an exercise in policy framing. More recently, Perrons has also suggested that 'effective gender mainstreaming would require a broader and more holistic conceptualization of the economy in order to secure greater gender equality' (2005: 389). Moreover, while Bacchi and Eveline are correct in noting that current approaches to GM tend to be largely ex post in nature, the importance of ex ante policy analysis is not explicitly absent from existing frameworks. Even if it is not always operationalized as such, the significance of having GM integrated in all steps of the policy process has been highlighted (Burt and Hardman 2001). This includes the ex ante policy development phase that consists of all activities that take place from the time a policy ideal is conceived until a policy is set into motion.

Bacchi and Eveline's proposal is important, however, in that it highlights the limitations of most conventional approaches to GM, which are largely caught up in vetting or proofing existing or proposed policies to test their impact on women and men and exploring how they can be introduced with fewer negative effects (2003: 110). They illuminate the importance of developing an approach to GM that can consistently and systematically interrogate the framing principles and objectives of policies under question, and inquire how such values and goals produce social relations and particular kinds of subjects. Arguably, GM cannot be effectively utilized without first understanding, for example, that 'gender practices are pre-existing the mainstreaming practices' (GPWG et al. 2003: 14). Clearly, this approach has the potential to expose how 'difference' emerges from relationships of power rather than inhering in individuals and members of particular groups. And it is consistent with the original intention of GM 'to make explicit various power relations, between women and men, among women, and among men' rather than an 'apparatus to render power relations invisible' (ibid.: 13). Developing GM analysis in which the broader political, social and economic contexts are examined and critiqued is key to mitigating the effects of neoliberalism on women's lives, especially on those women who are most vulnerable and marginalized. Focusing the examination in this way may also help identify policy windows within neoliberal contexts that would make it possible to implement GM. Bacchi and Eveline (2003) set the course for an approach that can produce different kinds of information, broaden policy debates among key stakeholders, and make policy-makers and decision-takers more aware of the objectives, rationale, and assumptions that shape nation states and underpin their institutions, programs, and policies.

Taking British Columbia as an example, the implications of this alternative GM approach would potentially be two-fold. First, in purporting to develop a gender-sensitive approach to public policy, politicians and policy-makers would become more aware of the contradictions of focusing on targeted women's issues such as violence and employability without examining how the fundamental aims of government further entrench a variety of gender inequalities, while at the same time they render gender issues 'subservient to wider political agendas' (Bacchi and Eveline 2003). For example, in emphasizing the need to improve women's employability, the B.C. government is assuming that women should accept current working conditions without tackling the disproportionate responsibilities for caregiving that are taken on by women and that create barriers to employment. The focus on labour force participation also creates a policy window to use the type of gender analysis proposed by Bacchi and Eveline to illuminate the extent to which health care restructuring, and home care and community care policies create gender inequities. The current government agenda thus creates 'a space to draw attention to women's inordinate contribution to care and maintenance of the working population' (Bacchi et al. 2006: 54).

In the growing body of B.C.-based research on the gendered effects of liberal government policies and programs, explicit links have been made between the changes and retrenchment of the social welfare state in the province with wider international trends, including 'the global process of corporate colonization' (VSW 2004: 4) and 'neoliberal state values' (Morrow et al. 2004: 358). Yet, these types of associations are rarely made inside government. Under the scheme proposed by Bacchi and Eveline, there would be a shift from the often technical exercise of scrutinizing already proposed policies and programs against GM tools and checklists to considering and evaluating the broader contexts that inform government agendas and mould gender relations. And if properly applied, the analysis would move beyond 'male/female comparisons to consider how forms of globalization that benefit privileged women simultaneously have harmful effects on various vulnerable populations' (Hankivsky 2006b: 101). In general, using a broader analysis to be able to identify the importance of multiple subjectivities may also inform the province's current policies that prioritize Aboriginal populations and, in particular, Aboriginal women. In this way, GM may be seen to be consistent with and valuable for realizing current government agendas across sectors.

Second, those who engage in critical analyses of the current Liberal government in British Columbia by focusing on specific cuts in particular policy areas would be redirected to consider how these are linked to the underlying values, political goals, and trade-off choices of the government, which have influenced the framing of policy problems across sectors, and shape how variously situated citizens, including marginalized women, are perceived and responded to in policy. If one considers the strategic plans of the Liberal government since 2001, there is a definitive pattern in overall priorities, which have informed policy directions and affected numerous population groups in the province, including women. At the very beginning of its mandate, the government set out *Five Great Goals*, which are intended to inform all government priorities and activities until 2015–16. The goals are:

1 To make British Columbia the best-educated, most literate jurisdiction on the continent
2 To lead the way in North America in healthy living and physical fitness
3 To build the best system of support in Canada for persons with disabilities, those with special needs, children at risk, and seniors
4 To lead the world in sustainable environmental management, with the best air and water quality, and the best fisheries, bar none
5 To create more jobs per capita than anywhere else in Canada. (British Columbia 2005)

The current government's core values are: (1) integrity, to make decisions in a manner that is consistent, professional, fair, transparent, and balanced; (2) fiscal responsibility, to implement affordable public policies; (3) accountability, to enhance efficiency, effectiveness, and the credibility of government; (4) respect, to treat all citizens equitably, compassionately, and respectfully; and (5) choice, to afford citizens the opportunity to exercise self-determination (British Columbia 2005). Such goals and values, which can be interpreted as congruent with a neoliberal paradigm, have shaped both Liberal government agendas, and arguably undermine the legitimacy of gender and other marginalized dimensions of identity as focal points for equity-oriented initiatives (Teghtsoonian 2005: 323).

It is precisely because these goals and values have precipitated changes with a range of gendered effects at all levels of government that GM must focus its efforts on understanding the implications of such broader policy frames in order to 'put neoliberal agendas into question' (Bacchi and Eveline 2003: 99). This type of analysis has the potential to provide insights regarding the ends or goals of policy-making and illuminate what is required to bring about real structural change so that GM may be used to set policy agendas rather than to simply integrate considerations of gender into existing policy agendas. Indeed, 'policies do not simply "impact" on people – they "create" people' (2003: 110). Similarly, in my own work, I have critiqued dominant GBA policies in Canada, arguing that by focusing primarily on gender, these policies tend to ignore various forms of oppression and how these interconnect and reinforce one another, and in the process, further discriminate against multiply marginalized women (Hankivsky 2005). In this way, 'Deep Evaluation' and its related Gendering-Based Assessment allow policy analysts "to reflect upon the full implications of pursuing a particular policy objective" (Bacchi and Eveline 2003: 111). Elsewhere Bacchi at al. have argued that even within the limits of neoliberal government agendas, policy actors find room to manoeuvre and to develop services and programs that are attuned to patterns of disadvantage. In the Australian context specifically, they observe that "at least some public servants are willing and indeed eager to debate the shape of the policies they are directed to implement" (2006: 55) and that there are real opportunities to "challenge the anti-intellectualism that characterizes the policy realm" (2006: 64).

A reconceptualized approach to GM may also encourage more citizen engagement; that is, an open public discussion and debate about the contexts, structures, and institutions emerging in an era of neoliberalism that shape existing gender relations and inequalities for various groups of women, which in turn are further entrenched with specific policy choices. As I have argued elsewhere, instead of prioritizing the '"voice of the market" or the "voice of the policy expert,"' there should be a forum for 'prioritizing the voice of the people, and in particular those vulnerable and at-risk populations, who have been, and continue to be, disproportionately affected by globalization and its related [neoliberal] policies' (Hankivsky 2006b: 102). In making this argument about an alternative approach to GM, one must acknowledge some of the limitations of this strategy. For example, GM is a government strategy and tool. Unless the private sector embraces this approach, gender mainstreaming is limited in its ability to address key issues about the relationship between governments and markets (Beveridge and Nott 2002), which is essential to disrupting neoliberal government policies. It is worth highlighting, however, that private sector leaders are beginning to demonstrate with facts and figures that GM is good for business and the bottom line (World Bank 2002). It is the potential for improving efficiency and effectiveness that makes GM an especially attractive strategy for the private sector. If GM is increasingly seen as an acceptable strategy, a window of opportunity may exist to use it to eventually question, in more progressive ways, neoliberal commitments that shape government policies and priorities.

Conclusion

Bacchi and Eveline (2003) turn our attention to the need for an alternative approach to GM that can challenge neoliberalism and bring about structural change. The overall lack of carefully thought through alternative conceptualizations and visions in the field makes their work a welcome and much needed addition. Their proposal, which is intended to ensure fundamental assessment of government ends or policy goals by examining broad political contexts and the way in which they shape citizens, paves the way to developing urgently needed GM strategies that are agenda setting rather than integrationalist in nature. By refocusing GM on ex ante considerations, in which the environment in which policies are being developed and implemented is made central to the analysis, they provide an opening to 'contest the neoliberal premises that currently infiltrate and constrain gender analysis and mainstreaming' (2003: 114). That is, they direct attention to the importance of effective critical analysis of policy as a crucial stage in moving towards contesting neoliberal policies and ensuring that GM is part of meaningful change processes.

   Applying this approach to British Columbia illuminates the underlying values of the B.C. Liberal government and redirects investigations into the gendered effects of government policies and programs to consider how the overarching contexts and goals of government shape policy development. This leads to more comprehensive understandings of how power relations, including gender relations, are constructed at various levels of decision-making. This GM method reveals the shortcomings in government commitments to gender analysis in policy that focus on women's 'special needs' while simultaneously creating a policy milieu that fundamentally undermines social justice and gender equality. It may also reveal strategic policy areas in which GM can be used to make broader change. In the final analysis, change is 'slow, messy and marked by unpredictable connections' (Bacchi et al. 2006: 62). Bacchi and Eveline's proposal does, however, contribute to a transformatory version of GM that is valuable not only for the case study of British Columbia but also for other jurisdictions nationally and internationally. It opens the door to seeing how GM can be used to make those unpredictable connections and to find ways to effectively analyse and ultimately challenge, resist, and oppose neoliberalism and its concomitant policies and programs.

Note

1 Reported in Status of Women Canada (1995).

References

Archibald, Ted, Dodie and Goldney. (2005). *Submission to the British Columbia Select Standing Committee on Finance and Government Services*. Prepared for the B.C. Coalition of Women's Centres. Electronic version retrieved 4 Jan. from http://www3.telus.net/bcwomen/archives/BCCWC_bcbudget2006_text.html.

Bacchi, Carol, and Joan Eveline. (2003). Mainstreaming and Neoliberalism: A Contested Relationship. *Policy and Society* 22(2): 98–118.

Bacchi, Carole, Joan Eveline, Jennifer Binns, Catherine Mackenzie, and Susan Harwood. (2006). Gender Analysis and Social Change: Testing the waters *Policy and Society* 24(4): 45–65.

Bakker, Isabella. (2003). Neo-liberal Governance and Reprivatization of Social Reproduction: Social Provisioning and Shifting Gender Orders. In Isabella Bakker and Stephen Gill (eds.), *Power, Production and Social Reproduction*, 66–82. New York: Palgrave.

Bashevkin, Sylvia (ed.). (2002). *Women's Work Is Never Done: Comparative Studies in Care-Giving, Employment, and Social Policy Reform*. New York: Routledge.

Beveridge, Fiona S., and Sue Nott. (2002). Mainstreaming: A Case for Optimism and Cynicism. *Feminist Legal Studies* 10: 299–311.

Booth, Christine, andV Bennett. (2002). Gender Mainstreaming in the European Union: Towards a New Conception and Practice of Equal Opportunities? *European Journal of Women's Studies* 9(4): 430–46.

Bourdieu, Pierre. (1998). Utopia of Endless Exploitation, The Essence of Neoliberalism: What Is Neoliberalism? A Programme for Destroying Collective Structures which May Impede the Pure Market Logic. *Le Monde Diplomatique*, Dec. Electronic version retrieved 5 April 2006 from http://mondediplo.com/1998/12/08bourdieu.

Bretherton, Charlotte. (2001). Gender Mainstreaming and EU Enlargement: Swimming against the Tide? *Journal of European Public Policy* 8(1): 60–81.

British Columbia, Government of. (2002). Government Strategic Plan 2001/02 to 2004/05, British Columbia Government.Electronic version retrieved 3 Nov. 2004 from http://www.bcbudget.gov.bc.ca/2002/StrategicPlan/default.htm#goal-1.

– (2003). *Guide to Best Practices in Gender Analysis*. Ministry of Community, Aboriginal and Women's Services. Electronic version retrieved 20 March 2006 from http://www.gov.bc.ca/bvprd/bc/search.do?navId=NAV_ID_8380&action=searchresult&qp=&nh=10&qt=gender%20analysis

– (2004). *A Women's Health Strategy for British Columbia: Advancing the Health of Girls and Women*. Ministry of Health. Electronic version retrieved 25 April 2006 from http://www.cw.bc.ca/WomensHealthStrategy.pdf.

– (2005). *Five Great Goals*. 15 April. Retrieved from http://www.bcliberals.com/309/5490/?PHPSESSID=ad2d15db49344126236a67b787139561.

– (2008). Ministry of Community Services 2008/09 – 2010/11 Service Plan, British Columbia Government. Electronic version retrieved 4 March 2008 from http://www.bcbudget.gov.bc.ca/2008/sp/cs/default.html#1.

British Columbia CEDAW (Convention on the Elimination of all forms of Discrimination Against Women). (2003). *Draft Report of the Committee on the Elimination of Discrimination Against Women: Consideration of reports of States parties, Canada*. Fifth periodic report. Electronic version retrieved 19 Jan. 2006 from http://www3.telus.net/bcwomen/archives/CEDAWdraftreport_jan_03.pdf.

Brodie, Janine. (1996). *Women and Canadian Public Policy*. Toronto: Harcourt.

– (2002). The Great Undoing: State Formation, Gender Politics, and Social Policy in Canada. In Catherine Kingfisher (ed.), *Western Welfare in Decline:*

Globalization and Women's Poverty, 90–110. Pennsylvania: University of Pennsylvania Press.

Burt, Sandra, Sonya L. and Hardman. (2001). The Case of Disappearing Targets: The Liberals and Gender Equality. In Leslie A. Pal (ed.), *How Ottawa Spends 2001–2002*. Don Mills: Oxford University Press.

Casqueiro Cardoso, João. (2000). Making Women Count in Portugal. In Fiona Beveridge, Sue Nott, and Kylie Stephen (eds.), *Making Women Count: Integrating Gender into Law and Policy Making*, 77–106. Aldershot: Ashgate.

Creese, Gillian, and Veronica Strong-Boag. (2005). *Losing Ground: The Effects of Government Cutbacks on Women in British Columbia, 2001-2005*. Vancouver: Coalition of Women's Centres.

– (2008). *Still Waiting for Justice: Provincial Policies and Gender Inequality in BC 2001-2008*. Prepared for the B.C. Federation of Labour and the University of British Columbia Centre for Women and Gender Studies, Vancouver.

Gender and Peacebuilding Working Group (GPWG) of the Canadian Peacebuilding Coordinating Committee (CCPC) and the Canadian Consortium on Human Security (CCHS). (2003). *Canadian Perspectives on Security, Conflict and Gender: Advancing Research, Advocacy and Policy*. Conference, 25–6 Aug., York University, Toronto.

Grace, Joan (1998). Sending Mixed Messages: Gender Based Analysis and the 'Status of Women.' *Canadian Public Administration* 40(4): 582–98.

Hafner-Burton, Emilie, and Mark A. Pollack. (2002). Gender Mainstreaming and Global Governance. *Feminist Legal Studies* 10(3): 285–98.

Hankivsky, Olena. (2005). Gender Mainstreaming vs. Diversity Mainstreaming: A Preliminary Examination of the Role and Transformative Potential of Feminist Theory. *Canadian Journal of Political Science* 38(4): 977–1001.

– (2006a). Reflections on Women's Health and Gender Equality in Canada. *Canadian Woman Studies: Canadian Feminism in Action* 25(3-4): 51–7.

– (2006b). Imagining Ethical Globalization: The Contributions of a Care Ethic. *Journal of Global Ethics* 2(1): 91–110.

Haraway, Donna J. (1991) A Cyborg Manifesto: Science, Technology, and Socialist-Feminism in the Late Twentieth Century. In *Simians, Cyborgs and Women: The Reinvention of Nature*, 149–81. New York: Routledge.

International Development Research Centre (IDRC). (2003). Institutionalising Gender Equity Goals in the Policy Process. Electronic version retrieved 22 Aug. 2004 from http://www.idrc.ca/en/ev-42969-201-1-DO_TOPIC.html.

Klein, Seth, and Andrea Long. (2003). *A Bad Time to Be Poor: An Analysis of British Columbia's New Welfare Policies*. Vancouver: Canadian Centre for Policy Alternatives.

Larner, Wendy. (2000). Neo-liberalism: Policy, Ideology, Governmentality. *Studies in Political Economy* 63: 5–25.

Morrow, Marina, Olena Hankivsky, and Colleen Varcoe. (2004). Women and Violence: The Effects of Dismantling the Welfare State. *Critical Social Policy* 24(3): 358–84.

OSAGI. (1997). United Nations Office of the Special Advisor on Gender Issues and the Advancement of Women. Electronic version retrieved 5 Feb. 2006 from http://www.un.org/womenwatch/osagi/gendermainstreaming.htm.

Perrons, Diane. (2005). Gender Mainstreaming and Gender Equality in the New (Market) Economy: An Analysis of Contradictions. *Social Politics: International Studies in Gender, State and Society* 12(3): 389–411.

Rankin, Pauline L., and Jill Vickers. (2001). Women's Movements and State Feminism: Integrating Diversity into Public Policy. Electronic version retrieved 29 July 2004 from http://www.swc-cfc.gc.ca/pubs/pubspr/0662657756/200105_0662657756_e.pdf.

Rees, Teresa. (2002). Gender Mainstreaming: Misappropriated and Misunderstood? Paper presented to the Department of Sociology, University of Sweden.

Ricciutelli, Luciana, June Larkin, and Eimear O'Neill (eds.). (1997). *Confronting the Cuts: A Sourcebook for Women in Ontario.* Toronto: Inanna Publications and Education Inc.

Squires, Judith, and Mark Wickham-Jones. (2002) Mainstreaming in Westminster and Whitehall: From Labour's Ministry of Equality to the Women and Equality Unit. *Parliamentary Affairs* 55(1): 57–70.

Sjoroup, K. (2001). The Case of Denmark. In U. Behning and A. Serrano (eds.), *Gender Mainstreaming in the European Employment Strategy.* Brussels: ETUI.

Standing Committee on Status of Women. (2005). *Gender-Based Analysis: Building Blocks for Success.* Ottawa: Report of the Standing Committee on Status of Women. Electronic version retrieved 15 June 2005 from http://www.parl.gc.ca.

Status of Women Canada. (1995). Setting the Stage for the Next Century: The Federal Plan for Gender Equality. Retrieved on 6 May 2003, from http://www.swc-cfc.gc.ca/pubs/gbaguide/gbaguide_e.html.

– (1998). *Gender-Based Analysis: A Guide for Policy-Making,* rev. ed. Ottawa: Status of Women Canada.

– (2002). *Canadian Experience in Gender Mainstreaming 2001.* Ottawa: Status of Women Canada, Gender Based Analysis Directorate.

Teghtsoonian, Katherine. (2000). Gendering Policy Analysis in the Government of British Columbia: Strategies, Possibilities and Constraints. *Studies in Political Economy* 61: 105–27.

– (2003). W(h)ither Women's Equality? Neoliberalism, Institutional Change and Public Policy in British Columbia. *Policy, Organization and Society* 22(1): 26–47.

– (2004). Neoliberalism and Gender Analysis: Mainstreaming in Aotearoa/New Zealand. *Australian Journal of Political Science* 39(2): 267–84.

– (2005). Disparate Fates in Challenging Times: Women's Policy Agendas and Neoliberalism in Aotearoa/New Zealand and British Columbia. *Canadian Journal of Political Science* 38(2): 307–33.

Teghtsoonian, Katherine, and Louise Chappell. (2008). The Rise and Decline of Women's Policy Machinery in British Columbia and New South Wales: A Cautionary Tale. *International Political Science Review* 29(1): 29–51.

True, Jacqui, and Michael Mintrom. (2001) Transnational Networks and Policy Diffusion: The Case of Gender Mainstreaming. *International Studies Quarterly* 45: 27–57.

United Nations. (1995). *Fourth World Conference on Women, Beijing Platform for Action.* Sept., Beijing, China. New York: United Nations.

VSW (Vancouver Status of Women), Feminist Working Group, and Women and Welfare Project (2004). *A New Era: A Deepening of Women's Poverty.* Electronic version retrieved 19 Jan. 2006 from http://www.vsw.ca/Documents/ANewEraMarch2004revised.doc.

Verloo, Mieke. (1999). On the Conceptual and Theoretical Roots of Gender Mainstreaming. Paper presented at the 1st meeting of the ESRC Seminar Series: The Interface between Public Policy and Gender Equality: Mainstreaming Gender in Public Policy-Making – Theoretical and Conceptual Issues, Centre for Regional Economic and Social Research, Sheffield Hallam University, 12 March 1999.

Woodward, Alison E. (2001). *Gender Mainstreaming in European Policy: Innovation or Deception?* Discussion paper FS 101–103. Berlin: Wissenschaftszentrum Berlin für Sozialforschung.

World Bank. (2002). *The Business Case for Mainstreaming Gender, from Integrating Gender into the World Bank's Work: A Strategy for Action.* Electronic version retrieved 17 Dec. 2005 from http://siteresources.worldbank.org/INTGENDER/Resources/strategypaper.pdf.

PART TWO

Reimagining Income Security for the Most Vulnerable

5 Abolishing Prostitution through Economic, Physical, and Political Security for Women

LEE LAKEMAN

In the view of the Canadian Association of Sexual Assault Centres (CASAC), prostitution is a globalized abuse of women (and a few men) that is best viewed as a form of violence against women, laced with economic exploitation. Prostitution in Canada feeds on women's relative poverty and economic insecurity, on women's physical and social vulnerability to men, as well as on men's sense of entitlement. This chapter will explain how current social forces emboldening the global sex industry are the result of governments' laissez-faire economic and social policies. Prostitution within Canada is racialized, simultaneously exploiting and creating a demand for transnational trafficking of women and children from Asia and the global South as well as from the impoverished Aboriginal communities of the North. Prostitution of adult women relies on, exploits, and creates the demand for the sexual exploitation and commercialized rape of children.

In Canada the recent publicity regarding the horrific multiple murders of prostitutes in Edmonton and Vancouver, along with a desire to 'clean up' the Downtown Eastside in Vancouver in anticipation of the tourism for the 2010 Winter Olympic Games and the property development related to them, has revived a strong interest in new prostitution laws. Decriminalization and legalization of prostitution are two possible alternatives considered by various groups advocating law reform. This chapter argues that neither the decriminalization nor legalization of prostitution would address its root causes or the harms it does. The position advanced in this chapter is that there are various possible policy initiatives that could support the abolition of prostitution within Canada, and that the latter approach would be facilitated by attending to issues of global economic fairness and international human rights.

This chapter therefore focuses particularly on domestic policy solutions that are consistent with the goal of effecting global economic fairness and international human rights law designed to reduce all forms of violence against women, including sex trafficking and sex tourism. It argues that women's economic security will be advanced only if these two sets of concerns are addressed simultaneously.

Canadian Legislation and the Current Debate

Canadian law criminalizes prostitution under the Criminal Code's solicitation laws, under the new anti-trafficking amendments to the Criminal Code passed in 2005, and by way of the international agreements to pursue sex tourists for crimes abroad.[1] According to Section 213 of the Criminal Code, 'Offence in Relation to Prostitution,' commonly known as 'the communication law,' all forms of public communication for the purposes of prostitution are illegal, including those relating to bawdy-houses (sec. 210 and sec. 211) and procuring (sec. 212; Canada 2005). The anti-trafficking amendments create offences that prohibit acts 'for the purpose of exploiting or facilitating the exploitation of another person,' prohibit persons 'receiving a financial or material benefit' that they know results from the commission of trafficking, and prohibit interference with the travel documents of those trafficked. Canadian courts have relied on 'regulation, prohibition, and rehabilitation' to manage prostitution and have offered little protection to victims of prostitution (Canada 2005: n.p.). This approach criminalizes prostitutes and prostitution, with women typically bearing the brunt of arrests and sentencing, and ignores the fact that prostitution is largely a practice of men exploiting women – especially women in need. Consequently, many otherwise progressive groups and individuals, including some feminists, argue that Canada's prostitution laws should be removed from the Criminal Code altogether. These individuals and groups, like most women's groups including those that represent prostitutes, want prostitutes to be protected by, rather than subjected to, criminal prosecution. A number of different positions are advanced by these individuals and groups. Some call for the legalization of prostitution, others for its decriminalization, while some go so far as to argue for the withdrawal of any state or international control or restraint from the global business of prostitution. No national feminist groups in Canada have called for the total decriminalization or legalization of prostitution.

Decriminalization and Legalization: Theory and Public Policy

One position advocating decriminalization of prostitution argues for exempting prostituted women from prosecution under Canada's Criminal Code, but without exempting prostitution itself from criminalization. The elements of this policy were first visible beginning in 1985 with the Fraser Report (Canada 2005). This report, a government study of adult prostitution in Canada, called for criminal sanctions to discourage street prostitution because it was seen to be destructive to the community; at the same time, the report also recommended acceptance of and a licensing system for indoor brothels (sometimes organized as escort services and massage parlours), claiming that these presented no harms to women.

Another version of decriminalization policy, under consideration by the Canadian Subcommittee on Solicitation Laws (of the House of Commons Standing Committee on Justice and Human Rights), calls for total deregulation or decriminalization of prostituted women and also of customers and pimps (Canada 2006). Decriminalization in this sense promotes the total deregulation of the sex industry and calls for the removal of all laws against johns, pimps, procurers, and bawdy-house owners as interference with 'ordinary businesses.'

Policies promoting the legalization of prostitution, as distinct from the decriminalization approach, allow, and even insist on, state interventions, particularly with regard to the regulation of prostitution and the taxation of its proceeds. They usually include proposals for 'industry standards,' government-authorized credentials for prostitutes, and for 'harm reduction' programs on the theory that one could encourage the trade and still ameliorate the impact of poverty and violence on individuals within the trade, as well as reducing the impact on the communities hosting it. Some who argue for legalization recommend regulation of certain forms of prostitution either through urban zoning laws designed to create and confine 'red-light districts' or through licensing prostitutes in designated numbers of women per site or throughout designated areas. The legalization approach deals with the sex industry in a way that is consistent with many other international, national, and local labour and industry policies under imperialism (or globalization as it is more commonly called). And, as in these other policisies of global industry and capital, governments and unions are being called on to institutionalize and normalize prostitution and to control it with regulations. This approach intends to embed prostitution in the local economy such that the government has an investment in maintaining the flesh trade, much as governments have done with gambling. While not always glorifying the sex trade, legalization accepts prostitution as an inevitable and permanent industry.

Problem with Decriminalization and Legalization Policies

There are a number of problematic ideas that underlie both decriminalization and legalization approaches. These include the notion that prostitution is an acceptable service to men, that it is an inevitable part of life for women, and that there are ideal conditions, namely, under free markets, where coercion can be eliminated so that only those truly wanting to be prostitutes will actually be in the business. Prostitution is imagined to be a situation where, under the best circumstances, 'choices' can be made between free agents – the prostitute and her client. In this sense, prostitution is seen as work and like any other type of work, needing employment protections to minimize exploitation. Some who hold, whether consciously or unconsciously, to the free-market approach are so wedded to the notion of the market as a solution to this issue that they see prostitution as no different in any way from any other job. Even those who understand the exploitative nature of the sex trade nevertheless focus on prostituted women as 'workers' in the sense that they need employment protections. The state's objectives under decriminalization, then, are to protect prostituted women from the harassment of the police, to maximize individual women's occupational choices, and to promote 'harm reduction strategies.' Often supporters of this regime can be identified by the contradictory messages of claiming to be protecting 'women on the street' by proposing to legitimize the indoor bawdy-house, massage parlour, and escort trade. The emphasis of legalization policy is on removing criminal laws and passing permissive legislation. Even local by-laws and other civil regulations under this regime would be curtailed. Municipal governments and civil law bodies would not be able to restrain or prohibit what has been deemed legal.

As a political term 'decriminalization' has changed meaning over the years with the growth of neoliberalism. In the 1970s and 1980s those who call for decriminalization proclaimed 'for the prostitutes and against prostitution.' During the conditions of the 1970s welfare state, with a women's movement still on the rise, a strong antipoverty movement, and with antiracist and anticolonial uprisings under way, a different outcome from decriminalizing prostitution might have occurred. Although then, unlike now, the policy framework of decriminalization presumed that only the women would be decriminalized, not the owners of escort services, massage parlours, and bawdy-houses, not the traffickers and slave traders, not the child rapists – there is no such thing as a child prostitute, since children cannot give consent (Lakeman 1993). Decriminalization once implied removing, as social control agents, both the 'hard cop' of the police and the 'soft cop' of the intrusive social worker while expanding the formal and informal supports of a connected community of more or less equals. It implied a provisioning government tending common resources for the common good. It presumed that even in government policy, 'community' trumped 'commerce.' It also relied on the mistaken belief of the time (of the welfare state) that society was moving steadily towards a future in which the common ground of the commonwealth was understood to be the result of the contributions of all and would be legally accessed and shared by each. In such circumstances decriminalization implied, even promised, to women affirmative political recognition, legal and social inclusion, and government-mandated entitlement to resources. With that assurance to the group, women would not individually choose prostitution. Why would they?

In contrast to the ideas of the 1970s, decriminalization policy now means the absence of legal protections against prostitution and trafficking of human beings in an economic and political environment that promotes prostitution (Lakeman 2005). There are a couple of exceptions to this completely laissez-faire approach. For example, all proposals for decriminalization, even in this context, allow an exception to protect children, since according to international studies 14 years is the average age for entering prostitution. (Sweden 2005). One other frequent exception allows for the prohibition of buying and selling women who can prove they were forcibly trafficked. In this frame, force requires not only crossing international borders but also proof of brutality (like a gun to the head).

The swing to the right in global politics has changed the context of the discussion of prostitution and the consequences of decriminalization as policy. The current context for decriminalization proposals is neoliberalism, structural adjustment programs, regressive immigration policy, Third World plague and destitution, a backlash against feminism, and a regressive approach to economic entitlements. The economic need has grown to the extent that our borders do not hold Third World destitution beyond our shores. Abysmal conditions can be found in many Aboriginal communities, in both remote reserves and in many city centres. The internal migration from Native reserves, coastal communities, and resource towns to city ghettos continues, interrupted only by urban renewal programs that push those ghetto populations to bleaker suburbs (Lakeman 2005).

One social, rather than commercial, objective claimed by supporters of both legalization and decriminalization as public policy is to reduce the prejudice against, and the stigmatization of, prostitutes and to address the situation by reducing any sense of moral superiority over prostituted women and children, and over johns, pimps, and procurers. This position argues for acceptance of prostitutes on the basis of diversity, welcoming them into the mainstream of society or even into the elite. And in the situation of legalization some prostitutes are indeed accepted into liberal elites. More often, however, what is accepted is the behaviour of the johns, pimps, and owners who are already there. It ignores or dismisses as collateral damage the continuing or even consequent denial of human rights and freedoms for whole groups, in this case the freedom of women as a group to 'substantial equality' as a basis for meaningful individual choice.

Another social objective claimed by those calling for decriminalization and/or legalization is the hope that either policy would increase the safety of women in the street trade by moving that trade into the light of brothels and massage parlours. However, as is evident in Australia and the Netherlands, not to mention the Asian markets, legalization of the indoor trade expands the illegal outdoor trade, and legalizing the adult trade increases the trade in children.

In the name of individual choice, this policy of legitimization or decriminalization of prostitution generally refuses to group, measure, and name the gender, social class, or race of those who would benefit from legalization and those who would be left with the problems such action would cause. It therefore fails to see the connections with other abuses and other possible solutions. Neither legalization nor decriminalization as a public policy accepts the possibility of the transformative imperative to end race, class, and gender oppression. So, it cannot imagine ending prostitution. Those promoting legalization and decriminalization refuse to be scandalized by the sexualizing and racializing antiwoman stereotypes in the everyday advertising for de facto legal bawdy-houses and escort services. They disassociate the reality of providing women for that domestic trade in massage parlours and bawdy-houses, advertising one race at a time, one fetish at a time, from the demand for more and more compliant, exoticized trafficked women and children.

So far, the policy framework stemming from the legalization and de-criminalization positions seems to uphold the human right of men to prostitute women and for women to agree to that right of men, but it cannot challenge the privilege of men to sexualize commerce and violence. It cannot challenge the privilege of men to commercialize and violate girls and women sexually. It cannot uphold the right of girls and women to refuse to be prostituted.

Yet, this is the policy framework promoted by the 2006 majority of the Canadian Subcommittee on Solicitation Laws (of the House of Commons Standing Committee of Justice and Human Rights). This policy framework indirectly proposes a mix of decriminalization and legalization (or regulation) by implying that all prostitution offences be removed from the Criminal Code (Canada 2006). As Maria Mourani, criminologist and then Bloc Québécois Critic for the Status of Women, points out, the law seems to have been framed on the basis of 'choice':[2] 'To accommodate and "protect" a tiny minority of individuals who "choose" to sell their bodies, Members of Parliament are considering accepting prostitution as the simple exchange of sexual services for money. Prostitution is much more than that, however. Prostitution is a system of exploitation whose victims are primarily women. It derives from and fosters unequal and violent relationships between men and women. Can we accept that?' (2006: n.p.).

While the Canadian Subcommittee on Solicitation Laws claims distance from those who advocate legalizing a sex industry by talking about some of the harms, the need for exit services, and the need for regulations, the responses to its report came quickly and delineate the points of disagreement. For example, in what follows Mourani cites a comparative study prepared for the Women's Rights and Gender Equity Committee of the European Parliament, which shows that 'the legalization of prostitution leads to child sex abuse, violence against women and a marked increase in human trafficking. This committee also concludes that the legalization of prostitution fuels demand and the purchasing of sex, including trafficking victims, and recommends that States recognize that reducing the demand for trafficking is crucial' (2006: n.p.).

It is a little hard to imagine how an absence of law (decriminalization) would make one of the 'harm-reduction' methods proposed by the subcommittee successful, that is, the 'two-woman-shared apartment/brothel.' The subcommittee seems to imagine that two drug-addicted women operating a small-business brothel in their home could defend themselves from the likes of the Vancouver or Ipswich killer[3] by hiring private security. The argument that private enterprise can buy such protection seems to replicate the old joke about chivalry in which 'Prince Charming' (an abusive husband or pimp) is seen as someone to own and control you to protect you from the violence of other men. Once again, quoting Mourani in her response to the Subcommittee's report: 'The individuals who are exploited and who have not really chosen a life of prostitution (which applies to the majority) need our help. They have no help at present and that is scandalous. It is unacceptable that women's right to a society that fosters equality and non-violence should be sacrificed for a very small minority of individuals who choose to sell their bodies. This so-called freely consenting choice applies to a minority, which cannot demand that society abandon its defence of egalitarian and non-violent relationships in its laws and regulations' (2006: n.p.).

Abolition of Prostitution

Abolitionism Policy

Abolitionism policy does not support the criminalization of prostitutes; it supports the criminalization of the exploitative activities that constitute the industry of prostitution. The aim of abolitionism is to eradicate prostitution, and in this it goes far beyond even the 1970s notion of decriminalization, where prostituted women and children would not be legally targeted. Abolitionism as a political framework unites, in feminism, the struggle for women's sexual autonomy, the struggle to end violence against women, and the struggle for women's economic security. It links the struggle of women within Canada to the transnational struggle, privileging the needs of the poorest for legal protections and socioeconomic and environmental entitlements. Abolition policy to meet feminist standards requires an integrated feminist approach. This is the position held by the Canadian Association of Sexual Assault Centres: to combine and address imperialism, immigration issues, racism, and poverty as state obligations to provision residents and to reduce violence against women. In conjunction with this, the state's obligation to democracy means it must cooperate with the self-organized uprising of women for equality. Faced with the incremental government decriminalization of violence against women and with the increased targeted criminalization of women who defend themselves from violence and poverty, CASAC passed interconnected resolutions: these resolutions call for an end to all forms of prostitution including pornography and the placement of prostitution within the context of worldwide violence against women and global women's poverty (2005).

Underlying Theory: Prostitution Is Violence against Women

Prostitution is a practice of men exploiting trapped women, and like all forms of violence against women, it is a sexist threat that has the effect of controlling all women. Catharine MacKinnon summed up the encompassing nature of violence that extends its harms beyond any one or any one group of women and beyond immediate corporal abuse: 'By violence against women, I mean aggression against and exploitation of women because we are women, systematically and systemically. Systemic, meaning socially patterned, including sexual harassment, rape, battering of women by intimates, sexual abuse of children, and woman killing in the context of poverty, imperialism, colonialism and racism. Systematic meaning intentionally organized, including prostitution, pornography, sex tours, ritual torture and official custodial torture in which women are exploited and violated for sex, politics and profit in a context of, and in intricate collaboration with, poverty imperialism, colonialism and racism' (2006: 29).

To be prostituted is to live at the whim and will of, and with only occasional and unreliable benevolence of, the patriarch, the patron. It creates 'a class of women [that] can be legally segregated from society to be used as instruments of male pleasure and sexual commodities' (Raymond 2001: 5).

The Economic Problem

Women endure prostitution because they are degraded and desperate and have few alternatives. In feminist economic terms, prostitution is a·practice forcing many girls and women, some of the time, to resort to this disabling and scarring, ever-available means of 'making a living.' Recent international studies put the median age for entrance of girls into prostitution at 14 years old (Sweden 2004: 2).[4] 'The majority of girls enter prostitution before they have reached the age of consent,' Donna Hughes (2000) pointed out at a lecture on Sexual Exploitation at Queen Sophia Center in Valencia, Spain. Prostitution is reserved, as a lifelong confinement, for a very few selected doll figures but mostly for those women who are considered disposable, those who never had or have lost masculine protection and patronage. Perhaps more importantly, prostitution is a commercial enterprise in which men create the demand for trafficking of human beings, mostly women and children.

Prostitution, according to feminist abolition theory, is a pillar of power relations supporting patriarchy and conflicts with any notion of women's sexual autonomy. Prostitution often rests on the economic deceit of women. While women are promised a living through selling their bodies, the mechanisms often create debt bondage that ultimately can diminish women's economic autonomy to the point of enslavement (Lakeman et al. 2004b). Whatever the circumstances of prostitution, there is no escaping the physical danger, health harms, social impairment, and patriarchal dependency. There is no evidence to suggest women normally, that is, other than a handful of women, find routes to long-term economic security through prostitution.

Abolition Supported by International Human Rights Agreements

For many, whether or not a woman 'consents' to prostitution (i.e., a woman's 'choice') is the primary issue to be respected. Women assisting rape victims regularly face the legal situation of courts legitimizing a claim by men accused of rape of a presumption of consent. Until very recently men could claim that they had a reasonable belief that a woman consented even if they had not asked her. They could claim consent even if she was debilitated by drugs and/or alcohol, and some claimed consent even when she was found tied up at knife-point. The 'consent' involved when a woman is controlled by economic necessity or physical threat to herself or her children requires scrutiny. As late as the 1990s CASAC women lobbied the Canadian government for changes to these legal loopholes.

The historical misuse of consent in Canadian law in a way that excused rape leads us to an analysis of the importance of the concept of 'consent.' Fortunately, there have been significant advances in the international arena regarding the issue of consent. The 1949 U.N. Convention for the Suppression of the Traffic in Persons and of the Exploitation of the Prostitution of Others (subsequently referred to here as the Convention) had sprung from the postwar articulation of human rights and human horrors. It was on the right track by making consent a non-issue in any cases involving profiting, bullying, threats, or deceit. Obviously such trickery renders consent either uninformed or not freely given. But even the antiprostitution reformers of that sharp-eyed postwar time could not anticipate the exponential growth of child exploitation, sales of body parts, the pornography industry, sex tourism, mail-order bride systems, or the mass migrations of poor women (Huda 2006). They could not anticipate the hotels, taxi services, airlines, and other businesses implicated in the billions of dollars that support the flesh trade (O'Connor and Healy 2006; Plamondon 2002). They did not anticipate AIDS or the Internet. Nevertheless, the U.N. Convention did begin the global agreement to protect four million victims and to prosecute traffickers (Raymond 2001).

Feminists articulated trafficking as 'female sexual slavery' (Barry 1985), based partly on the progressive reform concepts developed in the post–Second World War period and encoded in both the International Declaration of Human Rights and the consequent instruments like the 1949 Convention for the Suppression of the Traffic in Persons and of the Exploitation of the Prostitution of Others. By 1998 a United Nations process to update international agreements to restrain organized crime and three relevant protocols was under way: one being a protocol to deal with the trafficking in persons. In 2000 at a U.N. world summit in Palermo, Italy, eighty countries signed a protocol (the Palermo Accord) that embodied an understanding of the connections of trafficking between countries and prostitution within countries, between organized crime and prostitution, and between the realities of 'force' and 'consent.' The Palermo Accord began to link abstract concepts of prostitution and human trafficking to the lives and needs of real women and children:

> 'Trafficking in persons' shall mean the recruitment, transportation, transfer, harbouring or receipt of persons, by means of the threat or use of force or other forms of coercion, of abduction, of fraud, of deception, of the abuse of power or of a position of vulnerability or of the giving or receiving of payments or benefits to achieve the consent of a person having control over another person, for the purpose of exploitation. Exploitation shall include, at a minimum, the exploitation of the prostitution of others or other forms of sexual exploitation, forced labour or services, slavery or practices similar to slavery, servitude or the removal of organs; (b) The

consent of a victim of trafficking in persons to the intended exploitation set forth in subparagraph (a) of this article shall be irrelevant where any of the means set forth in subparagraph (a) have been used. (United Nations 2000: Article 3)

This international agreement signed by Canada says that coercion, debt bondage, deceit, or the more common lack of informed and free consent of women prostituted are the key markers of criminal prostitution and trafficking activity. Enforcing the Palermo Accord and the new law prohibiting sex tourism requires governments to protect those prostituted and to criminalize the trade in human beings (United Nations 2000). Signing this accord necessitated Canada writing domestic laws to enact it, laws that criminalize prostitution and that promise aid to women and children trafficked, including those trafficked for the purpose of prostitution. Canada is now bound to reconcile our regard for prostitution with our regard for trafficking; our obligations not to criminalize victims of trafficking with our habit of criminalizing women and children prostituted on our territory; our treatment of international victims with our treatment of victims from other parts of Canada; our requirements of free and informed consent in each of those situations of assessing woman abuse.

The Case for Abolition

According to abolitionists, nothing about prostitution makes it inevitable, necessary, or worthwhile. Its impact on individual woman and children, on women as a group, and on particular groups of women is devastating. By its nature negative, prostitution further damages the social relations between women and men. Feminist abolition calls for men to stop buying sex and to stop buying access to women and children. It envisions government policy that moves towards an end to the trade in sex, an end to the trade in women and children, and an end to all violence against women. Since the abolitionist position frames prostitution as the sexual enslavement of women, government policy about prostitution must not undermine the sexual autonomy of women. The feminist abolitionist position endorses prostitution law reforms that affect social, economic, civil, and political policy shifts to ensure personal and economic security for all people. This is an approach that understands prostitution to be an international and a national issue, and, at its heart, demands a provisioning of community and government protections against the kinds of economic and social policy that are integral to neoliberalism. The demand for an egalitarian economic and social future for all is key to the prevention of sexual exploitation.

Feminism is a politics that recognizes women are largely treated in society as a group. While feminism increasingly stresses the differences among women, it also recognizes that many issues confront women as a group, and it tries to advance the interests of the group, women, so that women collectively and therefore individually are not oppressed. As part of the tilt of governments in Canada towards the right, they have minimized their obligations to reduce oppression of women as a group. The end of the equality-seeking mandate of the Status of Women Canada and its funding of the independent women's movement, the cuts to the planned child care initiative, and the changes to the Canada Assistance Plan (CAP) program and the social transfer agreements that have resulted in the effective end of the right to welfare are only a sample. The loss of the Court Challenges program also means the almost total lack of access to the Constitution's Charter of Rights and Freedoms, since most all women cannot fund court cases demanding the equality promises of that Charter.

The feminist position on the abolition of prostitution, as represented by the Canadian Association of Sexual Assault Centres, insists that since Canada has signed the Palermo Accord, it must abide by the spirit of that international agreement in protecting women and children prostituted or trafficked between countries and within Canada:[5] 'Neither the young women of the small towns and impoverished First Nations' communities nor the young women escaping the impoverished developing world should be left to the rule of johns, pimps, procurers and traffickers. They should neither be criminalized nor economically abandoned by Canada' (CASAC 2006: n.p.).

'They are us,' was repeated over and over, as feminists debated approaches to policy at the CASAC Day of Feminist Dialogue. Women recognize that they might have found themselves with these women's limited choices but for some good fortune related to privilege of birth in social class, race, or particular patriarchal protection. Those working directly with women in Vancouver who have been sexually assaulted observed and recorded the link between women exploited on the street to girls who had been 'apprehended' from poor and/or Aboriginal mothers and raised in the 'care of the state.' It is easy to see the link between the male–female relations in prostitution and those in incest, and this understanding has enabled women's groups to challenge publicly the institutional power of men within the private realm of the family. Women working with abused women were able to record current incidents of sexual violence replicating famous pornography and misogynist iconography. Visible and recorded also is the vulnerability of girls to the surrogate fathers – priests and teachers – in residential schools (whether for the deaf or for Aboriginal children), and the link between the hypersexualization of girls and the propaganda of sex-role stereotyping and the hate literature of pornography.

No matter their form: as age-old myth, pornography, sex-role stereotyping, advertising, and popular culture, feminists have fought the stories that blame prostitution on women – of money-hungry, deviant girl-children and dangerous nymphomaniac adolescent stepdaughters and larcenous neighbours. The focus was on how women were seen, especially the cultural relativism that claimed communities of poor women or Third World women accepted or even venerated the life of prostitution as disciplined, artful, or even spiritual choice, and the colonial attitudes that claimed Aboriginal women and Black women enjoyed a primitive, animalistic hypersexuality that endured prostitution mindlessly. Those opposed to prostitution fought the notion that disabled women were so starved for affection and sex that all advances were welcome. These 'rape myths' helped attackers and their apologists to construct the unreasonable belief that women have consented to sex or even masochistic practices or inane brutality. And women still fight the twentieth-century notions of 'the disposable woman,' so embroiled in the endless replay of the 'Jack the Ripper' story among the commercial media, the police, and urban rapists, as described by Jane Caputi in her book, The Age of Sex Crimes (1987).

The Policies of Abolition

LEGAL PROSECUTION
Criminalizing the women and children bought and sold is neither useful nor just. The point of abolition is to protect, not criminalize the women and children trapped, endangered, and abused. All forms of violence against women suffer for lack of long-term, concerted effort on the part of the criminal justice system. The recent research by CASAC reveals regular failure at the levels of policing, investigating, prosecuting, arguing, adjudicating, and sentencing crimes of violence against women. Nevertheless, women against prostitution persist. Some of the public compassion towards prostitutes, results, in recent times, from more

than thirty years of escalated and concentrated feminist public educa-tion and advocacy supporting prostitutes. Canadian feminists still or-ganize against violent predators and police neglect, but also against po-lice harassment, gendered prosecution, fines, or jail sentences for what can be described as women's poverty crimes (CASAC 2001).

Criminal censure against prostitution should reflect censure against other forms of violence against women. Criminal law cannot end vi-olence against women or poverty, but it can censure both the acts of sexist exploitation in prostitution itself and the layer of exploitation heaped on top of the already unbearable inequities borne by some women. And while law and order, even in its most progressive and democratic forms, cannot eradicate violence against women, protection by both government and non-government players in the fields of so-cial, political, economic, and civil human rights might (Lakeman 2005). In a liberal democratic justice system it should be part of the design that criminal justice happens in open courtrooms and within legal pa-rameters and is best done with legal representation, recorded verdicts, and recorded judicial reasons including for sentencing. It should not be effectively decriminalized by diversion to restorative justice initia-tives, family courts, circle sentencing, offender-victim mediation, civil restraining orders, or johns' schools. None of these forums are yet suit-able for an equality-seeking undertaking.

While antiviolence abolitionists call on men to voluntarily end the demand for prostitution, governments must also criminalize those who continue to create profit by demanding and supplying flesh in trade. The abolition of prostitution does not entail criminalizing women and chil-dren (or the rare man) bought and sold in prostitution; at the same time, it does involve criminalization and prosecution for pimping, procuring, running bawdy-houses, or purchasing sex. Certainly there should be no tolerance for trafficking of people, whether across recognized national borders or within them. The definition of consent (in the international protocols like the Palermo Accord) is key: it does not require proof of force but only indications of deceit, profit, or coercion. These consent-destroying factors are all present in domestic prostitution. The point of declaring prostitution to be violence against women is to place the blame on those who promote or profit from prostitution – including the 'johns' – and to see the connection to liberation. But it also reminds us that all violence against women is currently badly policed and badly prosecuted in court. Improvements are needed because all forms of vio-lence against women function as enforcers of inequality.

Feminists will need to continue to monitor the impacts of government policy and lack of policy on women, all women. That monitoring and evaluating approach applies to trafficking of people within the country as well as international trafficking, to policing as well as the refusal to police, to ensuring immigration status as well as borders, to pay equity, pensions, and welfare not just the profitability of international trade deals. Clearly feminists demand consultative status on all these policies regarding prostitution not only for the few prostituted women who want to show that they are content with their lot, but also for those women who wish to avoid, escape, and end the trade.

Many, in the name of either the right or the left, who would minimize government control of the sex trade, also eschew use of the state to interfere in other forms of violence against women. In citing the racism and class bias of the state, some suggest women should, as a matter of principle, hesitate to call on police even to interfere with men who overpower them. Antiviolence workers in my collective say it is possible to challenge the bias of the state without abandoning women to brutal men and that it is possible to enforce laws against sexist violence without expanding police powers.

According to Statistics Canada there were 171 known murders of prostitutes in Canada between 1991 and 2004, including a dramatic increase in 1995, when social programs began to suffer from the end of federal funding from the Canada Assistance Plan (CAP) to the provinces. In 2004 sixty-two wives were killed by spouses or ex-spouses (Statistics Canada 2005). Between 1 April 2005 and 31 March 2006 nearly 106,000 women were admitted to shelters to escape violence, according to a Statistics Canada Transition House Survey (Statistics Canada 2007). The conviction rate in virtually all states, on all crimes of violence against women, including for traffickers, pimps, johns, and procurers, is still shamefully low compared with any other major crime (CASAC 2004). For instance, in an article recently appearing in the British newspaper, the Guardian, it states: "If a man commits a rape, then he has on average, a less than one percent chance of being convicted" (Bindel 2007: n.p.). There have been incidents engineered by states (rarely by vindictive women on their own behalf) for rape crimes. But arresting men who abuse women is nowhere popular enough to be in danger of contributing to the legitimacy of a right-wing state. Men arrested and jailed are disproportionately poor men, Aboriginal men, and men of colour, but that is not an indicator that innocent men are criminalized; rather it makes visible that too many of the moneyed men and white men who have committed violence against women are not targeted, investigated, arrested, or convicted. Environmental degradation, war, and impoverishment of nations of the South and indigenous peoples create the conditions that snare victims of sexual slavery. It follows that ending prostitution requires support for those peoples in their own lands before the herding and luring can happen.

Social Supports and Feminist Transformation

It is notable that the 2007 Standing Committee on the Status of Women assigned to address the question of trafficking insisted on integrating the issues of prostitution and pornography in their report, called Turning Outrage into Action to Address Trafficking for the Purpose of Sexual Exploitation in Canada. This all-party committee approached the issues as a matter of women's equality and therefore produced recommendations ranging from raising the age of consent, to changing immigration policy to protect women, to legal and social provisions for those trafficked into Canada. The report clearly identifies the key factors to be women's poverty, racism against women, particularly Aboriginal women, war, pornography, and the local demand created by men buying sex: 'The Committee supports the definition of trafficking contained in the Protocol. However the Committee considers the definition to be weakened by its lack of clarity with respect to what constitutes sexual exploitation. For that reason, the Committee wishes to clarify that prostitution and pornography are forms of sexual exploitation, wherever they occur – on the street, in massage parlours, modelling agencies etc., or through escort agencies' (Status of Women Canada 2007: 3).

They also minced no words on consent of trafficked persons. They point to the U.N. definition and Canadian trafficking law language in which one cannot consent to any of the activities (of being exploited) and point out that 'the vast majority of witnesses who testified before our committee saw prostitution as a form of violence against women in and of itself' (2007: 4): 'The Committee came to the conclusion that prostitution is closely linked to trafficking in persons. We believe that prostitution is a form of violence against women and a violation of human rights. The Committee feels that the prostitute's consent is irrelevant, because you can never consent to sexual exploitation' (2007: 5). Clearly, approaching the problem with the status and liberty of women at the forefront shapes the understanding and recommendations of this all-party parliamentary committee.

Feminist abolition policy as developed by the autonomous women's movement would require universal social systems of public health and education. It would still require specific programs that focus on ameliorating and interfering with violence against women, including supports for victims such as exit strategies for prostitutes and internationally trafficked women and children. But more than that would be needed. It would require a challenge to men's entitlement to abuse women or even to be sexually serviced. A key economic strategy shift would understand wealth differently, understand women's economic contributions differently, and foster a more fair and equitable redistribution of resources and income. This mixture of universal programs and economic shifts to prevent poverty and specific programs to aid prostitutes and others victimized by violence needs to be designed by women themselves through the processes of debate, representation, and continued monitoring to see that women's objectives in policies are met.

One example of this process was the meeting of many Canadian feminist organizations in Pictou, Nova Scotia, for two days in September 2004 to explore a concept of fair sharing of Canadian resources, rather than people having to rely on charity or social work once they are in poverty. This gathering proposed a feminist version of a Guaranteed Livable Income through the Pictou Statement, as a more equitable redistribution of resources and income (*Lakeman et al.* 2004a). The Pictou Statement, adopted by CASAC in 2005, envisioned a feminist economic agenda integrated with concern for sustaining the earth and establishing equality. It decried the fact that Canadian federal policy not only resists this direction but has shifted over the past few decades to increasingly avoid government's obligation to provide for its residents, to end poverty, and to reduce women's vulnerability to sexist violence. Economic change occurred gradually over time, but major events occurred in 1995 both through Paul Martin's devastating budget cuts (Cohen 1997; Cohen and Brodie 2007) and by the end of the Canada Assistance Plan's federal/provincial national standardization and cost-sharing arrangements. In every significant area cuts and restrictions affected women's organizing. Cuts to funding for women's advocacy groups were particularly significant and had a devastating affect on women's ability to communicate with each other on policy issues. Also, the shift of responsibility from the federal government to the provincial governments for many social programs made the experiences of women across the country both more diverse and more precarious.

For the government to assume the obligation and or intention to establish the rights of women to economic equality, national welfare standards must recognize that although pay equity and affirmative action strategies are important, a Guaranteed Livable Income is the most promising strategy on the horizon. This would be an especially effective if it were connected to the provision of universal social programs for health, welfare, education, and worldwide sustainable environmental practices.

Protection from Violence

State protection from violence is a crucial element in the elimination of prostitution. Enacting the demands of women for better responses to all forms of men's violence against women requires improving law, policing, prosecution, court processes, sentencing, social programs, and public education, as well as creating a better relationship with women's independent equality-seeking groups through government consultation and funding. It requires recognizing prostitution as violence against women.

Recognizing the specifics of women's economic insecurity draws our attention to the fact that prostitution and sexual exploitation both result from and compound women's impoverishment. Women's economic vulnerability creates an undignified and dangerous dependency on men. Men's exploitation of that vulnerability is antisocial and often criminal – physical threat as well as economic exploitation, deceit, and coercion legally eliminate consent.

Conclusion

Feminist abolitionism calls for men to stop buying sex and to stop buying access to women. Legalization and incremental decriminalization policies outlined in the Justice Canada review of solicitation laws do nothing to prevent men from buying women; in fact, these policies promote the prostitution of women. It bears repeating that it is men who create the demand for sexualized services: 'If people are being prostituted, there are necessarily "prostitutors" – almost always we men – the people who buy or market the "sexual services" of the women and youths being merchandised. Male privilege, desire and sexist culture have a lot to do with this institution. Indeed, prostitution would not exist without our will and our money. By "disappearing" the role of men, the federal report obscures this relationship of dominance' (Brodeur et al. 2006: n.p.).

Abolitionists call on men to voluntarily end the demand for prostitution, but governments must also restrain organized crime and criminalize those who continue to profit by buying and supplying flesh in trade. The United Nations points the way forward and calls on governments to reconsider the short-term economic security of women according to their human rights. To ensure that there is equal access to shared benefits, privileges, and resources of society rather than abandoning women and children to the street, a long-term, feminist social transformation is needed.

Notes

1 See, e.g., the case of Donald Bakker in Vancouver, charged under Canada's 'sex tourism law': 'In 2004, he pleaded not guilty, claiming that Canada has no right to police people while they are outside its jurisdiction. Much of the evidence against him was videotapes that Bakker himself made. Some of these show Bakker torturing Vancouver area prostitutes. Other videos show him having sex with girls in Cambodia, the oldest of whom was 12. On 1 June 2005 he pleaded guilty to 10 counts of sexual assault to avoid a trial' (Wikepedia 2004: n.p.).

2 Mourani was removed by the Bloc as critic for women's equality once she participated in the Status of Women Committee report that opposed the decriminalization or legalization of prostitution. This will be discussed later in the chapter.

3 Robert Pickton is on trial for killing 26 women after scores of sex workers disappeared from Vancouver's notorious east side over the past three decades. In May 2005 Statistics Canada's Roy Jones told a parliamentary subcommittee that 79 prostitutes had been murdered in Canada between 1994 and 2003 – all 'in the context of their involvement in this industry.' Notably, the annual murders increased in 1995, the pivotal year in which social policy changed away from national and universal programs and away from any guarantee of welfare (Lakeman 2005).

4 Cherry Kingsley, spokesperson for the Experiential Women's Coalition, reported this statistic to the CASAC gathering on 30 April 2005 and at the Rape Relief anti-prostitution evening at Wise Hall in Vancouver on 10 Oct 2003.

5 This agreement builds on Convention on the Elimination of All Forms of

Discrimination Against Women (CEDAW) and Violence Against Women provisions and the other rights of migrant populations.

References

Barry, Kathleen. (1985). *Female Sexual Slavery*. New York: New York University Press.

Brodeur, Jacques, James Douglas, Nicolas Doyon, Martin Dufresne, Philippe Robert de Massy, and Jacques Saintonge. (2006). Pas de prostituées sans prostitueurs Electronic version retrieved 13 Sept. 2007 from http://sisyphe.org/article.php3?id_article=2557.

Bindel, Julie. (2007). Why Is Rape So Easy to Get Away With? *Guardian*,1 Feb. Electronic version retrieved 29 June 2007 from http://www.guardian.co.uk/print/o329702204-10477000html.

Canada. (2005). *Report and Recommendations in Respect of Legislation, Policy and Practices Concerning Prostitution-related Activities*. Ottawa: Department of Justice Canada.

– (2006). *The Challenge of Change: A Study of Canada's Criminal Prostitution Laws*. Report of the Subcommittee on Solicitation Laws (of the Standing Committee on Justice and Human Rights). Ottawa: House of Commons.

Canadian Association of Sexual Assault Centers (CASAC). (2001). *Women's Critical Resistance from Victimization to Criminalization*. Convention Proceedings. Ottawa: CASAC.

– (2005). Anti-trafficking Policy and Work: New CASAC Policy. Electronic version retrieved 1 July 1 from http://www.casac.ca/english/CASAC.convention.2005.htm.

– (2006) Protect Victims and Criminalize Profiteers. Report of the Subcommittee on Solicitation Laws. Electronic version retrieved 1 July 2007 from http://sisyphe.org/rubrique.php3?id_rubrique=109.

Caputi, Jane. (1987). *The Age of Sex Crime*. Ohio: Bowling Green State University Popular Press.

Cohen, Marjorie Griffin. (1997). From the Welfare State to Vampire Capitalism. In Patricia M. Evans and Gerda R. Wekerle (eds.), *Women and the Canadian Welfare State: Challenges and Change*, 28–70. Toronto: University of Toronto Press.

Cohen, Marjorie Griffin, and Janine Brodie (eds.). (2007). *Remapping Gender in the New Global Order*. Oxford and New York: Routledge.

Huda, Sigma. (2006). Statement on the 2nd Annual Report of the Special Rapporteur on the Human Rights Aspects of Victims of Trafficking in Persons,

Especially Women and Children. Geneva: United Nations, Human Rights Council. Electronic version retrieved 13 Sept. 2007 from http://action.web. ca/home/catw/readingroom.shtml?x=92105.

Hughes, Donna. (2000) Lecture on Sexual Exploitation. Presented at Queen Sophia Center, Valencia, Spain.

Lakeman, Lee. (1993). *99 Federal Steps toward an End to Violence against Women.* Toronto: National Action Committee on the Status of Women.

– (2005). *Obsession, with Intent: Violence against Women.* Montreal: Black Rose Books.

Lakeman, Lee, Angela Miles, and Linda Christinasen-Ruffman. (2004a). Feminist Statement on Guaranteed Living Income. *Canadian Woman Studies Journal* 23(3,4): 204–6.

Lakeman, Lee, Alice Lee, and Suzanne Jay. (2004b). Resisting the Promotion of Prostitution in Canada: A view from the Vancouver Rape Relief and Women's Shelter. In Christine Stark and Rebecca Whisnant (eds.), *Not For Sale,* 210–52. North Melbourne: Sinefex Press.

MacKinnon, Catherine. (2006). *Are Women Human? And Other International Dialogues.* Cambridge: Harvard University Press.

Mourani, Maria. (2006). The Majority Report of the Justice Subcommittee on Solicitation Laws: A Direct Assault on Women's Rights and a Gift to Organized Crime. Bloc Québécois Critic for the Status of Women. Electronic version retrieved 1 July 2007 from http://sisyphe.org/article.php3?id_ article=2501.

O'Connor, Monica, and Granine Healy. (2006). *The Links between Prostitution and Sex Trafficking: A Briefing Handbook.* Prepared for the Joint Project Coordinated by the Coalition Against Trafficking in Women (CATW) and the European Women's Lobby (EWL) on Promoting Preventative Measures to Combat Trafficking in Human Beings for Sexual Exploitation. Electronic version retrieved 13 Sept. 2007 from http://action.web.ca/home/catw/ attach/handbook.pdf.

Plamondon, Ginette. (2002). La Prostitution: Profession or exploitation, Une Reflexion a Poursuivre. Montreal Canada: Conseil du statut de la femme. Electronic version retrieved 13 Sept. 2007 from http://www.csf.gouv.qc.ca/ telechargement/publications/RechercheProstitutionProfessionOu Exploitation.pdf.

Raymond, Janice G. (2001) *Guide to the New U.N. Trafficking Protocol: Protocol to Prevent, Suppress and Punish Trafficking in Persons, Especially Women and Children, Supplementing the United Nations Convention against Transnational Organized Crime.* North Amherst, MA: Coalition Against Trafficking in Women.

Statistics Canada. (2005). *The Daily: Homicides*. Electronic version retrieved 13
    Sept. 2007 from http://www.statcan.ca/Daily/English/051006/d051006b.
    htm.
– (2007). Transition House Survey 3328. Electronic version retrieved 13 Sept.
    2007 from http://www.statcan.ca/cgi-bin/imdb/p2SV.pl?Function=
    getSurveyandSDDS=3328andlang=enanddb=IMDBanddbg=fandadm=
    8anddis=2.
Status of Women Canada. (2007). *Turning Outrage into Action to Address Traf-
    ficking for the Purpose of Sexual Exploitation in Canada*. Report of the Standing
    Committee on the Status of Women. Ottawa: House of Commons.
Sweden. (2004). Prostitution and Trafficking in Women. Fact Sheet, Ministry
    of Industry, Employment and Communications, Jan. Electronic version
    retrieved 13 Sept. 2007 from http://www.sweden.gov.se/content/1/c6/01/
    87/74/6bc6c972.pdf.
– (2005). Prostitution and Trafficking in Women. Fact Sheet, Ministry of In-
    dustry, Employment and Communications, Jan.
United Nations. (2000). *Protocol to Prevent, Suppress and Punish Trafficking in
    Persons, Especially Women and Children, Supplementing the United Nations
    Convention against Transnational Organized Crime*, Article 3. Electronic ver-
    sion retrieved 1 July 2007 from http://www.uncjin.org/Documents/
    Conventions/ dcatoc/final_documents_2/convention_%20traff_eng.pdf.
Wikepedia. (2004). Donald Bakker, Electronic version retrieved 1 July 2007
    from http://en.wikipedia.org/wiki/Donald_Bakker.

6 Lone Mothers: Policy Responses to Build Social Inclusion

LEA CARAGATA

Welfare and Work

In the past ten years or so Canadian welfare policy has been reshaped to require lone parents to participate in paid work, training, and/or volunteer activities to receive social assistance. These policies, modelled on U.S. welfare reform, are known variously as 'workfare' and 'work-first' programs. Related to these policy changes, between 1993 and 1998 the number of lone mothers in Canada with a child under the age of 6 years participating in the labour force at some point in the year rose from 48.8 per cent to 77.1 per cent (Vosko 2002). This increase is attributable in part to workfare initiatives that have had some success in their demands for labour market engagement. However, the nature of the work that these lone mothers undertake requires scrutiny, as does its effect on their families.

Current labour market options for less-skilled workers, or those without the supports to work full-time (e.g., those without adequate child care), tend to be low-paid employment involving irregular hours, shift work, and demands to work on-call (Smith and Jackson 2002; Caragata 2003), with women workers significantly over-represented in this precarious labour market. Overall, more than one-third of Canadian women (compared with 16.1% of men) work in what Statistics Canada classifies as 'low paid employment.' Among Canadian women workers, 69 per cent earn less than $8 per hour (Maxwell 2002; Morissette and Zhang 2005; Statistics Canada 2006b). Part-time work and holding multiple jobs are also gendered; women outnumber men in part-time work by three to one (Menzies 1998; Statistics Canada 2003) and account for 70 per cent of all holders of multiple jobs (CLC 1997). Demonstrating the gendered nature of labour-market precariousness, more than 50 per cent of families led by lone mothers have incomes that are less than half the national median income, compared with only 10 per cent of other family forms (Jenson 2003).

While part-time and low-paid work causes difficulty for anyone who is dependent on her wages, it is uniquely problematic for lone parents. Because of the difficulty in accessing flexible and affordable child care, most lone parents must confine themselves to work within the school day, limiting the work hours and the jobs available to them. If they pay for child care (and most have no other option), then their earnings are substantially reduced. These scenarios, of course, presume that child care is available at all. In Toronto there are long waits for subsidized spaces, and the cost of a non-subsidized day care centre space almost equals minimum wage earnings (ACTEW 2007; Noik-Bent 2008). The cost of non-subsidized day care ranges across the country from lows for home-based care of about $25 per day per child to fees in child care centres of $60 per day per child, all depending on hours, quality of care, and the ages of the children involved. Thus, the cost of child care alone requires that lone parents achieve higher levels of earnings to sustain themselves in the labour market.

Unfortunately, workfare programs have tended to focus on job training sufficient merely to access the labour market – 'the shortest route to work' – rather than building skills sufficient to ensure a sustainable level of earnings. Thus, lone parents, the vast majority of whom are women, are caught in a policy bind. Welfare requires work that does not pay enough to afford rent, food, and child care for a family; often leading the lone mother back into the welfare system to repeat the cycle. Programs that supported a transition to work by protecting some portion of earned income have largely been cut. In Ontario 50 per cent of all earnings are 'clawed back' from a social assistance recipient, which reduces minimum wage work to a net of $4 an hour, before the worker has even paid for child care and transit costs (Toronto Social Services 2007). Thus, 'reformed' welfare systems afford little opportunity for a welfare recipient to build work skills – and the potential to command more than the minimum wage – while still relying on social assistance provisions.

The policy dilemma is clear. Workfare programs require lone parents to obtain work with minimal job training, while the labour market increasingly offers low-skilled workers only minimum wage work, often part-time and at off-hours, without benefits or employment protections.

The number of state-subsidized child care spaces is inadequate, and without these and other supports lone parents are economically unable to sustain themselves in the labour market, necessitating a cycle of welfare-work-welfare. The problem seems sufficiently straightforward that it is hard to grasp why the state has not responded. This lack of response drives the analysis that follows. Why has welfare policy created such a bind for lone mothers? How is it in our collective interest to see a significant part of the population forced to raise their children in poverty? The answers to these questions lie in sets of values and social practices that are insufficiently explored and explained, 'stories' we tell ourselves about who 'these people' are and why they cannot meet their own needs. The problem with the policy and programs that currently impoverish and stigmatize lone mothers – by gender, race, and social class – is that they are driven by certain discourses that remain embedded rather than consciously acknowledged and constructed.

John Dryzek and Valerie Braithwaite suggest that 'discourse can be defined as a shared set of understandings embedded in language that enables its adherents to put together pieces of information and other sensory inputs into coherent wholes, organized around common storylines' (2000: 243). This chapter explores these discourses on the presumption that such understanding is a necessary, although still insufficient, precondition for challenging and changing the dominant social discourse that constructs lone mothers. Public policy can, of course, drive discourse change, and hence can, through careful crafting, also challenge prevailing social views. More conservatively, however, it reflects current dominant constructions. I suggest that the latter course is the current reality for lone mothers who live in poverty.

A variety of comments from lone mothers on social assistance show how these discourses are assimilated, as lone mothers reflect on how they are seen, how they see themselves, and even as they see and create social distance between themselves as 'good' lone mothers and the 'others.'

'Sophie' describes her experience, suggesting the fact that she is Black adds another layer in the negative social judgment that she feels is applied to her:

> discrimination, racial profiling. It's the same thing. I get looked at every day because I'm on social assistance ... It bothers me. It's embarrassing sometimes. You meet somebody and you can have an intelligent conversation with this person and have a lot of things in common, but

once they find out that you're on Social Services, they're like, 'Ew, I pay for you to live.' (Interview participant, as cited in Caragata 2008a)

'Kayla' acknowledges the same feelings of being judged and under surveillance:

'[It's] very difficult. Everybody thinks you're happy to sit on it [welfare] and get a free ride. What could be a free ride about something like that? [Welfare workers] are digging up your past; they're digging up everything. You have no privacy whatsoever.' (Interview participant, as cited in Caragata 2008a)

'Alice' sums up what she understands to be the general social view:

"You know tax payers; they don't like people on welfare." (Interview participant, as cited in Caragata 2008b)

'Ann' tells how these discourses shape the lone mothers' own subjectivities:

They look down at you and they talk down to you. You feel really bad about yourself. (Interview participant, as cited in Caragata 2008b)

Mary confirms this view:

Exactly, yeah, because you just don't feel good about yourself. You don't feel good inside. (Interview participant, as cited in Caragata 2008b)

Or, women protect themselves by presuming that the discourses apply to 'other' lone mothers. Mary says:

And there's a lot of people out there that use the system, you know? Like, they collect cheques at different addresses, or they'll have more kids just to get more money, type of thing. It – kind of, defeats the purpose of the people that really need welfare, that need it to survive, because there's people out there scamming them. (Interview participant as cited in Caragata 2008b)

Discourse is a powerful shaper of our social attitudes and no one is immune, from the taxpayers Alice speaks for, to the welfare workers delivering benefits to the lone mothers themselves.

How does this discourse become so pervasive – and what might confront and challenge it? Given the power of these views, how likely are policy outcomes that might address the real needs of lone mothers? I suggest that the policy problem that confronts low-skilled lone mothers, certainly in North America and the United Kingdom, and to a lesser extent in Western Europe, is a pervasive public perception that the problems faced by lone mothers are variously self-induced, born of sloth and/or moral depravity, and that deprivation is a necessary incentive for them to change, to 'improve.'

Accordingly this chapter analyses a number of dominant and shaping discourses relating to lone mothers and welfare. Thinking about the discourse of lone mothers and welfare through the lens of social exclusion provides a more complex and complete picture of the relational nature of the elements of the discursive practices involved in creating a welfare/lone mother universe.

Social exclusion is a contested concept (Alden and Thomas 1998; Watts 2001) that is popularly used to describe a wide range of social and personal issues, including general inequality; poverty, homelessness, and unemployment; racial prejudice, segregation, and even ethnic cleansing; individual feelings of interpersonal rejection; and experiences of 'superfluity, irrelevance, marginality, foreignness, alterity, closure, disaffiliation, dispossession, deprivation, and destitution' (Silver 1994: 539). Even a partial review of a vast literature reveals that the language of social exclusion is applied to almost any kind of social ailment and is sometimes used without definition or explanation (Bhalla and Lapeyre 1997; Alden and Thomas 1998; Watts 2001). As such, the term conjures a notion lacking in substance, and at the same time, can point towards a concept that is rich and complex. Thus, when using the terms 'social exclusion' and 'social inclusion,' we must acknowledge that these terms defy absolute definition and are, rather, concepts or theories with multiple meanings and interpretations that are applied in a piecemeal fashion to a variety of conditions and situations.

In this chapter, when exploring the topic of lone mothers on welfare, social inclusion/exclusion provides an analytical approach to conceptualize and articulate the multifaceted manner in which systems and structures have impacts on the lives of lone mothers. Our discursive constructions have real on-the-ground impacts as they shape the experiences of lone mothers as actors, as citizens. Thus, this critical lens of social exclusion permits an exploration of the effects of these shaping discourses in a number of different realms. This contrasts with the too familiar alternative wherein social exclusion is used not to analyse structures but as a tool to tally individual deficits (Good Gingrich 2003), which practice is, of course, most consistent with a residual welfare state that largely blames individuals (however sympathetically) for their lack of successful social and economic engagement. As Anver Saloojee (2003) asserts, a weak version of social inclusion focuses on changing the excluded while a strong version focuses on challenging power relations between the excluded and those doing the excluding and emphasizes structural change.

Here a stronger version of social inclusion/exclusion is adopted: this provides for a theoretical framework that allows for greater insight into the experiences of lone mothers enabling a more complex understanding of inclusion/exclusion, recognizing that people can be excluded in some areas and included in others, and that exclusion occurs at all levels of society. Disadvantages are cumulative and interrelated; people from minoritized groups are more likely to be unemployed and are more likely to have less political power, fewer social contacts, and so on (de Haan 1999). Thus, each point of exclusion can contribute to greater exclusion at another level; marginalization is cumulative. While acknowledging its limitations and flaws, the language of social exclusion/social inclusion offers us a framework for exploring the many intersecting facets of marginalization and the ways in which they reinforce and intensify each other (Bhalla and Lapeyre 1997; Alden and Thomas 1998; Watts 2001).

This version of social inclusion/exclusion theory posits that we need to extend poverty theory by reframing our analyses so that we see the more complex social processes, such as the discourses described here that act, especially on minoritized population groups, to effectively disengage or exclude from significant aspects of contemporary life. Other issues of concern identified include the nature of collective responsibility and appropriate policy responses if population subgroups, gendered and racialized, are left in precarious employment with limited prospects. Thus, social exclusion provides a framework critical to understanding the experiences of lone mothers, and the social and policy processes that shape these experiences and give them meaning. Amartya Sen (2000) suggests that the theoretical bases of social exclusion derive in part from capability deprivation (lack of freedom to undertake important activities) and from the realization that poverty is not simply a lack of goods (material deprivation), but also affects one's status in the public realm and feelings of public worthiness (relational

deprivation). The exploration of both capability and relational deprivation, in addition to material deprivation, is a major strength of a social
exclusion framework. Social exclusion provides a relational perspective
on the ways in which 'social disqualification' occurs (as cited in Bhalla
and Lapeyre 1997: 414). Thus, social exclusion can provide a framework
for analysing the combination of:

- The context-setting structural forces
- The experience of the groups being disqualified
- The role of the state in enabling or ameliorating these forces through
  policy

For the purposes of this chapter I use a social exclusion lens to analyse those discursive practices that foster and sustain particular social
values that enable our successful processes of 'othering': setting
aside and distancing some selected people we regard as not like us,
not needing or deserving or even wanting what we have and want.
Discourses are a critical expression of these context-setting structural
forces. The following four major areas in which social exclusion is
made visible lend focus to our task of identifying the discursive constructions that 'mark,' 'name,' and 'blame' lone mothers:

1. Economic exclusion: work, income, household budget, credit/debt,
   consumption, etc.
2. Sociopolitical exclusion: personal and social well-being and health,
   social networks, voting, religion, sexual orientation, culture, ethnicity, time in Canada, etc.
3. Spatial exclusion: housing type, neighbourhood, economic and
   social diversity, safety, crime, etc.
4. Subjective exclusion: self-perceptions of personal autonomy and
   power and control, expressed perceptions of lone mothers in relation to other members of society, etc.

The chapter proceeds with a discussion of some elements of the public
discourse in each of the above realms as it relates to lone mothers. I neither claim empirical wisdom with respect to how I have identified these
shaping discourses, nor do I suggest that I have undertaken an exhaustive discourse analysis. Rather, I have selected certain – and perhaps
obvious – elements of readily observable public discourse that seem
to me to have salience in our views of lone mothers and their social

situations. I suggest this approach has utility in understanding public policy and the experiences of this vulnerable population. On a personal level, I can recognize discursive elements shaping my own views with respect to particular stereotypes about lone mothers, ones that I must struggle against in spite of the fact that I 'know' at an intellectual level a quite different story. This experience illuminates the shaping power of discourse.

Discursive Elements Shaping Economic Exclusion

Economic inclusion/exclusion is increasingly powerful in contemporary Western society. Our roles as workers shape not only our material relations but define, at least to some extent, the three other aspects of exclusion, sociopolitical, spatial, and subjective. This shaping power of economic relations is not an abrupt change but rather a slow, continuing aspect of advanced capitalism wherein, as Hannah Arendt (1958) prophetically claimed, 'man's' excellence, his uniqueness and ability is no longer made visible in the public realm but expressed more singularly through his labour. Work defines the neighbourhoods we live in, the marketing that targets us according to income and lifestyle 'profile' and our sense of self and self-worth. Relatedly, and perhaps more recently, our attention has been drawn by Sen (2000), Fraser (1997), and others to the role of our economic status in shaping our willingness to self-righteously proclaim ourselves as 'citizens' with needs the state has a responsibility to meet, these claims apparently having a higher value than the claims of those who are needy.

'Wealth as worth' is a discourse so pervasive that it underpins many aspects of contemporary public policy. Andrew Herman (1999), in his study of philanthropy and the meanings of wealth, examines the ways in which the wealthy have come to be seen as the 'better angels of capitalism.' One sees this manifested as governments around the world rationalize tax breaks to upper income groups because of their presumed capability to generate jobs, their roles as 'wealth makers.' Money, in the hands of those who are better off, is presumed to have a higher use value than it has in the hands of the poor. This is in spite of the fact that we know that the poor spend almost 100 per cent of their income, and equally importantly, they spend it locally. As an instrument of job creation and an economic engine, compare these two scenarios. High-income earners can afford to save the money from their tax breaks, are more likely to save through employing non-domestic investment, and when they do spend, their spending can completely bypass the local economy through travel and tourism, foreign investment, and the purchase of imported goods. The presumption that tax breaks for the affluent are economic generators is now seemingly taken at face value; Herman (1999) suggests that it derives from a moral overvaluing of wealth and those who possess it.

If the rich are the 'angels of capitalism,' what then are the poor? It is, of course, through the binary nature of the contrast that the discourse works its magic, shaping and signifying. Herman suggests that conferred on the behaviour of the wealthy is a certain moral identity; thus through the moral economy of wealth, financial wealth is transformed into moral worth, and excess resources are accounted for as signs of the bountiful surplus moral value and virtue of the wealthy (1999). This binary effectively casts moral doubt on the poor. Why are they poor? Why are they not contributing? These questions are induced by the constructed discourse.

Herman adds a gendered perspective to his thesis, describing a narrative pattern of fortune and virtue, creating two fundamental social categories: that which is given and that which is accomplished. Men are the primary force by which the former is transformed into the latter, Herman suggests tracing these discursive constructions to Renaissance mercantile capitalism – thus, historically designated narratives of fortune and virtue enable 'wealthy men to construct their moral identity' (1999: 8).

The sovereign male that Herman describes, of course, shapes the 'other': 'The abjected "other" has taken on many forms ... the spendthrift, those who do not use their "talents," the slothful, the economically dependent' (1999: 256). Herein we can see some of the discursive constructions that have framed how we see lone mothers.

Morally Suspect Lone Mothers

Morality as both the basis for economic entitlement and as derivative of economic success has also long shaped how we rationalize state benefits. The concepts of the 'deserving' and 'undeserving' poor are well understood as historically and contemporarily relevant to 'who gets what.' Disabled people receive higher benefits than single employables in all Canadian provinces and territories, while those considered the most 'unworthy' are perhaps men with addictions. Beyond general conceptions of the poor as morally unworthy, there is a sliding scale of moral worthiness. These notions are especially relevant in the dis-

course on lone mothers. Through the early periods of industrializat
lone mothers began to pose a policy problem. In the early nineteenth
century, they were often consigned to workhouses, an unwanted economic burden even if they were then not generally seen to have caused
their impoverished circumstances. Evolving moral and legal discourses
left bastard children without the legal protection of any parent, while
mothers were threatened with criminality for neglect or abandonment
(Smart 1996). Victorian moral purity movements cast the lone mother
as a fallen woman and her motherhood was interpreted as immorality.
Carol Smart (1996) further suggests that the shame of illegitimacy continued through the Second World War years as a moral disincentive to
lone motherhood. Following the war, important distinctions began to be
made among different groups of lone mothers. Widows and educated
lone mothers were distinguished socially from young, never-married
lone mothers. And economically, through welfare policy, lone mothers were more worthy than unemployed singles, as reflected through a
separate welfare program and higher rates of benefits.

Changing divorce laws, mother's allowances, availability of abortion, contraception, growing awareness of abuse, and a host of related
social factors all led by the 1970s to a lone mother discourse wherein it
was harder to singularly and negatively characterize the lone mother.
This moment of promise was surprisingly short. The men's and father's
rights movements, an antifeminist backlash, rising neoconservative
politics, high levels of public debt, and a corresponding critical view
of welfare state spending all combined, by the early 1980s, to bring
into question generous state support for lone mothers. In the United
States, there was particular attention given to young, predominantly
Black women allegedly having babies in order to be eligible for welfare
benefits. Although some (Jencks and Edin 1995; Edin and Lein 1997)
questioned these suppositions, much of American welfare reform was
aimed at cutting off such access. Thus, the U.S. welfare reform debate
paid considerable attention to 'babies for welfare,' the lone mother as
a 'welfare scammer,' and overall, to the so-called disinclination of lone
mothers to work. This marked an important shift in valuing stay-at-
home parenting, so that while women were still seen as primary carers,
they were to combine this with productive roles in the labour force.

Work versus Care

In North America women's participation in the labour market has
been growing steadily and is now almost at par with that of men. In

Canada women account for 46.9 per cent of those in the labour market (Statistics Canada 2006a). Constructions of 'good mothers' adapted to mothers in paid labour, as long as mothers continued to undertake – as their primary responsibility – their family roles. So, we have an evolving discourse that still demands mothers as primary caregivers but also enables their engagement in the labour market. Thus, contemporary labour markets require low-waged (women) workers, and these needs have driven some of the changes in welfare systems, such that they are more directly and obviously tied to labour market demands (Peck 2005; Grover and Stewart 2002).

Economic growth in today's Western societies requires competitively priced labour. And competitive pricing must now be judged against the cheap labour in unregulated markets such as China and other booming Asian economies. A factor in the construction of lone mothers and others as 'economically marginal' is that our economy requires more than ever, 'a reserve army of the unemployed,' with certain forces compelling those who are unemployed to take such work as there may be: for low wages and with insecure attachment to the labour market. It is these employees who fill the labour needs of the service sector, a steadily growing sector of the Canadian economy (Statistics Canada 2007) that requires labour that is part-time, casual, and often during non-standard hours. Ensuring a low welfare benefit rate – even for lone mothers previously seen as more deserving – provides an incentive to take such employment. Across North America such work is now combined with workfare or work-first initiatives requiring welfare recipients to find work, often implicitly acknowledging that partial benefits may be received concurrently. As a model, it has met with unquestionable policy success – as mentioned, the number of lone mothers in Canada, with a child under the age of 6 years, participating in the labour force at some point in the year, rose from 48.8 per cent to 77.1 per cent (Vosko 2002). Chris Grover and John Stewart (2002) conceptualize this combination of financial incentives and disciplinary measures to make non-employed people take paid employment as 'market workfare' in order to demonstrate the ways in which social security and labour-market policy are being used to help reconstruct the reserve army of labour. This discourse masks itself as creating incentives for labour market engagement by lone mothers rather than revealing, as Jamie Peck (2005) describes, the intertwining of social assistance systems with labour market needs.

These historic and contemporary discourses shape our views of poor and/or low-skilled lone mothers as changes in women's education and employment have enabled middle-class lone mothers to claim good jobs and high incomes. Moral scrutiny has lessened for divorced or widowed mothers and, if their education and employment status is sufficiently high, even for never-married mothers. In a sense, economics trumps all in contemporary discourse. The lone mothers for whom there is a discourse of moral regulation or dependence are those who are also poor and more likely also to be racialized, disabled, 'othered.' As Herman (1999) suggests, despite almost all other factors, wealth equates with moral worth. The problem, however, is that being a lone mother is in itself a contributing factor to a woman's poverty, making wealthy lone mothers less than common.

Discursive Elements Shaping Sociopolitical Exclusion

A second element or area of social exclusion relates to citizenship and one's right to be a claimant in the public realm. As Sen (2000) notes, one's relative sense of worth or entitlement is shaped by material well-being, and this shapes one's sense of public worthiness. In this section I examine discourses relevant to shaping lone mothers' notions of citizenship, as well as those that shape how we understand the public realm and, hence, how we see those who make claims of the 'public.'

Women have a long history of trying to achieve status in the sociopolitical realm. Seen as the keepers of the private realm of the family (Arendt 1958; Pateman 1988; Fraser 1990; 1997), ignored in the construction of the social contract, women achieved legal and political status in part through their roles as mothers. Fraser (1990), Sassen (1998), and others describe women in civil society negotiating on behalf of their children for a variety of social goods, such as school entry and social and recreational activity, and negotiating with the bureaucracy to obtain social benefits. It is in their roles as mothers that women are often propelled into the public realm. In spite of these limited points of entry, women as political citizens remain an underrepresented construction, certainly as evidenced in North America (Paxton 2003; Trimble 2001; Tremblay 2000).

The history of Western capitalist society reveals a story of marginalized and /or minoritized population groups struggling for access to the public realm, for legitimate and legitimized access to public space. The enfranchisement of women; the Alabama bus boycott; first-elected Blacks, women, First Nations, gays, lesbians; the 'liberation' of public parks, swimming pools, and schools; women's 'take back the night' marches; dramatic productions such as the Laramie Project – all of these are important social signifiers of struggles for access to the political realm and to the spaces of our cities. The 1960s and 1970s represented a period of democratization of the public realm, or at least a move in that direction. As part of these processes, women became more fully public citizens.

The notion of citizen, of course, has its roots in ancient Greece, where it applied to men of property and of a certain social, economic, and ethnocultural position (Kimlicka and Norman 1994). Subsequently, the enfranchisement of 'others' beyond men has been a slow process. So what are our ideas of 'citizen' today? How is citizen portrayed?

Stergios Skaperdas (2003) suggests that one dominant contemporary notion is 'citizen as consumer.' He argues that economic growth has become a more singular societal goal and that its focus detracts from time spent engaging 'publicly,' as citizen, and considers the following facts:

1. Material growth increases the time spent working in the market while it reduces the time spent in gatherings, in symposia, with others.
2. Public discourse requires time – to read, think, and interact with others.
3. Public discourse is also assisted by the presence of a public space, the agora, the corner cafe, bar, or tavern, as well as the presence of media that can provide fodder for debate. (2003: 35)

Skaperdas's argument builds on and concretizes arguments perhaps more broadly expressed over time by Arendt (1958), Habermas (1989 [1962]), and many others. In short, the opportunity and enticement to engage as citizen, in the public sphere – or at least in civil society – are eroded by an increasing emphasis on one's life in paid labour. Opportunities diminish as work weeks increase in length, precarious work predominates, and our public engagement is reduced to shopping at the local mall. The lone mother living in poverty is unlikely to see herself as a successful consumer. Rather, she is a victim or a failure in a society that creates ever-new consumer needs that she cannot satisfy for herself. Thus, as she fails as consumer, at least according to Skaperdas's view, she also fails as a citizen of the contemporary 'public' realm.

Another dominant discursive construction is 'citizen as taxpayer.' This is often reflected in the views of groups such as the National Citizen's Coalition and others whose views suggest that the goal of the taxpayer/citizen is to demand a reduced role for the state, to minimize taxes, and to leave individuals to care for themselves and their families. This view is particularly problematic in extending the notion of citizen to those who are poor or who pay minimal taxes. Is one's degree of citizenship equated with a higher tax levy? If so, the poor and poor lone mothers are by implication, less than citizens. They are reminded, in contemporary discourse, that they are takers, relying on the system, even 'taking advantage' of the system rather than contributing. The notion of the citizen as reluctant taxpayer (paying voluntarily only for what is in 'his' shared individual interest) underpins American, and to a somewhat lesser extent, Canadian society (Mead 1986; Barry 1990; Kimlicka and Norman 1994). Our contemporary discursive construction of 'citizen' marks out lone mothers (and others) as unworthy, failing both as consumers and as taxpayers and having a set of interests quite at odds with those that ask of the state only the protection of their private interests.

Nancy Fraser's (1992; 1997) notions of deliberative democracy contest these limited notions of citizenship and, rather, suggest social processes through which citizens come to shared values and a commitment to a common good. The success of such alternative and contesting discourses is at the moment minimal, leading Fraser (1997) to doubt whether such change is possible in the present neoconservative era. This challenge is further diminished by the very forces that enable a narrow conservative, exclusionary construction of citizen to prevail, with fewer and fewer opportunities for such deliberative action as Fraser describes.

Discursive Elements Shaping Spatial Exclusion

In considering spatial, geographical segregation of the poor and poor lone mothers, the notion that the socially excluded are a 'kind' of people with certain kinds of deficiencies, rather than social exclusion as a set of processes by which society excludes, has relevance. From immigrant settlement patterns to the white, executive, gated community, we seem to be increasingly desirous of living with our own 'kind.' As cities have grown and land use regulations have become more specialized, the development patterns of cities have changed from what they were in the early part of the twentieth century (Sassen 1998). Then, neigh-bourhoods tended to be built with multiple dwelling types and adja-cent industrial/commercial development. 'Kinds' were less singularly economically determined, and moral worthiness could not be simply detected by one's presence in a particular neighbourhood (Kaus 1992). Because urban growth in North America has occurred largely in the past seventy years, most of urban North America has developed in a more specialized, singular identity form. The modern suburb is most revealing, miles of low-density single-family homes, often built to ac-commodate a narrow income band, with commercial and work places beyond its boundaries. Its low density militates against viable public transit, and there are few if any public spaces within its 'walls' – the access roads surrounding it. Shops and services are provided in the lo-cal mall, and the stores within the mall are carefully calibrated to the incomes of the users. Social messages are clearly conveyed about who lives where, and from these, discourses are constructed and confirmed (Sorkin 1992; Kaus 1992).

The suburbs of the 'others' are equally walled – often by freeways – and contain miles of public housing projects or high-rise apartment buildings, again with shops and services constructed to represent those who use them. Thus, the services available also conform to the dis-course about who the poor are and what they require. Commercial en-terprises, especially food stores that take advantage of neighbourhood segregation and the lessened mobility of the non-car-owning poor by charging higher prices and stocking poorer quality products, confirm our notions of worthiness.

This spatially segregated land use that I have briefly described has particular implications for lone mothers both in shaping their material realities and in confirming contemporary discourse. As Saskia Sassen (1998) suggests in the context of globalizing economic systems, indus-trial production has been relocated to be accessible to highways and airports, on the edges of cities. Thus, access to work can be doubly problematic for those who are poor, as there may be no or limited pub-lic transit options, no feasible way to live close to work, and a lack of essential services such as child care in any reasonable proximity to the workplace.

Douglass Massey and Nancy Denton (1998) point to the retention of many historical practices of apartheid in housing and schooling. A lo-cal housing authority in Toronto was recently criticized for sending all Caribbean applicants to the same public housing complex. The same story holds for schools as for shops: if a neighbourhood is spatially and economically segregated, so, too, are the schools. Access to social networks offering a range of resources is also circumscribed by spatial segregation. Barry Wellman and Scot Wortley (1990) have demonstrated that the most effective networks 'contain' a range of network members. If one lives in a neighbourhood only with one's own 'kind' and that 'kind' is excluded in several of the dimensions under discussion here, the resources available through the network will be more limited. Thus, the discourses of who lone mothers are, what they need, and where they 'belong' are affirmed and reconstructed as spatial land use patterns symbolize and signify.

Discursive Elements Shaping Subjective Exclusion

There may be some important and unintended benefits to lone mothers deriving from these spatially segregated neighbourhoods; this also relates to our final category, subjective exclusion. Karen McCormack (2004) has reported that poor women residing in mixed-class communities, interacting with the working poor, working, and middle classes, were palpably aware of the dominant discursive images discussed here and took steps to distance themselves from the putative welfare mother. Like the welfare mothers who I cited at the beginning of this chapter, poor women can construct themselves as 'not the other' by reviling the lone mother on welfare, creating distance and separation: 'I am not like her.' Women living in neighbourhoods surrounded by other poor people, however, appeared to be partially immune from the pernicious associations with the welfare mother. While they were not wholly unaware of the dominant discourse, they were also operating in a different field, one in which poverty and receipt of welfare were understood quite differently. The meanings of welfare produced by the recipients themselves can run counter to the dominant construction in environments where other constructions compete against the socially prevailing ones. McCormack (2004) cites Dodson's exploration of the lives of poor women and girls as she suggests that many alternative strategies exist in the margins, that women construct a range of responses to dominant constructions, ways that they try 'to make sense of their place in the world and to hold on to themselves' (as cited in McCormack 2004: 360).

Recent data from 'Lone Mothers: Building Social Inclusion,' a Canada-wide multi-method longitudinal research program, of which this author is the principal investigator, confirm these findings. Based on preliminary data from forty lone mothers on social assistance, interviewed in Toronto in 2006, a number of women see the buffering effect of their poor neighbourhoods. They offered comments such as, 'So I prefer being in that neighbourhood because they don't dress their kids a lot in name brand stuff. So my kid is not too picked on,' and 'I don't think neighbours [are judgmental] because everybody pretty much in this building is on assistance, and getting their cheque at the same time.' Another lone mother said, 'Yeah it's been a good experience in E, this area. There are many single parents with a low-income.' These views contrasted with those of lone mothers in more mixed neighbourhoods, almost all of whom reported experiences of being stigmatized or withholding personal information and/or withdrawing from social interactions for fear of being negatively judged.

The discussion above points to the critical elements of subjective social exclusion. Discourse is a powerful shaper of human perception, and those who are vilified by prevailing discursive constructions often come to share those dominant constructions. Thus, lone mothers may themselves perpetuate the discourse, calling welfare snitch lines, blaming themselves and others, developing a self-concept that assimilates social views that they are unreliable, morally weak, perhaps stupid, and, most of all, dependent. The danger and consequence of this assimilated view is that people who so regard themselves are unlikely to simultaneously demonstrate agency, independence, and drive. Then, in the absence of lone mothers exhibiting these attributes, we are confirmed in our assessments and the public discourse is reinforced.

Of course, not all of those who are 'othered' through the processes described above assimilate these dominant discourses. There are those who resist, who maintain their sense of agency and refuse to accept the theses of dependency and lack of moral worth. What happens to them? Some do well, buy the story of mobility as Mickey Kaus (1992) describes it, and continue to try to achieve in normative terms. Others resist more actively, understanding – perhaps intuitively – that there are structural processes in place and that their place as lone mothers is not deserving of public disparagement. Those who resist actively invoke another discourse tied to processes of criminalization and different forms of stigmatization. Active 'resistors' are often identified as trouble-makers, non-compliant service recipients, and the hard to serve. And, these social processes are effective in acting to constrain those who choose to resist.

Concluding Possibilities

A public discourse that includes historic and contemporary values related to women and mothering, the work ethic and individualism, autonomy and independence, wealth and citizenship has and continues to underlie our public policy responses to lone mothers. Discourse serves two functions: (1) it shapes and legitimizes lone mothers' social exclusion and (2) it legitimates the reluctant policy response that further acts to exclude.

In North America families have been seen, in policy terms, as private realms, the responsibility of their male head who is the dominant breadwinner. As men have not been urged through public policy to engage in caring functions (unlike in other countries, Sweden being especially notable in this regard), women as workers have been largely ignored in policy terms, despite their strong labour market ties. One of the self-reinforcing consequences of this policy neglect is the concentration of low-waged work among women and the fact that Canada and the United States are among the OECD countries with the highest share of women in low-waged work (Caragata 2003). And, yet, it remains the case that the focus of public policy is on the male as the primary earner in the family. Thus, the circumstances in which lone mothers find themselves result from the discursive constructions discussed here, which lead to a policy focus that ties benefits to attachment to the labour market. Overlooked are the unique sets of difficulties that arise when there is only one potential breadwinner in a family, coupled with the 'caring' demands of children.

Discourse clearly shapes policy and policy can be used – by determined states – to shape discourse. This is perhaps best demonstrated through Sweden's use of a paternity benefit intended to foster men's provision of family care (Bergman and Hobson 2002). With respect to lone mothers, we see the compounding effects of economic exclusion, from which, in the contemporary era, so much else is derived. Our work (income) shapes our neighbourhoods, our social networks, and our patterns of consumption, and these in turn reinforce our social and political status. As well, the globalized workplace demonstrates capriciousness and rewards ever-changing work practices, limiting the opportunities of those who are less skilled and less flexible as workers. All of these phenomena shape our sense of entitlement as citizens, as we are disproportionately valued according to our status as economic contributors, as taxpayers and consumers. And, as we feel more or less like citizens, we have more – or less– right to demand that our needs and agendas be part of the public discourse, debated in the public realm. This speaks, of course, to Sen's (2000) articulation of one of the values of the social exclusion lens in highlighting the importance of understanding relational deprivation, which traditional poverty analyses miss. Sen describes relational deprivation as feeling unworthy, not feeling entitled as a citizen to make claims, to be in the public realm. This returns us to Herman's (1999) idea of 'wealth as worth' and returns us also, perhaps, to an Aristotelian notion of the public in which the public is comprised of citizens and citizens are men of property. This construction of citizen puts women at risk, along with those people who are poor. This increasingly includes lone mothers, immigrants, those who are racialized – multiple constructions of the 'other.' If a consequence of such exclusion is the feeling of being unworthy to be in the public realm, then we have lost ground that must be regained with gendered policies that acknowledge caring roles as well as those of breadwinner, recognizing the importance of discursive constructions that give messages of inclusion. This last point is rather acutely articulated by a quotation from Carole Steedman: 'I think I would be a different person now if orange juice and milk and dinners at school hadn't told me, in a covert way, that I had a right to exist, was worth something ... its central benefit being that, unlike my mother, the state asked for nothing in return' (Segal 2000: 23).

The covert message that Steedman derived from a school lunch program is one of inclusion, of her 'right to exist' that speaks volumes about discursive practices; the ways in which material realities and social practices shape and signify. One of the important signifiers in Steedman's experience is that of our overall worth and our sense of belonging, our right to be and the importance of our being, in the public realm.

References

A Commitment to Training and Employment for Women (ACTEW). (2007). Putting Women in the Picture, Employment Facts, Childcare, June. Toronto: ACTEW. Electronic version retrieved on 15 Nov. 2007, from http://www. actew.org/projects/pwpsite/snapshots/childcare_ACTEW_June07.pdf.

Alden, J., and H. Thomas. (1998). Social Exclusion in Europe: Context and Policy. *International Planning Studies* 3(1): 7–13.

Arendt, Hannah. (1958). *The Human Condition*. Chicago: University of Chicago Press.

Barry, Norman. (1990). Markets, Citizenship and the Welfare State: Some Critical Reflections. In Raymond Plant and Norman Barry (eds.), *Citizenship and Rights in Thatcher's Britain: Two views*. London: IEA Health and Welfare Unit.

Bergman, Helena, and Barbara Hobson. (2002). Compulsory Fatherhood: The Coding of Fatherhood in the Swedish Welfare State. In Barbara Hobson (ed.), *Making Men into Fathers: Men, Masculinities and the Social Politics of Fatherhood*, 92–124. Cambridge: Cambridge University Press.

Bhalla, Ajit, and Frederic Lapeyre. (1997). Social Exclusion: Towards an Analytical and Operational Framework. *Development and Change* 28: 413–33.

Canadian Labour Congress (CLC). (1997). *Women and Work Project*. Toronto: CLC.

Caragata, Lea. (2008a). Good Welfare Moms: Stories of Caring Labour. *Journal of the Association for Research on Mothering, Special Issue on Carework* 10/1: 66–81.

– (2008b). Constructing the Welfare Mom. Unpublished paper.

– (2003). Globalization and the Social and Economic Marginalization of Women and Families. *International Sociology* 18(3): 559–80.

de Haan, A. (1999). *Social Exclusion: Towards a Holistic Understanding of Deprivation*. London: Department of International Development.

Dryzek, John S., and Valerie Braithwaite. (2000). On the Prospects for Democratic Deliberation: Values Analysis Applied to Australian Politics. *Political Psychology* 21(2): 241–66.

Edin, Kathryn, and Laura Lein. (1997). *Making Ends Meet: How Single Mothers Survive Welfare and Low-Wage Work*. New York: Russell Sage Foundation.

Fraser, Nancy. (1997). *Justice Interruptus: Critical Reflections on the 'Postsocialist' Condition*. New York: Routledge.

– (1992). Rethinking the Public Sphere: A Contribution to the Critique of Actually Existing Democracy. In Craig Calhoun (ed.), *Habermas and the Public Sphere*, 109–42. Cambridge, MA: MIT Press.

– (1990). Rethinking the Public Sphere: A Contribution to the Critique of Actually Existing Democracy. *Social Text* 25/26: 56–72.

Fraser, Nancy, and Linda Gordon. (1994) A Genealogy of Dependency: Tracing a Keyword of the U.S. Welfare State. *Signs* 19: 309–36.

Good Gingrich, Luann. (2003). Theorizing Social Exclusion: Determinants, Mechanisms, Dimensions, Forms and Acts of Resistance. In W. Shera (ed.), *Emerging Perspectives on Anti-Oppressive Practice*, 2–23. Toronto: Canadian Scholars Press.

Grover, Chris, and John Stewart. (2002). *The Work Connection: The Role of Social Security in British Economic Regulation*. London: Palgrave Macmillan.

Habermas, Jurgen. (1989) [1962]. *The Structural Transformation of the Public Sphere*. Translated by Thomas Burger and Frederick Lawrence. Cambridge, MA: MIT Press.

Herman, Andrew. (1999). *The 'Better Angels' of Capitalism: Rhetoric, Narrative, and Moral Identity among Men of the American Upper Class*. Boulder: Westview Press.

Jencks, Christopher, and Kathryn Edin. (1995). Do Poor Women Have the Right to Bear Children? *American Prospect* 1(20): 43–52.

Jenson, Jane. (2003). *Redesigning the Welfare Mix for Families: Policy challenges*. Discussion paper F/30. Ottawa: Canadian Policy Research Networks.

Kaus, Mickey. (1992). *The End of Equality*. New York: Basic Books.

Kimlicka, Will, and Wayne Norman. (1994). Return of the Citizen: A Survey of Recent Work on Citizenship Theory. *Ethics* 104: 352–81.

Massey, Douglass S., and Nancy A. Denton. (1998). *American Apartheid: Segregation and the Making of the Underclass*. Cambridge, MA: Harvard University Press.

Maxwell, Judith. (2002). *Working for Low Pay*. Presentation to Alberta Human Resources and Employment. Ottawa: Canadian Policy Research Networks.

McCormack, Karen. (2004). Resisting the Welfare Mother: The Power of Welfare Discourse and Tactics of Resistance. *Critical Sociology* 30(2): 355–83.

Mead, Lawrence. (1986). *Beyond Entitlement: The Social Obligations of Citizenship*. New York: Free Press.

Menzies, Heather. (1998). *Women and the Knowledge-Based Economy and Society*. Ottawa: Status of Women Canada.

Morissette, René, and Zhang Xuelin. (2005). Escaping Low Earnings. *Perspectives on Labour and Income* 6(4). Electronic version retrieved on 15 Nov. 2007, from http://www.statcan.ca/english/freepub/75-001-XIE/10405/art-2.htm#aut#aut.

Noik-Bent, Sherry. (2008). No Greater Investment. *Globe and Mail*, 21 Feb. Electronic version retrieved on 15 Nov. 2007, from http://www.theglobeandmail.com/partners/free/globeinvestor/alternative/feb08/return.html.

Pateman, Carole. (1988). *The Sexual Contract*. Cambridge: Polity Press.

Paxton, Pamela. (2003). Women's Political Representation: The Importance of Ideology. *Social Forces* 82(1): 87–113.

Peck, Jamie. (2005) *Workfare States*. New York: Guilford Press.

Saloojee, Anver. (2003). *Social Inclusion, Anti-Racism and Democratic Citizenship*. Perspectives on Social Inclusion Working Paper Series. Toronto: Laidlaw Foundation.

Sassen, Saskia. (1998). *Globalization and Its Discontents*. New York: Free Press.

Segal, Lynne. (2000). Only Contradictions on Offer. *Women: A Cultural Review* 11(1/2): 19–36.

Sen, Amartya. (2000). *Social Exclusion: Concept, Application, and Scrutiny*. Social Development Papers No.1. Manila: Asian Development Bank.

Skaperdas, Stergios. (2003). Turning 'Citizens' into 'Consumers': Economic Growth and the Level of Public Discourse. *Rational Foundations of Democratic Politics*, 30–43. Cambridge: Cambridge University Press.

Silver, H. (1994). Social Exclusion and Social Solidarity: Three Paradigms. *International Labour Review* 133(5/6): 531–78.

Smart, Carol. (1996). Deconstructing Motherhood. In Silva E. Bortolaia (ed.), *Good Enough Mothering? Feminist Perspectives on Lone Mothering*, 37–57. London: Routledge.

Smith, Ekuwa, and Andrew Jackson. (2002). *Does a Rising Tide Lift All Boats?* Ottawa: Canadian Council on Social Development.

Sorkin, Michael. (1992). *Variations on a Theme Park: The New American City and the End of Public Space*. New York: Noonday Press.

Statistics Canada. (2007). Labour Force Survey. Ottawa: Statistics Canada.

– (2006a). Labour Force and Participation Rates by Sex and Age Group. *The Daily*, 17 July. Electronic version retrieved on 15 Nov. 2007, from http://www40.statcan.ca/l01/cst01/labor05.htm.

– (2006b). Women in Canada. *The Daily*, 17 March. Ottawa: Statistics Canada.

– (2003). Labour Force Information. Ottawa: Statistics Canada.

Toronto Social Services. (2007). Income Policy. Electronic version retrieved 25 Feb. 2008 from http://www.toronto.ca/socialservices/Policy/Income.htm#treatment.

Tremblay, Manon. (2000). More Feminists or More Women? *International Political Science Review* 21(4): 381–405.

Trimble, Linda. (2001). The 2000 Federal Election and the Electoral Glass Ceiling. *Bulletin du Centre de Recherche sur Femmes et Politique* 1(2): 2–4.

Vosko, Leah. (2002). Re-thinking Feminization: Gendered Precariousness in the Canadian Labour Market and the Crisis in Social Reproduction. Robarts Canada Research Chairholders Series, 11 April, York University, Toronto, Ontario.

Watts, A.G. (2001). Career Guidance and Social Exclusion: A Cautionary Tale. *British Journal of Guidance and Counselling* 29(2): 157–77.

Wellman, Barry, and Scot Wortley. (1990). Different Strokes from Different Folks: Community Ties and Social Support. *American Journal of Sociology* 96(3): 558–82.

7 Gender Equity and Social Welfare Reform: Supporting Economic Security for Lone Mothers on Assistance

SHAUNA BUTTERWICK

The ongoing debate about welfare and lone mothers focuses on welfare-to-work transitions, employment-based solutions to welfare 'dependence'[1] and reducing welfare (state) expenditures. The struggle, sometimes referred to as the 'welfare wars' (Fraser 1989), is an ideological one in which the best interests of women and their children often lose out to neoliberal policy objectives. The notion of a good society that would offer greater support in order to reduce poverty is greatly weakened by neoliberal policy that prefers market-based solutions to poverty. Neoliberal policy prescriptions, informed by the idea that future success is entirely dependent on the actions and choices of individuals, promote a combination of market-based solutions to poverty with reductions in government expenditures. These are the two main drivers behind the recent changes in welfare structures in Canada.

The purpose of this chapter is to analyse ways to best support lone mothers' transition from welfare (income assistance or IA) into paid work.[2] The argument developed here pushes conventional evaluations of welfare-to-work transitions by assessing what it means to support mothers' transition into forms of paid employment that pay a living wage. The analysis presented is a review of evaluations[3] (many government funded) of welfare reforms in Canada, the United States, Australia, and New Zealand. Many of these evaluations of welfare systems were conducted prior to the most recent round of cuts to welfare experienced in British Columbia and elsewhere in Canada in the past decade. Although some of the welfare programs evaluated reflect an earlier policy era, reviewing the studies is instructive in relationship to the current changes occurring in Canada because the studies review a range of possible interventions and program components, illustrating which approaches are more or less effective in not only reducing welfare expenditure and moving lone mothers into paid work (the focus of contemporary welfare reforms in most provinces), but also in reducing poverty.

The argument advanced in this chapter is that it is possible to support mothers who move from welfare by providing forms of employment that pay a living wage. The next section examines the effectiveness of various welfare program components and concludes with a discussion of priorities for creating a welfare system based on gender equity.

General Findings on Program Effectiveness

Most welfare-to-work evaluation studies are concerned with 'employment effects' and measure success in terms of employability outcomes alone. But the definition of 'success' in welfare policy is itself significant. While a focus on improving client employability seems to be the dominant goal in most policies, there are alternative perspectives about what constitutes 'success.' Some evaluations focus on the nature of the work being performed (Dickinson 1986). Others focus less on reducing the welfare rolls and more on the conditions experienced by welfare recipients. For example, Spalter-Roth, Hartman, and Andrews question the overall goal of reducing the welfare rolls, noting that 'many of the current proposals to cut welfare spending are inspired by politics and ideology, not hard information about the actual behaviour of welfare recipients' (1992: iii). Others, such as the Institute for Women's Policy Research based in Washington, D.C., understand 'success' as being able to reduce poverty simultaneously with reductions in welfare expenditures.

It is clear, however, that many studies (Dean 2001; Abromowitz 2006) find that neither welfare nor full-time low-wage work (the kind most likely to be obtained by the majority of lone mothers receiving welfare) provide enough income to raise these families out of poverty, or even to cover their basic expenses. These studies suggest that a range of income-packaging strategies would be necessary to allow recipients to mix benefits, paid work, and other sources of income. These income-packaging strategies, however, do not accept the low-wage labour market as a given, as is usual in most current policy. An alternative antipoverty policy, then, would be a jobs-based strategy, involving reform of the labour market with a 'focus on improving pay in low-wage jobs, changing the low-wage labour market and improving access to higher wage jobs' (Spalter-Roth and Hartman 1994: 12). In the remainder of this section, I review evaluations of welfare policy studies that provide recommendations based on differential assessment and targeting, training and education, job search, wage and earnings subsidies, self-employment, and active gender-equity policies and labour market intervention.

Differential Assessment and Targeting

Generally, welfare policy constitutes lone mothers receiving income assistance as an undifferentiated social group, ignoring how they may be more or less skilled, more or less educated, younger or older, with or without limiting disabilities, members of a racialized minority, and so on. In a study of lone mothers on social assistance in France, Jean-Claude Ray (1990) found this client group further differentiated by time, that is, where they were in the cycle of receiving API (Allocation de Parent Isole), the lone-parent allowance, and by the number and ages of their children, noting how the economic situation of women with three or more children actually worsened if the mother became gainfully employed. Ray also found problematic the categories of 'inactive,' 'unemployed,' and 'employed,' often used to differentiate single parents: '[Rather than] the undifferentiated treatment of all lone-parent families ... assistance has to be adapted to a variety of employment-related needs' (1990: 234).

Not only does much welfare reform regard lone mothers as an undifferentiated group, it is also fuelled by stereotypes and negative assumptions of the vision of the 'welfare mother' (Abromowitz 1996; Little 1998; Chunn with Gavigan 2004). Findings of many studies challenge these assumptions. For example, Georges Lemaître's three-year analysis of long-term recipients in British Columbia showed that approximately one-third of this population left the system permanently within that period and that 30 to 70 per cent (depending upon the grouping) had earnings from employment as well as assistance; these statistics belie the popular perception that 'social assistance is ... an all-or-none state' (1993: 7). Similar findings in the United States were reported by Spalter-Roth et al., who found that, over a two-year period, 70 per cent of Assistance to Families with Dependent children (AFDC) recipients participated in the labour force and that 75 per cent combined AFDC with other income of some kind: 'Recipients actively attempt to achieve the best living standard they can, subject to many circumstances they cannot control' (1993: 11), including a low-wage labour market, low benefit levels, lack of child support and child care, lack of health insurance, changing assistance rules, and stigmatizing ideologies.

Edin and Lein's (1996) U.S. study had similar findings, noting that the range of strategies available to both welfare recipients and low-wage working mothers was largely determined by each mother's private social safety net and the social-structural characteristics of the city in which she lived. Relying more on personal networks than on work and local agencies was found to be more conducive to moving from welfare to work. Mothers, however, do not have freedom of choice among strategies; their decisions are constrained by their own personal circumstances, the circumstances of the local community, and local welfare regulations.

Clearly, 'one size fits all' approaches do not work, as any particular barrier will not necessarily present itself as such for all individuals: 'Whether a particular issue prevents, limits or does not affect an individual's employment potential depends upon the interplay of this issue with her other personal characteristics and life circumstances' (Olsen and Pavetti 1996: 7). Issues that can make a difference relate to access to housing and transportation, physical health limitations, mental health problems, children's health or behavioural problems, alcohol and drug use, low basic skills and learning disabilities, and domestic violence (ibid.). Cynthia Andruske's (2002) three-year study of welfare mothers found poor health to be a major barrier, one that was exacerbated by low welfare rates and the low wages of entry-level work. The lack of quality and affordable child care, however, including child care that is available for women who work irregular schedules, remains a persistent barrier for most lone mothers (Cleveland and Hyatt 1996).

Recent changes to welfare regulations that require welfare clients to declare any income, including child support, have limited mothers' strategies even more. In many instances, receiving both social assistance and other income is now defined as fraud, and those who receive both have become criminalized. This was the case with Kimberley Rogers, an Ontario lone mother on assistance, who in the spring of 2001 was placed under house arrest for receiving both welfare benefits and a student loan (Chunn with Gavigan 2004).

The above studies illustrate that lone mothers on assistance are not an undifferentiated homogeneous category of recipients. Yet many policies and programs bring this rigid and narrow view reinforcing gender, race, and social class inequalities, as well as stigmatization. Effective programs for lone mothers on assistance must be flexible and recognize and provide resources to address lone mothers' multiple and changing needs and circumstances.

Education and Training Programs

Generally speaking, low levels of education and literacy are one of the main factors in maintaining poverty, particularly for lone mothers. Effective programs, therefore, support income assistance clients to upgrade and acquire educational credentials and skills-training for jobs that pay a living wage (Gittell, Schehl, and Fareri 1990; Smith 1998; Morissette and Picot 2005). Education and training programs can be further differentiated as classroom training, on-the-job training, literacy training, and life skills training, although these can all be offered in combination. Because training is also frequently offered as a component of larger strategies, it is difficult to determine to what extent program outcomes can be attributed to the training alone. Effective programs should include training as only one part of an overall strategy, one based on assessment of local labour market conditions and strong links to employers. Training for jobs that pay low wages will do little towards increasing self-sufficiency, neither will training for work in surplus occupations, as noted by the United States General Accounting Office (1994), which found that the majority of JOBS training programs in the United States (part of the welfare-to-work strategy) lacked an employment focus.

Training built on partnerships with potential employers will likely have a higher level of success. Robert Fay (1996) found that targeting employers, not only job seekers, works best as employers must recognize and value the training that participants receive; if they do not, it will do the trainees little good in helping them find jobs. Making connections with established educational bodies whose credentialing is widely recognized can overcome this problem, as noted in the 1996 Human Resources Development Council study (HRDC 1996), which found that classroom training of a more vocational nature, or directed towards specific occupations, is more likely to result in increased workforce participation and decreased social assistance dependency.[4] A B.C. Ministry of Social Services report (1992) discovered similar variations, with classroom training (in particular academic and adult basic education) combined with on-the-job training having the greater effect over the long term. A New Zealand study found that in addition to income, welfare clients who were are able to obtain one additional year of education also experienced wider health and social benefits (Johnson 2004). The 1996 HRDC report noted above also emphasized life skills training. The benefit of this training, however, depends a great deal on whether sufficient time and resources are provided for this part of the curriculum, whether programs are designed based on knowledge, respect, and appreciation of the lived reality of participants, and if they are part of a larger strategy that includes other industry-specific training for jobs that pay a living wage (Butterwick 2003).

To successfully participate in industry-specific training, however, many clients need to upgrade their basic education and literacy skills. Effective adult basic education (ABE) and literacy programs are found in community-based organizations (CBO) and colleges (Folkman and Rai 1999; Sheared, McCabe, and Umeki 2000). These programs balance the 'teaching for personal growth and development and training for employment' (Sheared et al. 2000: 79) and provide a variety of services and resources; local, familiar and welcoming locations; and culturally relevant and learner-centred curricula. Shauna Butterwick and Caroline White (2006) examined the effectiveness of British Columbia's college-based literacy and ABE programs during a time (1996 to 2002) when welfare regulations allowed income assistance recipients to attend college for English as a second language (ESL) and academic upgrading while receiving benefits. During this policy era, welfare monies were also provided to colleges to support these students, many of whom had never imagined furthering their education.[5] Once they finished their upgrading or ESL, support continued for those students as they moved into specific skills-training programs,[6] where the vast majority of graduates found employment that paid a living wage. Effective programs had committed and informed staff, strong links to the community, provided ongoing personal support and counselling services, and had strong linkages to both the welfare system and local labour markets.

There are examples of effective comprehensive programs such as the Minority Female Single Parent Demonstration project (Gordon and Burghardt 1990), which offered remedial basic education, job skills training, and supports to minority lone mothers in four U.S. communities. One of these sites, the San Jose Center for Employment and Training, which integrated a job skills curriculum with remedial basic skills training (or 'general employability training'), compared with the other three sites (that offered basic skills training alone), produced the largest increases in employment and earnings after twelve months, with the greatest net benefits being achieved by those participants who faced the greatest barriers. In Canada, the Women's Work and Training Program (WWTP) was created with federal and provincial funding by several female carpenters in 1997 in Regina, Saskatchewan. WWTP was a women-only carpentry apprenticeship program that trained sixty-four women, most of whom were poor lone mothers of Aboriginal ancestry (Little 2005). A key aspect of this program's effectiveness was the Regina Women's Construction Company, which provided a safe and supportive work site where participants could practice and expand on their carpentry skills. At the end of the program, several participants were on their way to becoming journeyed carpenters (one was the first Aboriginal woman in Canada to pass the Level 4 provincial exam), and most were working and no longer receiving welfare. Participants also acquired life and cooperative business skills: '[These] women ... defy the current attack on the poor that describes them as lazy, dependent, and unworthy of help ... [with] lone mothers being increasingly demonized' (Little 2005: 2).

Job Search Assistance

Job search assistance is offered through job clubs, re-employment bonuses, counselling, and interviews, and is generally the most inexpensive type of intervention, one that now dominates much welfare programming. It is, however, usually only effective for those who are most job-ready and who face few, if any, obvious barriers to employment, and thus is not generally useful for the long-term unemployed or lone parents. This was noted by the B.C. Ministry of Social Services 1992 evaluation of the B.C. Job Action programs, which showed a short-term reduction in welfare dependence (about eight months), but no reduction over the longer term. Encouraged to become quickly employed after the program, participants may have taken inappropriate jobs. The relatively low cost of these programs, if provided for the appropriate participants, make them quite attractive to governments with limited resources.

The cost efficiency of job search programs, however, has been challenged. For example, Adams and Tait's (2004) evaluation of the B.C. Job Placement Program pointed to the issue of 'deadweight loss,' noting that programs were actively screening out people with multiple barriers and selecting and being paid for assisting people who would have found work on their own. Fay (1996) suggests that the use of 'profiling' techniques and econometric models can address the deadweight loss problem by determining participants' risk of long-term unemployment. As with other kinds of interventions, job search assistance also seems to work well in combination with other initiatives, but the timing of the job search component is critical.

Work Experience

Work experience programs seek to develop basic skills and work habits and to provide the actual job experience that may help participants meet the requirements of the labour market. Work experience has become central to welfare programs in Canada and the United States, but evaluations (e.g., HRDC 1996) indicate that, while there are often short-term gains in employment and earnings and reductions in reliance on social assistance, these do not tend to translate into similar long-term results. An evaluation of two community service programs in Winnipeg (Stevens 1997) illustrated how these work experience programs generated considerable social assistance savings in the short term, but the long-term effects were unknown since participants were tracked for no longer than one and one-half years (and most returned to social assistance within one year). Since participants' wages were very low (less than minimum wage for the first two months of one program), and there were no earnings exemptions and few other services provided (outside of transportation costs), it is not surprising that low costs were maintained.

Work experience is central to 'workfare' programs, many of which require participants to work to receive benefits, without any additional wages. While workfare is nothing new, making it mandatory and incorporating job shadowing and community job placement is a shift from earlier approaches (Quaid 2002). Workfare's greatest weakness, according to Sherri Torjman (1998), is its simplistic 'one size fits all' approach that fails to recognize the complexities of poverty and the wide-ranging reasons for reliance on welfare. This approach contrasts with welfare regulations during the time of Lemaître's study (1993), where those mothers who were able to combine benefits with paid work tended to have higher incomes than either those who relied on assistance alone or those who left it for full-time employment. These results present an obvious 'economic justification' for allowing clients to receive benefits and engage in paid part-time work. The New Hope Project in Milwaukee, Wisconsin, is an example of this approach (Brock et al. 1997). Participants who were employed thirty or more hours per week were given wage supplements to bring them above the poverty line, child care assistance and health insurance were provided, and they were allowed up to ten hours per week of education or training with pay. Almost half of the participants were employed in unsubsidized jobs. Although wage levels were not specified, the difficulties that these people had previously had in finding jobs have led to some optimism that this program may turn out to be fairly effective for this 'hard-to-employ' group.

Wage Subsidies

Wage subsidies are direct payments to employers who hire welfare recipients, thus providing 'an incentive for firms to hire workers they would not otherwise hire, and so posit[ing] that slow adjustments in labour markets can be remedied through policies directed at labour demand' (Robertson 1994: 4). Well-targeted subsidies can be more cost-effective than many other programs and can also increase participants' long-term employability, especially for groups such as lone mothers who are at high risk of becoming long-term unemployed (Robertson 1994). However, some of the problems connected with wage subsidies include high deadweight, substitution, and displacement effects.[7] One Belgian study estimated a 53 per cent deadweight loss[8] and a 36 per cent substitution effect[9] from subsidy programs (Fay 1996). Other difficulties stem from program misuse, where employers use programs as a permanent workforce subsidy, and where there is collusion between employer and participant to create 'shadow jobs.' Other problems include low take-up rates and stigmatization. Most of these negative consequences could be minimized through careful control and monitoring (Robertson 1994).

The method of targeting participants was central to the Australian subsidy program JOBSTART (Fay 1996), where those who had been unemployed the longest qualified for more subsidies. Employers approached the Public Employment Service directly, rather than using a voucher system. Although the deadweight loss was still quite high, at 66 per cent, JOBSTART was considered one of the most successful subsidy programs in terms of participant employment rates (60% vs 30%) for the comparison group two years after program exit.

Earnings Supplements

In contrast to wage subsidies, earnings supplements allow people who are on assistance to work and receive a wage top-up (up to a specified limit), which is paid to the recipient directly, as a 'financial incentive' to take work that will hopefully outweigh the disincentives of earnings exemptions and low entry-level wages. In general, such programs are based on assumptions that there are job opportunities available to social assistance recipients and that wages will increase with time to the point where these jobs will offer self-sufficiency for participants. These assumptions informed the HRDC's Self-Sufficiency Project (SSP), a pilot project offered in British Columbia and New Brunswick between 1992 and 1998 (Social Research Demonstration Corporation 1996). Participants ('takers'), 95 per cent of whom were women, were randomly chosen from people in the target group who found full-time jobs (at least 30 hours per week) within one year. Earnings supplements for up to three years, equal to half the difference between their wages and a set annual wage level ($37,000 in British Columbia and $30,000 in New Brunswick) were provided.

The hope was that participants 'will become strongly attached to the work force and will develop marketable work skills and human capital' (Greenberg with Robins 1991: 1) and that, when their supplement period ended, they would either be self-sufficient through their jobs or at least have a considerably reduced 'dependency' on social assistance. Since the SSP was designed to test the results of the financial incentive alone, no other services were provided: no job search assistance or training, and participants had to make their own child care arrangements. Early evaluations of the SSP suggested positive results, at least in the short run, in addressing the project's 'dual goals' of reducing poverty while encouraging self-sufficiency. Participants' employment rates, hours of paid work, and earnings all increased significantly, while the amount of income assistance received decreased. Although program costs were relatively high, the net cost was significantly less than the gross cost, because of these income assistance savings.

In a six-year follow-up, however, Ford et al. (2003) found that the earnings of participants in this experiment had not improved. Without additional interventions, SPP participants had simply moved from being poor while receiving welfare to being the working poor. Both takers and non-takers cited child care as one of the major obstacles to taking up the supplement, and many thought the program would be improved with an educational or training component. Furthermore, more flexibility was seen as definitely desirable, particularly regarding the thirty-hour work requirement. Another point relating to flexibility arises from the greater relative benefits received by parents with fewer children or with higher potential wages.

Self-Employment

Few self employment programs that provide subsidies or grants for starting a business and sometimes training and other supports have been evaluated, making it difficult to generalize results (Fay 1996). Evaluations tend to indicate positive effects, including increased income, self-sufficiency, self-confidence, skills, and employability, but only for a small subgroup of clients – generally younger (under 40), male, and relatively well-educated individuals (Weicker and Company 1994). In 1994 HRDC commissioned a study to evaluate its Self Employment Assistance Program (SEA; Raheim and Bolden 1995). This program, which replaced the Self Employment Incentive Program (SEI), was intended to increase self-sufficiency through self-employment for both unemployment insurance and social assistance recipients. UI claimants received their regular benefits or a training allowance (whichever was higher) plus supplementary allowances (for expenses), while social assistance recipients (SAR) received the training allowance plus supplementaries. SEA had a training focus, as well as emphasis on monitoring and follow-up, a structural improvement over SEI. Under SEA, however, the proportion of SAR participants decreased significantly from 39 per cent to 17 or 18 per cent. Reductions were linked to a lack of referrals from Ministry of Social Services offices, the fact that many SAR participants received less money than when on income assistance, and the small amount of equity SAR clients could contribute to their businesses. A flat-rate allowance system was recommended. Although 53 per cent of the SEA participants surveyed were women (many giving child care concerns as a reason for choosing self-employment), low-income women face many barriers to successful self-employment, including 'lack of access to information, capital, technical expertise, business management experience, and informal networking opportunities' (Raheim and Bolden 1995: 144).

Raheim and Bolden pointed to some ways to reduce these barriers, noting that many of the more than 200 self-employment development programs in the United States that specifically served women, combined training, financial assistance, and technical assistance. Those that did not have a lending component formed linkages with willing financial institutions. Some provided financing through peer-lending groups, which substitute 'accountability to one's peers for collateral because most low-income women have no assets to serve as collateral' (Raheim and Bolden 1995: 148); loan amounts may be increased as a 'credit history' is developed. They noted a particular program, the Self-Employment Investment Demonstration (SEID), which offered training, counselling, technical assistance, loans or aid in getting credit, and help in waiving Assistant to Families with Dependent Children (AFDC) regulations so participants would not lose their grants during their first year of business. The removal of these barriers and provision of such supports, Raheim and Bolden reported, were seen as great aids to the viability of self-employment as an 'economic self-sufficiency option' for such women (1995: 148–9).

Mixed Strategies

Mixed strategies are the most effective kinds of strategies overall in increasing employment rates, offering a variety of the above options to participants, including personal needs assessment and counselling; education and training services; job-finding assistance; child care access assistance; training and job opportunities through employers; and links to other services, such as housing, transportation, and financial counselling. Given that the individualized focus and flexibility are the major reasons for these strategies' success, it is important that careful attention be paid to determining which services are most appropriate for each participant. This approach requires a good deal more input from participants than may be sought in less-flexible programs. These kinds of programs may also be (and perhaps should be) more amenable to different, and innovative, approaches.

An example of such a project is the Ottawa-Carleton Opportunity Project (OP), run by the Regional Municipality of Ottawa-Carleton Social Services Department (1996a; 1996b). This program used an 'investment model' of delivery, in the belief that 'if recipients are allowed to take the time they need – right now – to address their barriers, they will be better able to reduce and/or end their dependency on the system in the future' (1996a: 1). Randomly selected participants went through an assessment of their situation and barriers, setting personal goals and developing an action plan (done with their workers), and a referral to and co-ordination of access to services. Training and reduced caseloads for workers were provided to aid them in assisting clients. Some social assistance requirements (such as mandatory job search) were also waived so that clients were allowed to do the activities best suited to their needs. Strong community linkages were stressed, and developing networks was a main objective. The project was directly accountable to a Community Management Committee, comprised of community organization members, government representatives, and clients. One of the project's objectives, along with increasing employability, was to increase active community participation; both goals were achieved.

Active Gender-Equity Policies and Labour Market Development

A number of studies indicate that neither welfare nor full-time low-wage work help lone mothers on welfare escape poverty (e.g., Ray 1990; Karier 1998; Ford et al. 2003). A strategy of income-packaging, as noted earlier, practised by many assistance recipients, is generally more effective at getting families out of poverty, even if, in many welfare jurisdictions, receiving income from other sources while on income assistance is not strictly speaking 'legal' in terms of welfare legislation.[10] A mixed strategy allows recipients to mix benefits, paid work, and other sources of income.

The problem is that such an approach accepts the low-wage labour market as a given. Spalter-Roth et al. (1992) challenge the 'rhetoric of dependency' and the perceived need to 'encourage self-sufficiency,' which tend to assume that full-time employment is the way out of poverty for most lone-parent families. They note how the volatility of the low-wage labour market prevents self-sufficiency because of the preponderance of part-time and short-term jobs, and how the unreasonable burdens of full-time work placed on lone parents, already expected to be both parents to their children, make this unlikely. Thus, effective welfare-to-work policies for lone mothers receiving income assistance need to be buttressed with active labour market development initiatives that lead to more full-time, well-paid employment with benefits. Gender-equity policies are also needed in order to address women's unreasonable burdens of full-time work and full-time care of children. Nordic countries[11] (Haavind and Magusson 2005) have been regarded as exemplary in relation to policies that provide generous paid parental leave for both mothers and fathers (along with guaranteed job security) and state-subsidized child care. While these policies have contributed in significant ways to fathers becoming more actively involved with child care, Hanne Haavind and Eva Magusson (2005) note that there remains a gap between men's and women's wages, women continue to do the bulk of housework, and women continue to participate more than men in part-time work. They also find that even with these gender-equity policies, there has been no significant decrease in violence against women.

These contradictory tendencies remind us that 'welfare' and 'gender equality,' however they are defined, are not just matters of rights and opportunities, but just as much the products of efforts to transform everyday practices of men and women and equalize the power relations between them (Haavind and Magusson 2005: 233).

Summary and an Alternative Vision

The aforementioned studies provide ample evidence of what works in supporting lone mothers receiving assistance to not simply find low-waged jobs, which only reinforces their vulnerability and poverty, but to achieve long-term economic security. Overall, effective programs are more long term, comprehensive, and flexible, and include a mix of strategies based on differential assessment and targeting that recognizes women's different and changing needs. Examples of such comprehensive and flexible programs from Canada, the United States, and France have been outlined. Unfortunately, many have been cut entirely, and for those that remain, program components that are key to effectively helping lone mothers escape poverty have been eliminated.

Moving forward requires that the benefits of these programs to individual women and their families, as well as to communities and to government, be clearly articulated and that the key principles of such programs be reimagined within an alternative vision, one that avoids simply calling for the reinstatement of lost programs, wherein 'the benefits they provide are system-conforming ones that reinforce rather than challenge basic structural inequalities' (Fraser 1989: 145). An alternative vision and plan of action must recognize how, as Lea Caragata notes, globalization has created changes that are 'profoundly gendered and racialized' and that 'declining welfare state provisions have combined with the total marginalization of many already poor families from the economic marketplace to render an underclass not seen in the developed world since the 1930s' (2003: 559–60). An alternative orientation to social welfare policy is based on both the needs and rights of lone mothers. This requires interventions within multiple policy jurisdictions such as welfare, food security, housing, health care, labour laws, and free trade agreements.

Welfare benefit rates must be raised so that they are adequate and meet the basic needs for food, transportation, clothing, health, security, and shelter. Examining and reforming labour regulation is also needed in order to address workers' rights and, in particular, lone mothers' vulnerability to exploitation such that obtaining paid work is not based on the discretion or whim of a husband, employer, or state official. The living wage movement is an important element of an alternative vision that disrupts the 'drive to the bottom' of wages occurring under globalized capitalism. Equal pay for work of equal value is another policy move that is needed to disrupt income discrepancies based on gender, race, and class discrimination, among others. A key element of an alternative vision would directly address women's unequal burden of primary care work; this would involve the public recognition of the essential labour that women do in caring for children, the elderly, and community. A well-supported publicly funded child care system, wages for child and elder care, and adequate welfare benefits would reflect such values. An alternative vision would also involve equal sharing of the important work of elder and child care, which requires that such care is understood to be a social and not simply private matter. Family-friendly work policies are yet another arena of policy analysis and intervention that would be part of an alternative vision. We need to bring a social justice framework that uses the lens of gender, race, and class, among others, to analyse and organize against, perhaps through international coalitions, the negative impact of free trade agreements on all of these policy arenas.

The goal of this chapter has been to review studies of welfare effectiveness from a variety of jurisdictions in order to identify effective program components. It is hoped that this information can support welfare advocates, policy researchers, and program providers in their struggles for social justice for lone mothers on income assistance.

Notes

1 Dependency has become a much-maligned problem of the welfare state, a notion that 'carries strong emotive and visual associations and a powerful pejorative charge' (Fraser and Gordon 1997: 123). Extending that analysis, Kittay (1999) points to how everyone is dependent and at some point in their life needs to be cared for, and therefore, those offering such care work (such as single mothers on assistance) should be valued and supported.

2 Workfare orientations currently dominate welfare reform, and thus this chapter focuses on research that outlines effective interventions that support lone mothers receiving income assistance to move into paid work. This policy orientation, however, fails to recognize the unpaid caring work that women do. A fully realized antipoverty orientation would recognize, support, and reward women's unpaid caring work. Current ideological views ignore and devalue this labour, as evidenced by the inadequate welfare payment for mothers with children and the requirement that women find work regardless of the ages of their children.

3 Parts of this chapter are based on an earlier 1998 report co-authored by Anita Bonson and myself entitled, *Identifying Keys to Successful Transition from Social Assistance to Paid Work: Lessons learned from Canada, the United States, Australia and Europe*, funded by Human Resources Development Canada (HRDC) and the B.C. Ministry of Human Resources and Ministry of Advanced Education, Training and Technology.

4 See earlier note that critiques the notion of 'dependency.'

5 This policy was in effect between 1996 and 2002. Following radical welfare reform by the provincial Liberal government, funds to colleges to support welfare clients were cut, and except for those with disability status, welfare clients could no longer attend college programs.

6 Once students began a skills training program, they had to take out a student loan.

7 Displacement refers to how subsidized IA clients can displace other workers or others in a training program.

8 As noted earlier, deadweight loss refers to expenditures on clients who would have found work or met other program goals without state intervention, hence, the sense that they are 'deadweight' and there is a loss or waste of funds.

9 Substitution effect, in the case of income subsidies, refers to how these subsidies can have the effect of employers retreating from raising the wages of their workers because the wages are subsidized by the state.

10 In many welfare jurisdictions, income assistance recipients can no longer receive any additional income through such measures as child support, earnings supplements, or student loans. Indeed, not declaring this extra income is considered illegal, as with the Ontario case, mentioned earlier, where a single mother on welfare was found guilty of fraud and placed under house arrest because she had received both welfare benefits and income from student loans.

11 E.g., Denmark, Finland, Iceland, Norway, and Sweden.

References

Abramovitz, Mimi. (1996). *Under Attack, Fighting Back: Women and Welfare in the United States.* New York: Monthly Review Press.

Adams, Peter, and Cathy Tait. (2004). *Evaluation of the Job Placement Program and the Training for Jobs Program.* Prepared for Employment Initiatives, Branch Ministry of Ministry of Human Resources, Victoria, B. C.

Andruski, Cynthia Lee. (2002). *I'm Not Sitting on the Couch Eating Bon Bons! Women's Transition from Welfare to Paid Work and Education.* Unpublished doctoral dissertation, Department of Educational Studies, University of British Columbia, Vancouver.

B.C. Ministry of Social Services. (1992). *Routes to Independence: The Effectiveness of Employment and Training Programs for Income Assistance Recipients.* Victoria: Research, Evaluation and Statistics Branch.

Brock, Tomas, Fred Doolittle, Veronica Sellerath, and Michael Wiseman, with David Greenberg and Robinson Hollister, Jr. (1997). *Creating New Hope: Implementation of a Program to Reduce Poverty and Reform Welfare.* New York: Manpower Demonstration Research Corporation. Electronic version retrieved 28 Sept 2007 from http://www.mdrc.org/publications/347/textonly_abstract.html.

Butterwick, Shauna. (2003). Life Skills Training: 'Open for Discussion.' In Marjorie Griffin Cohen (ed.), *Training the Excluded for Work: Access and equity for women, immigrant, First Nations, youth and people with low income,* 161–77. Vancouver: UBC Press.

Butterwick, Shauna, and Caroline White. (2006). *A Path Out of Poverty: Helping Income Assistance Recipients Uupgrade Their Education.* Ottawa: Canadian Centre for Policy Alternatives.

Caragata, Lea. (2003). Neoconservative Realities: The Social and Economic Marginalization of Canadian Women. *International Sociology* 18(3): 559–80.

Chunn, Dorothy E., with Shelley Gavigan. (2004). Welfare Law, Welfare Fraud, and the Moral Regulation of the 'Never Deserving Poor.' *Social and Legal Studies* 13(2): 219–43.

Cleveland, Gordon, and Douglas Hyatt. (1996). *Childcare, Social Assistance and Work: Lone Mothers with Preschool Children.* Hull: Human Resources Development Canada.

Dean, Hartley. (2001). Working Parenthood and Parental Obligation. *Critical Social Policy* 21(3): 267–86.

Dickinson, Nancy S. (1986). Which Welfare Strategies Work? *Social Work* (July–August): 266–72.

Edin, Kathryn, and Laura Lein. (1996). Work, Welfare, and Single Mothers' Economic Survival Strategies. *American Sociological Review* 61: 253–66.

Fay, Robert G. (1996). *Enhancing the Effectiveness of Active Labour Market Policies: Evidence from Programme Evaluations in OECD Countries*. Paris: OECD.

Folkman, Daniel V., and Kalyani Rai. (1999). The New Role of Community-Based Agencies. *New Directions for Adult and Continuing Education* 83: 69–82.

Ford, Reuben, David Gyamati, Kelly Foley, Doug Tattrie, and Liza Jimenez. (2003). *Can Work Incentives Pay for Themselves? Final Report on the Self-Sufficiency Project for Welfare Applicants*. Ottawa: Social Research and Demonstration Corporation.

Fraser, Nancy. (1989). *Unruly Practices: Power, Discourse, and Gender in Contemporary Social Theory*. Minneapolis: University of Minnesota Press.

Fraser, Nancy, and Linda Gordon. (1997). A Genealogy of Dependency: Tracing a Keyword of the U.S. Welfare State. In Nancy Fraser (ed.), *Justice Interruptus: Critical Reflections on the 'Postsocialist' Condition*, 121–49. New York: Routledge.

Gittell, Marilyn, Margaret Schehl, and Camille Fareri. (1990). *From Welfare to Independence: The College Option*. New York: Ford Foundation.

Gordon, Anne, and John Burghardt. (1990). *The Minority Female Single Parent Demonstration: Short-Term Economic Impacts*. A Technical Research Report, Into the Working World Series, Lessons from Research. New York: Rockefeller Foundation.

Greenberg, David H., with Philip K. Robins. (1991). *Issues in the Design of the Canadian Self-Sufficiency Project Experiment*. Hull: Applied Research Branch, Human Resources Development Canada, Research Paper R-95-6.

Haavind, Hanne, and Eva Magusson. (2005). The Nordic Countries: Welfare Paradises for Women and Children? *Feminism and Psychology* 15(2): 227–35.

Human Resources Development Canada (HRDC). (1996). *A Review of Programs for Integrating Social Assistance Recipients into the Workforce*. Ottawa: HRDC.

Johnson, Grant. (2004). *Healthy, Wealthy and Wise? A Review of the Wider Benefits of Education*. New Zealand Treasury Working Paper 04/04. Wellington: New Zealand Treasury.

Karier, Thomas. (1998). Welfare Graduates: College and Financial Independence. Policy Note 1998/1. New York: Levy Economics Institute of Bard College. Electronic version retrieved 9 Oct. 2007 from http://www.levy.org/pubs/pn/pn98_1.pdf.

Kittay, Eva Feder. (1999). Welfare, Dependency, and a Public Ethic of Care. In Gwendolyn Mink (ed.), *Whose Welfare?* 189–213. Ithaca: Cornell University Press.

Lemaître, Georges. (1993). *Single Parents on Social Assistance: A Longitudinal Analysis*. Hull: Applied Research Branch, HRDC.

Little, Margaret. (1998). *No Car, No Radio, No Liquor Permit: The Moral Regula-*

tion of Single Mothers in Ontario, 1920–1997. Don Mills: Oxford University Press.

– (2005). *If I Had a Hammer: Retraining that Really Works.* Vancouver: UBC Press.

Morissette, René, and Garnett Picot. (2005). *Low-Paid Work and Economically Vulnerable Families over the Last Two Decades.* Ottawa: Statistics Canada, Catalogue No. 11F0019MIE–No. 238.

Olson, Krista, and LaDonna Pavetti. (1996). *Personal and Family Challenges to the Successful Transition from Welfare to Work.* Washington, DC: Urban Institute.

Quaid, Maeve. (2002). *Workfare: Why Good Social Policy Ideas Go Bad.* Toronto: University of Toronto Press.

Raheim, Salome, and Jacquelyn Bolden. (1995). Economic Empowerment of Low-Income Women through Self-Employment Programs. *Affilia* 10(2): 138–54.

Ray, Jean-Claude. (1990). Lone Mothers, Social Assistance and Work Incentives: The Evidence in France. In Elizabeth Duskin (ed.), *Lone-Parent Families: The Economic Challenge.* Social Policy Studies No. 8: 223–40. Paris: OECD.

Regional Municipality of Ottawa-Carleton Social Services Department. (1996a). *The Ottawa-Carleton Opportunity Planning Project Evaluation: Report for Phase I.* Ottawa: Author.

– (1996b). *The Ottawa-Carleton Opportunity Planning Project Evaluation: Report for Phase II.* Ottawa: Author.

Robertson, Heather. (1994). *Wage Subsidies to Encourage the Hiring of Unemployment Insurance Claimants.* Hull: HRDC.

Sheared, Vanessa, Jennifer McCabe, and Donna Umeki. (2000). Adult Literacy and Welfare Reform: Marginalization, Voice and Control. *Education and Urban Society* 32(2): 167–87.

Smith, Janet. (1998). *Literacy, Welfare and Work – Year II: A Case Study of the Lives of Seven Adults.* Ottawa: HRDC, Coalition for Brandon Literacy Services and National Literacy Secretariat.

Social Research and Demonstration Corporation. (1996). *When Work Pays Better than Welfare: A Summary of the Self-Sufficiency Project's Implementation, Focus Group, and Initial 18-Month Impact Reports.* Vancouver: SRDC.

Spalter-Roth, Roberta M., and Heidi I. Hartmann. (1994). The Clinton Round: An Analysis of the Impact of Current Proposals to 'Free' Single Mothers from Welfare Dependence. Paper presented at the Meetings of the American Sociological Association, 8 Aug., Los Angeles, California.

Spalter-Roth, Roberta M., Heidi I. Hartmann, and Linda Andrews. (1992).

Combining Work and Welfare: An Alternative Anti-Poverty Strategy. Washington, DC: Institute for Women's Policy Research.

Spalter-Roth, Roberta M., Beverly Burr, Heidi I. Hartmann, and Lois Shaw. (1995). *Welfare that Works: The Working Lives of AFDC Recipients.* Washington, DC: Institute for Women's Policy Research.

Stevens, Harry. (1997). The Effectiveness of Community Employment Programs for Social Assistance Recipients: An Evaluation of the City of Winnipeg's Community Services Programs. *Canadian Journal of Program Evaluation* 12(1): 71–85.

Torjman, Sherri. (1998). *Welfare Reform through Tailor Made Training.* Ottawa: Caledon Institute of Social Policy. Electronic version retrieved 24 June from http://www.caledonist.org/Publications/PDF/94159152.pdf.

U.S. General Accounting Office. (1994). *Welfare to Work: Current AFDC Programs Not Sufficiently Focused on Employment.* Report to the Chairman, Committee on Finance. Washington, DC: U.S. Senate.

Weicker, Ference, and Company. (1994). *Evaluation of the Self-Employment Assistance Program as It Relates to Social Assistance Recipients.* Report to the Community Futures Branch. Ottawa: HRDC.

8 Guaranteed Annual Income: A Feminist Approach

MARGOT YOUNG[1]

This chapter examines the idea of a guaranteed annual income as a solution for the economic and social inequality experienced by Canadian women. The argument that follows takes seriously the claims that different feminist activists and academics have made in favour of this path of policy reform. It also considers the cautions that have issued from individuals and groups equally concerned with social justice and women's equality. Ultimately, this chapter argues that, while the idea of a guaranteed annual income has tremendous immediate appeal, the current political climate and the complex nature of women's economic and social exclusion make the clarion call for a guaranteed annual income too risky and incomplete a political strategy. The conclusion the chapter reaches is one more marked by political caution and substantive concern than those urging implementation of a guaranteed annual income will like. The stakes of welfare reform are high, and it is critical that a conversation about economic justice for women be responsive to all feminist perspectives on the debate.

The discussion that follows begins with a brief reminder of the social and economic context that makes consideration of policies of economic redistribution so critical for women, and for some groups of women in particular. This is followed by an overview of the ways in which current social assistance provisions so badly fail low-income Canadian women. The third section provides an overview of what is meant by a guaranteed annual income. The fourth and fifth sections review some advantages and disadvantages, respectively, of guaranteed annual income proposals, from a feminist perspective. The final section concludes with some thoughts on policy directions indicated by these discussions.

Women's Poverty in Canada

Like the United States, Canada 'discovered' postwar poverty in the late 1960s. We remain today a nation increasingly characterized by deep and growing income and wealth inequality (Yalnizyan 2007; CCPA 2006; Lee 2004). More generally, our society is increasingly composed of two groups: distributional winners and distributional losers. Winners are highly skilled workers and two-earner households, while losers are disproportionately immigrant families, lone mothers, younger households, unemployed, and work-poor households (Esping-Andersen 2001).

The economic and political restructuring that marked neoliberalism's arrival on the Canadian scene has not been gender-neutral in its impact. Women have disproportionately experienced increased and more severe poverty (particularly in female-headed households), seen their consumption curtailed and work load increased as a result of loss of household income, been most directly affected by cuts to social services spending, and seen reductions in quality and conditions of paid employment options in both the private and public sectors (Brodie 1995). The simple and clear outcome is that progress towards gender equality has been significantly stalled.

Nowhere is this more evident than in low-income or poverty statistics. In 2003, 53 per cent of low-income Canadians were female (Statistics Canada 2005). Unattached women, Aboriginal women, immigrant women, women with disabilities, senior women, and women of colour are also disproportionately poor, both when compared with other Canadian women, and with their male counterparts. For example, in 2003, according to Statistics Canada (2005), 36 per cent of Aboriginal women, 23 per cent of immigrant women, 29 per cent of women of colour, and 26 per cent of women with disabilities lived in poverty; as well, 19 per cent of senior women were poor. Of Canadian families headed by lone-parent mothers, 38 per cent in 2003 had incomes that fell below Statistics Canada's after-tax low income cut-offs (LICOs), compared with 13 per cent of families headed by lone-parent fathers and just 7 per cent of non-elderly two-parent families with children (ibid.).[2] Many of these groups intersect: for instance, Aboriginal and African-Canadian women are more likely to be lone-parent mothers.

This situation in Canada has come in for international criticism. In January 2003 the Committee on the Elimination of Discrimination against Women conducted its fifth periodic review of Canada under the United Nations Convention on the Elimination of All Forms of Discrimination against Women (CEDAW). In its Concluding Comments, the Committee expressed astonishment about 'the high percentage of women living in poverty' (United Nations 2003: par. 257). A similar statement was made in 2006 by the United Nations Committee on Economic, Social and Cultural Rights (United Nations 2006: par. 15).

This chapter's consideration of a basic income focuses on the group of women with the highest rate of low-income status: lone mothers. While certainly not a new phenomenon, families led by lone mothers are increasingly a common and unexceptional family form. In 2001 there were 1,311,190 lone-parent families in Canada, of which 81.3 per cent were led by lone mothers (CCSD 2007). Divorce, or relationship breakdown, is the main reason for the incidence of lone-mother families (National Council of Welfare 2004). While these numbers reflect a series of evolving norms in Canadian society, they represent a hard-fought victory for women to be able to choose their sexual and life partners, and to choose whether or not they will raise their children in a conjugal relationship with another parent. A woman's ability to parent outside a traditional family form is a necessary freedom in any society that lays claim to basic respect for women's equality.

Yet, families headed by single mothers have by far the lowest income of all family types: their income is 38 per cent of the average income for non-elderly two-spouse families with children, and less than 60 per cent of the average income of lone-parent families headed by men (Statistics Canada 2005). Between 2001 and 2003 the average income of lone-mother families dropped, while the average income of other family types rose (ibid.).

There are good reasons for using the needs and circumstances of lone mothers as a context for thinking about basic income. First, this group represents key foci of gender analysis – family formation, division of labour, assumptions of dependency and independence – that are critical to policy discussions. They represent an important nexus of feminist concerns about women's caregiving responsibilities, economic resources, and political and social citizenship (McKeen 2004). Second, these women really are among the poorest of the poor in Canada, so solutions to poverty must take their needs into account. Third, renewed calls for what is being called a guaranteed livable income are coming from feminist grassroots organizations for which families led by lone mothers are paradigmatic of the need for the benefit (Women's Livable Income Group 2006). And, fourth, the circumstances of these women and their families, because these families disproportionately must rely on social assistance schemes, illustrate the problems with the current income support system, not the least of which is a benefit level that is grossly and cruelly inadequate.

Lone Mothers and the Current Welfare System

Welfare typically is formally conceived of as a program of last resort – a safety net for those whose basic needs are not met by individual or family personal wealth, earned income from the paid labour force, or some other government program. In practice, of course, this seriously understates the central role that welfare has come to play. Point-in-time numbers show that, in 2003, 1.7 million children, women, and men (5.5% of Canada's population) were on social assistance (Battle et al. 2006).

Welfare programs, which are provincially based, are plagued by inadequate benefit provision, unfair and unduly difficult access to benefits, stigma, punitive and coercive treatment of applicants and recipients, and unnecessary complexity and lack of transparency (Battle et al. 2006). Details of provincial welfare plans as they pertain to lone-mother families show that two phenomena are particularly striking. First, benefit levels are set so as to insure that lone-mother families reliant on welfare remain the poorest among the poor. For example, in British Columbia, the monthly income on provincial welfare for a Vancouver family with one adult and two children over the age of 5 years was $1,623.82 as of April 2007. This amount reflects all available income, including the base welfare rate of $1,036, tax credits and benefits, and the National Child Benefit. This (even recently raised) total is only 74 per cent of Statistics Canada's the after-tax LICO for this same family.[3] Indeed, the Dietitians of Canada have noted that welfare rates in British Columbia fail to provide an income adequate for meeting core nutritional needs (2006).

Second, the rules that structure these families' eligibility for income support and related benefits are, in most provinces, strikingly inconsistent with basic values asserted elsewhere in our political and social system. Rhetoric, both government and private, abounds about the central social importance and sanctity of the family, of children, and of meaningful employment. Yet social assistance programs, as they relate to lone-mother families, stand in sharp contradiction to these professed values. Welfare programs ensure that the children of these families face malnutrition, inadequate child care, and substandard housing. The mothers, forced to take available work as soon as their youngest child is 3 years old (in British Columbia) or even 2 months old (in Alberta), have limited opportunity for combining meaningful employment or training with their care responsibilities.

The best one can say about current welfare provision is that it is geared for short-term alleviation of the worst effects of poverty for these women. It is true that the current welfare state, to the extent that it gives some women economic independence from patriarchal relations within the family, has emancipatory effects (Fox Piven 1990). But, welfare provisions are shaped with the goal of 'reinserting' women into those institutions – the market and the nuclear family – that are most ill-suited for their own and their families' current needs and circumstances (McKay 2005: 87).

A number of recent reports examining Canada's income security system from a range of perspectives all agree that the system is a failed one. The Caledon Institute of Social Policy, for instance, calls for 'a new "architecture" of social policy for the twenty-first century' (Battle et al. 2006: 1). The National Council of Welfare observes that 'income irregularity is increasing and for most Canadians income security is decreasing. Our many programs have become a tattered patchwork' (2007: 1).

It is not surprising that alternative and novel forms of collective economic provision for the most vulnerable among us are tremendously appealing. Current policy proposals promise to cut through the dilemmas of welfare. Leading the pack – if volume of argument is any guide – is the raft of proposals for a guaranteed annual income.

Guaranteed Annual Income

This chapter uses the terms guaranteed annual income (GAI) and basic income (BI) interchangeably. Types of GAI are as varied as the commentators who propose them and go by a number of names, such as negative income tax, citizen's income, social wage, and social dividend. The model that this chapter uses for its discussion is a basic version: the provision of a floor income provided on a continuing basis, regardless of work effort, to all members of society. Thus, this chapter deals with the most straightforward and strongest form of GAI proposed. It is also the GAI model most like the reform currently advocated by a number of grassroots Canadian women's groups (e.g., see Pictou Statement, Lakeman et al. 2004).

The distinguishing characteristics of this GAI model are universality and unconditionality. As a universally granted benefit, the income would be equally available to every individual adult member of society. Such a benefit is in contrast to targeted or means-tested benefits, which selectively deliver benefits to a more narrowly defined subgroup on the basis of some characteristic, say, income level. The only distinguishing trait of those in receipt of a universal GAI would be age (say, over 18 years), although the benefit could be extended (probably at a lower level) to children.

Payment could be made either to households or to individuals, or to both at different levels. This chapter assumes payment to individuals, regardless of living arrangements. The reasons for rejecting the household as the sole benefit unit are to avoid the significant gendered issues of intra-household economic distribution and to reduce the regulatory 'curiosity' of the welfare state into women's personal and intimate relations. With payments to individuals, however, there remain equity concerns about the economies of scale that larger households with two or more adult recipients might achieve.

As an unconditional grant, the benefit payment would be independent of such behavioural factors as participation or non-participation in the labour force, how money is spent, or social living arrangements (McKay 2005). No conditions would attach to the continued receipt of the benefit, in contrast to current welfare provisions. This benefit would be considered a basic entitlement of membership in Canadian society, a right of citizenship, as central, say, as the right to vote. This GAI benefit would be financed through general state revenue funds, delivered by the national government directly to all residents of Canada.[4]

The dollar amount at which a guaranteed annual income would be set is obviously a matter of importance. This is not a question I take up here, but it would involve consideration of various poverty lines and of what constitutes a minimum livable income. The assumption made for the sake of this argument is that a GAI must be paid at a level sufficient to satisfy basic needs, to allow a degree of meaningful social inclusion, perhaps at a benefit level somewhere around the after-tax LICO levels set by Statistics Canada.

Feminist Assessments

The history of Canadian feminism's involvement with the idea of a guaranteed annual income is varied. In 1970 the Report of the Royal Commission on the Status of Women recommended the payment of a guaranteed annual income by the federal government to the head of all one-parent families (Canada 1970: 325). The next decade, however, saw more cautious feminist assessment and, indeed, rejection of the policy proposal by significant feminists. Feminist commentaries on the MacDonald and Forget commissions' proposals for variants of a guaranteed annual income, for instance, were critical of the family orientation of proposed GAI plans. In a representative article entitled 'A Good Idea Goes Bad: Guaranteed Income or Guaranteed Poverty?' Marjorie Cohen (1987) castigated the range of GAI proposals in circulation at that time as dangerous sell-outs – intentionally or naively – to business and market forces. In recent years there has been a resurgence of calls by some feminists for a guaranteed annual income (see Pictou Statement, Lakeman et al. 2004), but these calls have been met with silence or with vocal suspicion from other feminist commentators and opinion leaders. Feminist politics on the issue of a guaranteed annual income, thus, remain split.

The next sections examine some of the attractions and some of the disadvantages of a guaranteed annual income from a feminist perspective. Discussion here does not purport to canvas fully all of the arguments that one might muster on either side of any debate one might have over the idea of a GAI. It will not, for example, engage fully in arguments about the impact a GAI might have on the labour market or on economic incentive structures. Rather, the purpose is to map out, rather broadly, the arguments that, in the feminist debate over GAI policy, are most referenced. The goal is to ground the chapter's rather cautious conclusions about the political desirability, from a perspective of feminist politics, of a guaranteed annual income. Or, at least, the purpose is to signal that the issues that surround successful invocation of a guaranteed annual income should be considered complex and far from straightforward.

Potential Benefits of a GAI

The appeal of a guaranteed annual income is immediate. A GAI holds the promise of eliminating poverty and of bringing about a more equal sharing of society's resources (Theobald 1965). If set at a decent minimum level, and with all other things equal, a GAI would raise lone-mother families out of their current levels of material and social deprivation. This would lead to a fairer and more equitable society – one that delivers on the promise of social citizenship.

More specific benefits cluster around the dual features of universality and conditionality. As a universal payment, a GAI would eliminate a number of significant problems that persist with targeted or means-tested programs. Universal benefits reduce the stigma of receiving welfare and promote social cohesion by minimizing stratification through selective benefit receipt and dependence. Universal programs are cheaper to administer, more efficient, less intrusive, and encourage middle-class support for the benefit (Lerner et al. 1999).

Furthermore, when structured in terms of the individual and not in terms of a family income, a GAI offers to free women from coercive private economic relations with men. Mothers are recast as independent economic agents and no longer understood by social policy as, ideally, dependent homemakers or labour market participants only. Adoption of a basic income could communicate a particular positive set of ideas about women and about social organization generally (Brodie 1995). Importantly, it would protect women from economic coercion to stay with abusive partners (Mosher et al. 2004).

As an unconditional grant, the signal feature of the guaranteed annual income is that it breaks the long-standing link between income and employment, making an individual's economic well-being independent of involvement in the paid labour force. Unemployed status would not constitute a problem for benefit eligibility, and such a form of income security could not be justified a launching pad into the paid labour force. The GAI grants a 'right to discontinuous waged work and a right to disposable time' (Beck 1999: n.p.)

A GAI is attractive for lone mothers because of their vulnerable status in labour markets. Specifically, lone mothers are more likely to experience both exclusion from and marginalization within the labour force. Women who must leave the labour force to care for their children or other family members are at greater risk of having only non-standard employment available to them. Some lone mothers are necessarily separated from the paid labour force for so long that they are left living in poverty and being dependent on welfare for the long term. Others are involved within the paid labour force but work in casual, low-level jobs. Such employment is often associated with low wages; unemployment; under-employment; few pension, health, or other benefits; as well as and a limited career path. Some non-standard employment (such as in domestic work and farm work) falls outside the protections of labour standards legislation, with the result that its workers are denied overtime protections, minimum wage guarantees, maternity and paternity leave, and vacations. Linking these individuals' income security to labour market participation does little to address their poverty. For caregivers, justice tied to the workplace is often not justice at all (Ackerman and Alstott 2004).

Proponents argue that a guaranteed annual income would enable an individual to structure her work activity in ways most responsive to the changing circumstances of her life cycle, to make 'real choices with reference to economic and non-economic activities' (McKay 2005: 107). Programs that incorporate conditionality based on specific patterns of labour force involvement or availability mismatch the life circumstances of women – and mothers, in particular – and thus virtually guarantee many women's vulnerability to poverty (McKay 2005).

A guaranteed annual income – because of its unconditional decoupling of income security and paid employment – holds the promise of enhanced liberty, freedom to choose not to work at all, or not to work under exploitative and poorly remunerated conditions. Different theorists have different ways of understanding this aspect of a GAI. Carole Pateman (2004) stands out by arguing that this freedom is best understood as self-government or autonomy, not merely economic liberty. This connection with self-government is, for Pateman, the central reason to support a GAI. A basic income becomes a 'badge of [political] citizenship' (Lister 1992: 453).

Pateman writes how a basic income could 'end the mutual reinforcement of the institutions of marriage, employment and citizenship' (2004: 90). She argues that, within the Anglo-American social insurance system, the assumption is that wives are their husbands' dependents and women's economic well-being is a product of private status, not a citizenship entitlement. Male-pattern employment dictates the central terms of our income security system, and marks the citizen. Other social contributions – notably care work – are unacknowledged, unvalued, and thus irrelevant to social constructions of citizenship, as Pateman points out (2004).

A basic income removes the necessity to judge whether an individual's poverty is her own fault or the product of systemic factors, and a GAI, therefore, could remove the policy relevance of the distinction between deserving and undeserving. A guaranteed annual income could set in force a new order of social citizenship – of what the individual can demand from the collective. Lone mothers, in particular, would no longer be cast as a problem for the state: as undeserving, employable but not employed, and as dependent in the worst sense of that notion (Fraser and Gordon 1994; Brodie 1995).

Others promote a guaranteed annual income as the best path to the kind of economic flexibility that the labour market now demands, given globalization and rapid technological change. This flexibility would allow a wider range of paid work, such as part-time and temporary jobs, contract work, and so on. A GAI would also recognize and value unpaid work and activities that are integral parts of a cohesive and rich society (Lerner et al. 1999).

In summary, this list of positive claims for a GAI is potent: an end to poverty, recognition of women's citizenship, valuing of women's caring responsibilities, facilitation of a broader, more socially responsive range of human activities, a significant reduction in the punitive and disciplinary intervention of the state in women's lives, and empowerment of women to escape domestic violence. No wonder many feminist groups are calling for a guaranteed annual income.

Potential Negative Aspects of a GAI

In the face of the dire economic needs of low-income women and the attractiveness of what a GAI can offer these women, criticism of a guaranteed annual income can be uncomfortable. Nonetheless, there are a number of outstanding concerns about proposals for a GAI. First , there are straight-up concerns about the merits of the idea. Second, there are concerns about the pragmatic dangers attendant upon its implementation. I will deal with the concerns about the merits in this section and leave the pragmatic concerns to the conclusion.

Concerns about the substance and merits of proposals for a GAI, just like arguments in favour of a GAI, focus on the characteristics of universality and unconditionality. Traditional concerns so structured are not notably feminist, but these concerns nonetheless provide important structure to the existing debate within the feminist community.

The strongest of the traditional concerns argues that, most simply, paying a benefit to everyone, independent of labour market involvement, raises the issues of prohibitive costs and negative work incentives (McKay 2005). These two common critiques are straightforward, in that they are easy to understand and anticipate, and challenging to meet. The cost issue depends much upon the level of the benefit, tax-back rates (not always a feature of GAI proposals), and savings that result from the abatement of poverty, and the rationalization, simplification, and possible elimination of other social welfare delivery systems and programs. A fully adequate guaranteed annual income will likely mean radical redistribution of resources and priorities.

The traditional issue of work disincentives is widely explored in the literature and the critique gains cogency from the image of the lazy, able-bodied lout, more than eager to take the benefit and spend it surfing, skiing, or simply lying around. Bound with this critique is the moral principle of reciprocity – i.e., one ought not to receive something for nothing – in addition to more pragmatic concerns about the impact on the economy and economic growth of large numbers of individuals opting out of paid work.

In response to the second concern, Philippe Van Parijs, perhaps the best known international proponent of a guaranteed annual income, has argued that a GAI would actually enhance labour market flexibility. A basic income – functioning as an employment subsidy to the potential worker – would increase workers' options in job selection and even job creation,[5] abolish or reduce the unemployment trap by making work always mean a positive income differential, and finally, encourage job-sharing by better allowing part-time work or sabbaticals from work (1996). The argument is that a GAI, rather than discouraging active labour market participation, would be an aid to establishing a labour market more responsive to technological and work-pattern changes. The result, it is argued, is an income security policy that promotes both social justice and economic efficiency (McKay 2005).

The critique of this defence of a GAI is that this argument assumes formal labour market involvement is always something to encourage. The assumption ignores other positions with regard to economic and non-economic activities and presents a limited approach to the issue of social policy reform. Indeed, the focus on paid work, and on avoiding paid work through reliance on a GAI, is as Pateman (2004) argues, a particularly androcentric concern. Traditional social programs, and traditional defences of a guaranteed annual income, have, although from different perspectives, an obsession with paid work. Arguments about rational economic behaviour that structure the GAI debate apply best to men, whose lives are much more culturally accountable in terms of 'the traditional work-and-pay relationship' (McKay 2005: 113), while the 'life experiences of women are largely ignored' (ibid.: 114). Reform of social security policy that better fits the pattern of women's – and of mothers' – lives necessarily must depart from this norm.

The answer, Alisa McKay (2005) argues, is recognition of the positive contribution of non-work activities: not all human interactions and activities can be explained through appeal to market-based economic structures. Much of the caregiving work and family sustenance work that women traditionally do falls outside a model of productive work. Furthermore, argues McKay, without the inevitability of justifying income maintenance measures in terms of the workings of the market economy, new conceptions of the desired outline and workings of income maintenance policy can be imagined. She concludes, however, that this more gynocentric perspective will not satisfy traditional concerns about the efficient operation of the paid labour market in the face of universal and unconditional adequate income support.

So, the debate over impact on work incentives is a detailed one, with an interesting feminist perspective on labour market impact and the kinds of activities a GAI will allow to be recognized and affirmed, including activities that lie outside a traditional market analysis. But the fact remains that a benefit program that does not, in some manner, assume that traditional productive labour is somehow connected to benefit receipt is controversial. A GAI sits in clear violation of the principle of reciprocity, strictly understood. And, in contrast to Van Parijs' argument about improved labour market flexibility as a good thing, others point to the risk that a GAI will result in even worsened exploitative conditions. From this angle, the GAI is simply a way to compensate for what is perceived to be the 'inability of a large section of the workforce to be absorbed by the economy at an adequate wage' (van der Veen 1998:140). An unconditional basic income would constitute a floor beneath labour market earnings, enabling employers to offer less than a living wage. Some advocates argue that this is good, enabling 'continued participation of low earners in paid work' (ibid.: 140). From another perspective, a GAI simply institutionalizes low wages and enables enhanced socialization of business costs (Lerner et al. 1999: 32). Of course, advocates of a GAI argue, in turn, that the assurance of a guaranteed income would enable workers to refuse work at sub-subsistence wages, thereby ensuring employers had incentive to make employment more attractive (Standing 1998: 104).

Whatever the case is about work incentives – whether unconditional income is good or bad for paid work involvement – and leaving aside the albeit important debate about the effect on wage levels of a GAI, what is ignored in this debate is that women who have children stand in a more complicated relation to paid employment than is acknowledged by the assertion that separating income security from employment is liberating. Here the feminist discussion of a guaranteed annual income adds substantially to the debate.

A general movement of women into the Canadian paid workforce is a feature of the twentieth century. Most families led by lone mothers, despite this family type's disproportionate reliance on social assistance schemes, derive the majority of their household income, not from the social assistance system, but from paid work (Statistics Canada 2005). Furthermore, it is not clear that removal of the assumption of paid employment is an ideal solution for mothers. Indeed, some studies of mothers in Europe show that the majority of women would, in fact, choose some mix of their caregiving work and employment – quality employment – in the labour market (Esping-Andersen 2001). Some women will want to stay out of the labour market completely during their child-rearing years; others will want to continue in full-time paid employment. But many women may want some mix that works well for both their caregiving work and involvement in paid work.

A basic income will not fix this issue of paid and unpaid work. It will not make the workforce more compatible with being a primary caregiver of children. Indeed, as Pateman points out, a basic income may turn caregiving work into even more of a trap for those women who wish some employment involvement. A basic income may strengthen the 'norm,' the assumption that women will stay home to look after their children – because now they financially can. The result? Women remain without full liberty to balance being a parent and a worker as they wish, and men will continue to free-ride on the caregiving work of women (Pateman 2004).

More specifically, a guaranteed annual income would do nothing, commentators argue, to increase the relative value of women's unpaid domestic work or to change the traditional gendered division of labour within the domestic economy. Instead, a GAI might reinforce these traditional features (Orloff 1990, as cited in McKay 2005). Implementation of a GAI thus risks the further institutionalization of women's location within the family, with the consequent failure to liberate women from the very social assumptions and hierarchies that construct the domestic characterization and devaluation of women's work (McKay 2005). Constraints on women's actions, constituted by pre-existing gender-based social rules, norms, and preferences, would continue to delimit women's choices and to structure the allocation of care work and 'affiliative work' between women and men in traditional, and unequal, ways. Even if a woman did decide to work outside the home, the worry is that she would face reinforced public and intimate strictures to also do the traditional work of women, with the paradoxical result being 'decreases in wives [sic] standards of living, particularly in regard to time for rest and recreation' (Nelson 1996: 74). A guaranteed annual income could mean an increase in leisure and self-development opportunities for some, but it is unlikely that those individuals will be mothers.

The irony, then, is that in striving to ensure women's economic independence, this emphasis on economic security for mothers reinforces the separation of women from the public realm. At the same time, of course, as Pateman (2004) notes, it is true that women's private economic security could enable a more public citizenship for women. Nevertheless, in a society where an important 'public' arena is the paid workplace, women's choice to be present in this public sphere must be facilitated, acknowledged, and reinforced by public policy.

Perhaps the call should not be for freedom from paid employment, but for freedom from coercion to do paid work and to do badly paid work, and for freedom from coercion to withdraw from paid work. Advocacy should be for freedom to engage in activities that do not traditionally code as 'work,' like provisioning and other 'non-productive' yet critical activities (McKay 2005). Certainly, from a feminist perspective, the call must be for freedom from the assumption that the caring work of society is properly only – or even primarily – women's work: that is, it should include the freedom to not do unpaid care work. Only this complete package of 'freedoms' promises radical and fully progressive social reform for women who are mothers (McKeen 2004). We must recognize the importance of care work to our society, but not fix women within this role.

The lesson of feminist analysis of the state is worth repeating. As Janine Brodie (1995) argues, women are not simply acted upon by the state, do not merely react to state actions as a group of social actors standing outside any one state manifestation, but come to understand their material situations, their social options, gender relationships, and their distinct identities and interests through state action and policy. What comes to be regarded as natural, as normal, as incontestable is strongly influenced by the forms of institutions embedded in society by the state. Of course, these understandings are anything but these things – they are historically specific, political, and partial, but different state forms 'weave different meanings into our everyday lives,' and these meanings are normalized by law and policy, not merely imposed through state programs and institutions (1995: 27). Social welfare reform must be careful about what it is institutionalizing and normalizing.

Calls for a guaranteed annual income ignore critical feminist recognition of the oppressive function that the public/private split has for women in another way, as well. GAI proposals typically overemphasize the importance of private purchasing power and thus inadvertently, at least, ignore the roles that public responsibility, public provision, and public ordering of, say, the labour market or community institutions ideally play in securing individual and community welfare. A program for women's economic security, or, more specifically, for mothers' economic security, that emphasizes only the provision of a basic income risks reinforcing the classical liberal divide between the public, the market, and the private family. This 'sociopolitical map' (Walzer 1984: 315) of classical liberalism, and now neoliberalism, rests on the insistence that whatever is a private concern or subject to individual sovereignty, such as the family or the market, is out of reach of collective or public reordering or interference. Feminist theorists have long disputed the notion that this divide is natural and ahistorical. Their critiques reveal that this separation reflects particular political manipulations that work to deny the role that public interests play in shaping and coercing private relations. Indeed, the line between the public and the private shifts constantly, the two spheres both determine and define each other, and the divide, far from being natural or inevitable, implements one selective and historically located set of political and economic interests.

The economic redistribution that a basic income represents does recast the boundaries between the state or the public and the distributional outcome of the market. It widens the realm of the public by engaging the state to redistribute base income more fairly. However, emphasis on a basic income alone as the centre piece of social welfare provision leaves intact and separate from collective purview much of the workings of the market – both its provision of services and its treatment of workers. We know how crucial this partition is to the perpetuation of unequal and oppressive class, gender and racialized relations.

Moreover, many proposals for a guaranteed annual income cast citizenship primarily in terms of the citizen as consumer, empowered by that citizenship to purchase social welfare needs in the market. Thus, ironically, such a progressive and often well-intentioned proposal for welfare reform can reinforce what Pierre Bourdieu has termed 'the undivided reign of the market and the consumer, the commercial substitute for the citizen' (1998: 25). The result is that the 'public good' of social welfare becomes a 'private good' (ibid.). And public expectations about what ought to be collectively provided change accordingly (Brodie 1995). Yet, not all necessary social welfare goods can be provided adequately by the private market alone, or even at all. Many require collective, public provision – like medical care, forms of insurance, education, and so on. No matter how adequate a GAI might be, there will still be services and goods that individuals will need – and that any just society would not see them go without – that such an income spent in the private market could not obtain.

This brings my discussion to the last point about the ways in which a guaranteed annual income has troubling resonances with neoliberal assumptions about and preferences for social and economic ordering. Typical GAI proposals inadequately challenge the formal (rather than substantive) equality aspirations of dominant neoliberal political discourse. The idea that economic and social needs can be best met by a universally established basic income that delivers (roughly) the same amount to everyone ignores that some individuals and groups of individuals have significantly different and more extensive needs and ought therefore to have greater and different entitlements from the collective universal benefit.[6] For example, a universal and fixed grant of health care access would overinsure some and underinsure others. All universal programs run afoul of this concern about the false equality of formal equality alone.[7] But any reform to the welfare state must recognize that key areas of human welfare require more than equal allotments of cash. Some GAI proposals take this into account, but not all.

To conclude this section on criticism of a GAI, two points distinct to a feminist perspective on a GAI stand out. First, social welfare reform must be sensitive to the complex nature of women's relationships to paid work. Simply discounting the need for women who are parents to have some meaningful involvement in the paid labour market may misstate what is actually desired by many women. Second, some calls for a GAI lend support, albeit unknowingly or unintentionally, to assumptions of social and economic ordering that are suspect: the gendered division of labour, an underemphasis on public citizenship and substantive equality, and a shrinking of public service provision. So, while one must be careful to recognize that there is much that is liberatory for women – particularly the most oppressed and poorest women – in aspirations of liberal economic individualism and the formal equality that underpins it, one also must be cautious in engaging such an alignment uncritically.

Conclusion

Left undiscussed so far is the issue of political salability and feasibility: the pragmatic considerations in actually bringing about a guaranteed annual income program in Canada. In turning to this issue, it should be noted at the outset that the political resonances with neoliberalism and traditional gendered notions of labour are greatly troubling. Particularly worrying are the inevitable compromises involved in achieving social policy proposals in this age of ascendant Canadian neoliberalism and what this might mean for a GAI in practice. The ideological resonance of a GAI with plans for the dismantling and recasting of the welfare state already in progress should make us uneasy, at least. There are a number of specific issues of concern.

First, because it will be difficult to sell the idea of a GAI that grants an adequate level of income, for the reasons of cost and reciprocity discussed above, the adequacy of the benefit is likely to be subject to political compromise. This risks what Bruce Ackerman and Anne Alstott call the 'chump change' problem – that benefits under any GAI that is politically feasible will be miniscule and trivial (2004: 52). In the guise of providing all that is liberating about a GAI, the neoliberal state will provide an income that is far from adequate, using the legitimacy of the progressive argument, while ensuring continued impoverished conditions for many Canadians. The problem of poverty will appear to have been addressed; the reality will be that the poor – particularly the very poor such as lone-mother families – will be less and less visible or credible as objects of political concern and attention.

Some progressive proponents of a guaranteed annual income see a strategy of gradual implementation as the answer to this issue. But they often ignore that, conjoined with such a version of GAI, could very well be the continued or even enhanced dismantling of existing social welfare programs. That is, the right will support the left's advocacy of a GAI because a GAI will serve as a means of getting rid of our messy welfare state. Other publicly provided income security benefits will be folded into the GAI, and other publicly provided benefits and services – like child care, and so on – will have no political viability. The public goods of the Keynesian welfare state will become the private goods distributed through the neoliberal market. The outcome would be the worst of both worlds: an inadequate GAI enabling the reduction or continued non-provision of all other aspects of the social welfare state. Instead of gradually acclimatizing the public to the idea of an adequate GAI and a fuller welfare state, the implementation of an inadequate GAI will normalize minimal and residual state presence in economic security provision.

Let me give an illustration of a vision that supports such a 'solution' to the failings of current income security provision. In 1986 the Macdonald Commission on the Economic Union recommended a version of a guaranteed annual income. This version had four features: (1) the amount of income guaranteed was about one-third of income at the poverty line; (2) all other social programs, including housing, unemployment insurance, welfare, and transfer payments from the federal government to provinces, would be cancelled; (3) minimum wages would be kept low and pay equity ineffective; and (4) the GAI would function as a wage top up, or subsidy to employers, so that Canadian corporations could keep wages low and remain competitive in free trade, a move also recommended by the Commission. The politics of this use of a GAI are not unique, nor have they become outdated. Arguably, they have become stronger and more powerful – and clever enough to co-opt more progressive calls for a GAI.[8]

Nonetheless, there is much that is engaging and empowering about the idea of guaranteeing every Canadian a decent and fair share of economic resources. The insistence on substantive equality and economic citizenship that underpins the aspirations of progressive GAI proponents has to be part of any reform to our income security programs. But I would add three other essential elements to income security reform, elements particularly essential to the economic health of families led by lone mothers.

First, we need to think specifically about the continued and enhanced collective provision of essential goods – goods and services that everyone should be able to access. These are such things as schooling, health care, child care, social housing, and so on. These goods are best provided on a universal basis by government. Without the base of a well-developed welfare state, people will remain in need, despite basic income grants. So, a 'fully developed welfare state may deserve priority over Basic Income because it accomplishes what Basis Income does not; it guarantees that certain specific human needs will be met' (Bergmann 2004: 117).

Second, labour market policy is critical, especially for those most vulnerable in the paid labour market, such as lone mothers. We must ensure that it is not contradictory to be both a primary caregiver for children and a paid worker. This will take such things as a higher and decent minimum wage, better caregiving leave for days when children or other family members are sick, timetable flexibility and other family-friendly workplace practices, decent maternity and parental leave, and so on. Labour market policy must be an important focus of women's calls for social welfare reform. Parenting and wage work should both be possible, without 'suffering from the second-class work citizenship of part-time workers in a world run by full-time workers' (Orloff 1990: 4–5, cited in McKay 2005: 109).

Third, from a feminist perspective on women's economic security, all roads lead to universally available, affordable, accessible, and quality public day care. Child care is covered by the first point about essential goods, but it is so central to women's equality that it deserves mention again. With good employment policies and universal, affordable quality child care available, significant proportions of lone mothers will leave their poverty behind. Sweden, for example, has a poverty rate of 5 per cent among its lone mothers, a number that Esping-Andersen (2001) attributes to not only a more substantive welfare system but, also, importantly, to sound employment policies and day care availability.

Finally, it is unlikely that any one single social program can provide fully the range of services and income support our society ought to provide. A guaranteed annual income captures powerfully at least part of what a just and fair society will guarantee to everyone: an adequate degree of unconditional economic independence and empowerment; however, a GAI alone cannot capture the collective and public provision of fully adequate social welfare to which we must aspire.

Notes

1 Thanks to Jim Mulvale for intellectual comradeship, generally, and comments on this chapter, particularly. Comments from the editors and anonymous reviewers are also gratefully acknowledged and appreciated. Opinions and errors in this piece are, of course, mine alone. Funding support was received from the Economic Security Project, funded by the Social Sciences and Humanities Research Council of Canada through its Community-University Research Alliance Program.
2 The figure of 38% represents the numbers across Canada; it is higher, however, in some regions. Notably, in 2004 British Columbia had a rate of poverty for families led by lone mothers of 49%, a considerably higher figure (Pulkingham 2006).
3 Statistics Canada's LICOs are one of the most widely used measures of low income. These figures, generated by Statistics Canada, vary by household size and area of residence. Statistics Canada defines a low-income household as one that spends a disproportionate amount on basic necessities,

which are food, shelter, and clothing. LICOs are generated using either pre-
or post-tax income.

4 Most advocates argue that this basic income should not be taxed, although
a variety of different tax schemes have been proposed for income earned on
top of the GAI. I leave these delivery details for another time.

5 E.g., GAI recipients could start up their own business ventures and thus create employment for themselves where none existed before. This would be
possible because of their independence from needing to find paid work.

6 Some GAI proponents argue for benefit rates that take account of such
features as family size, disability, and age; however, the point persists that
all important differences cannot adequately be factored into a universal
program.

7 My thanks to Hester Lessard for this insight.

8 The MacDonald Commission proposal was roundly and effectively criticized by a range of groups. The problem of the capture of progressive calls
for reform by regressive policy is not unique to GAI proposals. However,
for the reasons set out above, this is a particular risk for a GAI platform.

References

Ackerman, Bruce, and Anne Alstott. (2004). Why Stakeholding? *Politics and Society* 32(1): 41–60.

Battle, Ken, Michael Mendelson, and Sherri Torjman. (2006). *Towards a New Architecture for Canada's Adult Benefits*. Ottawa: Caledon Institute of Social Policy.

Beck, Ulrich. (1999). The New Statesman Essay: Goodbye to All that Wage Slavery. *newstatesman.com*, 5 March. Electronic version retrieved 5 Aug. 2007 from http://www.newstatesman.com/199903050020

Bergmann, Barbara R. (2004). A Swedish-Style Welfare State or Basic Income: Which Should Have Priority? *Politics and Society* 32(1): 107–18.

Bourdieu, Pierre. (1998). *Acts of Resistance: Against theTyranny of the Market*. New York: New Press.

Brodie, Janine. (1995). *Politics on the Margins: Restructuring and the Canadian Women's Movement*. Halifax: Fernwood Publishing.

Canada. (1970). *Report of the Royal Commission on the Status of Women*. Hull: Information Canada.

Canadian Centre for Policy Alternatives (CCPA). (2006). *Growing Gap, Growing Concern: Canadian Attitudes towards Income Inequality*. Toronto: CCPA.

Canadian Council on Social Development. (2007). *CCSD's Stats and Facts:*

Families: A Profile of Canadian Families. Electronic version retrieved 1 Jan. 2007 from http://www.ccsd.ca/factsheets.

Cohen, Marjorie. (1987). A Good Idea Goes Bad: Guaranteed Income or Guaranteed Poverty? *This Magazine* 21(2): 19–23.

Dieticians of Canada. (2006). *Cost of Eating in British Columbia: Annual Report 2006.* Vancouver: Dieticians of Canada, B.C. Region and Community Nutritionists Council of B.C.

Esping-Andersen, Gøsta. (2001). Households, Families and Children. Paper prepared for the RC 19th Annual Conference 'Old and New Social Inequalities: What Challenges for Welfare States?' 7–9 Sept., International Sociological Association, Oviedo, Spain.

Fox Piven, Frances. (1990). Ideology and the State: Women, Power and the Welfare State. In Linda Gordon (ed.), *Women, the State, and Welfare,* 250–65. Madison: University of Wisconsin Press.

Fraser, Nancy, and Linda Gordon. (1994). A Genealogy of Dependency: Tracing a Keyword of the U.S. Welfare State. *Signs* 19: 309.

Lakeman, Lee, *Angela* Miles, *and Linda Christiansen-Ruffman.* (2004). [Pictou Statement] Feminist Statement on Guaranteed Living Income. *Canadian Woman Studies Journal* 23(3,4): 204–6.

Lee, Marc. (2004). *New Perspectives on Income Inequality in B.C.* Vancouver: CCPA, B.C. Office.

Lerner, Sally, Charles Clark, and Robert Needham. (1999). *Basic Income: Economic Security for All Canadians.* Toronto: Between the Lines.

Lister, Ruth. (1992). *Women's Economic Dependency and Social Security.* EOC Research Discussion Series No. 2. Manchester: Equal Opportunities Commission.

McKay, Alisa. (2005). *The Future of Social Security Policy: Women, Work and a Citizen's Basic Income.* London: Routledge.

McKeen, Wendy. (2004). *Money in Their Own Name: The Feminist Voice in the Poverty Debate in Canada 1970–1995.* Toronto: University of Toronto Press.

Mosher, Janet, Patricia Evans, and Margaret Little. (2004). *Walking on Eggshells: Abused Women's Experiences of Ontario's Welfare System.* Final Report of Research Findings from the Women and Abuse Welfare Research Project, 5 April.

National Council of Welfare. (2007). *Solving Poverty: Four Cornerstones of a Workable National Strategy for Canada.* Ottawa: Minister of Public Works and Government Services Canada.

– (2004). *Poverty Profile, 2001.* Ottawa: Minister of Public Works and Government Services Canada.

Nelson, Julie A. (1996). *Feminism, Objectivity and Economics*. London and New York: Routledge.

Orloff, Ann. (1990). Comment on Ann Withorn: Is One Man's Ceiling Another Women's Floor? Paper presented at conference 'Basic Income Guarantees: A new welfare strategy?' 6–8 April, University of Wisconsin-Madison.

Pateman, Carole. (2004). Democratizing Citizenship: Some Advantages of a Basic Income. *Politics and Society* 32(1): 89–105.

Pulkingham, Jane. (2006). Bucking the National Trend: Poverty among Lone Mothers. *CCPA BC Commentary* 9(3): 5.

Standing, Guy. (1998). Seeking Equality of Security in the Era of Globalisation. Speech on file with author. Published in Sally Lerner, Charles Clark, and Robert Needham (eds.) *Basic Income: Economic security for All Canadians* (Toronto: Between the Lines, 1999, 101–6).

Statistics Canada. (2005). *Women in Canada 2005: A Gender-Based Statistical Report*. Ottawa: Statistics Canada.

Theobald, Robert. (1965). *Free Men and Free Markets*. New York: Anchor Books.

United Nations. (2003). *Report of the Committee on the Elimination of Discrimination against Women*. Twenty-eighth session (13–31 Jan.), Twenty-ninth session (30 June–18 July). New York: General Assembly Official Records, Fifty-eighth Session Supplement No. 38 (A/58/38).

– (2006). *Consideration of Reports Submitted by States Parties under Articles 16 and 17 of the Covenant*. Thirty-sixth Session (1–19 May). New York: United Nations.

van der Veen, Robert J. (1998). Real Freedom versus Reciprocity: Competing Views on the Justice of Unconditional Basic Income. *Political Studies* 46(1): 140–63.

Van Parijs, Philippe. (1996). Basic Income and the Two Dilemmas of the Welfare State. *Political Quarterly* 67(1): 63–6.

Walzer, Michael. (1984). Liberalism and the Art of Separation. *Political Theory* 12(3): 315–30.

Women's Livable Income Working Group. (2006). *Women's Economic Justice Project: An Examination of How Women Would Benefit from a Guaranteed Livable Income*. Victoria: Victoria Status of Women Action Group.

Yalnizyan, Armine. (2007). *The Rich and the Rest of Us: The Changing Face of Canada's Growing Gap*. Toronto: CCPA.

9 Re-visioning the Environment of Support for Lone Mothers in Extreme Poverty

PENNY GURSTEIN AND SILVIA VILCHES

This chapter takes as its starting point the experiences of lone mothers on income assistance who have young children, and asks the question: how can public policies better respond to the support needed by these women to adequately care for their children and themselves? Income support reductions in the province of British Columbia are putting increasing pressure on lone mothers to rely on social support networks outside the public arena, primarily networks of family and friends. This can be seen as a way to shift public responsibility onto private social networks, and of reducing government responsibilities. In this chapter we examine the way the regulatory pressure is putting women and their children in an even more precarious situation because of the fragile nature of the complex webs of support on which they are forced to rely.

The problem for these women is not only poverty, but also the way that the public and private systems are conceptually divided by the regulatory regime. Strell and Duncan (2001) identify various national strategies in Europe regarding what Evers, Pilj, and Underson (1994) have discussed as a 'welfare diamond' (cited in Jenson and Saint-Martin 2003). Jenson and Saint-Denis identify the particular constructions of relationships between the family, community, state, and market sectors as 'citizenship regimes' organized by conceptions of rights and responsibilities, and note that there has been a shift to 'responsibility' and 'future investment' as opposed to support from the state for the family. Janine Brodie (2003) further problematizes the relationship among these sectors, noting that neoliberal politics and the concept of globalization contain a slippage of scale that defers responsibility from the public/macro-scale to the private/micro- or family scale. Brodie wonders whether this scalar slippage may explain the shift to a rights discourse that also tends to support the same language of atomization, aligning with the shift from collective responsibility to individual responsibility. Luxton (2006), Bezanson (2006), and Brodie (2003) also draw attention to the neglect of social reproduction as necessary work that is ignored in the slippery shift in focus that obscures not only the collective need to provide for children and families, but also the necessary work that women do in creating social structure and the necessary supports of future labour.

In this chapter we focus on re-visioning the policy framework to recognize the roles and responsibilities that women with young children have, rather than imagining mothers on income assistance as separate from, and a drain on, civil society. This opens the way to moving beyond the public/private dualism that underlies current Canadian public policy approaches. Understanding and re-visioning the public/private divide may enable lone parent mothers to care for themselves and their children in all ways, including financially.

The analysis presented in this chapter is based on multiple in-depth interviews with twenty-two lone mothers with preschool children, undertaken as part of a five-year qualitative longitudinal study[1] that focused on how reductions and changes in income assistance benefits and regulations have changed the goals, eligibility, and expectations of people on income assistance. In-depth interviews were conducted every six months over three years. Half of the study participants identified as Aboriginal, and six lived in the northern part of the province, while the others lived in East Vancouver.

The longitudinal nature of the study provided opportunities to reflect on the ongoing interactions between life circumstances and policy changes, revealing the gap between aspirations and achievement, as well as the interaction between public and private constraints and supports. It also provided an opportunity to better understand whether the social capital that theoretically enables individuals and communities to engage in society is enhanced or hindered in this regulatory environment. Finally, the longitudinal study adds to an understanding of the gendered effects of the new government policies by examining the interaction between parenting responsibilities and social networks.

The Policy Context – Lack of Public Supports

The province of British Columbia provides an ideal ground in which to conduct this study, because the B.C. government initiated the most extensive welfare and social services restructuring that has yet been attempted in Canada (Goldberg and Wolanski 2005). In January 2002 it announced that the operating budget of the ministry responsible for social assistance would be cut by $581 million (or 30%) over the next three years. This cut has since grown to $609 million. The ministry eliminated 459 full-time equivalent positions, and 36 welfare offices across the province were closed. A combination of cuts to welfare benefits and a further tightening of eligibility rules achieved the remaining budget savings.

The policy changes for lone parents have been dramatic. Single parents in the Expected to Work (ETW) category, which excludes those designated as Persons with a Disability (PWD) or Persons with Persistent Multiple Barriers (PPMB) are now expected to work when their youngest child reaches the age of 3 years, rather than 7 years, as was previously the case.[2] These 'employable' lone parents used to receive a support allowance for food and necessities of $377 per month; subsequently, this allowance was reduced to $325.58. For families with more than three people, including the parent, the shelter allowance has been cut in the range of $55 to $75 per month on amounts that were already 60 per cent of the average market rental costs in Vancouver. Employable lone parents were previously entitled to a flat rate earning exemption of $200 per month, but earnings exemptions have now been completely eliminated. Before the reforms, these parents were also entitled to keep $100 per month of child support income they received from ex-partners; now, all child support payments are deducted. There has also been elimination of many work entry assistance benefits. Full-time students in accredited post-secondary programs that are eligible for B.C. Student Financial Assistance (loans) are no longer eligible for income assistance. Emergency grants were capped at $20 for food per person per month, one month's shelter annually, and $100 per person for clothing annually. Most importantly, there is a new emphasis on returning to work; lone mothers in the ETW category whose youngest child is 3 years of age or older must comply with mandated requirements to return to work or risk reduction of already minimal support amounts. Non-compliance with the mandatory employment plan is penalized through a $100 reduction in the monthly support allowance. Not declaring gifts of material support, including gifts in kind with material value, potentially subjects women to a life-time eligibility ban.

Unlike in the United States, social service cutbacks have also had an impact on spending at the program level, by reducing and consolidating the number of support programs and reducing the financial flow to agencies like neighbourhood houses, women's shelters, and family support services. Child care spending, another key support to lone mothers, was affected by reductions in operating grants, parent subsidies, and wage supports to child care workers. Government priorities, directed towards 'capacity development' and away from core operating funds, are reportedly shifting the delivery of child care from paid staff to volunteers and private charitable donors. The closure and consolidation of government offices, in combination with the reduction and consolidation of programs particularly affected northern and rural communities because this occurred during an economic downturn in the primary industries of the region. In addition, instability in the child protection services, including contracted family support services, was created by the process of transfer to Aboriginal governance authorities. The lack of public supports has resulted in an increasing reliance by impoverished women on the social supports of family and friends to obtain basic necessities, while in turn, increasing family and friends' reliance on them (Vilches and Gurstein 2006).

The Positioning of Dependency in Social Care Frameworks

The relationship of the state, the market, the family, and the voluntary or community sector are often connected as the four corners of a 'diamond' (Jenson 2004). The welfare diamond, originally formulated as 'the state,' 'the market,' and 'the family,' by Esping-Andersen was expanded by Evers, Pilj, and Ungerson (1994, as cited in Kershaw 2005: 3) to include the voluntary sector. This structure may be used, as Strell and Duncan (2001) have done, to classify and compare regulatory regimes according to the emphasis they place on the relationships between the sectors. As they point out, some regimes, as in Austria and the Netherlands, provide strong support for adults to care for young children. These types of regimes do not require caregiving parents to look for work until their children are youth or leave home. The Scandinavian countries, in contrast, provide strong labour market engagement support, but make it difficult for adults to stay at home beyond the early years. The relationship of the state to the market is thus malleable and interacts with, and controls, caregiving. Women are particularly vulnerable in differing regimes because of the disproportionate responsibility they have for caregiving (Kershaw 2005; Turnbull 2001). Rooke and Schnell (1983) argue that the constructed dependency of children is primary to understanding the way women are caught in cycles of dependency, a view that is confirmed by Strell and Duncan's (2001) comprehensive analysis.

The lone parent mother straddles the divide between being a financial provider to her family and a caregiver to her children. This dual-role presents at least two challenges to the prevailing neoliberal social care framework because of the way mothers' situations cut across the idealized conceptual organization of state-market interactions. First, the neoliberal imperative to provide or finance care within the privacy of the family is challenged by the fact that lone mothers typically cannot finance the care of their children with the resources they are able to generate through the market. Also, they are often only able to provide care themselves with state income support. Thus, a woman's status in the market amplifies and implicates certain gendered effects of social policies, highlighting and drawing attention to the inequalities between citizens. Second, caring work and the obligations to care can be considered to be a microcosm of the kind of 'contractual relations' that are theorized to occur within the dimensions of the market, pointing to similarities, rather than differences, in the kinds of relationships possible in these ostensibly distinct and separate spheres of activity.

Dolfsma et al. (2005) describe three distinct ways of conceiving the relationship between the market and the state, which have implications for understanding the effects of policy reconfigurations of social care frameworks: (1) as separate competing spheres, (2) as nested cooperative spheres, and (3) as interlocking spheres of multiple contractual relations. In a separate sphere perspective, it is possible for a person to be alienated from, or by, the market. This generates a need for the state to ensure 'attachment' to the labour force, or else to support individuals who are 'external' to the market. This kind of 'alienation' from the market is not possible in the second model, where the state is conceptualized as part of the market, either equilaterally, or with the market encapsulating society. The difference between preferences for privatization or distributive justice results out of the priority one gives to intervention in the market versus allowing the market to set social rules. The third model conceptualizes the market-society relationship as one comprised of many contractual arrangements, a view that incorporates diversity and diminishes the potential for single sources of responsibility or control. The market is present in the 'social' sphere, and vice versa, and specific implications change depending on the goal of a particular inquiry. This model may offer more opportunity for an 'agentic' view of the individual.

Contextualizing the relationship of the state to the individual in terms of state and market obligations to provide support, and between fiduciary and caring responsibilities, helps to describe the changing context that lone parent women on welfare are experiencing. Changes to the British Columbia welfare system represent an attempt to push fiduciary responsibility to the market: this is clearly evident in mandatory employability programs and reductions in state supports. Our question and inquiry then focuses more narrowly on the microenvironment that the women live in, and their everyday experiences. In this way, we analyse how macro-state policies influence individual well-being, the ability to cope, and the effectiveness of the recent policy changes.

Social Support as a Crucial 'Context'

Turning from the structural or macro-level to the micro-level, we focus on social supports: what is important to lone parent mothers on welfare in terms of surviving and getting ahead and how policy affects their daily lives. In a review of welfare research, Williams, Popay, and Oakley (1999) compared structural analysis with the emerging theoretical interest in coping, stress, and individual capacity. They suggest that welfare research is moving to incorporate a view of the individual as an agent operating within the constraints of conditions set by state policies and the market. At this level, research reveals the ability of people to offer resistance, to comply, to cope, and to strategize. Research that focuses on individual capacity may add to our understanding of how policies can better support lone parent families by revealing the effects of intra-family interactions, as well as the effects of individual actions on and within micro-systems.

Before looking at the everyday experiences of people, it is important to understand how the theories of social support, social networks, and social capital may be used to interpret these interactions. Social support is defined as 'something received by an individual in order to enhance their well-being' (Weber 1998: 2). Social support is also characterized along four dimensions: emotional, instrumental, informational, and appreciative (Universiteit Twente 2004). Kanaiaupuni et al. (2000) point out that the two-way nature of much social support is typically ignored; nevertheless, they note that in their research with Mexican families, social supports form an inherent strength in the context of thin public supports.

Social supports should not be confused with social networks, and methodologically conflating the two is not helpful in terms of clarifying their value and utility (Williams et al. 1999). Bjornskov and Tinggaard Svenson (2003) suggest that network theory refers to quantity and presence, rather than quality of interactions, and actual networks can be difficult to measure because of controversies over what actually constitutes a network and to whom. To make the micro-level more complex means describing and delineating to whom and to what extent supports are made available, and under what circumstances.

Weber (1998: 21), citing Hare-Mustin (1991), notes that much social support research ignores gender by either obscuring gender differences (such as women's relative lack of power) or using the male experience as a norm. Williams et al. (1999) suggest that the study of social supports is a profoundly gendered inquiry, requiring an explicit consideration of the role of gender in the study of expectations and environments that impact the lives of individuals.

Distinguishing social supports and social networks from social capital, Bjornskov and Tinggaard Svenson (2003) describe social capital as 'networks and norms that govern the interactions among individuals, households and communities' (2003: 8). Portes (1998), though, strongly advises against automatically ascribing the attributes of individual networks to communities, and instead, recommends carefully focusing research and findings on particular levels, or scales, of environment. Social supports should therefore be conceptually distinguished from social capital because social support describes the milieu of the individual, while social capital is composed of dynamic interactions among individuals together in community. In examining the lives of the marginalized, DeFilippis (2001), among others, critiques approaches to social capital that ignore the exercise of power, and argues that policies that engage social capital as a resource should be examined for their effects on, and interactions with, the lives of the marginalized.

The Findings: A Precarious Social Network

The social support systems that are evident through the participants' stories reveal relationships that are bound in a reciprocal set of obligations that balance needs with giving. Needs met through these systems are not only for companionship, but also for basic necessities such as food and shelter, which are a regular struggle to provide:

My kids got to have something first before I [eat]. I don't care if I don't eat.
I always say that [to myself], I don't care about me but I care about you.
(Olivia)

Bezanson similarly noted, when interviewing women about the effects of the 1996 neoliberal restructuring of Ontario's welfare system,
that food was the most flexible element of women's household budget
(2006: 189). Bezanson found that the cost of food meant that women did
not buy clothes (for years), ate once a day or maybe less, opted between
essential but unsubsidized medication and as for eating, at times abso-
lutely relied on food bank hand outs as their primary source of food.
Like Olivia, they fed their children first, so that literally, the policy was
'consuming women.'

In British Columbia, the explicit neoliberal goal of 'enhancing community capacity' by shifting responsibility to the private sector was
relayed as expectations that women would turn to friends and family
for support. However, the networks the women in this study relied on
have limited resources, and often people in these networks have also
been affected by the same cutbacks. In addition, the lone mothers are
not always recipients, but also key social supports for a circle of family
and friends, as well as providing for their own children. Neysmith and
Reitsma-Street (2005) conceptualize this as 'provisioning' and explicitly
use this concept to make women's contributions both inside and outside the home more visible.

Organizing for the Future

'Nancy' exemplifies some of these complex relationships. Although
Nancy is on income assistance and caring for her three young children
in a four-bedroom townhouse, she is also sharing her space with two
sisters, one sister's partner, and this couple's children. The groceries
and daily routine are a burden, but she does not like to ask her sisters
for help. Her perception that it would not be fair to them is tied to the
past and her judgments about how she was raised.

I'm really mad at my mom for putting all that responsibility on me, and
I'm trying not to do that with my kids. Like, if they want to do it, then they
can do it, but I'm not going to say, 'Oh, you dress your sister and bathe
your sister' and 'take your sister here and there.' If they want to help out

then they'll help out, but if they don't, then that's fine with me because it's my responsibility not theirs. And like, with my sisters, I try not to get them to watch my kids too much also, especially my younger sister. (Nancy)

In addition to illustrating the complexity of strained networks, this example also begins to paint a portrait of the way the past is tied to the future. In this example Nancy establishes a normative regime for the giving of care, a regime that is similar to the Bjornskov and Tinggaard Svenson definition of social capital. She claims the responsibility for giving care, and sets the boundary for her own and others' acceptable behaviour. As Neysmith and Reitsma-Street (2005) point out, she is provisioning for the future. For example, part of her care is given in the expectation and hope that her sisters will attend and complete high school.

I'm very proud of her being in school still, because my other sister that just moved in – the older one … didn't go to school or anything. So, I told her to keep it up and to stay in school. Because for a while she was wanting to have a baby. Like, how are you going to go to school? I said, 'Look at it, I have three kids, my youngest one is 19 months, and I still haven't finished school.' I said, 'Stay in school, later, after you're done your school, and you get job training and everything, then you can have a baby.' (Nancy)

It is important to note the reciprocal nature of this relationship. Her sisters are not simply staying with her for 'free,' irrespective of their financial contribution. There is also an obligation or expectation, whether they choose to comply with it or not, that Nancy relays to them. She herself maintains an understanding of her actions as bettering her sisters' possibilities for the future. She is investing in her family's future, building social capital. The view from the state side, that she is a recipient only, is contravened here by the multiple people she provides for, not only now, in the moment, but for the future. She is a bridge to future labour market engagement and is working towards it for those who depend on her.

Reciprocal Networks

In the example above, Nancy is in control and making the decisions. However, more often the women were in sharing relationships that were comprised of give and take with others. For example, while Nancy is a source of support to members of her immediate family, she also receives support from a 'dear friend' who is also a neighbour.

> She's the one that's been helping me out quite a bit. My son has really bad asthma and he had these re-occurring ear infections and it was really bad. I was changing him. And then next thing you know I looked and saw red on his ear. I said, 'Oh my God, his ear was bleeding.' It cracked. So, she helped me get his ear better and so she's been helping out quite a bit. (Nancy)

This kind of helping is both what is called 'affective' or emotional helping, as well as instrumental. This relationship, once it began to build, became one of mutual aid. The two friends made an arrangement; when the neighbour had trouble getting income assistance she looked after Nancy's children and got paid through a child care subsidy. Because Nancy is receiving support for child protection concerns, she was able to get her friend a supplement to bring the wage up. Thus, although the friend helps her by taking care of her children and they look out for each other, Nancy has also reciprocated with material support. This exchange of help characterizes the complex relations between the market, state, voluntary sector, and social supports. In the following passage it is apparent that this exchange is 'common currency' that women consciously develop as a form of 'investment' for future needs.

> I have really good supporting friends, and we help each other out, invite each other over for dinners, or just help, every little bit. I even try to help my other friend out. They'd give us like a bunch of rice bags, so I was able to give her some, because she was struggling. It's good to help, because then later on something good will come. (Andrea)

Interactions between Formal and Informal Supports

Social support garnered through informal relationships was augmented by support from formal aid agencies, such as government social workers, non-profit societies contracted by the government to provide public services, and voluntary organizations. What each of these entities provided was often key to survival. For instance, when Nancy's apartment had cockroaches, the building owner insisted she get rid of all of her things. A bin was provided and she threw out many of her possessions. While government financial assistance workers helped by providing her with some money to replace the items, it was not enough and other agencies stepped in.

> My daughter's church helped us out with a lot of stuff too, because they get donations of furniture and stuff like that. They just dropped by, on last Thursday, with this really nice bed for my sister. (Nancy)

Although this appears to be a charitable act on the part of the church, it would seem that they are likely paid or subsidized to run some children's programs as well, since Nancy does not pay for the programs. At this level we begin to see the interaction of systems, as money and assets flow through various channels, connecting in this case, the state through the voluntary sector to her family.

The flow of support from the voluntary sector also has a countervailing action, in that there is also an attempt to regulate this flow through public policy. This impacts private support networks as well as what is sometimes called the 'privately delivered/publicly funded sector.' For example, when Andrea moved to safer, better housing she could not receive government assistance for the move. Welfare regulations only provide moving expenses if the rent for the new residence is lower than for the previous place, or when it is recommended by a social worker for child protection reasons. Since Andrea took the initiative to assure the safety of her children without meeting either of those conditions, income assistance staff told her to rely on her informal social networks for support. However, this has material consequences for those in her social network as well as for her. Andrea used all her grocery money to pay for moving costs because she had no car and no friends with a car.

> Well, later on when I do run out (of grocery money), and I am really stuck, their [government] position is use up what resources you have, friends, family. And when that is all gone then I can get a crisis grant for the month … I haven't yet, but I will end up borrowing money from [my mom], which is tough because we're going out to see her at the end of the month. She doesn't know we're going though, so it's a surprise for her … And I don't have any family here expect for the boys' dad. And he's unemployed and unreliable. (Andrea)

Andrea was clear that both the reductions in income assistance amounts and denial of crisis grants forced her to lean more on informal and formal supports. Andrea shielded those she cared for from the effects of the government policy, though, by balancing her need with resources from her own social network. It was ironic that the person she turned to was her mother, because this extended the gendered effect into the previous generation. The gate-keeping effect of the policies thus ensures that the flow of supports has particular characteristics, and actually keeps women in their 'place.' The regulatory advice has the effect of causing Andrea to use her social support resources whether they are offered or not, violating the voluntary nature of these relationships. Just as Nancy consciously developed her social support into a network, so does the government explicitly require Andrea to exhaust hers. For those whose sources of support were in a precarious states, this put the whole social network at risk.

In a contrasting case, very different from Nancy's, 'Molly' has an extended family who are both able and willing to offer support, and who are encouraging her to move on in a career. Molly already has post-secondary education, and she is anxious to get off welfare. Confusion over regulations tripped her up, though.

> They say that if I work, I can have part of what I earned, but I didn't know that now they just take everything. I was feeling really bad, because I was working to have some more money and when my welfare cheque came, it was nothing. It was enough to buy food, but I couldn't buy any clothes for her [daughter], I couldn't buy any shoes. I have my cousin, and I have [a] friend, they gave me all the clothes … was thinking, okay, I can maybe buy something for Christmas for her, and I can give something to my cousin too, like a little present. And suddenly, there was nothing. I mean, if she gets sick, it's really tough for me to buy the medicines, and all those things, you know. It also says in the book [information pamphlet] that at Christmas they will give you a bonus or something, and they didn't even tell me this changed. And so then I didn't have anything to buy her for Christmas. I applied to people to buy things for you [charity], whatever you need. So they gave me all the presents, and my aunt and friends, they gave presents [for my daughter], so I feel okay. But I feel a little sad, you know, because I was planning to use that money. I was waiting for that money. (Molly)

In this excerpt Molly is engaged in reciprocal relationships where she receives instrumental support. She does give back by providing after-school care for her cousins for 'free' every day, but she would still like to give back through her own resources. She exerts a normative assessment of this situation, one that suggests certain kinds of expectations. This urge was so strong that Molly took a job in the fall with the express intent of saving money for Christmas. What happened to Molly was a result of lack of information that ended up rendering her labours for nought; she actually lost money and became even more dependent on family and friends. In this regulatory environment information is itself a currency, and lack of information required her to draw on her network of supports, negatively impacting everyone. Even as a relatively well-resourced woman, she still loses, and dramatically so, in the case of lack of money for her child's needs, such as for medicine.

Managing the Instability

The ideology that is translated into policy through legislation, and communicated to staff who then relay it to income assistance recipients as they try to goad them to move off welfare, is that the women only have value as income earners in the marketplace. This deliberately singular focus results in the regulatory environment impeding the development of social capital. Sometimes it also works to undermine existing social support systems, as in the cases of Molly and Andrea. In other cases, the pressure to use non-state resources goes beyond undermining the women and actually puts these women and their children at direct material and other risks, as it does in the cases of Nancy and Olivia.

The need for support often drives women to rely on the fathers of their children, but this could be a risky and complicated strategy. 'Regine' and the father of her children were on good terms and, in exchange for helping out, she let him use her place as an address and home base when he was in town from seasonal work. However, this backfired.

> [Their father] hasn't done his taxes since 2000 up until now. Four years. It screwed everything up. They [government] have been taking money, left and right. So they took the whole Child Tax benefit, Family Bonus. They took all the GST [tax credit] – what I've been receiving normally because he hasn't done his taxes … Like, he comes around and then leaves. You know, like a freeloader. Comes around when I've got money. Or, you know, he knows the Child Tax came, and he'd be around. Yeah. So now I'm not getting it until he does his taxes. (Regine)

As a result of this sequence of events, Regine's formal sources of support were drastically reduced, putting her and her children at severe financial risk. Without the regular federal tax credits, she could not sustain herself. However, the father supplied extra money when he was around, which she also needed. Trying to balance the two sources of support risked her whole system. Regine did not have the kind of networks to draw on that Molly and Andrea had, difficult as those were. As a result, Regine turned to a riskier source, one that ultimately failed both because the father did not acknowledge her risk and because government sanctioned her, not the father, when they were caught contravening the rules. Thus she takes a double risk to receive occasional help, which she requires in order to manage. The partnership, though, is illusory. There is no social capital development here.

The risk of being put at financial risk is not only the chance of being punished. It is also the case that some women are exposed to violence by maintaining contact with abusive ex-partners. Olivia has had three ex-partners, two of whom have been abusive. She recounts:

… about two years ago, he came after me. He always used to come to my place, and want to see my kids, or if he needs a place, he'll come. And I said I'm not one of those people to forgive anybody if they mistreated me. And [he] did mistreat me. He went and beat me up. So, I said, 'You can sleep on the floor, or get out.' And so he comes back and forth, right? And when I go to conferences he would babysit for me – I had to pay him, and I said, 'No, I can't do that no more, so you get out for good.' But when I kicked him out and I meant seriously, he thought, oh, this is it, you know, she meant it, right? So, he went to a lawyer. He wants support, he wants spousal support, he wants the kids, he wants this, and he wants that. I went to the court – he didn't show up. Court says, 'Oh, well, we'll give him another week.' So we waited next week for him to come back, still no show. Five times, no show. So I said to the judge, 'Well, what's going to happen now'? I said, 'He wanted this, he wanted that.' And I said, 'I don't have nothing to give him.' And so the judge says, 'Well, we'll just give you the kids.' And, you know, [that] is not fair, it's wasting my time all this, for him not just to show up. (Olivia)

For Olivia, the alternative to not having her partner babysit was to be alone and to forego the support. On the other hand, Olivia had travelled to this region with her partner, and when the relationship broke down, she was 'stuck' in an alien place.

It's just that I'd been married and the only people I know is my husband's parents and his friends. And you know, that's what I call my so-called friends. I don't have nobody. (Olivia)

In these cases, the fathers of the children are sometimes the closest thing to a real support that the women have, but as with Olivia or Regine, this could be a difficult choice.

The assumption that there were support networks of family and friends on whom the women could rely proved to be tenuous. As Side (1997) found, women's friendships were fragile in that they were both voluntary and an outcome of intentional work. Lack of reciprocity in what were considered basic moral obligations was likely to result in breakdown, as was overinterference or the appearance or demand of what might be judged as dependency. Luxton (2006), who investigated how friends responded to medical emergencies, found that friends tended to hold back if they felt family could provide or was present (read the fathers of these women's children, for instance), and that, alternatively, the medical and economic systems had little way of recognizing, supporting, or engaging the participation of friends. Some of the women in this study did have 'dear friends,' who helped them materially or emotionally or otherwise, but they also referred to the fragility of these friendships, their need to reciprocate, and the lack of time to have friends or isolation from others because of lack of money. In addition, as some women pointed out, even their neighbourhoods were risky places to go for support.

We live in a building all of single moms, I'm telling you the truth ... And the children they're really violent; they're angry. So one day you have friends, one day you don't have [a] friend. (Natalie)

The sense of responsibility the women have in caring for others interacts with normative expectations of reciprocity to make social support networks both fragile and obligatory. It is not 'free' help, and in some cases, because of the need driving them, puts these women at increased financial risk or even violence. Ministry policy not only pressures women to use these networks, it also works against the development of social capital by preventing women from reciprocating except by giving their time, something already in short supply. Material need forms a counterbalance, however, locking these mothers into the need to act, and narrowing their choices. The social networks that we have identified cannot build even fragile 'social capital' because social interactions within the wider community are inhibited, rather than facilitated.

The Environment of Support

The impact of government policies on the daily lives of the participants in this study is very evident. Lowering of income assistance rates precipitates both housing and food insecurity. Without the financial resources for safe, affordable housing women have to resort to inadequate, unhealthy housing, or in some cases, periods of homelessness and reliance on their social network to provide shelter. In turn, with their finances depleted every month, all of our participants have at some point relied on food banks to tide them over until they receive their next income assistance money. For many of our participants food banks were not an emergency situation but an ongoing provisioning strategy.

Unhealthy living conditions and food insecurity put the health and safety of mothers and their children at risk. Many of the mothers reported serious health problems such as diabetes and asthma for themselves and their children, which also increase the risk of their inability to manage. As Table 9.1 illustrates, the fragile system in which they are embedded makes their work as caregivers and provisioners harder to navigate. In a study of informal caregiving, Luxton (2006) reaches similar conclusions and maintains that neoliberal policies that stress reliance on informal support networks leave people vulnerable, impose undue burdens on caregivers, and undermine the support that people rely on.

The government requirement that women exhaust all available capacity in their social networks also amplifies the gendered impacts of their position as caregivers. For women trying to leave unstable or abusive partners, this requirement in combination with isolation from friends and family intensifies their vulnerability to ongoing unhealthy interactions. For women without family, who are able or healthy, the requirement means a temporary shifting of inadequate resources, pouring one half-full glass into another, with an ever-reducing capacity. This stresses the entire social support network, leaving the women, their children, and their families with little capacity to face catastrophic emergencies. It also amplifies a gendered effect, as was demonstrated by how Andrea turned to her mother while Regine and Olivia suffered by turning to the fathers of their children. Thus, the consequence of public policy that

Table 9.1.   Social Supports: A Two-Way Street of Complex Webs of Interaction and
Reciprocal Obligations

A Fragile System for Women	Stresses on the System
• Women balance need with giving. • Women are source of support to immediate family and others. • Women receive support from others. • Women build social support systems through material, emotional, and information exchange.	• Social networks do not always equal 'social capital.' • Women forced to resort to their social networks can be put at risk of violence. • Women can weaken others in their networks. • Women can obligate women to return 'favours.' • Such obligations invite remarginalization along gender lines.

treats these networks as 'social capital' that could be further utilized
by the women undermines and exhausts the private side of the care
framework for women in extreme poverty, rendering them even more
vulnerable to future dependence on the state and to exploitation. This
has particularly ominous potential for women who are trying to come
off the streets, heal from addictions, or who have fragile mental health.
In these cases the burdens risk the entire family cohesion.

The caring responsibilities that these women not only wanted to carry out for their children, and which they were legally obligated to fulfil,
could be depicted on a Venn diagram (Figure 9.1) that highlights the
way the women's needs are co-constructed by overlapping and conflicting ethics in the public sphere. It is important, as Bronfenbrenner
(1979) stressed so many years ago, to consider the whole family within
the context of its supports or else the whole family as a system becomes
at risk. This is especially clear when considering the health and well-
being of young children who are dependent on their parents. But as can
be seen from this study, the health and safety of women is also put at
risk by their duties as mothers in combination with such policies. We
argue that policy needs to address and support the deficits in the in-
terconnections between these essential components of life, rather than
considering the lone parent mother as morally deficient because of her
dependency on income assistance and lack of market engagement. The
need to care for children is undermining attempts to move away from
financial dependence on income assistance supports, as demanded by

Figure 9.1.   Overlapping constraints.

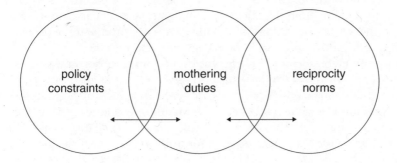

policy. Thus, 'mothering' is catching these women in a dual bind, and the current regulations are weakening the capacity to care.

Policy Implications: Re-visioning Social Supports in Context

The disconnection between policy expectations and the lived experiences of these women increases their reliance on their private social networks. However, these social networks are often fragile, resulting in further impoverishment. We argue that a policy framework based on an 'ecological' model can better address the provisioning of services because the sources of support are organized within the totality of a person's environment. This means attending to the particular supports that a woman needs in light of the resources that are available to her and to those she supports. The woman/lone parent must not be viewed in merely socioeconomic terms, but as embedded within and part of a vital set of supports that operate in both the formal and informal sectors. This moves away from both the state responsibility model that Dolfsma et al. (2005) describe, as well as the private sector responsibility model, to recognize individual women's agency within an unequal and gendered division of privileges and social exchange systems.

For policy systems to be able to 'see' the client as an agent of her own network involvement, as the third model proposed by Dolfsma et al. suggests, requires more latitude and accountability at the level of the case worker to ensure that certain outcomes are attained, much in the same way that the model for working with children at risk that Bronfenbrenner (1979) developed is designed to achieve ongoing developmental supports for children in specific, articulated ways within accepted standards of care. In this model, a case worker's role is to facilitate and understand the micro-system of supports of each family. To enable the system to sustain itself, those who are intimately involved in supporting the family could be recognized and remunerated. At the community level, social programs vested in voluntary sector agencies are seen as part of a system of support, and not just as resources that meet a particular need. Social support agencies could function as focal points to stabilize networks, but they would need long-term secure funding to do so. The state could more fully enact its dual responsibility to sustain an environment of support for individuals, as well as to mitigate against systemic market failures for individuals, whether because of caring responsibilities or gender inequity, or other issues. Recognizing the interaction of systems of support could potentially enable the market to function in an economically productive way for individuals by permitting women to partially engage in paid work without being penalized.

Redefining responsibilities calls for a radical change to the way we think about financial dependence, not just tinkering with policies to adjust for market conditions. If the caring responsibilities of families are to be preserved (and this study shows that this is at risk), then the support networks that mothers use and create need to be supported in conjunction with market engagement. The policy solution is therefore not to focus on the inabilities of income assistance recipients to cope financially, which is too narrow, as others have suggested (Brodie 2003; Bezanson 2006; Luxton 2006), but on how public policies, the private market, the community sector, and personal networks can work together to facilitate the necessary capacity and access for these women as well as the crucial caring work – that must be someone's responsibility.

The current policy model limits public responsibility to the provision of money, replacing provisioning by a male provider or breadwinner by the state, as Strell and Duncan found (2001). While clearly lack of money, or extreme poverty, is a serious problem, we argue along with Luxton (2006) and Bezanson (2006), that it is not the foundational impediment in these women's lives. To have a social justice solution, we need to put women in charge of organizing their resources, and to have the policy context support that endeavour. In this way, sources of support from family and friends, formal support agencies, and public policy initiatives interact to sustain lone parent women and their families. This revisioned policy framework includes not only income assistance policies but all policies regarding the everyday experiences of women as mothers, including housing policy, child care, labour market strategies, transportation, and food security. Policies need to include supports for fathers, to strengthen networks for women, as well as to permit informal support while recognizing dangers and risks. Local, provincial, regional, and federal policies also need to be linked together with a common ethic to create a context of support.

Re-visioning the family as an essential support system that is part of a larger community also addresses the problem of vulnerable mothers, such as those with fragile mental health, because then the mother does not have to hold all the answers herself. Instead of being critically stretched, a mother who needs healing or special supports can be added to a co-supportive web of interactions that permits her to contribute but does not penalize her for need. The contrasts are between a system where such a woman could access health supports while her children are well cared for in stable, professional, early childhood care centres versus another scenario where she becomes involved in substance abuse because she is too stressed and her children are removed from the family, at considerable tragedy to the extended family and expense to the public system. This contrast in policy highlights the problems with the individual responsibility model versus an ecological framework model. While proposing a sharing vision of care seems utopian in the present policy context, it is utterly achievable with a different vision of what constitutes work and responsibility within families and community.

Notes

1 This five-year study, The Income Assistance Project, is funded through the Consortium for Health, Intervention, Learning and Development (CHILD), a Social Science and Humanities Research Council (SSHRC) Major Collaborative Research Initiative (MCRI) project.
2 A criterion of the recruitment of study respondents was that their youngest child was less than 6 years old at the commencement of the study in order to document what occurred when their employment status changed.

References

Bezanson, Kate. (2006). The Neoliberal State and Social Reproduction: Gender and Household Insecurity in the Late 1990s. In Kate Bezanson and Meg

Luxton (eds.), *Social Reproduction: Feminist Political Economy Challenges Neoliberalism*, 173–214. Montreal and Kingston: McGill-Queen's University Press.

Bjornskov, Christian, with Gert Tinggaard Svendsen. (2003). *Measuring Social Capital: Is There a Single Explanation?* Department of Economics Working Paper 03-05. Aarhus: Aarhus School of Business.

Brodie, Janine. (2003). Globalization, In/security, and the Paradoxes of the Social. In Isabella Bakker and Stephen Gill (eds.), *Power, Production and Social Reproduction; Human In/security in the Global Political Economy*, 47–65. London and New York: Macmillan and Palgrave.

Bronfenbrenner, Urie. (1979). *The Ecology of Human Development: Experiments by Nature and Design*. Cambridge, MA: Harvard University Press.

DeFilippis, James. (2001). The Myth of Social Capital in Community Development. *Housing Policy Debate* 12(4): 781–806.

Dolfsma, Wilfred, John Finch, and Robert McMaster. (2005). Market and Society: How Do They Relate, and How Do They Contribute to Welfare? *Journal of Economic Issues* 39(2): 347–56.

Evers, Adalbert, Maarja Pilj, and Clare Ungerson (eds.). (1994). *Payments for Care: A Comparative Overview*. Aldershot, UK: Avebury. Cited in Paul W. Kershaw, *Carefair: Rethinking the Responsibilities and Rights of Citizenship* (Vancouver: UBC Press, 2005, 3).

Goldberg, Michael, and Kari Wolanski. (2005). *Left Behind: A Comparison of Living Costs and Employment and Assistance Rates*. Vancouver: SPARC.

Hare-Mustin, Rachel T. (1991). Sex, Lies and Headaches: The problem Is Power. *Journal of Feminist Family Therapy* 3: 39–61. Cited in Martha L.Weber, *She Stands Alone: A Review of the Recent Literature on Women and Social Support* (Winnipeg: Prairie Women's Health Centre of Excellence, University of Winnipeg, 1998, 21).

Jenson, Jane. (2004). *Canada's New Social Risks: Directions for a New Social Architecture*. Ottawa: Canadian Policy Research Networks.

Jenson, Jane, and Denis Saint-Martin. (2003). New Routes to Social Cohesion? Citizenhip and Social Investment State. Canadian Journal of Sociology 28(1): 77–99.

Kershaw, Paul W. (2005). *Carefair: Rethinking the Responsibilities and Rights of Citizenship*. Vancouver: UBC Press.

Kanaiaupuni, Shawn Malia, Theresa Thompson-Colón, and Katharine M. Donato. (2000). *Counting on Kin: Social Networks, Social Support and Child Health Status*. CDE Working Paper No. 2000-10. Madison: Center for Demography and Ecology, University of Wisconsin-Madison.

Luxton, Meg. (2006). Friends, Neighbours, and Community: A Case Study of the Role of Informal Caregiving in Social Reproduction. In Kate Bezanson and Meg Luxton (eds.), *Rethinking Social Reproduction: Feminist Political Economy Challenges Neoliberalism*, 263–89. Montreal and Kingston: McGill-Queen's University Press.

Neysmith, Sheila, and Marge Reitsma-Street. (2005). Provisioning: Conceptualizing the Work of Women for 21st Century Social Policy. *Women Studies International Forum* 28: 381–91.

Portes, Alejandro. (1998). Social Capital: Its Origins and Applications in Modern Sociology. *Annual Review of Sociology* 24: 1–24.

Rooke, Patricia T., and R.L. Schnell. (1983). *Discarding the Asylum: From Child Rescue to the Welfare State in English Canada, 1880-1950*. Lathan, MD: University Press of America.

Side, Katherine. (1997). *In the Shadow of the Family: Women's Friendships with Women*. Unpublished doctoral dissertation, Women's Studies, York University, Toronto.

Strell, Monica, and Simon Duncan. (2001). Lone Motherhood, Ideal Type Care Regimes and the Case of Austria. *Journal of European Social Policy* 11(2): 149–64.

Turnbull, Lorna A. (2001). *Double Jeopardy: Motherwork and the Law*. Toronto: Sumach Press.

Universiteit Twente. (2004). Theorieënoverzicht TCW: Social Support, The Netherlands. Electronic version retrieved 6 Oct. 2005 from http://www.tcw.utwente.nl/theorieenoverzichht/Alphabetic%20list%20of%20theories/index.html.

Vilches, Silvia, and Penny Gurstein. (2006). Income Assistance Rules Exhaust Women's Resources. *SPARC News* 23(2): 20–1.

Weber, Martha L. (1998). *She Stands Alone: A Review of the Recent Literature on Women and Social Support*. Winnipeg: Prairie Women's Health Centre of Excellence, University of Winnipeg.

Williams, Fiona, with Jenny Popay and Ann Oakley. (1999). *Welfare Research: A Critical Review*. London: University College of London.

PART THREE

Rethinking Labour Market and
Employment Support Policy

10 Income Security for Women: What about Employment Insurance?

MARTHA MacDONALD

How well does Employment Insurance (EI), the leading income security program in Canada, meet the economic security needs of women? The introduction of the Employment Insurance Act in 1996 considerably revamped Canada's Unemployment Insurance program (UI), introduced in 1940. EI created a complicated system of deserving and less-deserving unemployed through an intricate maze of targeting measures. The aim of the EI Act was to reduce 'dependency' on the state for income support, while generating surpluses to help eliminate the federal deficit. Almost as soon as the act was implemented minor changes were made, and the program has been tinkered with continually over the decade. Anne Porter (2003) has examined the evolution of UI as a gendered program: she found that during the UI period women's labour force attachment was suspect, and many women's jobs and unemployment risks (such as child-bearing) were not covered, or poorly covered, by the UI program in the early years. Not surprisingly, therefore, gender biases in the EI reform were identified before the new program came into effect (HRDC 1996b), and these issues have been debated in the courts and in the research ever since (Pulkingham 1998; Salhany 1998). Have the ensuing changes moderated the negative impacts of EI on women? Of particular concern are the implications for different types of work (part-time, seasonal, self-employed, etc.) and different types of workers (with respect to, e.g., age, income, dependents). What changes would make EI better serve the income security needs of women?

While most examinations of EI focus on a particular type of benefit (e.g., regular, maternity/parental, fishing), it is instructive to look at the evolution of the program as a whole. So, for example, while women's entitlements have deteriorated under regular EI, their entitlement to maternity/parental benefits has dramatically expanded. In addition, the new Compassionate Care Benefit offers funded leave to employees (most of whom are women) to provide end-of-life care to family members. The contrasting discourses on regular and special benefits are also interesting. While women's child-rearing and other caregiving responsibilities receive some support under the special programs, they are invisible and effectively penalized within regular EI.

Welfare State Restructuring and Gender

The introduction of EI, as well as the Canada Health and Social Transfer (CHST), was premised on reduced state expenditures, targeted social security spending, and the primacy of employment for meeting economic security needs. Canada, like other liberal welfare regimes, was responding to changes in demographics, labour markets, family structure, and political ideology. In the metaphor of the welfare diamond, the changes continued the shift towards a decreased role for the state and an increased role not only for the market but also for family and community. The reforms have been interpreted as consolidating a neoliberal welfare state (McKeen and Porter 2003; MacDonald 1999).

The new welfare state is not just about cuts, but also about a different conception of social policy that has become clearer in the post-deficit period. To the extent that the state promotes equality, it is equality of opportunity, not of outcomes. Thus, the state may invest in human and social capital to enable individuals to support themselves through the market. However, not all investments have equal expected value. Thus, children are obvious targets for future-oriented spending and are the new 'deserving poor' (Wiegers 2002; Dobrowolsky and Jenson 2004). The form of social spending also differs in this new welfare state and is distinguishable from either the Keynesian or the social democratic state. Tax expenditures (targeted tax breaks for the 'needy') are preferred, because it is a market approach to social issues that puts money in the hand of 'consumers' rather than delivering services; where services are involved, the state is inclined to be a purchaser rather than a provider; and income security entitlements are even more targeted to those most in need financially, rather than provided on the basis of the principle of universality.[1] Each of these spending methods relies on the market, implicitly or explicitly, to deliver critical social supports and services.

The mid-1990s reforms reflect the erosion of the male breadwinner model as the basis of social policy. The feminist welfare state literature focuses on the relationship of production and reproduction and the underlying assumptions about gender roles implicit in state policies. In the liberal welfare regimes, the male breadwinner model clearly predominated. Adult men were assumed to be the family breadwinners, and they received social security entitlements through their market activity. Programs such as the Canada Pension Plan, Unemployment Insurance, and workers' compensation were all policies designed around male models of employment. Adult women were assumed to be caregivers and received social security entitlements mainly through their connection with male earners, or in their absence, through second-tier state benefits such as social assistance, if they were destitute, and Old Age Security benefits if they were old and destitute. While the male breadwinner model is still an assumption in the design of much Canadian social policy, the model of an 'adult worker,' 'citizen worker,' or 'universal worker' has emerged and is reflected in the major social policy reforms of the past decade. This model takes as its premise the expectation that adults be self-supporting, whether or not they have caregiving responsibilities. Social policy is then framed to foster and support the primacy of labour market participation and economic self-sufficiency. As Ruth Lister points out (2004), even the emphasis on children reflects their value as future 'worker citizens,' not as 'child citizens.' Nevertheless, feminists emphasize that, although the adult earner model may seem to be gender-neutral, the realities of male and female earners remain very different, and caregiving remains profoundly gendered. Gender-blind policies based on a universal earner model have deeply gendered impacts.

Both the welfare regimes literature and the feminist welfare state perspective point to a crisis of social reproduction in the current context (Esping-Anderson 2003; Lewis 2001). Analysts observe a vacuum in caregiving created by women's labour force attachment, state funding cuts, and an aging population. The policies associated with the adult worker model have not adequately addressed these challenges for social reproduction. The default approach of the state is to count on women increasing their work burden to meet care needs as they juggle paid work, child-rearing, elder care, and community volunteer work (Baines 2004; Williams 2004). While women have long suffered the consequences of this approach by the state, its broader social and economic feedback effects are now being manifested in falling birth rates and stress-related productivity problems.

The new configuration of the welfare state relies heavily on women's work of social reproduction as well as on their labour force participation. The universal breadwinners in the new model are by no means equal, and it is not a universal caregiver model, where each adult is expected to take on caregiving responsibilities (Stark 2005). To view EI through this lens is instructive, as assumptions about women's roles as workers and caregivers are intricately interwoven in the program. New policies retain elements of the male breadwinner model, since the prototypical work pattern is implicitly 'male,' and the generic caregiver is implicitly female.

Several themes common to recent welfare state restructuring will be used in this chapter to examine the past decade of EI changes: these changes increasingly rely on approaches that privilege individual responsibility, the primacy of employment as the source of economic security, the privatization of care (to the family, or the market), more means-testing based on family income so that all benefits are increasingly like 'welfare,' the increased use of the tax system for the targeting and delivery of benefits, and a focus on children as the most deserving group for state benefits. Alternatives to these types of expectations of public policy that would better serve the economic security needs of women will also be raised.

Regular Employment Insurance

As already noted, the 1996 reform of regular UI benefits hurt women more than men (Pulkingham 1998; CLC 1999). With the change to an hours-based system (with the first hour of work counting), more women became contributors but fewer were able to qualify for benefits.[2] The translation of weeks required for UI to hours required for EI used a thirty-five-hour work week as the 'norm,' clearly a male norm. This formula increased the amount of work needed to qualify for people working less than thirty-five hours a week, disproportionately women. Women were further affected by the tough new entrant/re-entrant (NERE) rules, where the number of hours needed to qualify for benefits jumped to 910 for those who had worked less than 490 hours (or equivalent EI benefit weeks) in the year preceding the qualifying period, thus penalizing anyone with an irregular work pattern or anyone who takes time out in relation to caregiving – again, a requirement that is more likely to affect women (Phipps and MacPail 2000; HRDC 1999).

The underlying aim of the reform was to encourage continuous labour force attachment and provide incentives for people to take any and all available work. Several penalties were built in for this purpose. The intensity rule penalized repeat users of EI by gradually lowering the benefit rate from 55 per cent to 50 per cent of insurable earnings; the high-income claw-back also had an escalating rate based on past EI use, and the benefit formula used a 'minimum divisor' to calculate average insurable earnings, resulting in lower benefits for those who qualified with less than fourteen to twenty-two weeks of work (depending on regional unemployment rates).[3]

People were affected differently depending on the nature of their work. Part-time workers (predominantly female) were hurt in terms of both eligibility and duration of benefits, so much so that a court challenge claimed discrimination based on gender (Salhany 1998).[4] Seasonal workers with long hours (predominantly males) could qualify more easily, but were hurt by measures that penalized repeat users (HRDC 2001b; 2001c). Seasonal workers with low earnings or less than thirty hours of work per week (disproportionately women) lost significantly in terms of eligibility under EI (de Raaf et al. 2003). Holders of multiple jobs fared better under EI than under UI (HRDC 2001a). Meanwhile, the 'ideal' (male) worker with a full-time job, who rarely faced unemployment, would have noticed little difference. Self-employed workers – a growing proportion of whom are women – remained outside the system. Thus, while the male breadwinner ideology that permeated UI throughout most of its history was now absent, the adult worker model underpinning EI translated the inequalities of a gendered labour market into differential entitlements (Porter 2003).

These program parameters are consistent with the neoliberal welfare state's emphasis on the primacy of the market and its discouragement of dependency on state income security programs. 'Good' workers are rewarded and 'bad' ones are punished. The implicit assumption is that work is available for the asking. EI also continued the policy begun in 1977 of using UI/EI funds for 'employment benefits and support measures,' as they are now called, such as counselling, skills development, and wage subsidies. Women's access to training actually decreased, however, as training became almost exclusively tied to EI eligibility (Cohen 2003),[5] and the delivery model changed to one of partnership and individual responsibility, so that those who are eligible must contribute to the costs of their training.[6]

The parameters have been tinkered with over the past decade, mostly to remove so-called unforeseen work disincentives and enhance the EI program's original intent to promote labour force attachment. For example, the benefit formula discouraged workers from taking weeks of work with lower earnings, as this reduced average earnings and thus benefits. In response to complaints by employers and employees, and after a series of pilot projects, a 2001 amendment ignores 'small weeks' (earnings less than $225) in the benefit calculation if a person has more than the minimum divisor number of weeks (meaning many seasonal workers do not benefit from this provision). Also in late 2000 the intensity rule and the escalating claw-back for repeat users were dropped. These two changes were seen as political, given the intense opposition in regions with high concentrations of seasonal work. Both were bigger issues for men than for women, given that more repeat users and high earners are males (Stratychuk 2001; de Raaf et al. 2003).

Another area that has seen modest change is the NERE requirement. It was quickly recognized that parents returning from child-related leaves could be 'inadvertently' classified as re-entrants. Thus, as of 2000, parents who have received maternity/parental benefits in the previous five years are subject to only the normal EI eligibility rules (420–700 hours). However, parents who did not qualify for maternity/parental benefits, discussed below, still face the requirement of 910 hours, as do people who take time out for other kinds of caregiving – again, mostly women. NERE rules continue to create pressure on workers to maintain continuous labour force attachment, consistent with the adult worker model. Women and other workers in precarious jobs have difficulties meeting this ideal. For seasonal workers, for example, there is extreme pressure to stay on the work/EI treadmill, as finding 910 hours of work can be impossible.[7]

The latest area to be tinkered with is the benefit formula. Average insurable earnings are based on the last twenty-six weeks of work, subject to the minimum divisor. This can seriously lower the benefits of those with irregular or fluctuating earnings, or those who qualify with limited weeks of employment, such as substitute teachers, casual workers, and seasonal workers. The 'small weeks' provision did not fully address this problem. Presentations to the Task Force on Seasonal Work called for the use of the best twelve weeks of earnings (FFAW 2004). In October 2005 a pilot project to use the best fourteen weeks (out of 52) in calculating average earnings began in high-unemployment regions. Note, however, that this leaves the minimum divisor in place, which is of particular concern to seasonal workers. While the change to the fourteen best weeks will be welcomed by precarious workers, it also enhances the availability to employers of a flexible workforce by making benefits less responsive to fluctuations in earnings. In the language of HRDC, it will 'promote labour force attachment,' or the willingness to take any and all work available.

Another change since 1996-97 also reflects the ongoing fine-tuning of work incentives in EI. In 2005 a pilot project in high-unemployment regions increased the allowable earnings while on EI (to $75 per week, or 40% of benefits), encouraging people to work while on EI, as it reduces the effective 'tax' on earnings. Given that EI maximum benefit levels were lowered to $413 a week in 1996, and stayed there for ten years, allowing claimants to supplement their benefits (rather than raising benefits) is consistent with making EI more like welfare (keep benefits low and increase the pressure to be an 'earner'). Thus, it seems that regular EI is becoming more of an income supplement than an earnings replacement program in these regions, supporting a precarious, low-wage workforce.

A final change relates to the duration of benefits: the maximum number of weeks was reduced to forty-five under EI, and dramatically reduced for part-time workers. A 2004 pilot project increased the duration of benefits for eligible workers in high-unemployment regions. According to the findings of the pilot project, 'some part-time, seasonal and workers with short employment periods, because of the very nature of their work, face situations where their EI benefits end before finding new employment' (Service Canada 2007: n.p.). This pilot project provides five additional weeks of regular benefits to such workers with 'few employment alternatives' (ibid.).[8]

While women's work patterns resulted in loss of eligibility for EI compared with UI for many women, some women who continued to qualify for EI saw their benefits increase because they were in low-income families with children and so also qualified for the family supplement (FS). The idea of differentiating workers with dependents from those without is not new in UI. In fact in the early years of UI, such a differentiation existed. However, at that time it was in the context of an unemployment insurance scheme based on the male breadwinner model, where claimants (mainly men) with dependent spouses, or those who were the main supporters of dependent children, got higher benefits (Porter 2003: 44). This provision was dropped in 1975 as a cost-cutting measure, but returned in 1994 to soften the blow when the benefit rate was reduced to 55 per cent of insurable earnings; low-earning claimants with dependents under the age of 16 received a benefit rate of 60 per cent of their individual insurable earnings. Note that this model did not reward those who are supporting spouses, as all adults are expected to be workers. With EI, support for dependents took another turn by basing eligibility on family income, not individual earnings. The use of family income to evaluate need is associated with welfare and moves the program away from a more narrowly cast social insurance model that adopts a singular earnings replacement ratio for eligible claimants based on employment criteria alone. Most feminist economists argue that a real universal earner policy would base entitlements on individual earnings, and then separately deal with income support for children (MacDonald 1998). The family supplement, like social assistance, targets the neediest; furthermore, it divides the unemployed into more deserving (those with children) and less deserving (those without children). Lone mothers benefited from the increased generosity of the family supplement, while mothers with higher-income spouses lost eligibility (Phipps et al. 2001). Such supplements do not address the fundamental problem that women's low EI benefits mirror gender inequality in the labour market.

In summary, although the changes to regular EI over the past decade have addressed some of the concerns that workers and employers had with the initial 1996 reform – and most changes were certainly welcomed – the major gender concerns have not been addressed. These include the impact on part-time workers, the implications of NERE rules for caregivers, and the pressure to take any and all available work. Interestingly, most of the changes have enhanced the incentives to take precarious work; however, women and men in some precarious jobs continue to be poorly served by the minimum divisor and the exclusion of the self-employed. Beneficiaries in low-income families with children have benefited from the more generous family supplement, consistent with the neoliberal welfare state's focus on children as the only 'deserving poor.' In fact, it could be argued that women have a stronger claim on EI now as mothers than as workers, given the precariousness of many of their jobs. Under regular EI, the female adult worker is poorly insured – unless she is also a mother.

Maternity/Parental Benefits

As under UI, most provisions developed for regular EI benefits in the 1996 reform were applied to maternity and parental benefits. For example, the benefit rate calculation was the same (including the family supplement), the NERE rules and two-week waiting period applied, and the self-employed were not covered. The maximum number of eligible weeks of maternity, parental, and sickness benefits combined remained at thirty, where it has been since 1990 (Perusse 2003).

As under UI, EI maternity/parental benefits differ from regular EI benefits in that eligibility and duration are fixed and not related to regional unemployment rates. The previous eligibility requirement of twenty weeks was translated into 700 hours, and as with regular benefits, women working less than thirty-five hours a week find it harder to qualify, especially in high-unemployment areas. In addition, the high-income claw-back is not applied to maternity/parental benefits. Thus, the program parameters combine some of the logic of regular benefits (around labour force attachment and benefit levels, with emphasis on work incentives) with the logic of supporting caregiving (particularly the set length of benefits).

The potential impact of the change from weeks to hours was dramatic. A part-time worker could have qualified under UI with as few as 300 hours (15 x 20), compared with the 700 hours now needed. There was also concern that qualifying would be particularly difficult for women who already had children, as they would be more likely to work part-time (Salhany 1998). However, an HRDC evaluation found that 90 per cent of those who left jobs for maternity-related reasons (as shown on their ROEs, records of employment) had the required 700 hours; the evaluation also found little difference for those who already had children. In a related study, Shelley Phipps (2001) found that, while the UI/EI change did not reduce overall eligibility, younger mothers, those in casual employment, and those who worked for smaller firms were less likely to qualify under either UI or EI rules. It should also be noted that, in 2000, about 20 per cent of mothers who were eligible did not participate in the parental benefits program (HRDC 2004a: 20), perhaps for reasons related to other program parameters, such as benefit levels. Furthermore, many participants returned to work early, especially younger workers, lone parents, those whose spouses did not work full-time, and those with post-secondary education (Phipps 2001).

There was considerable objection to the 700-hour entrance requirement, including a court challenge (Salhany 1998). Furthermore, women who took maternity might find themselves caught by the higher NERE requirement with subsequent children. In response to these concerns, the required hours were decreased to 600, and the NERE rules were adjusted to exempt those who had received maternity or parental benefits in the five years before the qualifying period. In addition, the two-week waiting period was dropped for the second parent. The rationale for these December 2000 changes was that maternity/parental benefits had been inappropriately and inadvertently caught in the logic of regular benefits (specifically the NERE rules, the two-week waiting period for each claim, and the use of thirty-five hours to translate into a UI week). At the same time maximum weeks of parental benefits were increased dramatically, from ten to thirty-five, with a combined maximum benefits period of fifty weeks of sickness, maternity, and parental benefits (raised to 65 weeks in 2004).

Several empirical studies have examined the impact of these changes. The reduction in the number of hours required to receive maternity benefits resulted in a 4.4 per cent increase in women qualifying and a doubling of total benefits paid between 2000 and 2002 (Perusse 2003). The proportion of all new mothers receiving benefits increased in 2001, but 12 per cent of new mothers were employees who did not meet the entrance requirements for benefits, and another 5 per cent were self-employed and thus excluded from the program (Marshall 2003). Phipps finds that significant differences persist among women with regard to the likelihood of receiving benefits, with lone parents, younger mothers, those with less education, and those with other children being less likely to report receiving benefits (2006: 43). Not surprisingly, the length of leave taken has increased (Marshall 2003: 6); however, lower earnings were associated with an earlier return to work.

While the 2000 changes addressed some (although not all) of the eligibility concerns, no changes were made in benefit levels. Human Resources and Skills Development Canada (2005a) found that low benefit levels were the main complaint about the program. Average weekly benefits remained unchanged, at $295 per week. Dominique Perusse (2003) reports that women beneficiaries had fewer hours and lower insurable earnings (and therefore benefits) compared with men. As with regular EI, how parents fare depends on their type of work and also, because of the family supplement, their family income. Phipps (2006) reports changes over time in the entitlements of new parents, relative to their work and family characteristics. Total benefit entitlements of the 'typical' new mother have increased dramatically since 1971, but weekly benefits have actually declined, even since 1997, as the real value of maximum benefits has decreased along with the benefit rate. The effective weekly replacement rate for high-earning mothers has also declined, given the freeze in maximum insurable earnings (MIE; Phipps 2006).

The program clearly reflects an adult earner model: stay-at-home parents do not benefit. Fairly continuous labour force attachment is needed to remain in the system (note that eligibility decreases with more children, as it becomes more difficult to meet this norm). Also, as with regular benefits, non-standard work is penalized compared with full-time work, and recent changes increase the incentive for workers to take on more precarious work.[9]

Although parental benefits appear to be gender-neutral, it is significant that the interaction of the program parameters with gendered labour markets leave women as the main recipients (93%; Perusse 2003) of parental benefits. The low benefit rate encourages the lower earner (usually the mother) to take the benefits. On the other hand, more men may be in a position to get benefits topped up by the employer. The program does not move us to a universal carer model. Also, the program is narrowly focused on the first year of child-rearing, leaving parents on their own to cope during the remaining years. The lack of flexibility in how time off can be structured is a key criticism of the program (Phipps 2006; Women's Network PEI 2004.).

The EI maternity/parental parameters can be compared with the new Quebec Parental Insurance Plan, implemented in January 2006 (Phipps 2006; Tremblay, chapter 11 in this volume).[10] The QPIP has more flexibility, offering an option of higher earnings replacement rates (75%) for a shorter duration (15 weeks of maternity, 25 shared parental, and 3 weeks father-only benefits), or a Plan B, with a longer duration but a lower earnings replacement rate (some weeks at 70% and some at 55%). The QPIP raises maximum insurable earnings (to $57,500) and thus increases benefits under either of its plans or options. These provisions address the concern of low effective earnings replacement rates under EI, especially for higher earners. Furthermore, the eligibility requirement is $2,000 in earnings, which is considerably lower than EI and includes self-employed workers.[11] There is no waiting period. These changes remove the tie-in between the rules and incentives for regular EI and maternity/parental benefits. The reasons given for excluding the self-employed from regular benefits (the 'moral hazard' argument that the self-employed can contrive to lay themselves off) makes no sense in terms of maternity/parental benefits.

The QPIP adds to the debate about whether maternity/parental benefits should remain within EI or be a separate program, as in most other countries. The Supreme Court of Canada confirmed the constitutionality of the federal government's provision of maternity/parental benefits through the Employment Insurance Commission (HRSDC 2005b), while allowing the transfer of EI funds to Quebec to support its own program. Many social policy advocates breathed a sigh of relief, as the ruling retains a national program for the rest of the country.[12] There was fear that if the program devolved to the provinces, many would choose – or only be able to afford – to offer less than is now available.

There remains the option of keeping the maternity/parental program federal but taking it out of EI. Again, the likelihood of getting agreement in the current context is low, as we have seen with a national child care strategy. Furthermore, there is some political advantage in having a broad set of employment interruptions legitimized and insured under EI. The Quebec program gives a concrete example of how the major weaknesses of maternity/parental benefits – lack of access for many women in non-standard paid work, lack of coverage for the self-employed, low earning replacement rates, and inflexibility in the structure of the leave – could be addressed even within EI (Phipps 2006). Maternity/parental benefits are the warm face of EI, and it is possible that experiments within this program could lead to positive changes in the parameters for regular benefits. It is likely, for example, that the self-employed will be first brought into maternity/parental benefits.

Compassionate Care Benefits

In 2003 a new EI benefit, the Compassionate Care Benefit (CCB) was introduced (Bill C-28, effective January 2004) to address the needs of workers who provide care to dying family members. The Speech from the Throne (2002) stated that the government was committed to modifying existing programs 'to ensure that Canadians can provide compassionate care to a gravely ill or dying child, parent or spouse without putting their jobs or income at risk' (HRDC 2004b: 2). Such a program was recommended in the Kirby Report, and is consistent with the Romanow Report's call for direct support for the informal caregivers on whom health care restructuring has relied (Fletcher 2006; HRDC 2004b).

HRDC's background materials on this program indicate that Human Resources and Development Canada sees the CCB as part of a 'global movement toward more family-friendly labour legislation' (2004b: 4). The CCB is firmly situated within an adult worker model, where many care responsibilities also reside with the family. The state facilitates the provision of care in the private sphere by adults (mainly women), who are expected to also be employees. HRDC notes that while Sweden, for example, provides up to sixty days leave at 80 per cent pay, comparable liberal welfare regimes like the United Kingdom and Australia have far more modest benefits. Canada's Compassionate Care Benefit is more generous than some, but still quite limited.

Eligibility for the CCB is based on the rules for other EI special benefits, including maternity/parental (as amended in 2000): 600 hours of insurable employment are needed to qualify for up to six weeks of compassionate care benefits (with a two-week waiting period). As with parental benefits, the leave can be shared among family members, and only one waiting period needs to be served. The calculation of benefits is the same as for regular EI and other special benefits. Claimants must obtain a medical certificate stating that the family member is gravely ill and that the claimant could provide care and support. There is a six-month window within which to take the six weeks of leave.

HRDC consulted widely with stakeholders before implementing the CCB (Cummings 2001; Fast et al. 2002a; 2002b). It was clear within the first year, however, that the take-up rate was considerably lower than the 270,000 expected. In 2004-05 less than 4 per cent of the $190 million EI budget for compassionate care claims was spent (Osborne and Margo 2005: 6). An evaluation has been under way since 2004 to better understand the problems with the program (HRDC 2004b). Critical reaction to the program centres on key parameters that limit its effectiveness.[13] For example, the definition of for whom one can provide care is narrow – one's child, parent or parent-in-law, spouse or common-law partner. The requirement for medical certification of impending death also poses a barrier, certainly on an emotional level. Furthermore, many people provide care for very ill family members who do, in fact, have a reasonable chance of recovery. In addition, the length of the leave is short, given the unpredictability of terminal illness. The concept of care is based on a narrow medical model: 'providing or participating in the care of the patient, or arranging for the care of the patient by a third-party care provider, or providing psychological or emotional support to the patient' (HRSDC 2004: n.p.). The CCB ends upon death, even if the six weeks have not been used up; however, the time following death may demand at least as much caregiving, under a broader notion of care. Although many of these concerns have been acknowledged, and the program is under review, no changes have yet been made to the legislation.[14]

A major concern about the CCB program is that it entitles only a narrow set of end-of-life caregivers to its benefits, namely, people who are employed and can meet the EI eligibility requirements. All the issues noted above for regular benefits apply, such as omission of the self-employed and difficulties for workers in part-time, seasonal, and other non-standard jobs.

The CCB program enables workers to maintain their labour market connection, and it also enables employers to retain workers. The CCB program is perhaps the prototype for further expansion of benefits for employment interruptions related to caregiving. For now, EI provides some support for the care of those at the very beginning and those at the very end of life, care provided mostly by women. There is much caregiving in between, which women handle as best they can, often by taking the very types of work that undermine their EI entitlements.

Conclusion

It has been a decade since implementation of the Employment Insurance reform began, and the program has continued to evolve. Changes to regular benefits have been mainly to fine-tune the original incentives, but those to special benefits have been more substantive. Some of the most punitive elements of the program have been withdrawn (e.g., the intensity rule), yet the issues raised about women's entitlements have not been addressed. Over the past decade, women have benefited only as mothers, with the changes to special benefits and the increased family supplement.

No change has been made in eligibility for regular benefits and the new entrant/re-entrant rules remain in place, despite widespread acknowledgment of the difficulties posed for workers in precarious employment. No change was been made in a decade to the level of minimum insurable earnings (the earnings ceiling for paying premiums), and therefore benefits, with the result that effective earnings replacement rates fell. Several changes have adjusted the benefit formula to encourage people to take all available hours of work, benefiting employers as much as workers. Encouraging and rewarding labour force attachment remains the hallmark of EI. The cut-backs, which were part of the original design, are essentially still in place and the savings have been realized.[15]

Women were hurt more than men by the original EI reform in 1996, losing eligibility and duration of benefits. The number of regular claims by women fell by 25 per cent over the decade, compared with a fall of 22 per cent for men (HRSDC 2006). Note that, while women made up only

40.5 per cent of regular EI claimants in 2004-05, they constituted 44.7 per cent of the unemployed in 2005 (Statistics Canada 2006). Women also received only 34 per cent of regular benefit dollars (in 2004-05), reflecting both their lower average insurable earnings and their shorter entitlements in terms of weeks (HRSDC 2006). While women now receive almost half of total EI payments, this is almost totally due to the increased generosity of the caregiving-related benefits (maternity/parental and compassionate care benefits). ⟩

Employment Insurance clearly reflects an adult worker model, and many of the changes over the past decade reflect the state's grappling with the caregiving tensions inherent in that model. Parental benefits have been enhanced, and the new CCB opens the door for insuring other care-related employment interruptions. Labour force attachment is necessary to access these benefits, and families are expected to provide the care. These policies are not gender-neutral. While the caregivers are overwhelmingly women, gender inequalities in work patterns (themselves partly related to caregiving) limit some women's access and/or benefits (most notably in the case of part-time workers and those who take time out of the labour force). The low earnings replacement rate means some return to work early, and it also reinforces women's continued responsibility for caregiving (the lower earner in a dual-earner family, typically the mother, is the 'rational' one to take the leave).

Women's responsibilities as income earners and caregivers permeate their experience of both regular and special Employment Insurance. These same norms, ironically, are applied to the caregiving benefits. While the state is providing more caregiving benefits, it is relying on – and reinforcing – women's responsibility for care. If gender equality is to be promoted, or caregiving integrated within an adult worker model, changes will have to be made to both types of benefits.

Women's income security needs would be better served by a program that improves the nexus with their employment and takes account of caregiving in the design of the full range of benefits. The implicit use of a male work norm (full-time and continuous work) in setting EI parameters must be addressed. All people with care-related work interruptions should be exempt from the NERE eligibility rules. Weeks of work, as well as hours, should be taken into account in determining part-time worker eligibility and claims' duration, so that the penalty to those working fewer than thirty-five hours per week is eliminated. The minimum divisor should be dropped, and the benefit formula should use the best twelve weeks of work over a longer time frame, say five years, so that it is neutral with respect to the timing of work. A benefit floor should be considered, given the low earnings of many women; and self-employed workers should be covered for both regular and special benefits. As Diane-Gabrielle Tremblay shows (see chapter 11 in this volume), the Quebec program provides an excellent example of how special benefits can be improved, in terms of both generosity and flexibility. The parameters need to be liberated from the logic of regular EI. The waiting period, the one-year qualifying period, the low earnings replacement rate, and other parameters to create work incentives make no sense for special benefits. Other incentives do need to be built in, for example, incentives that would encourage fathers to take more leave, or enable flexibility in the timing of leaves, including returning to work part-time.

Notes

1 Universality means benefits are delivered to the whole population in question (such as all families with children, or all seniors, or all unemployed) rather than to a particular subset (low-income families with children, poor seniors, unemployed people with dependents).

2 The 1998 *EI Monitoring and Assessment Report* showed a 20% decrease in claims by women compared with a 16% decrease for men between 1995–96 and 1997–98 (HRDC 1999). Various ways of calculating EI eligibility/unemployed also consistently show lower rates for women (HRSDC 2005a: 1005; CLC 1999; 2003).

3 Thus, for calculation of benefits, a seasonal worker in a high-unemployment region (where one needs 420 hours to qualify for EI) would have her earnings averaged over 14 weeks (even though 420 hours might be achieved in a 10-week season). One who needs 700 hours (in a very low-unemployment region) and has worked only 20 weeks would have her earnings averaged over 22 weeks. This results in lower benefit levels.

4 The ruling by the Umpire, Salhany, agreed the legislation discriminated against women and violated the Charter of Rights and Freedoms, but the government appealed the decision in a Federal Court of Appeal, where it was overturned.

5 This chapter does not discuss changes to these measures over the decade. Implementation took many years.

6 Training Purchases were gradually phased out and extended UI benefits for those in training programs ended.

7 A pilot project started in December 2005 in high-unemployment regions

allows NEREs with only 840–909 hours in the qualifying period to be eligible for EI if they agree to participate in 'employment measures' (such as counselling or career planning) to enhance their job prospects. A similar approach was taken by the The Atlantic Groundfish Strategy (TAGS) program, where applicants had to participate in 'active' labour market measures to get income benefits; however, the measures were often viewed as demeaning and inappropriate (HRDC 1996a).

8 Note that the testing ground for all of these pilot programs has been high-unemployment regions. This may reflect the political pressure from employers in such areas who depend on EI to maintain a flexible work-force. UI/EI not only maintains individual workers, it supports employers and communities. In high-unemployment areas it is also less reasonable to expect that workers can easily 'adjust' out of precarious work and into full-time stable employment.

9 Many of the changes over the decade to regular benefits also apply to maternity/parental benefits, including the pilot projects on using the 14 best weeks in the benefit formula and allowing more earnings while on EI.

10 For details, see the Quebec Parental Insurance Plan. Electronic version retrieved on 2 Feb. 2008, from http://www.rqap.gouv.qc.ca/index_en.asp.

11 It should be noted that there is a precedent in EI for using an earnings criterion and insuring the self-employed, namely, fishing benefits.

12 Groups that came out in support of the ruling included the Network on Women's Social and Economic Rights, the Canadian Centre for Policy Al-ternatives, the CAW, NUPE, and NAWL. However, all groups also urged the government to reform the EI program (e.g., to enable more women to qualify and to enhance earnings replacement rates).

13 See, e.g., the recent Health Council of Canada evaluation for a good sum-mary of these issues (Osborne and Margo 2005).

14 Former Minister Belinda Stronach announced in November 2005 that the government was planning to allow the patient to designate the appropri-ate caregiver, rather than limiting it to immediate family; however, this has not been implemented (HRSDC 2005c).

15 The *2005 Monitoring and Assessment Report* estimated an average annual savings of $1.4 billion per year from the 1996 reform (HRSDC 2006: 93).

References

Baines, Donna. (2004). Seven Kinds of Work – Only One Paid: Raced, Gen-dered and Restructured Work in Social Services. *Atlantis* 28(2): 21.

Canadian Labour Congress (CLC). (2003). *Falling Unemployment Insurance Protection for Canada's Unemployed.* Ottawa: CLC.

– (1999). *Left Out in the Cold: The End of UI for Canadian Workers.* Ottawa: CLC.

Cohen, Marjorie Griffin (ed.). (2003). *Training the Excluded for Work: Access andEequity for Women,Immigrants, First Nations, Youth and People with Low Income.* Vancouver: UBC Press.

Cummings, Joanne. (2001). *Report on Working Parents with Gravely Ill Children.* Canadian Alliance for Children's Healthcare. Submitted to HRDC, Ottawa.

de Raaf, Shawn, Costa Kapsalis, and Carole Vincent. (2003). Seasonal Work and Employment Insurance Use. *Perspectives on Labour and Income* 4(9: 5–11.

Dobrowolsky, Alexandra, and Jane Jenson. (2004). Shifting Representation of Citizenship: Canadian Politics of 'Women' and 'Children.' *Social Politics* 11(2): 154–80.

Esping-Andersen, Gosta. (2003). Women in the New Welfare Equilibrium. *European Legacy* 8(5): 599–610.

Fast, Janet, Linda Niehaus, Jaquie Eales, and Norah Keating. (2002a). *A Profile of Canadian Palliative Care Providers.* Report submitted to HRDC, Ottawa.

– (2002b). *A Profile of Canadian Chronic Care Providers.* Report submitted to HRDC, Ottawa.

Fish, Food and Allied Workers (FFAW). (2004). *Presentation to the Task Force on Seasonal Work.* Retrieved on 2 Feb. 2007, from www.ffaw.nf.ca/BriefDetails. asp?id=4.

Fletcher, Stephanie. (2006). The Canadian Policy Response to the Crisis of Care: Opportunities and Consequences for Women. Unpublished MA thesis, Women's Studies, Saint Mary's University, Halifax.

Human Resources Development Canada (HRDC). (1996a). TAGS: *The Atlantic Groundfish Strategy:Background Paper TAGS Household Study.* Ottawa: HRDC, Cat. No. SP-AH007E-BP1-01-96.

– (1996b). *Employment Insurance: Gender Iimpact Analysis.* Ottawa: HRDC.

– (1999). *Employment Insurance 1999 Monitoring and Assessment Report.* Ottawa: HRDC.

– (2001a). *EI Reform and Multiple Job-Holding.* Ottawa: HRDC.

– (2001b). *An Evaluation Overview of Seasonal Employment, EI Evaluation, Evaluation and Data Development.* Strategic Policy. Ottawa: HRDC.

– (2001c). *EI Reform and Seasonal Workers that Earn Less than $12,000. Final Report.* Employment Insurance Evaluations Strategic Evaluations, Evaluation and Data Development, Strategic Policy. Ottawa: HRDC, Cat. No. SP-ML013-12-01E.

– (2004a). *Evaluation of EI Parental Benefits, Evaluation and Data Development.* Strategic Policy. Ottawa: HRDC.

– (2004b). *Evaluation Framework of the Evaluation of EI Compassionate Care Benefits*. EI Evaluation, Program Evaluation. Ottawa: HRDC.

Human Resources and Skills Development Canada (HRSDC). (2004). A New Employment Insurance Benefit – Compassionate Care Benefit. Press release, 6 Jan.

– (2005a). *Summative Evaluation of EI Parental Benefits, Final Report*. Program Evaluation, Strategic Policy and Planning. Ottawa: HRSDC, Cat. No. SP-AH-674-01-05E.

– (2005b). Government of Canada Responds to the Supreme Court of Canada Decision on Employment Insurance Maternity and Parental Benefits. Press Release, 20 Oct. Electronic version retrieved 25 May 2006 from http://news.gc.ca/web/view/en/index.jsp?articleid=176459&.

– (2005c). Government of Canada Initiates Regulatory Changes to Expand Eligibility Criteria for the Employment Insurance Compassionate Care Benefit. Press Release, 28 Nov. Electronic version retrieved 24 May 2006 from http://news.gc.ca/web/view/en/index.jsp?articleid=186529&.

– (2006). *Employment Insurance 2005 Monitoring and Assessment Report*. Ottawa: HRSDC, Cat. No. SP-102-04-06E.

Lewis, Jane. (2001). The Decline of the Male Breadwinner Model: The Implications for Work and Care. *Social Politics* 8(2): 152–69.

Lister, Ruth. (2004). The Third Way's Social Investment State. In Jane Lewis and Rebecca Surender (eds.), *Welfare State Change: Towards a Third Way?* 157–82. Oxford and New York: Oxford University Press.

MacDonald, Martha. (1999). Restructuring, Gender and Social Security Reform in Canada. *Journal of Canadian Studies* 34(2): 57–88.

– (1998). Gender and Social Security Policy: Pitfalls and Possibilities. *Feminist Economics* 4(1): 1–25.

Marshall, Katherine. (2003). Benefiting from Extended Parental Leave. *Perspectives on Labour and Income* 4(3): 5–11.

McKeen, Wendy, and Ann Porter. (2003). Politics and Transformation: Welfare State Restructuring in Canada. In Wallace Clement and Leah F. Vosko (eds.), *Changing Canada: Political Economy as Transformation*, 109–34. Montreal and Kingston: McGill-Queen's University Press.

Osborne, Kate, and Naomi Margo. (2005). *Analysis and Evaluation: Compassionate Care Benefit*. Toronto: Health Council of Canada.

Pérusse, Dominique. (2003). New Maternity and Parental Benefits. *Perspectives on Labour and Income* 4(3): 12–15.

Phipps, Shelley. (2006). Working for Working Parents: The Evolution of Maternity and Parental Benefits in Canada. *IRPP Choices* 12(2).

– (2001). *Unemployment Insurance – Employment Insurance Transition: An Evalu-*

ation of the Pre-2001 Maternity and Parental Benefits Program in Canada. Strate-
   gic Evaluation and Monitoring, Evaluation and Data Development. Ottawa:
   HRDC, Cat. No. SP-AH133-03-00E.
Phipps, Shelley, Martha MacDonald, and Fiona MacPhail. (2001). Gender
   Equity within Families versus Better Targeting: An Assessment of the Fam-
   ily Income Supplement to Employment Insurance Benefits. Canadian Public
   Policy 27(4): 423–46.
Phipps, Shelley, and Fiona MacPhail. (2000). The Impact of Employment Insur-
   ance on New Entrants and Re-entrants. Final Report. Strategic Evaluation and
   Monitoring, Evaluation and Data Development. Ottawa: HRDC, Cat. No.
   SP-AH135 -11-00E.
Porter, Ann. (2003). Gendered States: Women, Unemployment Insurance and the
   Political Economy of the Welfare State in Canada, 1945–1997. Toronto: Univer-
   sity of Toronto Press.
Pulkingham, Jane. (1998). Remaking the Social Divisions of Welfare: Gender,
   'Dependency' and UI Reform. Studies in Political Economy 56: 7–48.
Quebec. (2006). Quebec Parental Insurance Plan. Electronic version retrieved
   3 July 2007 from http://www.rqap.gouv.qc.ca/index_en.asp.
Salhany, R.E. (1998). Reasons for Judgment in the Matter of the Employment
   Insurance Act and in the Matter of a Claim by Kelly Lesiuk, Winnipeg,
   Manitoba. Ottawa: Office of the Umpire for Employment Insurance Com-
   mission.
Service Canada. (2007). Pilot Project on Increased Weeks of Employment
   Insurance (EI) Benefits: The Purpose of the Pilot Project. Electronic version
   retrieved 12 Sept. 2007 from http://www1.servicecanada.gc.ca/en/ei/
   information/increased_weeks. Benefits shtml.
Stark, Agneta. (2005). Warm Hands in a Cold Age: On the Need of a New
   World Order of Care. Feminist Economics 11(2): 7–36
Statistics Canada. (2006). Labour Force Characteristics by Age and Sex. Labour
   Force Survey. Ottawa: Statistics Canada. Electronic version retrieved 4. Jan.
   2007 from http://www40.statcan.ca/l01/cst01/labor20a.htm.
Stratychuk, Lori. (2001). Repeat Users of Employment Insurance. Perspectives
   on Labour and Income 2(4): 5–12.
Wiegers, Wanda. (2002). The Framing of Poverty as 'Child Poverty' and Its Implica-
   tions for Women. Ottawa: Status of Women Canada, Policy Research Fund.
Williams, Cara. (2004). The Sandwich Generation. Perspectives on Labour and
   Income 5(9): 5–12.
Women's Network PEI. (2004). Looking Beyond the Surface: An In-Depth Review
   of Parental Benefits. Ottawa: Federal Labour Standards Review.

11 Quebec's Policies for Work-Family Balance: A Model for Canada?

DIANE-GABRIELLE TREMBLAY

Quebec's policies on child care, parental leave, and other measures to improve the work-family balance are often presented as a model for the rest of Canada. This chapter will compare and assess recent changes in both Quebec and at the federal level in Canada to ascertain the extent to which public policy addresses problems related to the balancing of work and family. In particular, it will examine the ways that current policies at the federal level and in Quebec affect gender equity in the labour market and the family.

The chapter will first set out a typology of family policies based on the classifications developed by Hantrais and Letablier (1996). Second, it will present a brief history of federal and Quebec policies regarding parental leave and child care services while attempting to situate them in relation to this typology. Recent federal policy orientations reflect a vision that differs greatly from Quebec's on family policy goals. It is argued here that the rest of Canada and the federal Conservative Party are pursuing a conservative or laissez-faire doctrine, while the federal Liberal Party seems to favour a policy aimed at alternating between work and family, which is also a conservative position. Quebec generally favours a policy of work-family balance that involves a combination of work and family and parental responsibilities, although the Action démocratique du Québec (ADQ, the opposition party) has proposed a policy that would lead towards a greater degree of conservatism. In Quebec, a shift to the right may, however, be difficult for any government to accomplish because of the extent to which new programs have encouraged paternal leave. In January 2006, the government of Quebec established a new parental leave insurance plan (QPIP), thereby implementing a different policy from that of the rest of Canada. Parental leave is now more flexible (either a shorter leave with a higher earn-ings replacement benefits rate or a longer leave with a lower earnings replacement rate), with three to five weeks of the entire leave period (of almost one year) reserved exclusively for fathers. There seem to be po-litical forces pulling in different directions at the moment, and since the present Quebec government is a minority government, family policy is high on the agenda.

The third objective of this chapter is to present available data on the use of parental leave and child care services as evidence of the impact of these policies on equity issues. This chapter will argue that Quebec's child care and parental leave policies would be good models for the rest of Canada. Data regarding parental leave show that the majority of users are still women, despite increasing participation on the part of fathers in child care, as well as in play and educational activities. Al-though throughout Canada the extension of parental leave to one year, in 2001, was viewed by some as constituting considerable progress in terms of employment equity, this policy could very well further rein-force traditional mothering roles without having a strong influence on the participation of fathers in parenting, and thus rather negatively af-fect the goal of labour force equality. Low-cost child care in Quebec ($5 a day per child at the beginning of this program, raised to $7 a day per child in 2003, versus approximately $30 a day per child before gov-ernment funding was introduced) is a progressive measure that seems to have affected female labour force participation rates and child care enrolment.

Since the new parental leave came into effect, Quebec has noted an increase in births, which were up to 82,500 in 2006 in comparison with 76,250 the previous year. This is the highest increase (8%) since 1909. It is clearly too early to attribute this increase to the new regime, especial-ly since some parents may have slightly delayed their project of giving birth to be able to take advantage of the new regime; nevertheless, the fertility rate in Quebec increased to 1.6, which is higher than the Cana-dian average, and up 0.1 point from the previous year. In the context of an aging population, fertility rates are of interest. The evidence in this chapter will demonstrate that it is mainly because of the more inclusive characteristics of the parental leave program that this program should be envisaged for implementation elsewhere. The new parental leave policy is more inclusive in that it provides more mothers with coverage (e.g., it includes the self-employed) and a better probability that fathers will participate in parenting since some weeks of leave are reserved for them. Parental leave policy is not the only element necessary to facilitate work-family life balance: child care, flexibility of working time, and telework (Tremblay 2002; Tremblay et al. 2006a; 2006b; 2006c; 2007b), among other measures at the firm level, are also important. If well designed, parental leave can contribute significantly to involving fathers in the care of children, the sharing of family responsibilities, and thus to work-family balance.

National Models

The forms that work-family relationships take vary according to country and geographical region, with northern and southern Europe holding clearly opposite positions, as do the United States and northern Europe. Work-family articulation takes on very different forms depending on the social, demographic, and cultural contexts, as well as on the public policies in place, the latter being our main research interest in this chapter.[1] Most countries are linked to a model without perfectly fitting into it, and this is also true of Quebec and Canada, as we will see.

Work-Family Balance or Cumulative Model

In the countries that draw on the work-family balance, or cumulative model, the aim of public intervention is to balance the demands of family life and work by allowing individuals, both women and men, to remain employed while assuming their family responsibilities. In other words, the work-family balance, or cumulative model (since it is possible to cumulate work and family) makes it possible to juxtapose family with employment without having to sacrifice one for the other. This model offers the best quality and the greatest variety of public measures for adjusting to the work-family relationship, that is, accessible and highly developed public child care services, excellent working-time arrangements, and paid and flexible parental leave.

In countries that draw on this model greater importance is given to the equal treatment of men and women than in countries that draw on other models. Laws and public policies related to work-family balance apply to both men and women to encourage a more equal sharing of both work-related duties and family responsibilities. Measures related to parental leave, for example, provide for special incentives to encourage men's participation. This type of family policy is based more on the notion of citizenship to the extent that it is first and foremost a policy of gender equality and a childhood policy, since children are considered to be future citizens. In a nutshell, work-family balance model underpins a policy of social integration (Hantrais and Letablier 1995: 44). Countries such as Sweden, Norway, Finland, and Iceland fit into the work-family balance model (Tremblay 2004; 2005)

Work-Family Alternating Model

The main aim of the work-family alternating model is not to juxtapose family with work, as in the work-family balance model, but rather to encourage employed parents, generally women, to opt for a strategy of entering and exiting the labour market to balance work and family by giving priority to one sphere over the other at different times. The state encourages women to leave their jobs or to reduce their work hours in order to take care of their children, and then to return to the labour market later, most often on a part-time basis when the children reach school age. This policy approach generally affects only mothers because, although it is desirable that work and family responsibilities be shared more equitably by both parents, it is rare that fathers leave their work or reduce their work hours to devote themselves to the family (Tremblay 2002; 2004). Countries oriented towards the work-family alternating model share a conception of the family that is based on the gendered division of roles, relying mainly on the mother's role in linking work and family. They share a 'privatist' representation of the responsibility for raising children, in the sense that public intervention leaves families with this exclusive responsibility. The work-family alternating model covers countries such as Germany, the Netherlands, and in some aspects, France. Germany, for example, offers little support for child care and has fiscal incentives for mothers to stay at home. Programs described as 'cash for care,' which give financial incentives to mothers who take care of children or who do not use the public child care system when available, are measures that fit into this model; they contribute to women staying at home, often for a few years, since the programs sometimes have higher incentives as the years go by or for a third or subsequent child.

Non-Interventionist Model

Countries oriented towards the non-interventionist model are characterized by the virtual absence of any state measures for adjusting the work-family relationship. Among these countries, a distinction should be made between those in which there is little or no state intervention due to insufficient resources as long was the case, for example, in some southern European countries (Spain, Greece, and Portugal), and those in which state intervention is weak based on principle, as in the United Kingdom and the United States. Both cases result in a purely privatist conception of the work-family relationship, where any accommodation between the two spheres is left entirely up to the initiative of individuals and employers. In this latter case, it can be concluded that collective bargaining at the company level must compensate for the lack of public policy and state intervention. This third model is characterized by weak state measures for adjusting the work-family relationship. Canada is often associated with the United States as representative of a non-interventionist model, but there are significant differences between the two countries, in particular with regard to the provision of the one-year parental leave and, until the January 2006 election, a proposed national child care program (which was, and remains, already in place in Quebec).

These models have distinct effects on women's participation in the labour market (Cette et al. 2007). The work-family balance model yields the most positive results for women's participation in the labour market in terms of the rate of participation, stability, and number of hours worked each week. The work-family alternating model also produces positive results for women's participation in the labour market, but causes more frequent interruptions in addition to reducing the number of weekly work hours – both are factors that have consequences for women's income, skills level, career opportunities, and so on. In contrast, the non-interventionist model yields more diversified results, depending on the context of the particular country: social gender relations, specific historical conditions, and the national economic situation, among other factors. This non-interventionist model usually has a more negative impact on fertility and labour market participation, but situations vary.

The Situation in Quebec

Quebec is close to the work-family balance model, although the large support for the ADQ in the 2007 election means that part of the population may be moving towards supporting a more conservative model, a model closer to the work-family alternating model. Although not all policy measures meet expectations in practice, and much remains to be done to catch up with the situation in Scandinavian countries, Quebec nevertheless clearly stands apart from the rest of Canada, and even more so from the United States, where the model of non-intervention predominates. Even so, there are some threats to the Quebec model: for example, the ADQ (the present opposition party) proposes a 'cash for care' measure of $100 a week for mothers who do not put their children in the child care system, a model that seems to be attractive to 'stay at home' mothers. The majority of the population, however, including mothers in the labour force, strongly favour maintaining the public child care system as well as developing more measures to strengthen the work-family balance model. The high participation rate in the labour force of women with children under 6 years of age seems to confirm the need and support for the cumulative, or work-family balance model.

History of Policies

The Quebec government's interest in family policy can be explained by two main factors: (1) sociodemographic changes, related to a drop in fertility, a decline in marriage, and an increase in marital instability; and (2) an increase in mothers' participation in the labour force. Women's increased labour force participation makes it essential to think about family and work-family balance policy and certainly explains the recent gains achieved by policies fostering this objective. Although the demographic changes are not unique to Quebec, their pace in Quebec represents a special case within Canada, and the measures adopted over recent decades also make Quebec a distinct case within Canada.

The 1960s were a socially determining period for Quebec. The government became increasingly interventionist, and the significant social changes that took place during this time are often referred to as the Quiet Revolution. Feminism became an important social movement, and women's participation in the labour market increased markedly. Over the years, public policies gradually began to take this fact into account. Laws and measures, such as maternity leave and subsidized child care, came into being as a result of the struggles of the women's movement and other popular movements. The first interventions regarding maternity leave came from the federal government. In 1971 the eligibility criteria for the Unemployment Insurance (UI, after 1996 Employment Insurance) program were broadened to include a seventeen-week maternity leave, whereby fifteen weeks were paid at 60 per cent of insurable earnings (now reduced to 55 per cent, but with the length of parental leave increased to about one year). This EI program, which still constitutes the only income security for many Canadian women, nevertheless contains important limitations that the new Quebec Parental Insurance Plan of 2006 addresses, as will be seen below.

From the 1980s onwards the Quebec government began to take a close look at the transformations in the family and women's participation in the labour market, with many policy statements published over the years (see, e.g., Tremblay 2008, 2004). An important 1987 statement on family policy was behind the creation of the Conseil de la famille, which became the Conseil de la famille et de l'enfance (Council of Families and Children). Together with the Conseil du statut de la femme (Council on the Status of Women), this organization was among the most vocal in public policy issues concerning women, family, and child care. Over the years, these two organizations published many analyses and called for policy changes; they were largely supported by women's groups and activists on gender equality. All these endeavours were important over the 1980s and 1990s, but the concrete measures were slow in materializing, except for some support for child care.

Then in 1997 a review process, which took place in many government organizations, led to the establishment of three goals: (1) to ensure equity through universal support provided to families and increased assistance to low-income families; (2) to facilitate a balance of parental and work-related responsibilities; and (3) to foster child development and promote equal opportunities (Québec 1997a: vii).

These goals were made top government priorities, but again, a number of years went by before concrete measures were proposed, except for support to child care services and the federal parental leave program. The Quebec government asserted that it had to obtain federal government funding to proceed with the new proposed parental leave plan. An agreement was concluded in 2005, and in January 2006 Quebec was able to implement its own Quebec Parental Insurance Plan. The work-family balance policy, which had been the object of consultation since 2003, did not require that funds be transferred; nevertheless, it was set aside by the Liberal government of Quebec, possibly because of opposition from employers, since a few employers' organizations were quite vocal in opposing any governmental intervention.

An explicit work-family balance policy, as envisaged in the 1997 review process, is to this day the main element missing that would situate Quebec clearly in the work-family balance or cumulative model. Indeed, while child care support is important, and comes first in the demands of Canadian mothers for a work-family balance, Quebec parents are more and more requesting that employers actively facilitate a work-family balance, with measures such as working-time flexibility, telework, flexible career plans, and the like. The demand for a work-family policy and for incentives and pilot projects along these lines remains present in Quebec.

Maternity Leave

In Quebec, up until January 2006, the financial support provided to mothers who were expecting a child or had had a child came from three different income replacement programs. One fell under federal jurisdiction (Canada) and the other two fell under provincial jurisdiction (Quebec).

The federal Employment Insurance program was the main parental leave benefits program administered by Human Resources and Social Development Canada (HRSDC). Benefits were paid to parents after a fourteen-day waiting period. The allowance corresponded to 55 per cent of insurable earnings. This leave, which used to last six months, was extended to one year in January 2001, and could be shared by both parents; however, unlike Sweden, incentive measures to encourage fathers' participation did not exist.

The Quebec Maternity Allowance Program (PRALMA) was under the responsibility of the Ministry of Employment and Social Solidarity (MES). Instituted to cover the fourteen-day waiting period imposed by the federal EI program, PRALMA offered a $360 maternity allowance to mothers who were eligible for employment insurance. Although not an immense amount, this program nevertheless supported low-income parents and would surely be welcomed by many Canadian mothers. The new Quebec regime covers the fourteen-day waiting period, and this program is thus no longer necessary, since it has been integrated into the new regime.

The Quebec Safe Maternity Program is administered by the Commission de la santé et de la sécurité du travail (CSST, or Occupational Health and Safety Board), and it allows a pregnant worker to stop working if her workstation or position poses risks for her own health or that of her fetus. During the first week of compensation, the employee receives her full salary from her employer. Subsequently, she receives compensation from the CSST through benefits that correspond to 90 per cent of her net income. This program is still in effect in Quebec.

The Labour Standards Act in Quebec stipulates that working women have the right to a maternity leave of eighteen weeks, but this leave is unpaid. This is the minimum to which women are entitled in any case, but if eligible for the new program, women are entitled to benefits.

Paternity Leave

Paternity leave, in particular paid leave reserved for the father, is not very common worldwide, although it is exists in Norway, Finland, and Sweden (2 months), as well as in Iceland (3 months). In general, where there is paternity leave, the tendency is to integrate it into general parental leave. In Canada, parental leave was extended in 2001 within the EI program, with the expectation that parents could share the leave between them, but there is still no financial incentive or time reserved specifically for fathers under the federal program. In Quebec, however, since January 2006 fathers have the right to take a three- to five-week paid paternity leave, based on the option chosen (longer leave with lower benefits or shorter leave with higher benefits). Combined with the parental leave, which has been extended to one year, this measure may favour a greater sharing of the leave between mothers and fathers, as has been observed in the Nordic countries, especially given the additional incentive offered by Quebec (better paid leave that is not transferable to the mother). Some analysis on the take-up of parental leave in Europe, however, indicates that fathers use what leave is reserved for them, but little more (Moss and O'Brien 2006). If the time reserved for them is long enough, as in Iceland – where three months are reserved for the father, three for the mother, and three can be shared – public policy can clearly lead to more sharing of parental responsibilities.

Parental Leave

Parental leave is in principle aimed at men as well as women, although in reality, it is mainly used by women. In relation to the goal of furthering gender equality, parental leave is supposed to play a key role, since it should help to distinguish between the physiological demands of pregnancy and childbirth on women, demands for which maternity leave was designed, and the care and raising of children.

Ultimately, the role of parental leave is to allow both parents to balance their work and family lives. It is essential that men participate in the same way as women; otherwise parental leave will translate into a kind of extended maternity leave, thus reproducing the traditional division of roles and the economic inequalities between men and women. However, since the Canadian government has not introduced any measures to encourage fathers' participation, the latter has not evolved greatly since extended parental leave was introduced. As women generally earn less than men, and the arrival of a child generally represents considerable expenses, the lower earner usually takes care of the baby. Parental leave was extended in 2001, and in the years 2001–04 only approximately 10 per cent of fathers took some part of parental leave, and on average they took less than one month. The Quebec plan was designed to remedy this problem by introducing clear incentives, that is, a period reserved specifically for fathers.

The 2006 Quebec Parental Insurance Plan

Since 1997 Quebec had been trying to adopt a parental leave plan that is distinct from that of the federal government, and it has requested that the sums needed for this purpose be transferred to it from the federal scheme. Following an agreement reached in 2005, the new Quebec Parental Insurance Plan came into effect in January 2006. The new QPIP has a number of advantages in terms of the population covered, flexibility in taking the leave, and the earnings replacement benefits rate, as will be seen below.

In Quebec the QPIP replaces parental leave measures under the federal program. The new provisions do not change the provisions stipulated in Quebec's Labour Standards Act, which specify the duration of maternity leave (18 weeks) and parental leave (52 weeks) for a total of seventy weeks without salary, as well as the rights and obligations related to departure from and return to work. The new QPIP does, however, introduce four major changes.

The first change provides for weeks reserved for the father that cannot be transferred to the mother, which is an innovation in Canada and North America. Quebec fathers are now entitled to a three- to five-week paternity leave with higher benefits than under the federal program, since the income replacement rates and maximum eligible earnings have also been increased. Indeed, the federal parental leave program provides for a leave that can be shared by the father and the mother, but Statistics Canada survey data indicate that this measure has not been enough to increase fathers' participation since mothers still took an average of eleven months off in 2004, and only about 10 per cent of fathers took part of the leave (Table 11.1 below) data from 2005 indicate an increase in fathers' participation, to 14.5 per cent. In Quebec, the take-up of leave by fathers was 22 per cent in 2005, and with the new QPIP leave scheme, this has increased to 36 per cent.[2]

The second change involves the increased income offered by the QPIP. In addition to abolition of the fourteen-day waiting period stipulated under the federal parental leave program (2 weeks without benefits, as is the case with EI, with which this program is associated), the new QPIP increases the maximum insurable income to $59,000, and not $40,000, as is the case with the federal parental leave. This has been shown to be important for fathers' participation, since countries where replacement earnings rates are higher have higher participation of fathers.

The third change relates to the introduction of more flexibility in the QPIP, since parents now have two options: a basic plan (longer leave with lower benefits) or a special plan (shorter leave with higher benefits). The latter might interest those who need a higher earnings replacement rate (especially if their employment income is relatively low) or else who cannot afford to miss work for very long because of various personal or work-related reasons. The federal program provides for benefits corresponding to 55 per cent of the maximum insurable income ($40,000) during the fifteen weeks of maternity leave and thirty-five weeks of parental leave (accessible to both parents, but with a fourteen-day waiting period in each case). The new Quebec basic plan offers benefits of 70 per cent of the average weekly income for eighteen weeks of maternity leave and for five weeks of paternity leave. The QPIP offers two options for parental benefits, that is, 70 per cent of earnings for twenty-five weeks and 55 per cent of earnings for twenty-five weeks. Adoption leave can be shared by both parents, and provides for twelve weeks of benefits at 70 per cent of earnings and twenty-five weeks at 55 per cent.

The QPIP special plan provides for higher earnings replacement rates, but for a shorter period. Under this plan, maternity and paternity leave benefits are equivalent to 75 per cent of the weekly salary and are paid for fifteen weeks and three weeks, respectively. Parental leave is compensated at 75 per cent for twenty-five weeks and can be shared by the father and the mother. Under this special plan, the mother can receive benefits for a maximum of forty weeks (versus 50 in the basic plan), and adoption leave can be shared by both parents, for twenty-eight weeks at 75 per cent of earnings.

Lastly, it must be underlined that the new QPIP is more accessible and will allow more parents, including self-employed workers and students, to receive benefits since it no longer requires individuals to have worked 600 hours over the previous fifty-two weeks, but simply to have earned an insurable income of $2,000. The funding of this program is based on additional contributions that employers, employees, and self-employed workers must pay into the QPIP. Employers and employees, of course, continue to contribute to the federal EI program for unemployment coverage.

It is evidently still too early to assess the full impact of this new QPIP on fathers' participation in parental responsibilities, since the experience of Nordic European countries has shown that it takes a few years for fathers' participation to increase. However, based on what has been observed in other countries that have introduced a paternity leave period not transferable to mothers (Moss and O'Brien 2006), it is clear that there will be an increase in the participation of Quebec fathers, at least for these reserved weeks, if not more. This is especially true since, compared with fathers in the rest of Canada, there seems to be a greater proportion of fathers in Quebec taking advantage of parental leave; furthermore, because the earnings replacement rate has been increased, it is now easier to take the leave at a time when financial needs are considerable. In Canada, on the whole, the rate of uptake has already increased to 23 per cent in 2006, an increase due to the important increase in Quebec fathers taking leave with the new regime. In Quebec, 32 per cent of eligible fathers took leave under EI in 2005. This rate increased to 56 per cent in 2006 with the new Quebec Parental Insurance Plan (Marshall 2008).

We have up until now dealt with paid leave, but it should be underlined that the Quebec Labour Standards Act was also revised in 2003 to take families' needs into account and to protect the part of the workforce not eligible for paid parental leave. In Canada 75 per cent of mothers who have a child under 12 months of age have insurable employment, entitling them to maternity leave and parental leave benefits (under the federal plan; Statistics Canada data for 2003, 2004 and 2005 present the same percentage). In Quebec workers who do not have access to this plan, nevertheless have rights under the Labour Standards Act, which provides for a number of rights related to departure from and return to work. Due to limited space, it is impossible for us to report on all aspects of this issue; however, it should be pointed out that since 1 May 2003 employees in Quebec have the right to miss ten days of work (instead of 5 days, as was previously the case) in order to assume family responsibilities.

Use of Parental Leave by Canadian Women

Since data on the use of parental leave under the new Quebec Parental Insurance Plan are not yet fully available, we will examine the effect of the extension, in 2001, of parental leave to one year, under the federal program (Pérusse 2003; Marshall 2003). Table 11.1 presents some interesting data, despite the fact that Statistics Canada's Employment Insurance Coverage Survey focuses mainly on mothers, since fathers are considered only as spouses who might take up part of the leave. It is hoped that with the incentives offered to fathers in Quebec, more interest will be shown in their leave patterns. Table 11.1 shows that, in 2003–04, three-quarters of mothers who had a child aged 12 months or less had insurable employment, entitling them to parental benefits; 65 per cent of these mothers received benefits, while 35 per cent did not. Among those who did not have insurable employment, 9 per cent were self-employed (a situation remedied by the QPIP, since it makes self-employed or independent female workers eligible for the plan). It should be pointed out that under the new QPIP, individuals are required to have earned $2000 during the previous year, including self-employed female workers.

It is also interesting to note that, whereas the average duration of leave was five months before the federal government extended the period of parental leave within its EI program to one year, it is now eleven months: 62 per cent of women take a nine- to twelve-month leave, 16 per cent take more than twelve months, but only 8 per cent take from zero to four months, and 11 per cent take between five and eight months.[3]

Thus, even though the parental leave under the federal plan can theoretically be equally shared between the two spouses, according to their wishes, women have extended their duration of parental leave while men have not made a lot of effort to take this leave. In fact, among spouses, only 11 per cent of fathers took up part of the parental leave, which is a lower proportion than that of mothers, since only 20 per cent of mothers took less than nine months of leave, putting the duration of paternal leave in the range of one to three months. Unfortunately, the surveys on EI do not provide specific data on this subject, since the number of participating fathers is small. However, in reply to our question, Statistics Canada indicated that, although the data are considered not to be totally reliable because of the small number of respondents, the proportion of participating fathers in Quebec was 22 per cent (vs an average of 11% in the rest of Canada) in 2004. The 2005 federal data indicate a 14.5 per cent parental leave participation rate by fathers, while the more recent Quebec government data on fathers' participation in the new scheme indicate a 56 per cent participation rate. The higher rate of taking up parental leave by Quebec fathers, even before the new regime, suggests that there is a more open attitude on the part of Quebec fathers, who would like to participate to a greater extent in the family sphere (Tremblay 2003). Indeed, it may be that the important coverage given to work-family issues in the media over the years and in recent elections in Quebec, but also the very strong commitment of women's groups, unions, and government bodies (e.g., Conseil du statut de la femme, Conseil de la famille et de l'enfance), explain the fact that Quebec fathers feel more comfortable in taking time off for their children. Although some of our research highlights that fathers are not fully comfortable in taking time off or with flexible working-time arrangements in some firms or sectors (Tremblay 2003), it nevertheless seems easier, or more legitimate, to take paternity leave in Quebec than in the rest of Canada.

Since our aim is to classify Quebec in relation to the main models of work-family balance, described at the beginning of this chapter, some elements of child care services will now be presented.

Child Care

Child care services constitute a fundamental measure for balancing work and family. The number of day care spaces, the operating hours of child care centres, their geographical locations, and their costs are constant issues of concern for employed parents. These aspects have a direct effect on the time-management problems faced by parents. An effective child care system allows parents to better plan their schedules and can reduce tensions between family and professional responsibilities. Thus, we will briefly describe the situation in Quebec in this regard. Since the 1990s, a network of child care centres has been created in Quebec to provide educational child care services to children 4 years of age and under.

Child care centres and day care in family homes provide reduced-

Table 11.1 Eligibility of Mothers for Maternity and Parental Benefits and Duration of Leave

	2003	2004
Mothers with child aged 12 months or less (n)	327,000	350,000
With insurable employment (%)	75.3	74.3
Received maternity or parental benefits (%)	64.7	65.9
Did not claim or receive maternity or parental benefits (%)	10.6	8.4
Without insurable employment (%)	24.7	25.8
Had not worked in two years or more (%)	16.0	16.6
Other (includes self employed) (%)	8.6	9.1
Mothers who received maternity or parental benefits as a proportion of mothers with insurable employment (%)	85.9	88.7
Mothers with known return plans or already returned to work, paid employees only (n)[a]	208,000	211,000
Average duration of planned leave (months)	11	11
Median duration of planned leave (months)	11	11
0 to 4 months (%)	8.3	8.9
5 to 8 months (%)	13.5	11.6
9 to 12 months (%)	59.0	62.7
More than 12 months (%)	19.1	16.9
Spouse or partner claiming or intending to claim parental benefits	33,000	30,000
Mothers with spouse claiming or intending to claim benefits (%)	11.1	9.5

[a] Excludes mothers who have not worked in two years and self-employed mothers, since the survey does not provide information on their intentions to return to work.
Source: Statistics obtained by the author from Statistics Canada division responsible for employment insurance survey data.

contribution services (currently $7 a day per child) for children and babies. However, the number of child care spaces is far too low to meet the demand and needs. The number of spaces seems to be insufficient, and the operating hours too restrictive for many parents who work on nonstandard schedules. A survey by the Institut de la statistique du Quebec (Québec 1997b) revealed that 28 per cent of parents would like services to be more easily accessible in the evenings, nights, and on weekends. This proportion corresponds to the proportion of parents who work on a casual basis or on non-standard schedules. Moreover, school holidays and after-school hours represent care issues for a great number of parents. Despite these criticisms, Quebec parents are strongly attached to their network of child care services, and they reacted negatively to the proposal of the federal Conservative government (elected in January 2006), which planned to cancel the contributions paid to Quebec for these services and offer instead $1,200 per year for each child under the age of 6 to women who stay at home to care for their children. The payment of the $1,200 amount was indeed implemented by the federal government. The Quebec child care services network took action to defend its gains, and the Quebec government has recognized that public support for child care is such that it needs to be maintained and even the number of places for children increased over the coming years.

Researchers at the Université de Sherbrooke (Audet et al. 2006) conducted a preliminary analysis of the policy reform proposed by the Conservative government, which involves replacing child care services funding with an annual subsidy of $1,200 for each child under age 6, paid directly to parents. Audet and colleagues (2006) assessed the impact that this policy would have on poverty and inequality should the Quebec government decide to reduce current public funding of child care services, something that had effectively been envisaged by Quebec. According to the authors, although the effects on poverty and inequality in the general population are not highly significant, they increase in scale when the population targeted by these policies is considered, that is, couples with children and lone mothers are obviously most affected. In the case of the latter, Audet and colleagues predict that observed poverty, based on an index that captures all the dimensions of poverty, may increase by 60 per cent. This may, of course, have consequences for women's labour force participation and fertility: it could lead to an increase in labour force participation, to the extent possible, but also to a decline in fertility.

Data from the Workplace and Employee Survey of Statistics Canada (Tremblay et al. 2007a; 2006a; 2006b) indicate that Canadian parents of young children do not necessarily have access to better living conditions than non-parents do because the availability of child care, elder care, and other measures appear to be related more to the type of firm than to the presence of children. This is also one of the elements that clearly influences women's participation in the labour market and equality in the labour market, and while it would take too long to go into this here, we find it important to mention the important impact of working hours and the possibility of working arrangements on participation and equality, beyond the impact of child care and parental leaves.

Conclusion

The effectiveness of the Quebec and the federal Canadian models in the area of work-family articulation can be assessed by comparing their results with those obtained in other countries that implement other models, in particular in terms of women's labour market participation rates. An analysis of women's rates of participation in the labour market in Quebec and across Canada shows that these rates are increasingly high, in particular for women of childbearing age and for women who have children. Currently, two-thirds of Quebec adult women are in the labour market, and the rate is higher than that in some Canadian provinces (e.g., Ontario). Consequently, the number of dual-earner families, that is, the number of families in which both parents work, has increased considerably. The proportion of employed women who had children between the ages of 3 and 5 years was 41 per cent in 1976; by 1991 this proportion had increased to 68 per cent, and it has remained steady ever since.

In the 1990s public policies, both federally and in Quebec, tended to evolve towards the work-family balance model. The federal government's extension of parental leave, under its Employment Insurance program, to around one year brings it closer to the work-family alternating model – or the conservative model. Similarly, the newer federal program that pays a lump sum of $1,200 per year per child to all mothers of children under 6 years of age, including those who do not enter the labour force, places Canada firmly in the conservative model, which favours alternating work with family and, in particular, the withdrawal of women with young children from the labour market.

With its child care service network and its new Parental Insurance Plan, Quebec more closely resembles the work-family balance model, especially since it provides more flexibility in the duration of the various kinds of leave. In addition, if the incentive to fathers' participation leads them to exceed the three to five weeks of leave specifically reserved for them, Quebec could be considered to be resolutely in line with the work-family balance model, in which family responsibilities are shared by both parents. Finally, it must be said that, while a good model for the rest of Canada, Quebec is still far from the Scandinavian standard, since the parental leave (including the time reserved for fathers) is shorter. Furthermore, some political parties (namely, the ADQ, which came second in the 2007 election) propose policies that are quite conservative, such as 'cash for care' – $100 a month for parents of children who are not in the day care system or a 'baby bonus' of $5,000 for the third (or subsequent) child. While this is apparently attractive to 'stay-at-home moms,' it is very risky for those less educated to stay out of the labour market for many years, since they lose their skills and often are at greater risk of being in poverty, especially if they end up as lone mothers. In any case, Quebec's family policy appears to be some-where close to the Nordic influence at the moment, although the ADQ's propositions would bring it closer to a conservative alternating model, were they ever to be implemented.

Finally, the absence of working-time reduction or arrangement meas-ures is a weakness of Quebec and Canadian policy regarding work-family issues. While recent Statistics Canada data have shown that Québécois have shorter working hours than do Canadians on average (and the difference is even more apparent when comparisons are made with Ontario and Alberta), it is shorter hours worked in the public sec-tor that largely contributes to this differential (35 hours vs 37.5 hours in many Canadian jurisdictions). At the same time, Quebec has done little in recent years in terms of working-time policy (Tremblay 2004).

The two main Quebec political parties of the moment (Liberals and ADQ) propose diverging views of the family and of the work-family balance. While the Liberal Party (and the Parti Québécois before them) supports policies that resemble the work-family balance model, the ADQ has a more conservative view and proposes 'cash for care' poli-cies, which would lead towards the alternating mode. However, it is interesting to note how family policy and parental leave have gained popularity and were at the top of the political agenda in the election in Quebec in spring 2007. A national child care system and measures such as the new parental leave of Quebec would certainly be an improve-ment for women and men with children in other provinces of Canada.

Notes

1 Elements of the typology presented in Tremblay (2004) will be used here; these, as well as those of Hantrais and Letablier (1995; 1996), can be con-sulted for more information on the various countries found in each of the models.
2 Québec, Ministère de la famille, personal communication (March 2007).
3 The reasons for these different durations could not be provided to us.

References

Audet, Mathieu, Dorothée Boccanfuso, and Paul Makdissi. (2006). L'impact de la politique conservatrice de réforme du financement des services de garde sur la pauvreté et l'inégalité au Québec. *Interventions économiques* 34: ch. 9. Electronic version retrieved from http://www.teluq.uquebec.ca/pls/inteco/rie.entree?vno_revue=1&vno_numero=4.

Cette, Gilbert, Dominique Méda, Arnaud Sylvain, and Diane-Gabrielle Tremblay. (2007). Activité d'emploi et difficultés de conciliation emploi-famille: Une comparaison fine des taux d'activité en France et au Canada. *Loisir et société (Leisure and Society)* 29(1): 117–54.

Hantrais, Linda, and Marie Thérèse Letablier. (1995). *La Relation Famille-Emploi: Une comparaison des modes d'ajustement en Europe.* Paris: Centre d'études de l'emploi.

– (1996). *Familles, Travail et Politiques Familiales en Europe.* Paris: Presses universitaires de France.

Marshall, Katherine. (2003). L'avantage du Congé Parental Prolongé. *Perspectives on Labour and Income.* Ottawa: Statistics Canada, Cat. 75–001:5–13.

– (2008). Fathers' Use of Parental Leave. *Perspectives on Labour and Income.* Ottawa: Statistics Canada, 9(4): 15–21.

Moss, Peter, and Margaret O'Brien (eds.). (2006). *International Review of Leave Policies and Related Research 2006.* Employment Relations Research Series No 57. London: Department of Trade and Industry.

Pérusse, D. (2003). New Maternity and Parental Benefits. *Perspectives on Labour and Income.* Statistics Canada Cat. 75–001:12–16.

Québec. (1997a). *Nouvelles Dispositions de la Politique Familiale: Les enfants au coeur de nos choix.* Quebec: Secrétariat du comité des priorités du ministère du Conseil exécutif.

– (1997b). Survey. Quebec: Institut de la statistique du Québec.

Tremblay, Diane-Gabrielle. (2002). Balancing Work and Family with Telework? Organizational Issues and Challenges for Women and Managers, 157–70. *Women in Management 17(¾).* Manchester: MCB Press.

– (2003). Articulation Emploi-Famille: Comment les pères voient-ils les choses? *Les politiques socials* 63(3–4): 70–86.

– (2004). *Conciliation Emploi-Famille et Temps Sociaux.* Quebec: Presses de l'Université du Québec et Octares.

– (2008). *Conciliation emploi-famille et temps sociaux,* 2nd ed. Québec: Presses de l'Université du Québec et Octares.

– (ed.). (2005). *De la Conciliation Emploi-Famille à une Politique des Temps Sociaux.* Quebec: Presses de l'Université du Québec.

Tremblay, Diane-Gabrielle, Renaud Paquet, and Elmustapha Najem. (2006a) . Telework: A Way to Balance Work and Family or an Increase in Work-Family Conflict? *Canadian Journal of Communication* 31(3): 715–31.

Tremblay, Diane-Gabrielle, Elmustapha Najem, and Renaud Paquet, (2006b),

Articulation Emploi-Famille et Temps de Travail: De quelles mesures disposent les travailleurs canadiens et à quoi aspirent-ils? *Enfances, Famille, Génération* 4. Electronic version retrieved from http://www.erudit.org/revue/efg/2006/v/n4/index.html.

Tremblay, Diane-Gabrielle, Catherine Chevrier, and Martine Di Loreto. (2006c). Le Télétravail à Domicile: Meilleure conciliation emploi-famille ou source d'envahissement de la vie privée? *Interventions économiques* 34 (June). Electronic version retrieved from http://www.teluq.uqam.ca/interventionseconomiques.

Tremblay, Diane-Gabrielle, Renaud Paquet, and Elmustapha Najem. (2007a). Work-Family Balancing and Working Time: Is Gender Determinant? *Global Journal of Business Research* 1(1): 97–113.

Tremblay, Diane-Gabrielle, Catherine Chevrier, and Martine Di Loreto. (2007b). Le Travail Autonome: Une meilleure conciliation entre vie personnelle et vie professionnelle … ou une plus grande interpénétration des temps sociaux? *Loisir et société (Leisure and Society)* 29(1): 191–214.

12 Are Wage Supplements the Answer to the Problems of Working-Poor Women?

ANDREW JACKSON

A 'New Idea' in Canadian Social Policy

The idea of addressing poverty through some kind of wage supplementation program has been around for a long time, but it has only recently moved back to the centre stage of Canadian social policy. Unlike the more visionary and progressive concept of a guaranteed citizen's income (GCI), paid out as a right to all adults irrespective of their attachment to the job market, wage supplements are intended to promote and support paid employment and, specifically, employment in low-paid and insecure jobs. They have been seen as more 'work-friendly' than traditional welfare programs, which are often believed by right-wing economists to create 'disincentives to work' (Myles and Pierson 1997). At the same time, wage supplements can also be seen as less punitive than very low social assistance benefits, and as a small carrot to supplement the stick of very low income supports for the jobless.

One widely cited model is the U.S. Earned Income Tax Credit or EITC, which provides a (low) annual income supplement to working-poor families. These are families that have low incomes and also participate in the paid job market. A similar plan in the United Kingdom has been expanded under 'New Labour,' and one is now planned for Canada at the national level. Saskatchewan and Quebec already offer modest wage supplement programs.

The idea of wage supplements for the working poor has been promoted as one element of welfare-to-work policies by several proponents of a 'new social architecture' for Canada, notably the Canadian Policy Research Networks (CPRN; Jenson 2004) and the Caledon Institute for Social Policy (Battle, Mendelson, and Torjman 2006). Wage supplements were recently highlighted in the May 2006 report of the Toronto-based Task Force on Modernizing Income Security for Working-Age Adults (MISWAA Task Force 2006), and indeed MISWAA was likely the prime mover behind recent federal government interest in this area. The MISWAA Task Force included a very wide range of community, business, and labour participants, and reached a broad consensus that the problem of working poverty (i.e., poverty in households with significant attachment to the paid job market) had to be seriously addressed.

Among other recommendations, the final MISWAA report called on the federal government to introduce a wage supplement of up to $200 per month for persons working at least fifty hours per month, to be fully phased out at an annual household income of $21,500. In combination with a refundable tax credit for all low-income working-age adults, the wage supplement would bring a single adult working thirty-two hours per week at the Ontario minimum wage to an income of about $16,000 per year, from the current level of $13,000 per year. It is important to note that the MISWAA Task Force reached a broad consensus in favour of a menu of measures, including reform of the Employment Insurance system, increases in the minimum wage, and improvements to social assistance programs, in addition to these new tax credits.

The 2005 *Economic and Fiscal Update* presented by the federal Liberals just before their parliamentary defeat in November 2005 called for a 'Working Income Tax Benefit' (WITB) to be introduced in 2008–09. The aim of the WITB is to 'make work pay for low-income Canadians' and to ease transitions from welfare to work (Canada 2005b: 128). The illustrative example envisaged a maximum benefit of $1,000 for a lone parent with one child, which would phase in as family earnings reached a threshold of $3,000, and would begin to phase out as net family income rose above $18,000, which is roughly the poverty line for one adult. The WITB would disappear entirely when family income reaches $28,000. The WITB, like family income-tested child benefits, was to be delivered through the income tax system. The newly elected federal Conservative government promised in its 2006 budget to 'push this idea forward' in consultation with the provinces and territories (Canada 2006: 70).

Leading proponents of a WITB conceive of its role in different ways, and have different views on how other income support programs for working-age adults, like social assistance and Employment Insurance, should be changed. They also differ on the mix of employment and social policies of which a Working Income Tax Benefit would be a part.

However, they all start from similar, correct, premises: (1) paid work in today's job market is no guarantee of escape from poverty, and (2) the 'welfare wall,' which traps many working-age families in poverty, needs to be lowered. A WITB is more progressive than the dominant neoliberal model of using low social benefits to force workers into low-wage jobs. The punitive application of welfare cuts has been a common approach of many provincial governments in recent years, including the Mike Harris government in Ontario, the Ralph Klein government in Alberta, and the Gordon Campbell government in British Columbia.

Previous debates in Canada over the concept of a guaranteed annual income (GAI) divided progressive social policy advocates. 'Realists' argued that precarious work and underemployment are here to stay and supported family income-tested supplements, as in the Canadian Council on Social Development's advocacy of a form of a GAI as a centrepiece of social policy through its Work and Income project in the early 1990s. Other progressive groups either opposed or focused on different solutions to the problem of the working poor. For its part, the Canadian Labour Congress insisted, in its policy statement on a GAI in 1988, that the key focus should remain on improving the quantity and quality of jobs within a context of high employment and improved social insurance programs, with income supplements and basic income guarantees playing a much more residual role. Today, important social advocacy groups, such as Campaign 2000, the National Council of Welfare, and the National Anti-Poverty Organization, as well as many women's organizations, similarly stress the need to focus on better jobs as the centrepiece of an antipoverty strategy.

Income supplementation for the working poor raises some important questions of economic and social policy design. It is argued here that wage supplements should, at a minimum, not be seen as a substitute for direct measures to raise low wages, progressive reform to other income support programs, such as Employment Insurance, and expansion of public and social services.

Furthermore, any evaluation of the pros and cons of wage supplements must take into account the specific situation of low-wage and precariously employed female workers. That wage supplements would be paid out on the basis of low family income rather than to supplement the low wages of individual women is deeply problematic from a gender-equity perspective. The same is true of the argument of at least some proponents that family income-based wage supplements should be financed in part at the expense of Employment Insurance benefits.

Currently, these are paid to individual workers, independent of family income. The danger is that a wage supplementation strategy does not recognize the economic autonomy of women, and it could even penalize women in low-paid and precarious jobs.

Low Wage, Insecure Jobs – Women Fare Worst

A significant group of adult Canadians participate on a regular basis in the paid workforce but will nonetheless live in poverty unless cushioned by the earnings of another household member. In round numbers, a single person must work full-time hours for a full year (2,000 hours) for about $10 per hour to reach a single adult poverty-line income (as defined by Statistics Canada's pretax low-income line). Yet, about one in four of all workers fall short of the line. This includes about one in five adult female workers between the ages of 25 and 54 years, and one in ten adult male workers who earn less than $10 per hour (Jackson 2005). One in five females working full-time (21.9%) are low-wage workers; this proportion rises to 36.4 per cent among recent immigrant women and to 40.1 per cent among recent immigrant women who belong to a visible minority group (Morissette and Picot 2005).

Statistics Canada studies confirm that the proportion of low-wage workers in Canada has not fallen over the past twenty-five years, and indeed that real wages have fallen or remained unchanged for the entire bottom half of the workforce over that long period. Moreover, many people are trapped in low-wage jobs. Of adult low-wage earners over the age of 25, about two-thirds of women, and half of men, remain low paid over any given four-year period (Morissette and Johnson 2005).

Women are much more likely than men to be employed in low-wage and insecure jobs, contributing greatly to a much higher risk of being part of the working poor unless cushioned by the earnings of a (usually male) partner.[1] The level of occupational and industrial segregation between women and men remains very high, and jobs where women predominate, especially in the private sector, are more likely to be low paid than jobs where men dominate. The large category of sales and service jobs includes many low-pay and part-time jobs, such as salespersons, chefs and cooks, hotel workers, security guards, and child care and home support workers. One in three women (32.2%) work in these occupations compared with just one in five men (19.8%). A recent report of the federal government's Pay Equity Task Force (Canada 2004) notes that women are still highly concentrated in a small number of traditionally female occupational categories and that they overwhelmingly dominate the very lowest paid occupations, such as child care workers, cashiers, and food services workers.

Women are more likely to be employed in what Leah Vosko and others have termed 'precarious' forms of employment, specifically part-time and temporary jobs and the most insecure forms of self-employment (Vosko 2006). This difference in types of jobs performed results in a significant gap (58% vs 51%) between the proportion of working men and women who are steadily employed, working full-time hours for a full year. Put another way, almost half of all employed women work part-time or part-year (Jackson 2005).

In the core working-age group of persons aged between 25 and 54 years, just 4.8 per cent of men work part-time compared with 21.2 per cent of women. Part-time jobs are, on average, much less desirable than full-time jobs, paying a median hourly wage of just $10 compared with a median hourly wage of $17.32 in full-time jobs in 2003. Part-time jobs are also generally much worse in terms of job security, access to stable work schedules, and pension and health benefits. Many adult part-time women hold these jobs because they cannot find full-time jobs, or because they cannot find quality, affordable child and elder care and must fit paid work around heavily gendered caring responsibilities.

In 2003, 13 per cent of all female employees compared with 11.9 per cent of male employees were in temporary jobs, defined as jobs that are casual, seasonal, or most often, have a defined end-date. Male temporary work tends to be associated with construction and the resource sector, and is better paid than female temporary work, which is usually in lower-paid service jobs. The incidence of temporary employment for women has doubled since 1989, and female temporary workers are much more likely to work part-time than temporary male workers. Women are also more likely than men to be found in the most insecure and badly paid forms of self-employment, which are often a disguised form of contract employment. A person working under contract to one business, and who is closely supervised, is legally a contract employee – covered by employment standards – but many in this position are told, wrongly, that they are self-employed. In 2000 almost half (45%) of all self-employed women made less than $20,000 per year compared with 19 per cent of self-employed men in that earnings category.

There continues to be a significant wage gap between women and men. In 2003 the median hourly wage for all workers was $16.00 per hour, and the median hourly wage for women was 80 per cent that of men at $14.43 per hour, compared with $18.00 per hour for males. The greatest part of the wage gap cannot be explained by objective factors, such as the educational level and job experience of women, but is created by pay discrimination and cultural assumptions concerning the value of particular forms of work (Drolet 2002). Occupational segregation is a major part of the problem. The earnings gap between women and men is even greater on a weekly and annual basis because women work fewer hours. Average weekly earnings of women are just 71 per cent to those of men, and average annual earnings are just 64 per cent to those of men (Jackson 2005).

Poverty is defined at the family income level. Households dependent on the income of one woman earner are especially vulnerable to poverty simply because of the high risk of low-paid and precarious employment, and vulnerability rises with the number of children since child benefits, even at low-income levels, do not match the costs of raising children. One in six children live in families with incomes below the poverty line (pretax Low-Income Cut Off, LICO). Research by the Canadian Council on Social Development for the Campaign 2000 Report Card on Child Poverty in Canada (2003) showed that the majority (56%) of the more than one million children living in poverty live in working-poor families where at least one adult worked during the year (Campaign 2000, 2003). One in five (19%) poor children live in lone-parent working families – a group that is particularly vulnerable to poverty because of reliance on the earnings of one, usually woman, worker; one in five (21%) poor children live in couple families with one earner, and almost one in five (17%) poor children live in couple families with two earners. Low earnings for women are a big factor behind poverty for single women, lone-parent families, and even in multi-earner households. Conversely, some low-wage women are protected from poverty by the earnings of a partner, as discussed below.

Employment Insurance and Low-Wage Workers

Many lower-wage workers with interrupted earnings will fall below poverty lines, especially now that only a minority of unemployed workers qualify for Employment Insurance (EI) benefits to replace lost earnings. The risk of periods of low hours of insured work has increased in recent years with the growth of contract jobs and solo self-employment, while the risk of unemployment is much higher among low-wage workers. The EI program has been repeatedly cut since its

high point in the mid-1970s, especially by the Liberal governn
1994 and 1996. Today, only about four of every ten unemployed
ers collect EI benefits, down from 80 per cent in 1990, and only one in
three unemployed women collect benefits, down from 70 per cent in
1990. Only about one in four unemployed workers in most major urban
centres now receive benefits at any one time, since many do not qualify
at all, and others quickly exhaust their benefits. The cracks in the EI
system have been detailed in research reports by both the Canadian
Labour Congress (2005) and the MISWAA Task Force (2006).

Employment Insurance coverage has shrunk mainly because of
changes to program rules that make it much harder for workers, especially female workers, to qualify and also because of cuts to the length of
time for which benefits can be collected. Under current rules, a worker
must have worked between 420 hours (in communities with very high
unemployment rates) and 700 hours to qualify for regular benefits, rising to 910 hours for new entrants and re-entrants to the workforce, such
as young people, recent immigrants, and women returning to work.
The shift to an hours-based entrance requirement in 1994 disqualified
many female part-time workers who would have previously qualified
based on weeks worked, and now only half of all part-time workers
would qualify for benefits if laid off from their current job (Canada
2005a). Only about one in five working-poor employees qualify for Employment Insurance benefits over a year. A large proportion of working-poor women who lose a job do not qualify for EI benefits because of
too few hours worked, or because they combine periods of temporary
work with self-employment which does not count towards qualifying
hours (Fleury and Fortin 2006).

Workers who do have enough hours to get into the EI system often
qualify for only a short period of benefits, which can be as low as fourteen weeks in a region with a low unemployment rate. As well, EI benefits have been cut to 55 per cent of insured earnings, and the maximum
insurable earnings was frozen from 1994 to 2006 at just $39,000. The
maximum weekly benefit is barely enough to provide a poverty-line income for a single adult, even for those who do qualify for the maximum
benefit, and falls well short for those with dependents.

The 'Welfare Wall'

Low and insecure earnings are a major part of the 'welfare wall' that
traps many people and families on social assistance, especially lone-

parent families headed by women and women with disabilities. Transitions from welfare to work are enormously difficult if income from low-wage and insecure employment does not replace even punitively low levels of income support from social assistance. This is often the case if the available work is low-wage, part-time, or contract employment. Many persons, especially women, cycle between social assistance and precarious, low-paid work, often not finding enough security in employment to qualify for a meaningful EI benefit. When between jobs, transitions from welfare to work are also made much more difficult by the provincial norm of clawing back earnings from welfare cheques at very low earnings levels, resulting in punitively high tax rates. The MISWAA Task Force report (2006) rightly pointed to the need for a more phased-in loss of income support .

Many lone parents of young children are only available to work in part-time jobs that offer regular shift schedules. These can be hard to find, resulting in longer spells on social assistance. Paid work also often means incurring major child care costs, especially for lone parents, as well as loss of health, and possibly social housing benefits. The need for transitional supports as families leave welfare has been increasingly recognized, and some provinces, notably Saskatchewan, Manitoba and Quebec, now temporarily help cover drug costs during the transition and also supplement the earnings of persons leaving welfare. A major focus of the MISWAA Task Force report (2006) is on the need for such transitional benefits.

Facilitating transitions from social assistance to employment does not require the kind of punitive sticks that are wielded in neoliberal welfare states like Canada and are characterized by very low benefits, and deeply stigmatizing and rigorously means-tested programs. The Scandinavian social democratic countries provide reasonably generous unemployment and welfare benefits, and genuinely invest in training and in active labour market policies. Also, the fact that jobs, even at the low end of the job market, are better paid and more secure makes transitions much easier. As Johnson and Mahon (2005) argue, there are two models on how to connect social policy and the labour market; a punitive neoliberal 'workfare' model, and a progressive 'social investment' model that stresses the importance of state investments in 'human capital' and in supportive services, such as child care. These approaches in turn need to be connected to progressive labour market policies.

What Is the Mischief to Be Remedied? – Low Pay or Family Poverty?

Living in poverty is defined as living in a household that has an income falling below a poverty line set for that household type, for example, a single person; two adults; or various combinations of adults and children. Statistics Canada's LICO lines, as well as other commonly used poverty lines, such as the market basket measure (MBM) and low-income measure (LIM), attempt to gauge if the economic resources available to a household are adequate to meet a threshold standard. This standard might be access to a defined basket of goods and services (MBM) or to resources that are adequate relative to the community standard (e.g., the LIM, which is set at half the median income for an equivalent household), or some combination of the two, such as in the LICO lines.

Many workers in low-wage and precarious jobs do not live in households that fall below the poverty line, mainly because they are cushioned and protected by the wages of other (often male) earners in the household. In fact, only one in four low-wage women workers live in low-income households, although this figure rises to more than one in three for immigrant and visible minority women (Morrissette and Picot 2005). These figures do not, however, fully reflect the reality that many low-wage women workers live in families that are only treading water a little above the poverty line, and would be condemned to poverty if they lost an earning partner.

A central underlying question is whether governments should respond to the reality of low-paid and precarious jobs by topping up low family incomes or intervene directly to ensure that there are better-paid and more secure jobs for individual workers. If the approach is to top up family incomes to push them above poverty lines, then the focus will be on family income-tested wage supplements. By contrast, if the problem is defined as low wages for individual workers, then the focus will be on higher wages and improved access to benefits designed to replace individual rather than family earnings.

A recent research paper on the working poor produced by the federal Department of Human Resources and Social Development (Fleury and Fortin 2006) explicitly argues that the key area of policy concern should be working-poor families, not low-wage workers. The study defines the working poor as non-students working more than 910 hours in a year, who also live in a low-income family. Unsurprisingly, this means that the incidence of belonging to a working-poor family is very heavily influenced by family size and by the number of earners in the family.

Similarly, critics of increases in minimum wages often like to point out that some adult women minimum-wage workers are not poor – because they live with a partner who has higher earnings. Some advocates of wage supplements see higher minimum wages as an 'inefficient' poverty-fighting tool since many minimum-wage workers are young people, and supposedly 'secondary' (mainly women) earners who live in families that do not fall below the poverty line. As TD Economics posed the issue, 'The question policy makers need to ask themselves is whether they want to help workers with low earnings independent of their family economic situation, or help workers who live in poverty' (2005: 27).

Drawing attention to family composition as a factor in poverty is a valid analytical point, but problematic in policy terms. The assumption is made that resources are fully shared in the household, even though this has not stood up to close scrutiny by feminist economists. For example, it has been found that how money is spent depends on who in the household earns it, with women spending more on children's needs than men. Most importantly, dependence on the earnings of a higher-earning partner to avoid poverty entails a loss of economic independence, usually for women low-wage workers. That a low-wage woman worker is 'protected' from poverty by the earnings of a male partner also renders her vulnerable to abuse and exploitation, and clearly forecloses options and choices that would come with higher earnings. Moreover, some women are protected from poverty by the earnings of a child – a teen or young adult – in the house, which compromises the economic independence of each. Finally, a focus only on the income dimension of employment removes from view other ways in which low-wage, precarious jobs are deeply problematic for women. Being trapped in such jobs means a lack of opportunities to develop talents and capacities, to access careers and job ladders, and to attain genuine autonomy as an individual. Paid work has many valued outcomes for the worker other than securing family income above the poverty line.

Should Labour and Social Policy Reformers Support Wage Supplements?

Interest in helping the working poor is a welcome turn from the punitive orthodoxies that dominated Canadian social policy from the mid-

1970s through the 1990s. Advocates of a Working Income Tax Benefit are on the progressive side of the political spectrum to the extent that they think that work should pay and believe that people who move from welfare to work should be better off as a result and that working families should not live in poverty. It is notable that, as part of the MISWAA process, these propositions have been broadly supported by some major business actors, for example, the TD Bank (TD Economics 2005).

The advantages of a Working Income Tax Benefit are clear. Depending on the level and precise design, supplements could provide a non-trivial income boost to working-poor families and lower the 'welfare wall.' They could also be an important part of the answer to providing a decent income to people who cannot be reasonably expected to work on other than a part-time or part-year basis, notably some persons with disabilities and lone parents of young children who reasonably want to work part-time. Income supplements could – along with access to continued access to health benefits, child care, and affordable housing – be an important part of policies to ease the transition from a deeply stigmatizing and degrading social assistance system to full participation in the paid workforce.

All that said, some important caveats and reservations should be made about the concept of income supplements for the working poor, especially when seen in the light of implications for women.

Putting the Main Focus on Raising Low Pay

We need a clear sense of what the balance should be between wage supplements, on the one hand, and policies to raise wages through higher minimum wages, stronger labour standards, and access to collective bargaining, on the other. 'Realists' argue that precarious work and underemployment are here to stay. The key focus should, however, remain on improving the quantity and quality of jobs.

Canada is, like the United States and the United Kingdom, a low-wage country. One in six men and one in three women working full-time earns less than two-thirds of the national median wage, roughly double the level of most continental European countries, and almost four times the level in the Scandinavian countries. Countries with relatively equal wages and low levels of low pay tend to have low levels of family income inequality and poverty. This is unsurprising at one level, because the task of topping up low wages from transfers to promote family income equality is easier if wages are relatively equal. More surprisingly, it is because countries with high levels of wage equality also tend to spend relatively more of their national incomes on social transfers and on public services (Jackson 2005).

In the abstract, it seems plausible to say that the market should set wages and that governments should offset market inequality through income transfers. In the real world, however, very unequal societies have generally not considered the redistribution of income and the alleviation of poverty to be very important. It is telling that the current U.S. Republican administration has rejected further improvements to the Earned Income Tax Credit for the working poor on the grounds that 'tax cuts should go to taxpayers.' The perverse reasoning has been that the net effect of the EITC has been to remove low-wage workers from the tax system. Since the credit is 'refundable,' paid to tax filers with no tax to pay, many low-wage workers receive rather than pay a cheque. As such, they were consciously excluded from Republican tax cuts for 'taxpayers.'

In comparison with the United States, in the Scandinavian countries few workers must put up with low pay because unions represent a large proportion of the workforce, even in private services where most lower-pay jobs are to be found. Collective bargaining raises the relative pay of workers who would otherwise be low paid (women, youth, people of colour, and the relatively unskilled) by compressing wage differentials and also by raising productivity. Even the OECD (1996) and the World Bank (Aidt and Tzannatos 2003) have conceded that it is possible to have widespread collective bargaining coverage and also high levels of employment, labour market adaptability, and good macroeconomic performance. The OECD has also conceded that a 'reasonable' wage floor set through a statutory minimum wage can counter low pay at no cost in terms of higher unemployment.

An adequate wage floor, whether set by high union coverage or a decent minimum wage, would accomplish many of the goals of wage supplements. It would 'make work pay,' increase work incentives, and reduce the risk of income loss in transitions from welfare to work. However, a wage floor also gives employers an incentive to boost productivity by investing in capital equipment and in training. Raising productivity in low-wage sectors, especially consumer services, need not come at the price of unemployment if other policies – macroeconomic and industrial policies plus expansion of public services – maintain close to full employment. In short, wage floors are an important economic tool with which to shift work to higher productivity and higher-paying jobs, and not just a tool of income redistribution.

A higher wage floor could be established over time by facilitating union representation of lower-paid workers. This probably requires new forms of representation and bargaining at a sectoral and geographical rather than workplace-by-workplace level, so as to take labour costs out of the competitive equation in economically relevant sectors. Successful organizing and bargaining to improve wages, job security, and access to training for low-wage workers have taken place, for example, among security guards, among child care workers in Quebec, in citywide hotel and building cleaning services agreements, and in provincewide agreements for workers in the broader health care and social services sectors.

Given the very low level of current union representation in low-wage sectors, an effective wage floor also requires increasing minimum wages to adequate levels. Many social advocacy organizations have recently argued that the minimum wage should provide a living wage sufficient to keep a single person working full-time, full-year above the poverty line – implying a minimum wage of at least $10 per hour, or about two-thirds of the median hourly wage. This was, in fact, the approximate level of the average minimum wage in real terms at its high level in most provinces in the mid-1970s. Since that time, not only has the real value of the national average minimum wage fallen in terms of purchasing power due to long freezes in many provinces, it has also fallen from 50 per cent to about 40 per cent of average earnings (Battle 2003). A higher level could be reached, as in the United Kingdom, by increasing the minimum wage at a somewhat faster rate than prices and average wages, giving the labour market time to adjust.

Attention also has to be paid to the need to raise and enforce basic employment standards. In almost all provinces, the system is individual complaints-driven, and virtually all complaints are filed after a job loss. Basic standards with respect to hours of work and payment of wages are routinely ignored on a day-to-day basis in low-pay sectors, and many precarious workers are excluded because they do not fit the standard definition of an 'employee.' There could and should be effective and proactive enforcement of standards to ensure employer compliance and better standards, with respect to such key issues as stable work schedules, equal pay, and coverage for mainly women part-time and temporary workers, and provisions for paid sick leave and family

responsibility leave to deal with caring responsibilities (Canadian Labour Congress 2006).

How Will Wage Supplements Be Paid For?

Unlike wage floors achieved through higher minimum wages or collective bargaining, wage supplements would have to be paid for through
taxes, and would come at the cost of alternative forms of social spending. The fundamental fact of the matter is that a reasonably generous
supplement to working-poor families would be quite an expensive
proposition, especially if it is only gradually phased out as income rises
and applies to the working poor as well as to those leaving welfare for
work. The total cost of providing an income supplement to poor families with children that would be sufficient to raise them above the poverty line has been calculated by Campaign 2000 (2003) to be $5.3 billion.
However, a realistic program would have to include low-income single
adults and persons with disabilities, and it would have to be paid out
to persons above the poverty line as part of a phase-out.

In the real world, it is hard to imagine that a major earned income supplementation program would not come at the expense of other areas of
social spending. In the past, advocates of basic income guarantees (e.g.,
the Macdonald Royal Commission; then Minister Lloyd Axworthy, in
his 'Green Paper' of 1995) have favoured cuts to Unemployment Insurance (now EI) and other income support programs to free up funds
for a new program (Canada 1985; 1994). Part of the argument has been
that EI regular benefits are an 'inefficient' tool for fighting poverty since
unemployed workers can collect benefits, even if their annual income
is above the poverty line, and since many unemployed workers have
employed partners.

The key purpose of EI, however, is to temporarily replace the lost
wage income of individuals, not to redistribute income to low-income
families. It is important to safeguard individual eligibility rather than
treat workers differently, based on their family circumstances. An unemployed woman needs a replacement income to cover a period of
temporary unemployment or a maternity or parental leave, even if she
happens to live with an employed man. Moreover, the current EI program plays an important potential role in stabilizing the incomes of
middle- and lower-income families. While seriously undermined by
the cuts of recent governments, EI has the potential to smooth out earnings interruptions among the working poor, and the program still dis-

proportionately benefits lower-income households because relatively few higher-income households experience unemployment.

The labour movement and antipoverty groups have advanced detailed proposals for EI reform that would significantly improve access to regular benefits, as well as the level and duration of benefits. While not targeted to the needs of working-poor families per se, these proposals would improve access to the system for (mainly women and young adult) part-time workers, about one-half of whom do not qualify for benefits when they become unemployed. They would also improve access for seasonal and temporary workers. The EI program should recognize that many workers experience great difficulty in finding enough hours and weeks of work, even in regions of seemingly low unemployment.

As Myles and Pierson (1997) note, earned income supplements often reflect joint advocacy by neoliberals and persons with a very narrow concern about the alleviation of poverty, neither greatly value broader social benefits. In fact, high levels of investment in public and social services would greatly reduce the need for wage supplements. Many working-poor families would not be poor, or would be a great deal less poor, if they had access to free or heavily subsidized prescription drugs, public transit, public recreation programs, good quality child care, public educational institutions that did not charge extra fees, and so on. Universal programs and equal access to services reduce dependence on earnings and market income, and equalize economic circumstances, opportunities and life chances – regardless of the wage level of earners. Scandinavian social democratic countries are much more equal and have much lower levels of poverty than Canada and the United States, in part, because of income support programs, but also because of much more equal wages and a much higher level of tax-financed public services which are allocated on the basis of social citizenship rather than paid for on the market. Again, this increases the economic independence of women, reducing dependence on household income.

Public provision of fundamentally important services is valuable from the point of view not just of minimizing poverty, but also of creating a more inclusive and equal society. For example, we value public education because it includes all children and equalizes life chances, not just because it serves the needs of the poor. The kind of child care system we want would be universal, and provided at reasonable cost to all, as opposed to just a subsidized pillar for welfare-to-work policies. Social housing programs can create quality, affordable housing within inclusive, mixed-income communities, as opposed to rent supplements designed simply to fill gaps between low incomes and market rents.

A Benefit Based on Family Income?

The cost of any specific wage supplement program will depend on the size of the earnings supplement, the rate at which it is withdrawn as family income rises, and the family income level at which it is fully phased out. Inherent in such schemes is the fact that some recipients could face quite high tax rates at rather low levels of income, perhaps as they move from part-time to full-time or from part-year to full-year jobs.

Wage supplements as they exist in the United States and the United Kingdom, and as have been proposed for Canada, are based on family income. It is on the basis of family income that people would qualify for a particular level of benefit. However, if earnings supplements are withdrawn on the basis of rising household income, then some people will face very high taxes on individual earnings. For example, the earnings of a female spouse or young adult child of a low-wage worker taking a part-time or temporary job could easily push family income to a level where the supplement is quickly lost. There are, at a minimum, major design problems from a gender- and generational-equity perspective to be considered. Effectively, family income-tested benefits push us towards a family income-based tax system, militating against the economic independence of women.

Impacts on the Job Market

Wage supplements can be seen as a potential subsidy to low-wage employers. Some economists argue that earned income supplements would further encourage and entrench low-wage and precarious work, especially in a context of high unemployment (Iacobacci and Seccarecia 1989). Certainly, they would take some of the pressure off employers to improve wages and conditions, even in a tightening job market, as opposed to wage floor policies that would work in the other direction. If wage supplements were quite generous in a context of high unemployment, they could allow employers to lower wages and effectively shift part of their labour costs onto governments.

A recent U.K. study (Azmat 2006) challenges the assumption that tax credits to alleviate in-work poverty mainly benefit workers. Azmat investigates the incidence of the Working Families Tax Credit in the United Kingdom, introduced in 1999, which unlike similar tax credit policies, is paid through the wage packet, increasing the connection between the employer and worker with regard to the tax credit. The study found compelling evidence to suggest that employers discriminate by cutting the wage of claimant workers relative to similarly skilled non-claimant workers and that there was a spillover effect onto the wages of both claimants and non-claimants, for both men and women.

Conclusion

High levels of employment in decent, rewarding, skill-developing jobs are central to social welfare. In any 'new social architecture,' the major emphasis must be on securing access to collective bargaining and raising minimum wages and employment standards. There must also be progressive reform of Employment Insurance and continued emphasis on the importance of social and public services. If such policies were implemented, there would be a significantly reduced need for earned income supplements to address poverty among the working poor, and transitions from welfare to work would be facilitated.

While this is the key message of this chapter, earnings supplements might play a useful 'back-up' role to meet some special circumstances. Even if we raise hourly wages at the bottom of the job market and make jobs less precarious, incomes from paid work for some women will continue to be inadequate to the extent that some will only be able to work part-time in order to care for young children or elders, or because of a disability. There is a case to be made for supplementing on an ongoing basis the wages of individual workers who are participating actively in the job market in part-time jobs. Moreover, some low-income women workers will continue to be self-employed, and would not benefit from improved access to the EI program unless some key changes were made. We have to think about how to supplement low incomes from self-employment through EI reform, or outside the EI program. Persons with disabilities, who may be able to work only intermittently or on a part-time basis, could be assisted through a refundable disability tax credit designed to increase income and also cover the, often considerable, costs of employment supports.

In summary, wage supplements may play a useful supporting role in assisting the working poor, but they should not be seen as the centrepiece of a new social architecture.

Note

1 This section draws heavily on data to be found in Jackson (2005, Chapter 5: Women in the Workforce).

References

Aidt, Toke, and Zafiris Tzannatos. (2003). *Unions and Collective Bargaining: Economic Effects in a Global Environment*. Washington, DC: World Bank.

Azmat, Ghazala Yasmeen. (2006). *The Incidence of an Earned Income Tax Credit: Evaluating the Impact on Wages in the UK*. London: Centre for Economic Performance. Electronic version retrieved 18 June 2007 from http://cep.lse.ac.uk/pubs/abstract.asp?index=2337.

Battle, Ken. (2003). *Minimum Wages in Canada: A Statistical Portrait with Policy Implications*. Ottawa: Caledon Institute of Social Policy.

Battle, Ken, Michael Mendelson, and Sherri Torjman. (2006) *Towards a New Architecture for Canada's Adult Benefit.*, Ottawa: Caledon Institute of Social Policy. Electronic version retrieved 18 June 2007 from http://www.caledoninst.org/Publications/PDF/594ENG.pdf.

Campaign 2000. (2003). *Honouring Our Promises: Meeting the Challenge to End Child and Family Poverty – 2003 Report Card on Child Poverty in Canada*. Electronic version retrieved 18 June 2007 from http://www.campaign2000.ca/rc/rc03/NOV03ReportCard.pdf.

Canada. (1985). *Royal Commission on the Economic Union and Development Prospects for Canada*. MacDonald Commission. Ottawa: Canadian Government Publishing Centre.

– (1994). *Improving Social Security in Canada: A Discussion Paper*. Hull: Human Resources Development Canada.

– (2004). *Pay Equity: A New Approach to a Fundamental Right*. Final Report. Ottawa: Pay Equity Task Force, Department of Justice Canada. Electronic version retrieved 19 June 2007 from http://www.justice.gc.ca/en/payeqsal/docs/PETF_final_report.pdf.

– (2005a). *Employment Insurance (EI) Monitoring and Assessment Report*. Ottawa: Human Resources and Social Development Canada.

– (2005b). *The Economic and Fiscal Update: Strong Growth, Health Finances and a New Plan to Promote Long-Term Prosperity*. Ottawa: Department of Finance Canada.

– 2006). *Budget 2006 – Focusing on Priorities*. Ottawa: Department of Finance Canada.

Canadian Labour Congress. (1988). *Adequate Incomes for all Canadians: Policy Statement on a Guaranteed Annual Income.* Ottawa: CLC Convention.

– (2005). *Left Out in the Cold: The End of UI for Canadian Workers.* Electronic version retrieved from http://canadianlabour.ca/index.php/Unemployment_Insuran/556.

– (2006). *Labour Standards for the 21ˢᵗ Century.* Ottawa: Canadian Labour Congress.

Drolet, Marie. (2002). *The 'Who, What, When and Where' of Gender Pay Differentials.* Ottawa: Statistics Canada, Human Resources Development Canada, Business and Labour Market Analysis Division.

Fleury, Dominique, and Myriam Fortin. (2006) *When Working Is Not Enough to Escape Poverty: An Analysis of Canada's Working Poor.* Ottawa: Human Resources and Social Development Canada, Special Paper SP-630-06-06E.

Iacobacci, Mario, and Mario Seccareccia. (1989) Full Employment versus Income Maintenance: Some Reflections on the Macroeconomic and Structural Implications of a Guaranteed Income Program for Canada. *Studies in Political Economy* 28 (spring): 137–73.

Jackson, Andrew. (2005). *Work and Labour in Canada: Critical Issue.*, Toronto: Canadian Scholars Press.

Jenson, Jane. (2004). *Canada's New Social Risks: Directions for a New Social Architecture.* Ottawa: Canadian Policy Research Network.

Johnson, Robert, and Rianne Mahon. (2005). NAFTA, the Redesign, and Rescaling of Canada's Welfare State. *Studies in Political Economy* 76 (autumn): 7–30.

MISWAA Task Force (Modernizing Income Security for Working-Age Adults). (2006). *Time for a Fair Deal.* Toronto: Toronto City Summit Alliance. Electronic version retrieved 18 June 2007 from http://www.torontoalliance.ca/MISWAA_Report.pdf.

Morissette, Rene, and Anick Johnson. (2005). *Are Good Jobs Disappearing in Canada?* Ottawa: Statistics Canada, Cat. 11F0019MIE2005239.

Morissette, Rene, and Garnett Picot. (2005). *Low Paid Work and Economically Vulnerable Families over the Last Two Decades.* Ottawa: Statistics Canada, Cat. 11F0019MIE, No. 248.

Myles, John, and Paul Pierson. (1997). *Friedman's Revenge: The Reform of 'Liberal' Welfare States in Canada and the United States.* Ottawa: Caledon Institute of Social Policy.

Organization for Economic Cooperation and Development (OECD). (1996). Earnings Inequality, Low-Paid Employment and Earnings Mobility. *Employment Outlook 1996*, Ch. 3. Paris: OECD.

TD Economics. (2005). *From Welfare to Work in Ontario: Still the Road Less Travel-*

led. TD Bank Financial Group. Electronic version retrieved 18 June 2007 from http://www.td.com/economics/special/welfare05.jsp.

Vosko, Leah F. (ed.). (2006). *Precarious Employment: Understanding Labour Market Insecurity in Canada*. Montreal and Kingston: McGill-Queen's University Press.

13 Abandoning Mandatory Retirement Policies: What Are the Safeguards for Women?

MARGARET MENTON MANERY AND ARLENE TIGAR
McLAREN

The trend towards abandoning mandatory retirement is currently being widely debated in Canada, but little discussion has focused on its
implications for various sectors of employment, especially those in
which most women are concentrated. The debate has rarely acknowledged that mandatory retirement provisions apply to only about half of
all workers. Workers who are covered by mandatory retirement provisions generally have secure jobs that they may have to forfeit at the age
of 65 years. Most workers with less secure jobs, however, are unlikely
to be subject to mandatory retirement. As a result, they will not benefit
from the abolition of mandatory retirement and may, indeed, suffer indirectly from the fact that mandatory retirement is intertwined with
other policies.

In light of the debate it is important to be aware of how legislative
changes to eliminate mandatory retirement may ultimately threaten
women's economic security needs for retirement. Not all employed
women are 'vulnerable' workers; nevertheless, the jobs that most wom-
en hold are insecure, low paid, with minimal benefits (the majority, e.g.,
lack private pensions), and little workplace representation. Increasingly, the labour market has become skewed with a smaller proportion of
'good,' well-compensated jobs and a growing proportion of unstable,
relatively poorly paid jobs (Luxton and Reiter 1997), with mostly white,
well-educated men and some women having access to the former (Scott
and Lochhead 1997) and the rest of the population confined to the latter. This population is made up disproportionately of youth, women,
and immigrants (Fudge and Vosko 2003; Creese 2006). Ironically, the
interests of those with 'good' jobs have come to stand for the interests of
all workers in the mandatory retirement debates. But we leave out the

experiences of vulnerable workers to the detriment of understanding the implications of abandoning mandatory retirement for different employment sectors and the public policy strategies that need to expand safeguards to protect retirement incomes. Public policy changes need to take into consideration the social and economic impacts of current labour market forces and the different policy interests of women and men regarding mandatory retirement during a time when the very face of retirement is changing. As Monica Townson observes, there is 'growing uncertainty about retirement – how and when it might happen and what form it might take' (2006: 9).

Although mandatory retirement provisions themselves do not apply directly to most disadvantaged workers – especially women, people of colour, and other disadvantaged groups – the repercussions of eliminating the provisions may be far-reaching. Understandably, those who have good jobs now, and want to keep them, do not want to be constrained by mandatory retirement policies that allow their employer to end their employment at a pre-set, specific age. This desire to abandon mandatory retirement policies, however, fails to appreciate that mandatory retirement plays a strategic role as a specific criterion to protect age-based access to pension incomes (private and public). In addition, in the changing social and economic context and the increasing vulnerability of workers, its elimination poses a threat to public pension eligibility. The debate about ending mandatory retirement serves as a window on potential developments in the public pension system, as well as more ammunition (by virtue of less resistance) to move in the direction of pushing back the age of eligibility for pension income. It also serves to deflect attention from the economic insecurity in employment faced by those who ultimately rely exclusively or disproportionately on public pensions and the economic hardships that enforced labour market participation beyond the age of 65 would mean for them.

In exploring how mandatory retirement policies are located at the nexus of social, legal, income, and employment policies, this chapter (1) examines ways in which mandatory retirement is not just an employment arrangement, but also a social policy; (2) shows how public pensions are central to retirement income supports for most employment sectors; (3) discusses the role of public policy safeguards within the context of the 'flexible' labour market; and (4), in the conclusion, turns to public policy recommendations for safeguarding women's economic security. We argue that public pensions and labour market supports need to be considered to ensure that safeguards are in place to prohibit the erosion of current protections and rights awarded to Canadians at the age of 65 years. More specifically, we suggest policies to better meet women's economic security needs, for example, expansion of public and private pension coverage, representation of older workers in the labour force, government promotion of independent living in old age, and implementation of a Royal Commission on the Status of Older Workers to consider the social and economic security of older women.

Mandatory Retirement and Social Policy

Although mandatory retirement is not based in law, it is a legal and binding agreement negotiated between employees (or their union) and their employer that sets a retirement age as part of an employment contract. Surveys estimate that only about one-half of the Canadian labour force is subject to some form of mandatory retirement provision, whether in a collective agreement or a company personnel policy (Gunderson and Hyatt 2005). Mandatory retirement occurs in particular industries and particular jobs and usually in combination with private pensions (Gillin, MacGregor, and Klassen 2005). Since only about 40 per cent of employees have private pensions (Statistics Canada 2004), a large proportion of the labour force is not covered by rules that specify a mandatory age of retirement. A survey of the literature shows that, moreover, few employees actually retire as a result of mandatory retirement regulations (Gunderson and Pesando 1988; Gunderson 2004). Other factors such as death, poor health, layoffs, and early retirement will likely claim most employees before the age of 65 (Dunlop 1979). A study in 1988 estimated that only about 7 per cent of those bound by mandatory retirement rules were actually constrained by them (Krashinsky 1988). In 1994 the General Social Survey indicated that this proportion was about 12 per cent (Gunderson 2004). A more recent estimate showed the same figure (Saint-Cyr 2005).

Mandatory retirement is, however, more than just an employment arrangement between employers and employees. It is also a social policy that establishes criteria for income support through the public pension system that structures labour market and employment supports. Mandatory retirement is linked to numerous social policies, and pension plans, which have developed over the years based on the belief that those over 65 years of age would withdraw from the workforce. This employment arrangement, which was based on the male standard of labour (in which the male was the breadwinner in the family), became the industry standard first with the introduction of the Old Age Pension Act of 1927, when provincial governments provided pension benefits at age 70. Public pension programs such as Old Age Security (OAS), Guaranteed Income Supplement (GIS), and the Spouse's Allowance, as well as the Canada and Quebec Pension Plans (CPP and QPP) began providing retirement income for Canadians in the 1950s and 1960s and currently pay their retirement benefits beginning at age 65 (with reduced benefits available at age 60 from CPP/QPP). As companies developed private pension plans, they designed them to complement and to be integrated with public pensions – both universal pensions such as the OAS and the employment-related pensions of CPP/QPP. As a result, many organizations adopted the age of 65 years as the mandatory retirement age in private pension plan design (Dunlop 1979). Generally speaking, the social security system is premised on 'the identical age-based entitlement criteria' (Adams 1992: v). And more specifically, many social welfare programs – including employee and social benefit schemes such as group life and disability insurance, pension plans, and tax structures – are predicated on 65 as the normal retirement age. These programs and institutions have developed over the years based on the belief that people would withdraw from the workforce when they reached 65 years of age. Those concerned with human rights have long recognized that the entitlement at age 65 to public and private pensions is deeply interwoven with mandatory retirement (B.C. Human Rights Coalition 2005). The widespread and long-standing reliance throughout Canada on the permissibility of mandatory retirement prompted Supreme Court Justice La Forest to say that it had become 'part of the very fabric of the organization of the labour market in this country' (Adams 1992: 13).

The debate about banning mandatory retirement is driven by many different concerns. For those whose jobs are constrained by mandatory retirement policies and who want to continue working beyond age 65, the setting of age restrictions, understandably, is a major problem. For example, some of the most vocal opponents to mandatory retirement come from relatively privileged groups such as university professors, who have above average incomes, generally good pensionable earnings, a high status associated with their jobs, and a strong attachment to the labour force (Kesselman 2004). The debate about banning mandatory retirement, however, is driven also in part by labour and skill shortages. For example, the University of Toronto has reached a tentative deal with its faculty association to end its policy of mandatory retirement for professors and librarians to keep valued staff members who would otherwise move on.

A further reason for employees with relatively good jobs to argue for the elimination of mandatory retirement is that, increasingly, private pensions have shifted from defined *benefits* to defined *contributions*. Historically, mandatory retirement provided a deferred pay system in the private pension system. Employers paid younger employees less, and older employees more, with the added provision that older employees could keep their jobs, typically until age 65, and retire with a pension that guaranteed benefits at a set rate for life (so-called defined-benefit plans). Labour market restructuring has changed the efficacy of retirement income supports. Defined-benefit pension plans – which entitle the employee to a pension guaranteed by the plan sponsor related to earnings and years of service, with a guaranteed rate of benefits usually paid out starting at age 65 – are much less common now; in their place defined-contribution pension plans have become widespread (Baldwin 2004). These plans do not provide any guaranteed retirement income and shift the entire risk of providing a retirement income from the employer to the employee, thus making it exceedingly difficult to financially plan for retirement. Consequently, those who have private pensions have reason to argue that working beyond age 65 may be not only a question of freedom and choice, but also an economic necessity.

The human rights argument to challenge mandatory retirement as a form of age discrimination that restricts the freedom of individuals to work no matter what their age, as long as they are competent, is important. The Supreme Court of Canada, however, has ruled that such discrimination can be 'reasonable' and demonstrably justified in specific cases (McDonald 1995; Townson 1997). Most jurisdictions banning mandatory retirement, for example, make exceptions in the case of bona fide occupational requirements. In practice that may mean a retirement age can be set under terms of employment in a pension plan or collective agreement.[1] Furthermore, mandatory retirement as a human rights issue can rest on the notion of 'freedom of contract' between employer and employee – as a normal component of the terms and conditions of employment (Dunlop 1979). In other words, the practice of mandatory retirement carries with it both burdens as well as benefits for the older worker, as it developed in conjunction with the spread of pension plans during the past few decades. Many trade unions in Canada want to be able to negotiate mandatory provisions into their defined-benefits pension plans contained in their collective agreements to get better pension benefits for their members. The labour movement's opposition to the abolition of mandatory retirement is reflected in Canadian Labour Congress Resolution No. 377 passed in 1980 and confirmed in 1982: 'be it resolved that the Canadian Labour Congress is opposed to the erosion of the mandatory retirement system and that the current permissive legal framework be maintained so that the unions that wish to accept mandatory retirement are free to do so and those that wish to eliminate it can do so through collective bargaining' (Adams 1992: 3).

Although many different groups have argued in favour or against mandatory retirement, they nonetheless generally draw on assumptions of a male standard of labour, and do not consider mandatory retirement implications for women. On the face of it, mandatory retirement is a neutral practice with regard to gender – both women and men are subject to it. But because of historical, systemic inequalities, women are less economically prepared than men for retirement at the age of 65. As a social practice, mandatory retirement takes the work experiences of men as the normative standard; it ignores the many ways that women's life experiences differ from men's and, therefore, how it may have discriminatory effects on women (McLaren and Manery 2001). As a result, human rights commissions (e.g., Ontario Human Rights Commission) have expressed concern not only about the age discrimination that mandatory retirement allows. They have also noted its adverse effects on such groups as women and new immigrants, who have interrupted employment patterns or who enter the Canadian labour market later in their lives (Ontario Human Rights Commission 2001).

While younger generations of women are benefiting from declining wage gaps between women and men, and are generally employed for longer periods than older women have been, they are still subject to an entrenched system of occupational and educational segregation, the many inequities associated with it, and the prevailing invisibility and devaluing of domestic and community work.[2] More recently, they are faced with the proliferation of non-standard jobs (Cranford et al. 2003; Law Commission of Canada 2004) and the decline of social and community services (Fuller and Stephens 2004), which gives them less support and increased responsibilities for the health and welfare of family and community members.

Despite the compelling argument that mandatory retirement adversely affects women, younger as well as older women, it would be nonetheless premature to conclude that mandatory retirement should be eliminated on behalf of women. Government legislation to remove mandatory retirement may help some women, particularly those who are covered by private pensions, are well educated, and enjoy other advantages; but such a step is not likely to address the pervasive structural problems shared by most women, who do not have private pension plans (Morissette and Drolet 2001). In addition, other differences among women need to be taken into account. The systemic factors that adversely affect women's economic position are compounded by indigenous status, visible minority status, immigration status, disablement, sexual orientation, and so on (Day and Brodsky 1991; 1999; Jackman 1995).

While mandatory retirement may be discriminatory against some women, it is but a small part of the much larger problem of systemic discrimination that needs to be addressed (Adams 1992). Rather than eliminating mandatory retirement, the former judge George Adams argues, other measures might be more effective in addressing the problem of women's interrupted work histories: 'For example, might not mandatory private pension plans, mandatory portability of private plans, adequate day care, and social security contributions for women who work in the home caring for our children be better responses to the interrupted work histories of many women?' (1992: 13–14).

As Donald Dunlop notes, 'whether mandatory retirement is a discriminatory act that requires redress by federal and provincial governments is essentially a value judgment based on the prevailing ethics of the society' (1979: xii). In addition, it needs to be emphasized that responses to this question may vary significantly depending on which group of workers one has in mind.

In assessing its adverse effects on women, public policy should not address mandatory retirement as an isolated practice, nor as the most important. It is part of a complex web of systemic obstacles that render most women's experiences invisible and fundamentally insecure. Other policies and practices (e.g., pension plans based on employee contributions, the lack of appropriate child care, and the use of retirement replacement ratios as an indicator of pension adequacy), which treat men's experiences as normative and standard, shield from rigorous scrutiny the complexity and the pervasiveness of the systemic discrimination that women experience. As the B.C. Human Rights Coalition has recently argued: 'mandatory retirement raises important human rights considerations but it also encapsulates economic, labour and social policy concerns. Thus these larger issues must be incorporated into any substantive human rights analysis' (2005: 1). To insist on the elimination of mandatory retirement without providing other safeguards could create even further adverse effects for vulnerable workers. If our public pension system revises the age of entitlement to benefits upwards, as has the United States, the claim to 'a right to work' by privileged groups of workers risks being transformed, for the less advantaged, to 'an obligation to work' past the age of 65 (Adams 1992: 9). As mandatory retirement has already been abolished in several jurisdictions, it is essential that the existing safeguards of eligibility for public pensions at age 65 be protected. A delay or a reduction in pensions would be particularly disadvantageous to workers who have few alternative sources of retirement income. Workers who are already poor, or who are subject to multiple forms of discrimination, will suffer more from the banning of mandatory retirement and a corresponding introduction of more private and flexible pension plans than from the current permissibility of mandatory retirement.

Public Policy and Retirement Income Supports

While three provinces abolished mandatory retirement in the 1970s and early 1980s (New Brunswick in 1973, Manitoba in 1974, and Quebec in 1982), today there is renewed momentum to expand the abolition of mandatory retirement to the most populated jurisdictions in Canada. Ontario recently passed such legislation, in 2005; effective 1 January 2008, British Columbia eliminated mandatory retirement, and the Saskatchewan government eliminated it in 2007. As a result, it is important to examine the labour market and pension implications for vulnerable workers, especially given the current social and economic climate in Canada and elsewhere of rapid change and restructuring. While the elimination of mandatory retirement is not itself a direct problem for vulnerable workers – after all, they are unlikely to be constrained by mandatory retirement – its elimination may contribute to a destabilization of the age of eligibility for retirement income supports. Existing research suggests that the pressure to increase the age of eligibility for public pensions and to end mandatory retirement is happening in tandem as part of an overall trend to contain pension costs and to increase individual reliance on private market income (OECD 2006). If mandatory retirement loses its permissibility across the country, federal legislation will be freer to shift the age of eligibility for public pensions (OAS/GIS and CPP/QPP) upward. If the age of eligibility for public pensions increases, it is workers without private pensions (and mandatory retirement provisions) who will be most adversely affected. The current debates and directions in retirement policy and pension provisions have failed to consider adequately how such proposed changes would jeopardize the security of the most vulnerable workers.

Although raising the official retirement age is not yet on the agenda in Canada, recent proposals in Quebec are 'proactively' responding to OECD comments that Canada needs to raise the actual retirement age (Le Goff 2004). As a result of public consultations, the Quebec government proposes to develop more 'flexible' retirement benefits to dissuade workers from retiring early (i.e., before age 65) and to stay longer in the workforce (beyond 65). Despite Quebec's elimination of mandatory retirement in 1982, the average retirement age in 1990 was 61.2 years, and in 2000 it was even lower, at age 60 (the national average in 2000 was 61.5 years; Le Goff 2004).[3] Concerned about the falling average retirement age, the Quebec government proposes disincentives to early retirement, including actuarial adjustments that increase pension entitlements of those who contributed to the pension plan for more than forty years in the workforce and reduce entitlements for those who have spent less time in the workforce.[4] The latter would likely include those who experience unemployment and/or underemployment, interrupted careers, later employment starts such as immigrants, and so forth. Such proposals run counter to the current QPP and the equivalent CPP,[5] which serve as employment insurance programs that help to protect older workers from poverty in old age, starting at age 60.

While proposed changes to encourage later ages of retirement might give those who want to work beyond age 65 more 'flexibility,' it is important to consider the long-term impact on retirement incomes and the funding of pensions for those who have less choice. As Gunderson and Hyatt argue, the debate must include concerns raised by the trade unions and others who represent workers' interests that 'banning mandatory retirement is starting down a slippery slope where benefits to seniors will be whittled away on the grounds that they can keep working' (2005: 149). For example, the OECD report, *Boosting Jobs and Incomes*, released in Toronto on 15–16 June 2006, promotes recommendations for such regressive policies as 'work-for-welfare, two-tier minimum wages, ending mandatory retirement, further restricting 'wage setting institutions' (i.e. unions and collective bargaining), cutting public pensions' (Peters 2006: n.p.). If the OECD's recommendations become the 'new normal,' working people may face lower wages, less secure work, fewer pension protections, and more poverty. Following the report's release, the Stephen Harper government discussed steps in that direction, of cutting back employer and worker contributions to the Canada Pension Plan (CPP) to put 'more money in people's pockets' (Peters 2006: n.p.). This approach promotes the idea of private, individualized savings accounts where the individual is responsible for the risk of securing her or his retirement income.

The movement to eliminate mandatory retirement is occurring with the growing dominance of neoliberal thinking and practices that promote the objective of a privatized system of individual savings accounts as an effective way to reduce the fiscal cost of public pensions (Beattie and McGillivary 1995). As many workers are facing more insecure working conditions and fewer social program supports, one needs to ask whether, within this context, the abolition of mandatory retirement would contribute further to the unraveling of the social security system. During the current period of government restructuring and shifts towards neoliberal social, economic, and labour market policies – which increasingly download responsibility for well-being to individuals and their participation in the labour force – it is also important to be aware of how changes to mandatory retirement policies may affect women's economic security in old age. As Mary Condon argues, 'retirement income provision in Canada is built on gendered assumptions, which produce material disadvantage for women. These inequalities are being exacerbated by current neoliberal trends towards the 'marketization' and individualization of pension provision, supported by tax, securities and corporate legal norms' (2001: 83). If these trends continue, they could undermine the 'universal' part of retirement income security provisions that are not dependent on earnings in the labour force – Old Age Security and the Guaranteed Income Supplement – and that have helped mitigate poverty among people past employment age.

Current protections and rights in Canada on behalf of people on low incomes, notably elderly Canadians living below the poverty line, include the right to public pension programs such as Old Age Security (OAS) and the Guaranteed Income Supplement (GIS) as of age 65. The Canada and Quebec Pension Plans (CPP/QPP) offer retirement benefits to those who do not want to or cannot work, beginning at age 65, with reduced benefits available at age 60. Most Canadians are able to receive such public pensions as OAS regardless of their employment history (Social Development Canada 2007).[6] If individuals have had few employment opportunities – whether because of limited skills, a shrinking job market, family responsibilities, and discriminatory or exclusionary practices – they will be highly dependent on their public pension (Women Elders in Action 2004).[7] If they have had limited employment opportunities throughout their lives, it is unlikely that such opportunities will materialize for them as they grow older. In their retirement, such older people will have few alternative sources of income. In contrast, workers with good jobs with well-defined benefits will likely have greater security in old age, with several sources of substantial income, including the CPP/QPP and private pensions.

One of the strengths of Canada's retirement income system is that the risks and responsibilities are shared in a relatively balanced and flexible way that responds to the different financial needs of individuals and families over the course of their lifetimes. The federal government was well aware of the phenomenon of Canada's aging 'boomer' population and took that into consideration in designing the Canadian public pension system in the 1960s (Statistics Canada 1991). This foundation has made it possible for former Finance Minister Ralph Goodale to claim that 'Canada is one of the few countries in the world with a rock-solid public pension system' (2004: 11). However, the federal government did not design the public pension system to provide 100 per cent of Canadians' retirement income. Rather, government policy encourages individuals to save for retirement through tax-advantaged private pensions and savings plans. Generally, retirement income needs to be about 70 per cent of pre-retirement earnings to maintain a similar standard of living in retirement, with CPP/QPP replacing on average 25 per cent of earnings, and OAS replacing about 14 per cent (Baldwin 2004). While the CPP/QPP is one program that is specifically designed to contribute to earnings replacement objectives, the flat rate OAS benefit contributes to this objective as well. Because of OAS's flat rate, these two programs provide a replacement rate that is higher at lower levels of earnings. OAS and CPP will replace just over one-half of pre-retirement earnings for those whose earnings were at half the average wage. These programs will replace about 20 per cent of pre-retirement earnings for those who had high incomes, at twice the average wage and salaries. But replacement rates rest on averages and do not take into account the low earnings of many Canadians. OAS/GIS and investment incomes are generally more important for women, as more women depend on these programs than men. CPP/QPP and workplace pensions are more important for men, who on average receive higher benefits than women (Baldwin 2004).

Much of Canada's retirement income system provides rights and protections that depend on an individual's relationship to the labour force. Non-standard labour has become the way of participating in the labour force for almost two million low-wage workers in Canada. About one in six employed people currently work for less than $10 an hour (Maxwell 2002; Saunders 2004; Chaykowski 2005; Morissette 2008). Immigrants, women, and unskilled workers experience the highest risk of poverty in old age. New immigrants are more likely to have low income than those people who have been in Canada for more than fifteen years or those who were Canadian-born (Chung 2004). Single women who live alone are among the most impoverished among seniors, but the number of single men who live alone and who are impoverished in old age is also growing (Chung 2004). The OAS/GIS and CPP/QPP are the only stop gap against poverty in old age. Public pensions are all the more needed to secure retirement income for people who face poverty in old age as the labour market has become more 'flexible.' Rather than recommending banning mandatory retirement restrictions on employment, the Ontario English Catholic Teachers Association, for example, recommends finding ways to 'organize and negotiate contracts for unorganized workers so that they can improve their incomes, working conditions, job security, and retirement benefits' (2004: 2–3).

The 'Flexible' Labour Market and Public Policy Safeguards

While labour laws designed to reflect a labour market based on full-time, permanent, paid employment are no longer applicable to over one-third of the Canadian workforce[8] – people who are either self-employed or work at part-time or temporary jobs – eligibility for most labour- and employment-related rights, benefits, and protections still remains based almost exclusively on the standard employment relationship (Law Commission of Canada 2004). Such protections, nevertheless, vary within non-standard employment. For example, whereas contributions to CPP/QPP, which are based on earnings, are shared between the employer and employee, each paying 4.95 per cent of all earnings to a maximum contribution,[9] self-employed workers pay both portions, equal to 9.9 percent of earnings (Social Development Canada 2007). The self-employed are even more disadvantaged than other non-standard workers, as they are not eligible for such social insurance programs as Employment Insurance. Many who work in non-standard labour markets are left unprotected by public programs and a labour market that is becoming increasingly precarious, indicating a lack of protection under collective agreements and employment standards legislation (Cranford et al. 2003). In a report for the Law Commission of Canada, Kerry Rittich (2004) argues that, in promoting labour market flexibility, many jurisdictions are serving employers at the cost of protecting workers. This reorganization of the workplace and the economy, she suggests, is occurring at a time of declining strength in worker representation and voice, in which 'a 'representation gap' contributes to the downward pressure on wages and working conditions and increases economic and other forms of vulnerability at work' (2004: 40). Rittich recommends that legal reforms be developed to promote new forms of worker representation, particularly of the most vulnerable workers, to improve the status of workers in the new economy; workplaces, for example, need to introduce new voice mechanisms and greater access to union representation of vulnerable workers to collectively bargain over the redistribution of risks and rewards and the reorganization of work (2004).

In addition, the Canadian Labour Congress (CLC) is concerned that the decline in unionization and access to arbitration to ensure the enforcement of employment standards and human rights has allowed deregulation of the labour market. During the Canadian Human Rights Act Review Panel, in 1999, the CLC proposed establishing Human Rights Workplace Committees, based on the model of health and safety committees 'to monitor compliance with human rights legislation, and to act as providers of information on how workers could bring forward complaints' (2005: 23). The CLC argues that the impact of labour market deregulation in the 1980s and 1990s has depleted employment standards authorities of the resources and political support needed to protect vulnerable workers (2005). A study in British Columbia, for example, shows that the provincial government's recent changes to nearly every aspect of employment standards law, administration, and enforcement have eroded workers' rights and economic security (Fairey 2005).

The situation is especially critical for unrepresented workers, who have limited access to resources against violations of labour standards due to both 'a real and perceived threat of reprisal against employees who complain about their employment while on the job' (Law Commission of Canada 2004: 22). For example, the Canadian labour force is increasingly more diverse: 'More than three in four immigrants are persons of colour (belong to visible minority groups) and immigrants now account for virtually all labour force growth' (CLC 2005: 24). Non-unionized workers, who may not have the knowledge or resources to carry complaints forward, could rely on 'Workplace Committees' to 'help fill this key gap' (CLC 2005: 26).

Furthermore, several studies recommend safeguards that do not depend solely on the relationship between employer and employee and labour market participation (Rittich 2004; Law Commission of Canada 2004; Vallée 2005). These studies suggest that legal rules and policies are needed to address a range of non-market issues and concerns from the perspective of social and economic equality. For example, the Law Commission of Canada (2004) recommends expanding the social safety net by acknowledging that workers' participation in the labour force over the course of a lifetime involves diverse forms of work, including such non-marketable forms of work as child and elder care (see also Vallée 2005).

The differences in public and private benefit coverage among unionized workers and unrepresented workers draw attention to important principles of universality and human rights. Without any form of workplace protection from illness, demands of family care, or long-term disability, or without private pensions, the most vulnerable members of the labour force are left outside the current reach of labour laws. The public pension system may be their only source of retirement or disability income, albeit one that is set well below the poverty line. Improvements to labour laws, which would enhance their health and well-being and improve conditions and opportunities to prepare for retirement, will serve their purposes far more than the elimination of mandatory retirement will.

Concluding Discussion

The move to end mandatory retirement today represents a potential threat to the provision of public pensions at the age of 65 years because it comes at a time when the public pension system has been under threat, and continues to be so. Successive amendments to the OAS Act, including the claw-back (which takes back benefits from higher-income families and pensioners), implemented in 1989, removed universality in income security provisions for seniors. The Harper government supports reducing employer and employee contributions to the CPP in order to leave more money in the hands of taxpayers. In the context of growing concerns about an aging population (the so-called silver tsunami; Gram and Kane 2006), calls to increase labour market participation, and a neoliberal market-driven agenda emphasizing privatization, commodification, debt reduction, and lowering taxes, pressure has grown to shift community norms and expectations about the reasonableness of raising the age of retirement and eligibility for pension income (OECD 2006).

The more recent initiatives to end mandatory retirement provisions, in particular, in two highly populated provinces in the country, will potentially escalate an erosion of public commitment to public pension income at age 65. Because the workers who benefit from its elimination are relatively advantaged economically, and therefore politically, any slippage in their stake in the need to access pension income at age 65 is a potential threat to public pension provisions at that specific age. This scenario is similar to the debate about the removal of universality in government programs and its replacement with income-tested measures: the most needy are the ones who remain vested in the continuation of the public program – and they have the least power, politically speaking, to defend the provisions and standards.

The elimination of mandatory retirement is not a panacea, and it does not serve everyone equally. For one, it is not clear to what extent employers are willing to keep on or hire older workers, nor to what extent they are willing to accommodate older workers' needs (Gatt 2006). While it is easy to say that banning mandatory retirement will give everyone more freedom and flexibility and that it will protect human rights, many people are more concerned about the problems of inadequate wages and pensions, the public pension system, and the need for more supportive social programming. The mandatory retirement debate often ignores poverty and economic insecurity in old age. Yet, increasingly workers have unstable private pensions and less access to full employment and good benefits. Any discussion about eliminating mandatory retirement needs to address the right to social security for seniors, the majority of whom are women. The 'right to work' after the age of 65 years should not become an 'obligation to work' in conditions that jeopardize the health and well-being of older people. In considering the debate on mandatory retirement, we need to look at the larger social context of increased polarization between those who are doing quite well under the current economic system and those who are not. It is also important to ensure that those in decent job,s who want to have the choice to continue working in old age, are not speaking on behalf of everyone else – including those in non-standard jobs or those who have no private pension plans. Their retirement experience is likely to be very different from that of people in higher socioeconomic classes.

As we have argued throughout this chapter, income inequalities in retirement are directly connected to income inequality during working life. To address the complex question of protecting workers against income insecurity in their senior years, it would be worthwhile to appoint ombudspersons to represent the interests of older workers, particularly those who are vulnerable. Furthermore, the establishment of a task force or royal commission for older workers could focus attention, for example, on a broader definition of work, how the public pension system can better protect low-income workers, how employers can accommodate older workers, and how employment and labour standards can protect older workers who wish to continue working beyond age 65. Such a task force or commission might want to consider policy strategies that ensure, for example, the following: all workers logging more than ten hours a week have access to workplace pensions; these pensions are portable and do not have to be vested; all pensions both public and private are fully indexed; the minimum wage is raised to enable all working people to live above the poverty line to benefit them both during their working years and in later life; and taxation is removed from income below the poverty line (Women Elders in Action 2004).

In pursuing recommendations to address women's issues, it is important to consider a broader definition of 'work.' In addition, if federal and provincial governments are seeking to entice older female workers into the labour force, they need to develop integrated and comprehensive, economic, social, and labour market policies to accommodate such workers. Policies need to ensure that safeguards are in place to protect women's economic security. Policies also need to allow older women a measure of well-being, without an obligation to participate in the labour force. Many women have suffered from social inequalities and their rights as citizens, and the worth of their contributions to society often goes unrecognized. Public policies need to take into account the many ways in which women, whether in the labour force or not, contribute to society and they must have equal rights to its entitlements.

Acknowledgements

We thank the Columbia Institute for its financial support of the research for this chapter. The research benefited considerably from insights and comments by reviewers Marjorie Griffin Cohen and Monica Townson. We also thank Jane Pulkingham for her helpful comments on an earlier draft.

Notes

1 New Brunswick, e.g., which banned mandatory retirement in 1973, allows an exemption for mandatory retirement in the case of bona fide occupational qualification, if the employer can establish that it is reasonably necessary to the accomplishment of a legitimate work-related purpose (New Brunswick Human Rights Commission 2004).
2 For discussion on the status of gender equality in Canada, see Brodie 2007.
3 Ironically, the elimination of mandatory retirement in some provinces and in federal government employment has done very little to alleviate labour shortage problems associated with an aging population (Shannon and Grierson 2004). Ontario has passed legislation to eliminate mandatory retirement at the age of 65, even though, as Ontario Labour Minister Steve Peters reports, 'It's expected that less than two percent of Ontario's 1.5 million people 65 and over would continue to work' (Brautigam 2005: A8).
4 Other recommended changes to the QPP include allowing workers to receive pension benefits starting at age 60 and still keep their jobs. Those who re-enter the workforce after they start receiving public pension benefits would have to contribute to the plan while they receive their pension (Le Goff 2004).
5 The CPP and QPP are similar, in that they both share the same contribution rates, insurable earnings, and income replacement rate, but the QPP provides more generous survivor benefits for spouses under age 65 and more flexibility for disability benefits for participants aged 60 to 64 (Le Goff 2004).
6 An individual must have lived in Canada for ten years to be eligible for OAS, and for forty years after the age of 18 to receive an average monthly benefit of $467.21 in October 2006 (Social Development Canada 2007).
7 Many developing countries do not have government pensions, or reciprocal agreements with Canada, and as a result, the number of immigrant seniors living in Canada who are not eligible for public pensions is growing (Women Elders in Action 2004).
8 'An estimated two million adult Canadian workers earn less than $10 an hour. Almost two thirds of low-wage earners are women. About one third are the only wage earner in their family. This would mean that about 667,000 workers, most of whom are women, are attempting to support their families on less than $10 an hour. These people likely live in extremely impoverished circumstances' (Law Commission of Canada 2004: 21).
9 According to the Law Commission of Canada (2004), in 2000, the self-employed represented 16% of all workers; almost half of self-employed women had incomes of $20,000 or less.

References

Adams, George W. (1992). *Mandatory Retirement and Constitutional Choices.* Current Issues Series. Kingston: Queen's University, Industrial Relations Centre.

Baldwin, Bob. (2004). *Pension Reform in Canada in the 1990s: What Was Accomplished, What Lies Ahead.* Research Paper No. 30. Ottawa: CLC.

Beattie, Roger, and Warren McGillivary. (1995). A Risky Strategy: Reflections on the World Bank Report 'Averting the Old Age Crisis.' *International Social Security Review* 48(3–4): 5–22.

Brautigam, Tara. (2005). Ontario Will Ban Mandatory Retirement. *Vancouver Sun*, 9 Dec.: A8.

B.C. Human Rights Coalition. (2005). *Newsletter 2(1), February.* Electronic version retrieved 1 April 2005 from http://www.bchrcoalition.org/files/News072005web.pdf.

Brodie, Janine. (2007). Canada's 3-Ds: The Rise and Decline of the Gender-Based Policy Capacity. In Marjorie Griffin Cohen and Janine Brodie (eds.), *Remapping Gender in the New Global Order*, 166–84. London: Routledge.

Canadian Labour Congress (CLC). (2005). *Labour Standards for the 21st Century.* CLC Issue Paper on Part III of the Canada Labour Code. Ottawa: CLC.

Chaykowski, Richard. (2005). *Non-standard Work and Economic Vulnerability.* Vulnerable Workers Research Series. Ottawa: Canadian Policy Research Networks.

Chung, Lucy. (2004). Low-Paid Workers: How Many Live in Low-Income Families? *Perspectives on Labour and Income* 5(10): 5–14.

Condon, Mary. (2001). Gendering the Pension Promise in Canada: Risk, Financial Markets and Neo-liberalism. *Social and Legal Studies* 10(1): 83–103.

Cranford, Cynthia J., Leah F. Vosko, and Nancy Zukewich. (2003). Precarious Employment in the Canadian Labour Market: A Statistical Portrait. *Just Labour* 3 (fall): 6–22.

Creese, Gillian. (2006). Racializing Work/Reproducing White Privilege. In Vivian Shalla and Wallace Clement (eds.), *Work and Labour in Tumultuous Times: Critical Perspectives*, 192–226. Montreal: McGill-Queen's University Press.

Day, Shelagh, and Gwen Brodsky. (1991). *Women and the Equality Deficit: The Impact of Restructuring Canada's Social Programs.* Ottawa: Status of Women.

– (1999). Women's Economic Inequality and the Canadian Human Rights Act. In Donna Greschner, Mark Prescott, Martha Jackman, Bruce Porter, Shelagh Day, and Gwen Brodsky (eds.), *Women and the Canadian Human Rights Act:*

A Collection of Policy Research Reports, 113–76. Ottawa: Status of Women Canada.

Dunlop, Donald P. (1979). *Mandatory Retirement Policy: A Human Rights Dilemma?* Ottawa: Conference Board of Canada.

Fairey, David. (2005). *Eroding Worker Protections: British Columbia's New 'Flexible' Employment Standards.* Vancouver: Canadian Centre for Policy Alternatives, B.C.

Fudge, Judy, and Leah F. Vosko. (2003). Gender Paradoxes and the Rise of Contingent Work: Towards a Transformative Political Economy of the Labour Market. In Wallace Clement and Leah F. Vosko (eds.), *Changing Canada: Political Economy as Transformation*, 183–209. Montreal and Kingston: McGill-Queen's University Press.

Fuller, Sylvia, and Lindsay Stephens. (2004). *Women's Employment in BC: Effects of Government Downsizing and Employment Policy Changes 2001–2004.* Vancouver: Canadian Centre for Policy Alternatives, B.C.

Gatt, Virginia. (2006). Thinking of Working Past 65? Think Again. *Globe and Mail*, n.p. Electronic version retrieved 5 Aug. 2006 from http://www.prime50.com/press/media_article_thinking_of_working_past_65_aug_05_2006.htm.

Gillin, C. Terry, David MacGregor, and Thomas R. Klassen. (2005). *Time's Up! Mandatory Retirement in Canada.* Toronto: James Lorimer.

Goodale, P.C., MP, The Honourable. (2004). The Economic and Fiscal Update. Presentation to the House of Commons Standing Committee on Finance, 16 Nov.

Gram, Karen, and Michael Kane. (2006). Premier Promises to End Mandatory Retirement. *Vancouver Sun*, 2 Dec. Electronic version retrieved 21 Jan. 2007 from http://www.canada.com/vancouversun/news/story.html?id=c0e60ec7–8851–4b67-ab4b-b808824f0f98.

Gunderson, Morley. (2004). *Banning Mandatory Retirement: Throwing Out the Baby with the Bathwater.* Backgrounder No. 79. Toronto: C.D. Howe Institute.

Gunderson, Morley, and Douglas Hyatt. (2005). Mandatory Retirement: Not as Simple as It Seems. In C.T. Gillin, David MacGregor, and Thomas R. Klassen (eds.), *Time's Up! Mandatory Retirement in Canada*, 139–60. Toronto: James Lorimer.

Gunderson, Morley, and James Pesando. (1988). The Case for Allowing Mandatory Retirement. *Canadian Public Policy* 14(1): 244–64.

Jackman, Martha. (1995). Women and the Canada Health and Social Transfer: Ensuring Gender Equality in Federal Welfare Reform. *Canadian Journal of Women and the Law* 6: 371–410.

Kesselman, Jonathan R. (2004). An Economic Primer on Mandatory Retirement. Presented to SFU Faculty Association, 24 Sept. Electronic version retrieved 21 March 2005 from http://www.ocufa.on.ca/retirement./

Krashinsky, Michael. (1988). The Case for Eliminating Mandatory Retirement: Why Economics and Human Rights Need Not Conflict. *Canadian Public Policy* 14: 40–51.

Law Commission of Canada. (2004). *Is Work Working? Work Laws that Do a Better Job*. Discussion Paper. Ottawa: Law Commission of Canada.

Le Goff, Philippe. (2004). *Public Pension Plans and the Labour Market: The Case of the Quebec Pension Plan*. Parliamentary Information and Research Services. Ottawa: Library of Parliament, Cat. No. PRB 04–54E.

Luxton, Meg, and Ester Reiter. (1997). Double, Double, Toil and Trouble … Women's Experience of Work and Family in Canada, 1980–1995. In Patricia M. Evans and Gerda R. Wekerle (eds.), *Women and the Canadian Welfare State: Challenges and Change*, 197–221. Toronto: University of Toronto Press.

Maxwell, Judith. (2002). *Smart Social Policy: Making Work Pay*. Submitted to the TD Forum on Canada's Standard of Living.

McDonald, Lynn. (1995). Retirement for the Rich and Retirement for the Poor: From Social Security to Social Welfare. Editorial. *Canadian Journal on Aging* 14(3): 447–57.

McLaren, Arlene Tigar, and Margaret Menton Manery. (2001). *Factors Affecting the Economic Status of Older Women in Canada: Implications for Mandatory Retirement*. Vancouver: B.C. Human Rights Commission.

Morissette, René. (2008). Earnings in the Last Decade. *Perspectives,* 12–24. Ottawa: Statistics Canada, Cat. No. 75–001-X. Electronic version retrieved on 10 July 2008, from http://www.statcan.ca/english/freepub/75–001-XIE/2008102/pdf/10521-en.pdf.

Morissette, René, and Marie Drolet. (2001). Pension Coverage and Retirement Savings of Young and Prime-Aged Workers in Canada, 1986–1997. *Canadian Journal of Economics* 34(1): 110–19.

New Brunswick Human Rights Commission. (2004). *Guidelines to Mandatory Retirement*. Electronic version retrieved 2 March 2005 from http://www.gnb.ca/hrc-cdp/e/Guideline-on-Mandatory-Retirement.pdf.

Ontario English Catholic Teachers Association. (2004). *Response (Revised) to the Minister of Labour's Consultation Paper on Mandatory Retirement*. Electronic version retrieved 2 March 2005 from http://www.oecta.on.ca/pdfs/retirement.pdf.

Ontario Human Rights Commission. (2001). Time for Action: Advancing Human Rights for Older Ontarians. Toronto: OHRC. Electronic version retrieved 2 March 2005 from http://www.ohrc.on.ca/english/consultations/age-consultation-report.shtml.

Organization for Economic Cooperation and Development. (2006). *OECD. Employment Outlook 2006: Boosting Jobs and Incomes.* Paris: OECD.

Peters, John. (2006). The Wrong Way to Boost Jobs and Incomes. *Socialist Project, E-Bulletin 29*, 19 July. Electronic version retrieved 1 Dec. 2006 from http://www.socialistproject.ca/bullet/bullet029.html.

Rittich, Kerry. (2004). *Vulnerability at Work: Legal and Policy Issues in the New Economy.* Ottawa: Report for the Law Commission of Canada.

Saint-Cyr, Yosie. (2005). The State of Retirement in Ontario. Electronic version retrieved 25 Feb. 2005 from http://www.visa.ca/smallbusiness/article. cfm?articleID=246.

Saunders, Ron. (2004). *Defining Vulnerability in the Labour Market.* Vulnerable Workers Research Series. Ottawa: Canadian Policy Research Networks.

Scott, Katherine, and Clarence Lochhead. (1997). *Are Women Catching Up in the Earnings Race?* Social Research Series Paper No. 3. Ottawa: Canadian Council on Social Development.

Shannon, Michael T., and Diana Grierson. (2004). Mandatory Retirement and the Older Worker. *Canadian Journal of Economics* 33(3): 528–51.

Social Development Canada. (2007). Old Age Security Benefit Payment Rates, January to March. Electronic version retrieved 3 March 2007 from http://www.sdc.gc.ca/en/isp/oas/oasrates.shtml#note.

Statistics Canada. (1991). *Population Dynamics in Canada.* Ottawa: Statistics Canada, Cat. No. 96–305E.

– (2004). Percentage of All Paid Workers. Ottawa: Statistics Canada, Cat. No. 74–507-XCB and 13F0026MIE-2004001.

Townson, Monica. (1997). *Independent Means: A Canadian Woman's Guide to Pensions and a Secure Financial Future.* Toronto: Macmillan.

– (2006). *Growing Older, Working Longer: The New Face of Retirement.* Ottawa: Canadian Centre for Policy Alternatives.

Vallée, Guylaine. (2005). *Towards Enhancing the Employment Conditions of Vulnerable Workers: A Public Policy Perspective.* Vulnerable Workers Research Series No. 2. Ottawa: Canadian Policy Research Networks.

Women Elders in Action (WE*ACT). (2004). *Pensions in Canada: Policy Reform Because Women Matter.* Vancouver: WE*ACT.

14 Canadian and International Policies on Prostitution: Labour Legitimacy, Social Change, and Decriminalization

EMILY VAN DER MEULEN

International policies on the sex industry vary widely from country to country. England, for example, allows individual prostitutes to work from home but not on the street. In the United States, the State of Nevada has heavily regulated legal brothels in designated areas, generally outside city limits. Countries like Australia and New Zealand have moved towards models of decriminalization for sex work policy. Conversely, in South Africa the sex industry is criminalized, and sex workers are primarily charged under nuisance and loitering bylaws. Taiwan voted roughly a decade ago to ban its once-legal sex industry, forcing licensed sex workers to change profession or risk arrest.

This chapter will focus on the prostitution policies of three specific countries: Sweden, the Netherlands, and Canada to show differences in approaches and the consequences of these differences. From these case studies it may be possible to not only understand the effectiveness of different types of policies, but also to see how Canadian policy might develop. The chapter begins with an introduction to two particular frameworks, namely, abolitionism in Sweden and legalization in the Netherlands. It follows with a discussion of the major changes to Canadian prostitution policy for adult sex work[1] from the 1985 Fraser Committee (Canada 1985) to the 2005 Subcommittee on Solicitation Laws Review (Canada 2003; 2005). Viable recommendations for change will be put forward on how to improve Canadian sex work policy and its process for implementation. I argue that in order to successfully develop legislation that supports the economic security of sex workers, sex-working communities need to be part of the public policy process. Furthermore, I locate sex work as a legitimate form of work that should be treated accordingly. As such, a policy framework of decriminalization is advocated. There are four basic approaches to the policing and regulation of prostitution: abolition, legalization, criminalization, and decriminalization. Abolitionist policies are those that criminalize only the actions of individuals seen to be exploiting or coercing sex workers (Davis and Shaffer 1994). This framework, applied in Sweden, supports the view that the way to abolish the sex industry is to actively punish those who are supporting it. Therefore, clients, 'pimps,' and 'traffickers' are charged and penalized, whereas sex workers, who are seen to be the victims, are not. Legalization, as in the case of the Netherlands, allows certain forms of sex work to exist as long as the industry and its workers abide by specific, often stringent, rules and regulations. Forced licensing and finger printing, regulated brothels, and 'red light' zones are common within legalized systems. Under criminalization, as in Canada, all aspects of prostitution are subject to various laws, and both the clients and sex workers are punished through the judicial system; in effect, the entire prostitution industry, its workers and supporters, are legally and socially stigmatized.

The fourth legal framework, decriminalization, is one in which all prostitution-related offences are removed from the Criminal Code. Sex workers most often advocate decriminalization, as it supports their right to work and allows harms or grievances to be judged under different Criminal Code sections. For example, extortion, rape, forcible confinement, threat with a weapon, public disturbances, and causing a nuisance are all regulated under other sections of the Criminal Code and can be dealt with accordingly. Decriminalization supports the argument that prostitutes should enjoy the same workplace rights and benefits as all workers under federal labour law.

Sweden's Stance on Abolition

Since at least the early 1980s Swedish feminists have almost unanimously argued that sex work represents the sexual exploitation of women and that therefore laws should focus exclusively on clients. Over a twenty-year period, with relatively little opposition, the Swedish government voted to criminalize the purchasing of sexual services. This section will briefly outline the major changes to Swedish sex work policy from 1980 to 1999. The case study demonstrates a policy framework that has been built on the understanding that sex work is violence against women and should be abolished. Swedish policies were not developed with the participation of sex workers themselves and do not have their support, nor do they have the support of most sex work researchers and allies.

The Swedish government initiated a commission in the early 1980s to investigate aspects of the country's sex industry. Its 1982 final report concluded that prostitution was a question of 'human dignity' as opposed to sexual choice or sexual work (Svanstrom 2004: 227). The results from the investigation and report led to initial changes in sex industry laws, specifically the banning of all public pornographic shows. In effect, this abolition of public pornography marked the beginning of Sweden's new way of conceiving of sex work as a moral and ethical issue instead of as a labour and employment issue. Roughly a decade later, in 1993, a second Swedish commission was coordinated to reinvestigate the county's sex industry. Both men and women from a variety of backgrounds (public servants, police officers, administrators, social workers, and others) were invited to join the commission that was chaired by the minister of justice. Its final report recommended criminalizing both the seller (prostitute) and the purchaser (client) of sexual services. Public response to the report varied. The police and the courts disagreed with the report's recommendations to fully criminalize the sex industry on the grounds that it would be too hard, too expensive, and too inefficient to police. Others concurred, including both the Conservative and Liberal parties, who argued that criminalization would only push the sex industry further underground (Gould 2002). Swedish feminists and members of the women's movement were in partial agreement with the commission's report. Interestingly, they contended that the way to abolish the sex industry, prostitution in particular, was through partial criminalization, not full criminalization, as recommended. They argued that only the purchasers of sexual services should be penalized.

The women's section of the Social Democratic Party was successful, in 1997, in influencing the party to officially adopt the position that only the clients should be criminalized. A year later the Social Democrats put forth a widely popular bill to this effect, arguing that that the person who sells the sexual service should not be punished. The criminalization of the 'purchasing of sexual services' became official Swedish policy on 1 January 1999. It has since been argued that the perceived threat of foreign-born prostitutes, criminals, and pimps were underlying factors behind the creation and implementation of the bill (Kulick 2003). Public fear of the migration of sex workers from other European countries to Sweden, in addition to anxieties about the nation's entry into the European Union, garnered increased public support and acceptance of the abolitionist legislation.

The changes to Swedish laws continue to be seen as feminist victories by the majority of the Swedish population (Ekberg 2004). The main instigators and current supporters of the abolitionist policy are from Sweden's well-developed and influential women's movement. Sweden prides itself on being a progressive nation in support of women's rights. Indeed, there has been a high level of statewide gender equality since the 1960s and as such Swedish women, compared with women in many other nations, have greater access to economic, social, and political rights and privileges (Gould 2002). Women make up half of the parliamentary cabinet and have been overwhelmingly successful in gaining generous national child care policies, parental leaves, social assistance, and other progressive social policies. Unlike other countries with active women's movements that have been divided on contentious issues, the feminist movement in Sweden has been remarkably homogeneous in its understanding of sex work. Swedish prostitution debates have not centred on the 'forced versus voluntary' distinction that has dominated sex industry debates. Instead, Swedes have primarily focused on whether to criminalize the entire industry (as in Canada) or to criminalize solely the client (the abolitionist position). Notions of decriminalization and legalization have not been actively considered.

The first reported effect of the legislation was an immediate decrease in the number of prostitutes seen working on Swedish streets.[2] A good deal of research, though, has led to conflicting conclusions and recommendations. For example, recent studies have suggested that the decrease in street-based sex work is less the result of legislative changes and more due to a greater ability to make arrangements with clients via cell phones and the Internet (Norway 2004; RFSU 2003). Other studies have shown that the visible decrease in street-based sex work is the result of a shift in the industry to more underground and less safe areas where there is more exposure to violence (Svanstrom 2004; Gould 2002; RFSU 2003). Both independent and government reports have concluded that the laws have indeed been unsuccessful and counterproductive to Sweden's goal of abolishing sex work.

A 2004 Norwegian government study on prostitution in Sweden and the Netherlands concluded that it has been difficult to discern whether there has been a decrease in violence towards sex workers in Sweden since passage of the 1999 law. Incidences of violence were not systematically reported prior to the legislative changes, and so there are no comparative statistics. And yet, the Norwegian report outlines, 'violence is an everyday occurrence for women involved in prostitution [in Sweden]. Women tell of violence in the form of major attacks, rape, threats with knives and with being locked up' (Norway 2004: 12). Despite conflicting reports on the scope and extent of violence, it can at least be concluded that the working and living conditions for sex workers have not improved since the 1999 abolitionist policy came into effect.

The Norwegian study further concluded that, because of the decreased number of clients looking for sexual services (through fear of arrest and clients seeking prostitutes in neighbouring countries), those who are left are generally more violent and aggressive towards sex workers (Norway 2004; Sambo 2001). The diminishing numbers of clients creates a more competitive market where women need to reduce their rates and are more likely to agree to sex without protection. Women are also forced to make split-second decisions about whether to accept a client's offer, as any conversation in public could lead to his arrest (Norway 2004). In a presentation at the Taipei Sex Worker Conference in 2001, Swedish sex worker Rosinha Sambo argued that, with the new law, a sex worker is forced to act as a protector of clients 'in order to keep them. She's exposed to all sorts of criminals, psychos, sadists, because she must protect the customer' (2001: n.p.).

Despite the evidence from both sex workers and research studies, Swedish opinion polls show overwhelming support for the continued criminalization of the 'purchasing of sexual services,' and the public largely sees it as a move towards increased women's rights (Ekberg 2004: 1204–5; Gould 2002: 203–4). Swedish supporters of this system argue that it has sponsored more collaboration between the police and social services and therefore has led to a more sensitive treatment of prostitutes (Kilvington et al. 2001). They also argue that women are more likely to report crimes and assault to police and other authorities and that the legislative changes are in the best interests of sex workers and the abolition of the industry.

Swedish prostitutes dispute these assertions: Sambo (2001), for example, argues that even though the law protects prostitutes from arrest, they are unlikely to call the police in times of need because they then become stigmatized by co-workers and clients. Johannes, another sex worker in Sweden, alleged that the current system is 'not very concerned with sex workers as human beings, but more with abolishing prostitution as an idea' (Clamen 2005: n.p., emphasis in original). Swedish sex workers and others are arguing that, since the laws on the purchasing of sexual services have come into play, prices for services have decreased, sex without condoms and violence have increased, clients are forced to go to neighbouring states, and the industry has been pushed further underground (Norway 2004; Sambo 2001; Kilvington 2001). Indeed, independent studies, as well as individual sex workers, are claiming an increase in violence from clients in addition to deteriorated working conditions (Gould 2002).

The Pragmatic Policies of the Netherlands

Dutch policies that regulate the sex trade have often been referred to as pragmatic. While this may indeed be the case, some sex workers and sex work organizations claim that certain policies and state practices are too stringent and do more harm than good. The Dutch case study demonstrates a policy framework that on the surface appears to support prostitutes' labour rights but underneath is a harsh system with a thriving illegal underground where many are at increased risk to their health and safety.

The eventual legalization of sex work in the Netherlands was the culmination of nearly twenty years of parliamentary reform and public debate. Prior to the 1970s, street solicitation was deemed acceptable only in specific municipally regulated red-light areas so long as the public wasn't 'disturbed.' Brothels were banned outright according to the Dutch Criminal Code. Marieke van Doorninck (2002), of the International Committee on the Rights of Sex Workers (ICRSW) in Europe, explains that the sexual revolution and economic upswing of the 1970s led to an increase in the number sex workers on the streets and working in illegal brothels. Police services, the vice squad in particular, boosted their street sweeps and arrests in response to the increased visibility of the sex trade. The police began to notice that sex workers who were being routinely arrested were heading right back to the streets to raise money to pay off their fines, much to the annoyance of the local residents. In turn, as more residents issued complaints to police about the rising number of street sex workers, the police continued to respond by escalating street sweeps; the cyclical situation needed to change.

A growing awareness of the sex industry and understanding of prostitution as an income-generating activity moved Dutch policy-makers and police services to begin conceiving of the sex industry in terms of consent and coercion. To legalize brothels, the prostitution-related sections of the 1911 Dutch Morality Acts had to be repealed and the

Penal Code needed to be modified. The first major attempt to legalize brothels was made in 1985 with Bill 18202: Repeal of the Brothel Ban. The then minister of justice proposed 'to modernize the Penal Code' around prostitution-related offences and to remove the provisions for work camps for convicted pimps (Outshoorn 2004: 188). During parliamentary debates, the majority of the cabinet was in agreement to strike the ban on brothels and let municipalities fully regulate their own sex industries.

The ground-breaking originality of Bill 18202 was the differentiation between forced and voluntary sex work. The wording surrounding prostitution changed from 'vices' and 'morals' to 'payment' and 'work.' At the time, it was a landmark proposition, one that still actively guides the Dutch legal framework today. The proposed bill was temporarily tabled in 1989 because of disagreements over provisions surrounding trafficking. Years of parliamentary debates followed over how to define 'trafficking,' how to distinguish between forced and voluntary, how to set about the process of regulation, and how much regulatory control to give to municipalities.

Finally, in 1997, the second Repeal of the Brothel Ban, Bill 25437, was introduced to parliament. Its primary concern was to regulate the exploitation of sex workers and to protect minors from entering the industry. Taking another three years to pass through both the First and Second Chambers of the Netherlands parliament, Bill 25437 officially came into effect on 1 January 2000. After nearly twenty years of sex industry debates, the Netherlands lifted its ban on brothels, exactly one year after Sweden criminalized the 'purchasing of sexual services.' In a speech to parliament, the Dutch minister of justice argued, 'Prostitution has existed for a long time and will continue to do so ... prohibition is not the way to proceed ... one should allow for voluntary prostitution' (Outshoorn 2004: 185). He also noted that all kinds of forced prostitution would be 'combated vigorously.' According to one observer, van Doorninck, the years of debate were useful to help integrate the mostly illegal sex trade into conventional society and provided the time for 'both civil servants and sex club owners ... to get used to the idea of doing business with each other' (2002: 197).

According to the current Dutch framework, forced prostitution is defined as trafficking in women, debt bondage, pimping without the consent of the worker, and under-age prostitution. Voluntary, adult sex work is seen and understood to be a consensual form of work, where workers are eligible for health and safety benefits, medical benefits including sick leave, regular access to nurses and other health care providers, STI testing, and counselling, as well as free syringes and drug addiction counselling (Norway 2004). Local governments are responsible for issuing brothel licences and ensuring that strict health and safety codes are in place. Of the estimated 25,000 practising prostitutes, about half are currently working in brothels (Norway 2004). Prostitution is considered 'special' work under Dutch labour regulations, which means that vacant brothel positions are not advertised in employment offices, and sex workers cannot be fired for refusing to provide services to a client.

The municipalities that have been most successful in creating and regulating safe working conditions in brothels and tolerance zones have been those that have included sex workers in the policy development process with police services, residents, and brothel owners. In these instances, brothel inspectors and nurses are more likely to be welcomed into establishments and sex workers are more likely to call police when needed. In some districts the police have reported a 30 per cent decrease in street crime since the legislative changes (Norway 2004). Not all districts, though, have actively consulted sex workers in policy development. Indeed, some municipalities and residents' organizations have been vocal opponents of the legalization of the industry and have lobbied for a return to banning it. Other municipalities have imposed excessively stringent and confusing licensing systems that are extremely difficult to navigate. Often each of the multiple offices required in the licensing process has its own framework to deal with prostitution, frequently their positions collide and contradict one another.[3] With so many strict and complicated regulations, it can be difficult for brothel owners to operate legally in some municipalities (Norway 2004). Additionally, social stigma and discrimination remains in some jurisdictions, so that many prostitutes do not want their sex-work-related employment to be officially documented. In response to this system, some sex workers have chosen not to comply and find it in their best interest to refuse licensing, remain anonymous, and thus work in illegal and clandestine ways.

Within the legalized framework, brothel owners will lose their licences if they are found to employ non-EU sex workers. As such, many migrant sex workers, some of whom had worked in the Netherlands for years, found themselves unemployed and at risk of deportation after the repeal of the brothel ban. Consequently, many migrant sex workers were forced to turn to illegal, and often dangerous, sex clubs for work.

Any non-EU citizen found working in the sex trade is treated as an illegal immigrant under the Dutch Aliens Act. This has created a thriving underground sex industry where the workers are unable to turn to police support for fear of deportation. The Netherlands, like most European countries, has historically hosted and employed undocumented and non-EU workers in the sex industry. Initially, in the 1970s, most immigrant sex workers had travelled from Thailand and the Philippines. This demographic changed in the 1980s, when the Netherlands began to see more women from Latin America and Southeast Asia entering the industry. Another shift occurred in the 1990s with an influx of women from east and central Berlin.

The legalized system of the Netherlands appeals to many left-leaning policy-makers because it seems to both respect the rights of sex workers and the interests of the government simultaneously. In actual fact, many sex workers, in the Netherlands and in other countries, are arguing that some legalized systems are overly regulated by state powers. While all industries are regulated to protect public and state interests, the sex industry in particular is governed to such a degree that it often inadvertently penalizes the workers and pushes them to underground areas. The series of rules and laws that prostitutes are forced to abide by (licensing, forced finger printing, curfews, red-light zones) can be too stringent and not in their interests as workers. Additionally, the social stigma that still surrounds the sex industry, especially in particular municipalities, continues to undermine the policies that have been created to support sex workers' rights to work.

Criminalization in Canada

Unlike Swedish abolitionist policies that penalize the purchasing of sexual services and unlike Dutch legalization policies that regulate all aspects of the industry, Canadian policy-makers have opted for a system of criminalization. It is not currently against the law to 'be' a prostitute in Canada, but it is difficult to work in this capacity. Indeed, while prostitution is technically legal, the Criminal Code of Canada makes it virtually impossible to practise without the constant fear of arrest. The main prostitution-related offences in the Criminal Code are related to the following parts of the act:

- Sections 210 and 211, keeping, being an inmate of, or bringing someone to a bawdy-house or place used for prostitution

- Section 212, a series of offences relating to procuring or living on the avails, usually called 'pimping'
- Section 213, communicating in public for the purpose of engaging in prostitution, including stopping a vehicle or person

For eighty years, from 1892 to 1972, prostitution in Canada was governed under the Criminal Code's 'Vagrancy C' laws. Almost entirely unchanged during these years, Section 164.1 of the Criminal Code defined a prostitute as 'everyone who commits vagrancy who, being a common prostitute or night-walker is found in a public place and does not, when required, give a good account of herself' (Canada 1970: 369). Women, and not men, could be forcibly removed from public places and fined if they could not justify their presence on the street. Women's organizations and civil liberties groups charged that the law was discriminatory, and in 1972 it was replaced with a series of summary conviction offences for 'solicitation.' After six years of confusion over the definition of 'solicitation' (was it a wink, a nod, a gesture, an approach?) in 1978 the Supreme Court ruled in *R. v. Hutt* that in order to be charged for prostitution, solicitation had to be 'pressing or persistent.' Much to the annoyance of policing services, this ruling dramatically decreased police powers to arbitrarily arrest prostitutes; pressing or persistent proof of solicitation was needed.

Citizens' groups and police associations in the 1970s and early 1980s were unsatisfied with the changes to the prostitution laws and lobbied the federal government to find more long-term solutions to the 'problem.' In response to public concerns, on 23 June 1983, the minister of justice appointed a Special Committee on Prostitution and Pornography, commonly called the Fraser Committee, after its chairperson Paul Fraser (Canada 1985). The Committee's terms of reference were fivefold: (1) to consider access to pornography and its effects; (2) to consider the laws related to prostitution; (3) to ascertain public views on how to deal with pornography and prostitution; (4) to consider international policy frameworks; and (5) to put forth recommendations. At the time, the creation of the Fraser Committee was seen as a manoeuvre to stall on the implementation of new legislation and policy on prostitution during an election year.

The Fraser Committee's review and report continues to be the most extensive on the topic to date in Canada. After twenty months, $1.6 million, and hundreds of presentations in twenty-two Canadian locations, the Committee released its controversial two-volume, 753-page report on 22 April 1985 (Canada 1985). The report itself drew heavily from direct quotes and testimonies from residents' organizations, religious groups and churches, national and regional women's groups, children's advocates, university societies, professional associations, mayors, police officers and commissioners, and a very small number of sex workers. The limited consultation with sex workers was due in part to the Committee's focus on pornography and in part because there were far fewer sex worker organizations active in Canada at the time than there are now.

The report released a series of 105 recommendations, 49 of which focused specifically on pornography and 16 on prostitution (Canada 1985). Many of the prostitution-related recommendations outlined the need to decrease social inequalities between the sexes, increase social programs to support women and children in need, improve sex education programs in schools, further research into how to best address the social phenomenon of prostitution, and increase exit programs for sex workers who want to leave the industry. The most controversial of the recommendations, which were immediately picked up by both the media and the public, included the loosening of brothel and pimping laws. The Fraser Committee advocated that 'criminal law relating to prostitution establishments should be drawn so as not to thwart the attempts of small numbers of prostitutes to organize their activities out of a place of residence' (Canada 1985 684). The Committee further argued that the existing procuring, or pimping, laws 'reflect[ed] the view which was dominant at the end of the 19th century that adult women were not capable of making their own decisions on career and lifestyle' (ibid.: 543).

Public and media reactions to the release of the report and its recommendations varied considerably. While some women's organizations and civil liberties associations, as well as individual social workers and sex workers, were in support of the findings, major criticisms came from municipal politicians and representatives of antiprostitution community and religious groups (McLaren 1986). Many sex workers and feminists, on the other hand, considered the report's recommendation to allow groups of sex workers to work from home as the most progressive to date.

Within six business days of the release of the Fraser Committee's final report, the federal Conservative government introduced Bill C-49. In fact, it was during the Fraser Committee's deliberations that Minister of Justice John Crosbie announced that he was working on a prostitution bill and might not wait for the Fraser Committee to release its report. Justice Minister Crosbie's prostitution bill would come to have devastating effects on prostitutes working in Canada.[4]

Crosbie's Bill C-49 recommended turning 'communication' for the purpose of engaging in prostitution a Criminal Code offence for both prostitutes and clients. The bill also opted to strike down the earlier ruling that solicitation had to be 'pressing or persistent.'[5] Additionally, it proposed turning parked cars into 'public' places, making it illegal to engage in paid sex within the confines of your own car. Bill C-49, which sought to increase police powers to arrest both sex workers and clients, was in direct contravention of many of the recommendations of the Fraser Report. Despite public criticism and opposition, Bill C-49, now Section 213 of the Criminal Code, passed through the House of Commons with a wide majority vote in December 1985.[6] A stipulation was included in the bill that a 'comprehensive review of the law is to be undertaken by a committee designated by the House of Commons' within three years of it coming into effect (Moyer et al. 1989: 5).

Roughly two years later, in 1987, the federal government commissioned the mandatory national review and found that, since the passage of Bill C-49, there had been a drastic inequity in the enforcement of prostitution laws. The review concluded that many sex workers 'simply have longer criminal records' as a result of the new legislation (Canada 1989: 118).[7] In Canada, women are disproportionately charged under prostitution laws despite that fact that there are considerably more men (mainly clients, hustlers, and pimps) involved in the industry than women (mainly sex workers). The review found that most charges against sex workers were laid by undercover police officers circulating in unmarked cars in known prostitution areas.[8] The review concluded that the legislative changes brought about through Bill C-49 had not succeeded in curbing prostitution, as it was originally intended to do. Indeed, 'perhaps the clearest conclusion of this evaluation is that police enforcement ... did not suppress the street prostitution trade in most cities. The main effect was to move street prostitution from one downtown area to another, thereby displacing the problem' (Canada 1989: 119).

In 2003, approximately fifteen years after the national review of Bill C-49, MP Libby Davies of the New Democratic Party called for the most recent review of Canada's prostitution laws. Davis' proposal to the House of Commons read:

'That a special committee of the House be appointed to review the solicitation laws in order to improve the safety of sex-trade women and communities overall, and to recommend changes that will reduce the exploitation of and violence against prostitutes' (2003: n.p.).

In light of the horrific violent crimes, including murder, committed against sex workers in Canada this latest review is particularly important.

Like the Fraser Committee, the Subcommittee on Solicitation Laws of the Standing Committee on Justice and Human Rights (SSLR) made its focal point presentations from police services, community members, residents' groups, and advocacy and rehabilitation organizations (Canada 2005). Unlike the Fraser Committee, though, the SSLR heard from large numbers of sex workers, sex work researchers, and sex work advocates. Despite the knowledge that parliamentary subcommittee recommendations rarely make legislative impacts, sex worker organizations pushed to have their voices heard. While the SSLR might credit itself for being more inclusive to sex workers voices, sex workers argue that it was their own efforts that brought them to the table. There were forty-three public hearings held across the country from 9 December 2004 to 22 November 2005. Hearings were generally scheduled twice weekly and were televised via the Government of Canada's online broadcasting service. Transcripts were made available on the official SSLR website.[9] In addition to the public hearings, an undisclosed number of in camera meetings were arranged with sex workers. To protect their anonymity, sex worker presentations were not broadcast and the transcripts have not been made public.

Valerie Scott, Executive Director of Sex Professionals of Canada (SPOC) and self-described sex worker/prostitute/whore, became active in the sex workers' rights movement just after the Fraser Committee hearings of the mid-1980s. In looking back at her presentation to the Subcommittee, she was sceptical about how much impact she had on its members, especially those who seemed to already have their minds made up. Scott argued that some of the SSLR members were unreceptive to sex workers arguments and that one in particular read a magazine during her presentation (Scott 2006). Similarly, sex worker rights' advocate and activist Jennifer Clamen (2006), member of the Coalition for the Rights of Sex Workers and co-founder of the Canadian Guild for Erotic Labour, was conflicted about how receptive the SSLR was to hearing from and engaging with sex workers. She argued that, on the one hand, the SSLR had to be receptive because it was their job to sit and listen, but on the other hand, specific SSLR members came to the process with so many of their own preconceived notions about sex work and prostitution that it was difficult for them to understand the arguments being presented.

Upon hearing of the SSLR's activities, PIVOT, a non-profit legal advocacy organization located in Vancouver's Downtown East Side, became concerned about the possible under-representation of sex workers in the review process. In response, they procured ninety-one sworn affidavits from former and current sex trade workers to submit to the SSLR. Of the affidavits gathered, all but one called for the repeal of the bawdy-house laws, all but one called for the repeal of the communication laws, and many argued that important aspects of the procuring laws inhibited their ability to create a safer working environment for themselves (PIVOT 2003: 22–3, 25). PIVOT's report called for the decriminalization of prostitution along with broader social and economic changes. It concluded that 'striking down the prostitution laws is a critical step, but is not exhaustive of the actions required to remedy the disadvantage and marginalization experienced by sex workers in Canada. The affidavits and legal arguments emphasize the need for legal, social and economic change' (2003: 226).

In Montreal, sex worker rights' organization Stella similarly pulled together the voices of sex workers at their tenth anniversary celebrations in May 2005. The main event was a four-day conference attended by 250 participants, entitled 'Forum XXX: Celebrating a Decade of Action, Designing Our Future.'[10] Jennifer Clamen, who co-coordinated the Forum, presented at the SSLR hearings in Montreal and brought with her the voices of hundreds of sex workers. She opened her declaration by stating that 'behind this testimony stands the 250 sex workers of the Forum XXX, and other sex workers around the world that testify to the harm, crime, and injustice of criminalizing sex workers in a victimless crime' (2005: n.p.). The overwhelming consensus of both the participants of Forum XXX and the affidavits from PIVOT advocated repealing the laws surrounding sex work. Indeed, of the hundreds of sex workers who were either consulted prior to the hearings or presented at them, the vast majority support decriminalization.

The Subcommittee on Solicitation Laws marks the first time in Canadian history where large numbers of sex workers engaged with policy makers in the policy development process. Despite the duration of the study and the gravity of the situation, its final report, *The Challenge of*

Change: A Study of Canada's Criminal Prostitution Laws, contained only six unanimous recommendations (Hanger and Maloney 2006). These included increasing police resources and training to prevent trafficking and youth involvement in sex work, increasing education campaigns to prevent people from entering the sex industry, as well as exit strategies for those wanting to leave, and greater government-funded research programs on prostitution. The report cited internal disagreements between its members on whether prostitution is an issue of human rights or an issue of violence against women as a contributing factor to their lack of agreement and recommendations. In the end, hundreds of sex workers and allies procured sworn affidavits, coordinated conferences, and presented at the cross-country hearings, yet, little, if any, of their proposals for social and policy change were incorporated into the SSLR's final report.

Recommendations: Labour Legitimacy, Social Change, and Decriminalization

The most important people in the policy equation, and the most frequently overlooked, are sex workers, the true policy experts and policy analysts. Their intimate knowledge of the system lends them greater authority on lasting and beneficial legislative changes. Sex worker activists and sex work researchers argue that in order to increase the health, safety, and economic security of sex workers three major transformations are necessary: labour legitimacy, social change, and decriminalization.

First, trade union organizing and association-building are imperative for sex workers to establish and maintain working environments with adequate health and safety standards that they themselves define. In her presentation to the SSLR, Professor of Criminology at the University of Ottawa, Christine Bruckert, argued: 'In terms of the labour conditions, the criminalization of the industry means that the women are outside the protection afforded other workers by federal laws, such as the Employment Insurance Act and employment equity ... If their rights as workers are denied or contravened, they are not in a position to lay claims before, say, the labour board. Nor are they able to organize into labour unions to negotiate better working conditions with their employers' (Bruckert 2003: n.p.). Labour struggles and union organizing are important aspects of most marginalized workers' lives. Collective bargaining agreements, professional associations, worker solidarity, and international and national labour organizations can all help to ensure sex workers' rights.

Second, significant social changes that include initiatives to address both societal and economic inequalities for women are necessary. Women, both sex workers and non-sex workers, need greater access to social supports and networks that address economic insecurity and employment availability. Many sex workers face social isolation due to the stigma surrounding their lives and work. Indeed, for sex workers to be able to work with safety and dignity, the social stigma and negative stereotyping need to end. Discrimination towards sex workers will begin to cease when there is a shift in the way we conceptualize the industry. If sex work is indeed an occupation, its workforce should not face ostracization, social intolerance, and unsafe work environments. Keisha Scott, administrative coordinator for the oldest sex-worker-run education project in Canada, Maggie's: The Toronto Prostitutes' Community Service Project agrees: 'Sex workers deserve the same rights and security that are offered to teachers, auto workers or politicians' (Maggie's 2006: n.p.).

Lastly, the laws surrounding prostitution-related activities need to be removed from the Criminal Code of Canada for full industrywide decriminalization. Decriminalization has been and continues to be the preferred option of sex workers and allies. Sex worker and sex industry labour organizer, Kara Gillies, articulates: 'These laws prevent us from negotiating safe work conditions and developing secure work sites, leading to violence, economic insecurity and poor work conditions. By continuing to criminalize our lives and work, Parliament sends the message that people working in the sex trade are deviant, disposable and undeserving of respect' (Maggie's 2006: n.p.). Social and labour-based legitimacy can be attainable through the decriminalization of the industry, strong union and association-building, and a social understanding that sex work is work.

Debates surrounding changes to prostitution policy frequently conflate and confuse decriminalization and legalization. Often the term 'legalization' is mistakenly used to define any situation in which prostitution is not criminalized. Legalization, as we have seen in the Netherlands, refers to a system of state control and regulation of the industry that can include special taxes for sex workers, forced licensing and finger printing, mandatory health checks, zoning laws, lack of privacy, and more. Oftentimes, within this framework, prostitution is regulated as labour but simultaneously understood as a social problem. Due to the stigma, many sex workers want to remain anonymous for fear of reprisal from family and friends. Anonymity can be impossible in a legalized system where licences are mandatory and often kept on public record. Overly punitive regulations that are unnecessarily stringent encourage sex workers to continue working in underground, illegal, and often dangerous areas out of state view.

Conversely, decriminalization refers to the complete removal of all prostitution-related offences from the Criminal Code for consenting adults. Prostitutes are still liable to arrest, but this occurs under other criminalized areas, just as for any other citizen. Decriminalization reduces the social stigma attached to sex work and recognizes it as an income-generating activity that many people, primarily women, rely on for economic survival. Prostitutes can work freely without the menace of criminal charges and police harassment. Licences are not made mandatory, and sex workers can work collectively for increased solidarity and protection. Decriminalization effectively respects the privacy of sex workers and allows them to enter and exit the industry over different times of their lives, as they choose to or need to, without state intervention or documentation.

In a decriminalized system, if a client becomes violent the sex worker can call the police and have him charged with attempted assault, forcible confinement, threat with a weapon, rape, etc. Indeed, the Criminal Code of Canada already has provisions to protect against sexual assault and sexual harassment. Brothels would still be subject to rules, regulations, and standards – as are all businesses. Any business causing a public disturbance or engaging in illegal activities faces fines and closure; sex clubs and brothels would be no different. Street solicitation, as with other public activities, would be subject to nuisance, loitering, littering, and trespassing charges where appropriate. Sex workers would be eligible for workers' compensation, health and disability insurance, and statutory holidays; they would also pay income tax. As Valerie Scott of SPOC argues, 'For prostitution policy to work in Canada it would have to work for prostitutes, for residents, homeowners, and the Canadian tax payer. The best policy is decriminalization. There's no question. Decriminalization is the ideal' (2006: n.p.).

New Zealand voted to decriminalize prostitution in June 2003. While more research is needed to fully assess the long-term impacts of the new system in that country, sex worker organizations in New Zealand and around the world are heralding it as the most progressive state policy to date. One of the more important points of the New Zealand

Reform Act is that the protection and legitimization of sex workers is of primary concern, and sex workers themselves are able to create health and safety guidelines for the industry.

Conclusion

It is incumbent upon policy-makers to actively listen to members of the sex trade when making policy decisions and recommendations. A system to decriminalize prostitution is in the best interests of sex workers and the general public. Canadian prostitution policies will continue to not meet the health and safety needs of sex workers if sex workers have not been active members of the policy development process. Prostitutes' expert opinions and testimonies should be the primary sources, and sex workers themselves should be members of review committees. Despite sex workers' best efforts to be heard, the Subcommittee on Solicitation Laws provides a contemporary example of the ways in which sex workers' voices are marginalized in discussions that directly affect their lives and work. Indeed, it is the policies that penalize sex workers that create the conditions for exploitation within the industry.

Abolition, legalization, and criminalization are flawed legal, social, and economic models for prostitution policy. The abolitionist Swedish system was strongly supported by feminists and policy-makers despite warnings from police services and sex workers. As it stands now, prostitutes are working in dangerous and violent underground areas with much less protection and even greater negative social stigma. Sex workers are forced to quickly enter sex transactions with clients in order to protect themselves from arrest. In the legalized Netherlands, policy changes have brought about many labour protections and health standards, but state control and regulations are often so oppressive that working outside the system, in illegal areas, can present a better option. Additionally, an underground sex trade is thriving in the Netherlands where undocumented and migrant sex workers cannot report abuse out of fear of deportation. The social stigma against sex workers perpetuates a system of discrimination and alienation. In Canada, where we criminalize both the workers and the clients, sex workers are faced with threatening behaviour from police, clients, and the public. As prostitutes have argued for decades, it is necessary to understand that sex work is work. It is an income-generating activity that many women engage in for financial security. Criminalizing prostitutes only serves to increase their risk and further marginalize their activities.

Notes

1 For a critique of the arbitrary divide between 'youth' and 'adult,' see O'Connor Davidson (2005).
2 Some reports indicate a 90% decrease (Kilvington 2001: 78, 84); others claim 50% (Norway 2004: 10), and still others profess a margin of 30% to 50% decrease (Ekberg 2004: 1193).
3 Key departments include the police, fire services, health inspectors, building and housing departments, law offices, zoning offices, tax authorities, immigration, and others.
4 Interestingly, this minister of justice solicited the support of Canadian-born pornography actress Shannon Tweed, *Playboy* magazine's 1982 Playmate of the Year, to bolster support for him at a fundraising campaign party (Burstyn 1987).
5 Without the stipulation of 'pressing or persistent,' sex workers would be liable for arrest at the mere suggestion of sex.
6 For, 111; against , 35.
7 In 1985 there were 1,225 prostitution-related arrests, and in 1986 there were 7,426 (83% increase;Wolff and Geissel 1993).
8 Entrapment is not illegal in Canada.
9 SSLR website: http://www.parl.gc.ca/sslr-e.
10 According to co-coordinator Jennifer Clamen, the purpose of Forum XXX was 'to share strategies, including a discussion around law reform. The result: a unified voice against the criminalization of sex workers, and support for the decriminalization of our lives and our work' (2005: n.p.).

References

Burstyn, Varda. (1987). Who the Hell Is 'We?' In Laurie Bell (ed.), *Good Girls/ Bad Girls: Feminists and Sex Trade Workers Face to Face*, 163–72. Toronto: Seal Press.

Bruckert, Christine. (2003). The Subcommittee on Solicitation Laws of the Standing Committee on Justice and Human Rights (SSLR). Meeting No. 4. Ottawa.

Canada. (1970). *Report of the Royal Commission on the Status of Women (RRCSW)*. Ottawa: Information Canada.

– (1985). *Pornography and Prostitution in Canada*, vol. 2. Special Committee on Pornography and Prostitution (Fraser Committee). Ottawa: Department of Supply and Services.

– (1989). Synthesis Report. *Street Prostitution: Assessing the Impact of the Law.* Department of Justice Research Section. Ottawa: Communications and Public Affairs.

– (2003). Subcommittee on Solicitation Laws of the Standing Committee on Justice and Human Rights, No. 1–5, 37th Parliament, Second Session, 2 Oct. to 4 Nov.

– (2005). Subcommittee on Solicitation Laws of the Standing Committee on Justice, Human Rights, Public Safety and Emergency Preparedness, No. 1–43, 38th Parliament, Second Session, 9 Dec. 2004 to 22 Nov. 2005.

Clamen, Jennifer. (2005). Recommendations for Law Reform: A Sex Worker Rights Perspective. Unpublished Presentation to the Subcommittee on Solicitation Laws Review, 30 May.

– (2006). Unpublished interview, 5 Feb.

Davies, Libby. (2003). Private Members' Business, House of Commons of Canada, 37th Parliament, 2nd Session Journals No. 55, 7 Feb. Electronic version retrieved 15 Sept. from http://www2.parl.gc.ca/HousePublications/Publication.aspx?DocId=682120&Language=E&Mode=1&Parl=37&Ses=2.

Davis, Sylvia, and Martha Shaffer. (1994). *Prostitution in Canada: The Invisible Menace or the Menace of Invisibility?* Electronic version retrieved 11 Jan. 2006 from http://www.walnet.org/csis/papers/sdavis.html.

Ekberg, Gunilla. (2004). The Swedish Law that Prohibits the Purchase of Sexual Services: Best Practices for Prevention of Prostitution and Trafficking in Human Beings. *Violence Against Women* 10(10): 1187–1218.

Gould, Arthur. (2002). Sweden's Laws on Prostitution: Feminism, Drugs and the Foreign Threat. In Susanne Thorbek and Bandana Pattanaik (eds.), *Transnational Prostitution: Changing Global Patterns*, 201–17. New York: Zed Books.

Hanger, Art, and John Maloney. (2006). *The Challenge of Change: A Study of Canada's Criminal Prostitution Laws.* Rerport 6. Ottawa: Communication Canada-Publishing.

Kilvington, Judith, Sophie Day, and Helen Ward. (2001). Prostitution Policy in Europe: A Time of Change? *Feminist Review* (spring): 78–93.

Kulick, Don. (2003). Sex in the New Europe: The Criminalization of Clients and Swedish Fear of Penetration. *Anthropological Theory* 3(2): 199–218.

Maggie's, Toronto Prostitutes' Community Service Project. (2006). Sex Workers Slam Parliamentary Report. Press Release, 13 Dec.

McLaren, John. (1986). The Fraser Committee: The Politics and Process of a Special Committee. In John Lowman, Margaret A.Jackson, Ted S. Palys, and Shelley Gavigan (eds.), *Regulating Sex: An Anthology of Commentaries on the*

Findings and recommendations of the Bagley and Fraser Reports, 39–54. Burnaby: Simon Fraser University Press.

Moyer, Sharon, and Peter J.Carrington. (1989). *Toronto Street Prostitution: Assessing the Impact of the Law.* Ottawa: Communications and Public Affairs, Department of Justice.

Norway. (2004). *Purchasing Sexual Services in Sweden and the Netherlands: Legal Regulation and Experience.*, Ministry of Justice and the Police, Working Group on the Legal Regulation of the Purchase of Sexual Services. Oslo.

O'Connor Davidson, Julia. (2005). *Children in the Global Sex Trade.* Cambridge: Polity Press.

Outshoorn, Joyce. (2004). Voluntary and Forced Prostitution: The 'Realistic Approach' of the Netherlands. In Joyce Outshoorn (ed.), *The Politics of Prostitution: Women's Movements, Democratic States and the Globalization of Sex Commerce*, 185–204. Cambridge: Cambridge University Press.

PIVOT Legal Society. (2003). *VOICES for DIGNITY: Call to End the Harms Caused by Canada's Sex Trade Laws.* Report compiled by PIVOT Legal Society Sex Work Subcommittee, Vancouver, B.C.

RFSU (Swedish Association for Sex Education). (2003). *Prostitution via Internet.* Stockholm.

Sambo, Rosinha. (2001). The Situation of Sex Workers in Sweden. Conference Presentation at the Taipei Sex Worker Conference, Taipei, China. Electronic version retrieved 3 Jan. 2006 from http://www.bayswan.org/swed/rosswed.html.

Scott, Valerie. (2006). Unpublished interview, 9 Feb.

Svanstrom, Yvonne. (2004). Criminalizing the John – a Swedish Gender Model? In Joyce Outshoorn (ed.), *The Politics of Prostitution: Women's Movements, Democratic States and the Globalization of Sex Commerce*, 225–44. Cambridge: Cambridge University Press.

van Doorninck, Marieke. (2002). A Business Like and Other? Managing the Sex Industry in the Netherlands. In Susanne Thorbek and Bandana Pattanaik (eds.), *Transnational Prostitution: Changing Global Patterns*, 193–200. New York: Zed Books.

Wolff, L., and D. Geissel. (1993). Street Prostitution in Canada. *Juristat Service Bulletin* 13(4). Ottawa: Canadian Centre for Justice Statistics.

15 Economic Security for Women: Organizing around Immigration Status and Work[1]

JILL HANLEY AND ERIC SHRAGGE

Labour rights are not enjoyed equally by all workers in Canada. In this chapter, we document the limitations of labour protection legislation and policy for migrants in general and women in particular, drawing on an examination of labour rights cases presented to the Immigrant Workers' Centre (IWC),[2] a Montreal migrants' rights organization in which the authors are actively involved, together with research interviews with migrant women workers.[3] We will focus on the situation of women with 'precarious immigration status' that denies them the permanent right to remain in Canada or enforces their dependency on a third party such as a spouse or employer. Many migrant women[4] (sponsored spouses, refugees, live-in caregivers, victims of human trafficking) are excluded from labour protections because of their status, their social location, or their employment in 'women's work' that is not covered by regular labour laws.

We discuss the link between women's precarious immigration status and their increased economic insecurity. Our focus is the experiences of migrant women living in Canada with precarious status, the implications for the work that they do, and the limited choices that they have in terms of defending their labour rights. These women face difficult conditions in the labour market and are vulnerable to economic exploitation. We will also share how, despite the weakness of formal labour protections, some of these women find the means to resist exploitation.

We begin with a discussion of the socioeconomic context that frames the presence of migrant workers in Canada, referring to both local and international forces that are transforming our economy and creating the impetus to migrate. We then discuss the policy context that creates the various categories of 'precarious immigration status,' and the policies that frame women migrants' access to social rights. Case summaries drawn from interviews and experiences from our work at the Immigrant Workers' Centre are then presented to illuminate migrant women's experiences in the workplace. We will discuss examples of human trafficking, gender discrimination, older women in factories and the challenges of unionisation in traditionally women's workplaces. The problems the women interviewed encountered are presented, as are their responses in resistance to these problems. This is followed by an analysis that juxtaposes the policies intended to protect labour rights against the experiences shared by the women interviewed. We find a number of loopholes and grey areas that allow migrant women's rights to be violated on a systematic basis. And in cases where migrant women are protected, on paper, by these policies, we find that the reality is often quite different. The chapter concludes with policy recommendations for improved labour protections for migrant women and a presentation of the implications for community organizing with migrant workers.

Migrant Workers in Canada: The Wider Context

The Push and Pull of Migration

If there is one major impact of neoliberal globalization, it is the migration of huge numbers of people seeking to better their economic and, sometimes, sociopolitical situations. The decision to migrate to another country is shaped by processes in both the countries of origin and of destination. Deliberate government policies and sometimes wider social, political, and economic contexts act as incentives. Many people migrate because of lack of economic possibilities or because of displacement due to war or political repression (Castles and Loughna 2003). There are also specific labour market needs in Canada that pull people, but as we will see below, this does not necessarily translate into positive realities. An excellent example of the intersection of 'push' and 'pull' factors are the Philippine government's 'Labour Export Policy' (as termed by critics), pushing people to migrate for work (and to generate over U.S. $2 billion a year in remittances; Parreñas 2001; POEA 2001), coupled with Canada's Live-In Caregiver Program, seeking cheap skilled labour for domestic work. At present, over 90 per cent of the women coming to Canada on this program are from the Philippines.

Canadian foreign and international trade and economic policy also negatively impact the political and economic circumstances of those who migrate to Canada from the Third World. Ottawa's foreign relations and international trade policies operate simultaneously, through bilateral aid relationships and Canada's involvement in such organizations as the World Trade Organization (WTO), the World Bank, International Monetary Fund, or regional development banks. Thus, another 'push' factor in the migration of people from Latin America, Africa, and Asia to Canada is the cumulative effect of neoliberal and export-oriented policy frameworks imposed on these countries over the past twenty to thirty years, and the consequent agricultural liberalization, erosion of workers' rights, closure of domestic industries, undermining of public services, and waves of privatization of other essential services (Castles and Loughna 2003; Parreñas 2001).

The need of migrants to provide for relatives in their country of origin is an important factor in their vulnerability to economic exploitation in the destination country, and women are increasingly the first to leave home. Not only are we seeing a globalization of the feminization of poverty, but we are also witnessing a feminization of migration (Wichterich 1999; Parreñas 2001). Ties of dependence and responsibility with families back home act to bind workers to low-wage work in their country of destination, enduring difficult conditions. The risks of challenging working conditions are high. The reality for many immigrant workers today is that they cannot return to their country of origin, either because of a political situation or because of family members' need for money. As we argue in this chapter, these policies and wider factors contribute to the precariousness of immigrant workers who must work regardless of labour conditions.

Outcomes for Migrants to Canada

In the past fifty years, the ethnic and cultural makeup of immigrant workers in Canada has changed significantly; over the same period, immigration has had a major impact on the makeup of Canadian society and the structure of the labour market. While earlier waves of immigration predominantly drew people originating from European countries, today the majority of immigrants come from the Southern hemisphere, leading to a large influx of non-white immigrants (Statistics Canada 2004). Picot and Sweetman (2005) report that, in recent years, the proportion of 'economic immigrants' (defined by their potential economic contribution to Canada and immigrating through the independent and economic class), increased. This category rose from 37 per cent of accepted permanent residents (including their dependents) in 1981 to 54 per cent in 2001. In addition, 42 per cent of recent immigrants have university degrees compared with 19 per cent in 1981 (Picot and Sweetman 2005: 5). Despite their training and the public belief that Canada faces a shortage of skilled workers, immigrants with credentials from their countries of origin face severe difficulty in having them recognized, thus forcing them to work in jobs that do not reflect their qualifications.

In addition, immigrant workers find themselves disproportionately in low-wage jobs and facing chronically high levels of unemployment and poverty. Picot and Sweetman (2005) argue that the traditional pattern of earnings for immigrant workers – that is, relatively lower income in the early years after their arrival and catching up with Canadian-born workers afterward – has not happened. For the group that entered Canada in the 1970s, this gap has not narrowed as quickly. For those arriving in the 1980s and 1990s the gap has increased, and periods of economic growth and shrinking unemployment have not reduced this gap as would have been expected. Earnings for immigrant men fell by 13 per cent and increased by 6 per cent for women between 1980 and 2000, while for Canadian-born men and women they rose by 10 per cent and 11 per cent respectively (ibid.: 6–7).

Furthermore, using the low-income cut-off (LICO) as a measure of poverty as a reference, immigrants face a deteriorating position. The proportion of recent immigrants with family incomes below the LICO rose from 24.6 per cent in 1980 to 31.3 per cent in 1990 and to 35.8 per cent in 2000. In contrast, poverty rates among Canadian-born residents declined from 17.2 per cent in 1980 to 14.3 per cent in 2000. In 1980 the poverty rate for recent immigrants was 1.4 times higher than for other Canadians; by 2000 the equivalent differential in the poverty rate had grown to 2.5 (Picot and Sweetman 2005). This deterioration of low-income rates is not restricted to new immigrants but includes all immigrant groups.

It is clear that despite high levels of education, immigrants tend to stay at the bottom of the job market. This information challenges the myth that new immigrants are economically upwardly mobile. Given the more recent concentration in the rate of immigration to Canada of people from countries of the Southern hemisphere, and given the jobs that most of these new arrivals hold, a new system of racial stratification is emerging in Canada today. Non-white migrants are doing the low-skilled 'dirty work' and are being held in those jobs for long periods, despite their qualification to be employed in better situations. Furthermore, the expectation of upward mobility after several years of residence in Canada is not obtaining for more recent immigrants.

Other research supports Picot and Sweetman's study and shows that the historical economic success of immigrants integrating into the labour market has been reversed in the past twenty years (Shields 2003). Underemployment and lack of recognition of professional credentials are identified as major elements impeding the integration process of immigrants and refugees (Austin and Este 2001; Krahn et al. 2000; Li 2001; Aldridge and Waddington 2001) and leading to an increase in poverty and homelessness.

Cutbacks in social programs, such as language and job training, have reduced the ability of new arrivals to integrate into Canadian society. As well, because of the nature of their jobs, they have difficulties attaining the employment conditions necessary to qualify for Employment Insurance benefits. Furthermore, there are many informal associations in immigrant communities but these lack funding, status, and recognition to function as effective pressure groups to influence government policy or do not have the capacity to provide support, on a large scale, for new immigrants and their families. Groups that have been in Canada longer are able to get themselves into the funding process, but this has become more difficult for emerging groups.

The immigrants we interviewed arrived in Canada in a period of transition in the labour market. Fordist production methods that provided significant employment in unionized blue-collar jobs were in decline and replaced by service sector jobs and new 'flexible' working arrangements associated with the emerging 'new economy.' Contingent work is also on the rise, work that includes 'those forms of employment involving atypical employment contracts, limited social benefits and statutory entitlements, job insecurity, low job tenure, low wages and high risks of ill health' (Fudge and Vosko 2003: 183). Contingent work is the fastest growing pattern of employment, and youth, women, and immigrants tend to be absorbed into the labour market through these jobs (ibid.). One set of consequences of these changes is a simultaneous rise in the number of people participating in the labour market and increasing poverty. This reality creates a category of immigrant worker who is expected to respond to the shifting and particularized demands and conditions of the labour market. As Hart argues, the 'ideal worker' in the new economy is a 'self-sufficient nomad, migrating with moving job possibilities, keeping specific ties to neighbourhoods, friends and families suspended long enough not to interfere with the need for mobility ... characterized by low expectations regarding pay, working conditions, and above all job security ... new jobs will not be enough for workers to get by, but will have to be combined with other employment ... as well as work associated with unpaid social and personal services. In short, the new workers will be "working like women" whose flexible working patterns have already made them into a preferred labour force in many instances' (1992: 88–9).

Immigrant workers are ideal as this 'generic worker.' They arrive in a situation in which their choices are restricted. They often come from contexts of desperation, leaving as refugees or because of economic hardship. They also carry responsibilities for families at home. The labour market conditions that migrants face (described above) mean that many (although not all) immigrants are forced to accept that their dreams of what Canada might offer are just that – dreams.

Women and Precarious Immigration Status

Government policies and programs create the conditions faced by the women described in this chapter. Canada's 2001 Immigration and Refugee Protection Act, for example, constructs several categories of precarious workers through provisions that allow Canada to refuse an individual the right to remain in Canada or to require the cooperation of a third party, most often a family member or employer, in sponsoring migrants (Oxman-Martinez et al. 2005; CIC 2001). In spite of the rise in 'economic' and 'independent' class immigration cases (these now form the majority), in 2005, of the 509,000 migrants to Canada, 81 per cent were admitted under terms that gave them precarious status. Women were more likely than men to enter Canada through such categories (85% of women vs 80% of men; CIC 2006a; 2006b).

In cases of family sponsorship, women form the majority (almost two-thirds) of spouses and parents who are sponsored (CIC 2006a). Although sponsored family members have the right to work in Canada, they are denied recourse to welfare or pensions (for three years in the case of spouses and ten years for other members of the family).[5] Women are also more likely to be dependent refugee applicants, where their refugee claims depend on the experiences of the principal applicant (usually a spouse). A family split (because of separation or divorce) prior to final refugee determination can mean deportation for the spouse, on the pretext that she is no longer in danger in her country of origin since she is no longer married to the person under direct threat. The vast majority (more than 90%) of those admitted through the Live-In Caregivers program, who provide care for children, people with disabilities, or the elderly, are women, and over 80 per cent of these women are from the Philippines (Oxman-Martinez et al. 2004). These women are required to complete twenty-four months of live-in domestic work, with a visa dependent on a specific employer, before applying for permanent residency from within Canada. And finally, women are disproportionately victims of human trafficking. The Conservative government recently created a ninety-day temporary visa for victims of trafficking, giving them access to health care, but there still remains a great deal of discretion in the treatment of victims in the event of escape or discovery. If trafficked in the sex or drug trade, women may face criminal prosecution, and women still have no guarantee of being able to stay in Canada after their ninety-day visas expire. They are expected to apply for Refugee Status or for Permanent Residency on a Humanitarian and Compassionate basis, two process that are far from sure in terms of success.

Other precarious statuses (of which there were 247,143 documented cases in 2005) include refugee claimants and temporary residents (workers and students). Citizenship and Immigration Canada reports that in 2005 men made up 59 per cent of refugee claimants and temporary residents (CIC 2006b). Refugee claimants face a long wait through a flawed process, and it is increasingly difficult to enter Canada, especially because of the Third Safe Country Agreement with the United States (CCR 2005; Macklin 2005).[6] Temporary visas are issued for those coming to work, study, or visit in Canada, but these visas are always time-limited, very difficult to obtain if a person is coming from a developing country, and dependent on a specific employer, school, or host. Another unofficial precarious status is undocumented migrants, individuals who are smuggled into Canada (either through clandestine entry or the use of false documents) and those whose legal documents have expired or whose refugee claim has been refused. The 15,000 undocumented migrants estimated by the RCMP to enter Canada every year (in addition to those who are already here but who lose their status; Oxman-Martinez et al. 2005) are excluded from virtually all social benefits.

Throughout Canadian history, government policy on immigration has been seen principally as a way to increase the labour force, and migrants have traditionally entered the bottom of the labour market, taking up the worst jobs. Official government documents clearly state that immigration programs are intended to respond to Canada's economic need for a young workforce, supporting economic growth, and international competitiveness, as well as supporting what remains of the welfare state (particularly pensions; CIC 2007; 2004). Canadian immigration programs such as the Live-In Caregiver Program (LCP) and the Seasonal Agricultural Workers' Program (SAWP) are excellent examples of this phenomenon. Both programs offer temporary residency status for migrant workers in jobs that employers cannot fill with Canadians because of the poor working conditions (hours, difficulty of work, and social stigma). To keep these migrants in the target type of work, visa restrictions are very strict, prescribing a specific employer, the length of contract, and even where the worker must live.

Those migrants who are accepted as permanent residents find themselves restricted to the bottom of the labour market through more subtle means such as lack of recognition of their education, professional qualifications, or foreign work experience. Racial and ethnic discrimination also plays an important role (Hou and Picot 2003; Jackson and Smith 2002). The Canadian government has recently been leaning towards increasing the use of 'guest worker' types of programs, with the idea that this would allow Canada to respond to short-term labour needs without any long-term commitment to the migrant workers.

Women's Work and Precarious Status

Our interviews with migrant workers confirm reports in the literature describing the gendered division of labour, especially among people of colour (Shah and Menon 1997; Osborne 2002; Spitzer et al. 2002). Immigrant women face this gendered division within the broader labour market, sharing this condition with Canadian-born women, but Canadian immigration policies compound the effect. As mentioned above, women are over-represented in the immigration categories that can be considered precarious, and these categories are often related to employment. For example, the LCP confines women to domestic and caregiving work, and the 'entertainer class' of work visa was until recently used to fast-track women migrants to work as exotic dancers in Canadian bars. Both of these types of 'women's work' face labour shortages because Canadian-born women tend to refuse this work at current pay and working conditions.

Within the broader economy, our interview participants described systematic sexual and ethnic division of labour within factories, restaurants, hotels, and other workplaces. Women were also concentrated in the garment and service industries. In general, women's work is reported to be isolated (either physically or because communication with co-workers is forbidden), in low-paying industries, and in jobs difficult to unionize. Because women's paid work often mirrors the unpaid work that women do in the home, involving caring for people both physically and emotionally, it sometimes incurs a strange blurring of employee, family, and/or friend status.

The working conditions of interview respondents varied, reflecting an evolving ethnic stratification in the labour market accompanying successive waves of immigration. For certain ethnic groups, with a longer presence in Canada (over twenty years), many had achieved stability in what can be described as traditional working-class jobs. Their mobility remains very limited, however, and many ended up in cleaning jobs over the long term. More recent immigrants faced a harsher labour market reality. The new conditions of the service economy, with subcontracting, precarious work, and low pay, along with the consequent lack of power for workers, structure the daily lives of new immigrants.

The women interviewed for these research projects reported other gender-based labour difficulties. Women working in a variety of settings (factories, private homes, hotels, etc.) reported experiences of sexual harassment. In these instances, employers and supervisors took advantage of the heightened vulnerability of women with precarious immigration status. The difficulty of finding a new job made it next to impossible for women with precarious jobs to quit, their status made it complicated to file complaints with the Labour Standards Board or the police, and threats of either being fired or being reported to Citizenship and Immigration Canada were enough to make many women feel trapped in a job where they were being harassed.

Pregnancy was used against women workers. We came across several cases (both in interviews and through casework at the IWC) where women were fired once their employer discovered they were pregnant. One domestic worker's employer brought her to the hospital, telling her it was for prenatal care. Once there, she realized the employer had arranged for her to have an unwanted abortion! Although it is illegal for employers to fire a woman because she is pregnant, women with precarious status are often in no position to complain and need to put their energy into finding another job.

Stories of Women's Labour Experiences: Problems and Resistance

Over the years, the IWC has come to recognize that much of its organizing addresses the specific needs of women migrants. Workshops addressing women's rights in the workplace (focusing on family leave, pregnancy, maternity leave, sexual harassment, and gender equality) have been developed and a course on computer skills and rights advocacy (Skills for Change) is targeted at older women who experience severe discrimination in the labour market. Women make up the majority of those coming to the Centre with workplace problems, and women make up the majority of activists, volunteers, and staff. One of the IWC's most successful public events is for the annual International Women's Day. This event focuses on the issues facing migrant women within Canada, as well as the situations in their home countries that force migration. At the initiative of the IWC, some fifteen grassroots ethnic women's organizations have come together to form the March 8th Committee of Women of Diverse Origins. The alliances formed through this committee have proven key to policy-related campaigns such as the campaign to include domestic workers in the Labour Standards and Health and Safety regulations. The situation of immigrant workers can be illustrated through a discussion of the range of issues and advocacy activities of the IWC in recent years. Although immigrant women came to the IWC as individual cases, the IWC approached and acted upon these cases as part of a wider set of issues. The Centre aims to link individual experiences to political issues and to support collective action to change the underlying causes of such problems.

Domestic Work Turned Human Trafficking

A Filipina woman found the Centre through various social connections and called for help. She was brought to Canada on a visitor's visa from Saudi Arabia to 'work' as a domestic in Montreal. Although the family is wealthy, they only paid her for three of the nine months that she worked for them in Canada. She was also socially isolated, and her employers threatened her with deportation if she complained. After her call, workers and activists from the Centre 'rescued' her by going by to pick her up when the employers were out for the day. When she went to the police to report her exploitation (including the holding of her passport), one of the officers remarked that he was not sure how to proceed since there was no longer the crime 'slavery' on the books. The calculation of her back salary and overtime pay came to $39,000.

The IWC sees this type of situation as an example of human trafficking. This woman's precarious immigration status (CIC considered her illegal because her visitor's visa had expired and she had been 'working' under the table) meant that she had limited legal protection. The Labour Standards Board declined to accept her complaint regarding wages because she did not have the legal right to work and the police could not find a criminal category under which to charge the employers. The best option available to her was to file a civil suit, suing for back wages and for other damages, but Citizenship and Immigration Canada was telling her that she had to leave the country immediately. A small committee at the IWC was formed to support her case, and it was able to pressure the employer to reach a settlement out of court.

Sexual Discrimination on the Job

Gender-based discrimination is also commonly reported at the IWC. One case involved an LCP worker who was fired from her job when her employer discovered that she was pregnant:

> I was not qualified to get my permanent residence. For that, you have to have 24 months of live-in work within three years. But because I got pregnant, I wasn't able and it was impossible; no employer would accept me to live-in with my son. I could not deny that I had my son with me and every time they found out how old he was, they rejected me. I did more than 12 interviews, until I found part-time cleaning. (Interview)

It is illegal for an employer to fire a woman because she is pregnant; but for women with precarious status, it is very difficult to defend this right. For the woman cited above, she was refused recourse by the Labour Standards Board because, when she lost her job, her work visa became invalid and she became technically an 'illegal' migrant. This loss of status also meant that she was denied the employment insurance for maternity leave that she had paid into while she was working. This individual was unable to find another job that fulfilled the requirements of the LCP and eventually was forced to engage in a political campaign with the IWC and other allies (led by grassroots organizations from the Filipino community) to avoid deportation. She won her campaign, but other LCP workers continue to find themselves in similar situations.

Discrimination against Older Women Workers and Shoddy Union Representation

The IWC regularly sees cases of older women factory workers, with long years of service, being harassed to the point of wanting to quit their jobs. Those who do not quit are often fired under trumped-up accusations. We recently worked with a woman who had thirteen years of service with a company but who was being surpassed in production – but mostly through willingness to give up their labour rights (e.g., working through lunch breaks, doing unpaid overtime) – by younger, more insecure workers. Her employer started harassing her, publicly embarrassing her, and despite her resistance, ended up firing her without proper grounds. Her in-house union seemed to collaborate with the employer and did nothing to defend her. Her collective agreement included provisions below the minimum labour standards.

Since being fired, this woman has filed complaints against her employer for illegal firing, and her union for not properly representing her; she has also sent the health and safety inspectors to the plant to investigate unsafe working conditions. She has referred co-workers to the Centre and is now joining us in outreach efforts to reach workers in other industrial areas. She has finally won her case through an out-of-court settlement. Although the Centre would have preferred a case to set legal precedents, this woman, like many others, did not feel she could make the years of time investment that it would have taken to see the case through.

Deciding to Unionize and Having the Factory Close

Another woman who came to the IWC for help worked at a company that distributes medication, having been referred to the job by friends. In the three years that she worked there, however, the working conditions deteriorated. She had no morning or afternoon breaks, and the company stopped paying double for overtime. Eventually, a union organizer knocked at her door and got her interested in challenging these conditions. The organizing campaign progressed, and ultimately, the workers voted in the union: 58 voted for the union and 8 against. The main issues they wanted to challenge were with respect to job seniority and problematic conditions such as the lack of breaks, overtime pay, holidays, insurance, and benefits.

Keen to challenge her conditions, this woman became part of the negotiating committee. Few of her co-workers were willing to participate because they were afraid that the manager would know who is active in the union and that they might lose their jobs. She adds, 'I'm not afraid because I know my rights' (Interview). The day after they started negotiations, however, the company closed, laying off all the workers. It then later reopened with a new name. At a demonstration to protest the company's actions, the workers met a lawyer who said she would help with the challenge. Unfortunately, however, this lawyer confirmed that there is no law prohibiting a company from faking a closure in order to lay off workers and then reopening with a new name. The struggle over the job loss continued for a while and brought her and other workers into contact with the Immigrant Workers' Centre. But they did not win. The unfortunate reality is that these workers were replaced by other equally marginalized immigrant workers.

The scenarios described above are simply meant to serve as illustrations of the kinds of difficulties facing migrant women workers as they seek to obtain economic security. Underlying their difficulties we can identify the racism and sexism present throughout Canadian society, but also policy gaps that worsen the experience for women with precarious immigration status. These experiences and others like them led the IWC to take on longer-term goals. These goals, as well as issues raised from our broader research, are discussed below in the Policy Implications section of this chapter.

Defending the Labour Rights of Women with Precarious Status: Policy vs Reality

The stories shared above bring out the ways in which Canadian labour and immigration policies often intersect to deny women with precarious immigration status basic labour rights. We have also discussed how it sometimes happens that even when such women are included in labour protection policies, their relative social location impedes them from exercising these rights. In this section, we will go through the various labour protections that exist for Canadian workers and discuss how these protections apply to workers with precarious immigration status. At the end of the section, we will turn to the ways in which this policy framework intersects with the social reality of migrant workers.

One of the first challenges in addressing the labour rights of migrant workers is the classic Canadian conundrum of provincial versus federal jurisdiction. Labour is a provincial jurisdiction, while immigration is federal. There is little communication between the two levels to determine the implications of their respective policies on the other, and this comes across clearly when dealing with the different bureaucracies in trying to advocate for an immigrant worker's rights. Each level tends to refer the problem to the other.

Labour standards, health and safety provisions, and workers' compensation law are all under provincial jurisdiction; although the exact details may differ, the basic trend described here can be seen across the country. We will use the Quebec example. These three policy areas have several important limitations when it comes to immigrant workers. First among them is that these protections do not apply to all workplaces. The few types of work excluded from the basic labour standards, health and safety rules, and workers' compensation happen to include domains where immigrant labour makes up the overwhelming majority of workers. Domestic work and agricultural labour have their own, inferior, standards, for example.

A second limitation is due to procedural problems, rather than clear policy exclusion. These three policies indicate in their texts that they apply to all workers in Quebec, without specifying anything about immigration status. In making a complaint, however, workers are required to demonstrate their legal right to work, either through citizenship, permanent residency, or a valid work visa. If unable to demonstrate this right to work (if the person is working without documents or – incredibly – if their work visa has been rendered invalid because they have lost their job), a person is unable to proceed with a complaint. Another common reason workers are refused the protection of these laws occurs when the work was paid under the table, even if it was against the workers' wishes, which is more often the case for migrant workers. These two policy gaps create a situation where unscrupulous employers can easily exploit the most vulnerable workers, knowing that they are unable to complain.

A third limitation is the way in which these laws require individual complaints. Workplaces are not inspected for standards regularly, as are restaurants, for example. Rather, authorities only intervene in response to a complaint from an individual. Although it is illegal for employers to fire or punish employees who try to defend their labour rights through these laws, immigrant workers know that, in practice, they are risking a lot by making any such complaints.

Another important form of labour protection that exists for Canadian workers is the federal Employment Insurance (EI) program. All legally employed workers (and their employers), including temporary workers, pay into the EI fund through payroll taxes. A Catch-22 emerges when temporary workers try to claim EI, however. Technically, temporary workers are only allowed to stay in Canada so long as they respect their visa conditions by working for the employer designated on their visa. If they stop working for that employer, even if it is due to layoffs or unjust dismissal, they are supposed to leave the country immediately. Immigration policy does not allow them to stay in Canada to seek other work or to see through a complaint against their employer. What results is uneven access to EI. Some offices accord benefits to temporary workers, reasoning that they paid into the fund and should therefore benefit from it when they have lost their jobs, while other offices refuse benefits, reasoning that these individuals no longer have the right to stay in Canada.

A related problem with EI is that it is denied to individuals who are fired from their jobs. The IWC sees many cases of immigrant workers being unjustly dismissed as a result of discrimination, language difficulties, lack of knowledge of their rights, and/or reluctance to enforce their rights. Unjust dismissal is long and difficult to prove, however, barring many workers from accessing EI.

Apart from the problems with labour policies, immigrant workers with precarious status face both economic (structural and personal) and immigration risks should they decide to defend their labour rights through government channels. Migrant workers' position within the greater economy places them at greater risk of having their labour rights violated and of simply losing their jobs. The new economy (based on flexible labour and free movement of goods) allows for quick company closures, false declarations of bankruptcy, temporary/contract hiring, easy replacement of workers, and subcontracting (both domestic and overseas). Migrant workers find themselves disproportionately in such industries and therefore they are at greater risk of facing financial difficulties.

On a personal level, loss of income is very serious for migrant workers. For many, sending remittances home is their primary reason for migration, making job loss devastating not only for those in Canada but for those in the countries of origin who depend on them. Many categories of precarious status are denied access to income security programs, as well. There are the problems with EI, mentioned above, but in addition, many categories of migrant workers have difficult or no access to welfare or pensions. Finally, financial difficulties can eventually turn into immigration difficulties when migrants are denied permanent residency because they are unable to demonstrate their economic independence.

In terms of clear immigration problems, undocumented workers face possible deportation once identified to state authorities, and consequently many prefer to remain below the government radar. Those who are in Canada legally but without the right to work may lose future chances to become a permanent resident. And, although there is no basis in policy, many of those who do have the legal right to work in Canada fear that they will be refused permanent residency if they have a history of 'trouble-making.'

Implications and Conclusions

Our research and practice experience underscores the ways in which having a precarious immigration status seriously impedes a woman's ability to achieve and maintain her economic security. The stories we have gathered, as well as our policy analysis, lead us to identify both policy implications and possible organizing strategies to improve the labour conditions of migrant women workers.

Policy Implications

In the past, the labour movement and unionization provided an important basis for defending workers. The most recent wave of immigrant workers, however, finds itself in jobs that are difficult to unionize, and even the presence of a union does not necessarily improve working conditions. Our interviews suggest that if women migrants' rights are to be protected, changes need to be made in the areas of workplace regulation, worker income security programs, and immigration programs. In terms of workplace regulation, both Labour Standards and Health and Safety regulations must clearly protect all workers, regardless of their immigration status or the type of workplace. Hiring non-status workers should not excuse an employer from extending to all workers employed the same set of rights. This also removes some of the incentive to hire non-status workers and might lessen pressure on legal workers to lower their demands for better wages and working conditions. Enforcing workplace regulations should not involve verifying workers' immigration status, as this creates a major barrier to individuals' stepping forward with problems. Workplaces should be investigated once a complaint is made, in addition to the formal hearings on the specific case. A final change should be the establishment of spot checks on workplaces for working conditions, not immigration status. This removes some of the onus from employees to complain individually, thereby risking the loss of their own job.

Revisions are also necessary in terms of the eligibility criteria for Employment Insurance and Workers' Compensation. If migrants pay into these insurance programs, they should be eligible to receive benefits from them, even if losing their employment has meant a change in their immigration status. This principle is already in place for the Canada Pension Plan.

Some of the underlying provisions of our immigration programs must also be revised. The concept of immigration sponsorship (whether family- or employment-related) should be abolished. Having ties to family or employment in Canada should simply strengthen a person's immigration application, not create a complete dependency on a third party. Those coming on temporary work visas should be able to choose between temporary visas or permanent residency, in recognition of their contribution to Canada, and especially since we never meet the set immigration quotas. The current system seems to enforce immigrants' position at the bottom of the ladder (e.g., the LCP and SAWP), rather than addressing the working conditions that make these jobs so unappealing to Canadians.

Organizing Implications

For such policy changes to take place, community organizing must build from the individual all the way up to the policy level. Our interviews suggest several organizing strategies that might be more effective. Individual advocacy is a first step in supporting women to demand their labour rights. Individual rights education, case support, rights advocacy, and leadership development are all ways to help women enjoy what rights they do have, highlight rights gaps, and – hopefully – lead to spreading the word to others about the possibilities.

Collective organizing and advocacy are key in trying to build work-

place-based responses, bringing together people from the same industry to address common concerns and provide participatory research to
back up the campaigns. Workshops on rights are a way for individuals
to realize that others have similar experiences and, in some cases, to
create bonds for action.

Finally, individual advocacy and collective organizing raise issues
that clearly require policy campaigns: regularization campaigns to address immigration problems, health and safety campaigns to broaden
eligibility and workplace enforcement, LCP campaigns to abolish the
program and tackle the gendered framework of domestic and caregiving work, and labour standards campaigns.

In this chapter, we have shared the experiences of migrant women
workers, contextualizing their labour challenges within a broader economic and policy context. We argue that precarious immigration status
combines with gender and labour market forces to threaten migrant
women's possibilities in ensuring their economic security. Organizing resistance to gender-based labour exploitation is key in working
towards creating a critical mass of people such as the woman we interviewed who said that her experience in Canada has taught her to
improve her working conditions. She tries to encourage other workers
who are not too keen to challenge their conditions:

> If I am experiencing this kind of exploitation in the workplace and I do
> nothing about it, what will happen? So, I work for change, to give warning
> to these companies not to do it again. (Interview)

Notes

1 This chapter draws on two interrelated research projects undertaken in
   cooperation with the Immigrant Workers' Centre: 'Learning to Resist:
   Immigrant Workers' Experiences' (Shragge et al. 2004), as part of *Work
   and Life Long Learning (WALL) in the New Economy: National and Case Study
   Perspectives* and a FQRSC postdoctoral project, Organizing for the Rights of
   Undocumented Migrants.
2 The IWC is central to this chapter. The co-authors have been involved in
   this organization since it began in 2000. The stories and experiences discussed in the chapter are derived from the immigrant workers who came
   to the Centre either for help or to contribute to its development (volunteer
   members) or who were recruited for interviews through the Centre. One of

the major activities of the IWC is its engagement in alternative organizing practices.

3 Fifty interviews were conducted between 2003 and 2005 with three distinct groups: workers who came for help to the IWC or were involved in the Centre; workers from Latin America and had been in Canada for at least 10 years; and workers with precarious status such as refugee claimants, temporary workers, or undocumented workers. The interview guide explored issues such as migration trajectory, their work experience, and their resistance in the workplace where appropriate.

4 In this chapter, we have use the term 'migrants' to refer to all migrants to Canada, regardless of their immigration status. The term 'immigrant' refers to migrants who have been granted permanent residency. We make an exception in using the term 'immigrant worker' to refer to migrant workers in general, as this term is used in popular parlance.

5 Access to welfare is possible if the sponsored family member is willing to declare that the spouse has failed to provide for her or him and then sue the sponsor for support. This is not a viable option for many sponsored family members, especially in situations where they still have good relations with their sponsor but the sponsor is simply not able to provide adequate financial support because of illness, unemployment, etc.

6 In the first year after the implementation of the Safe Third Country Agreement, the number of refugee claimants dropped significantly, from 25,521 in 2004 to 17,975 in 2005 (CCR 2005: 3; CIC 2006b).

References

Aldridge, Fiona, and Sue Waddington. (2001). *Asylum Seekers' Skills and Qualifications Audit Pilot Project.* Washington, DC: National Organization for Adult Learning.

Austin, Christopher, and David Este. (2001). The Working Experiences of Underemployed Immigrant and Refugee Men. *Canadian Social Work Review/Revue canadienne de service social* 18(2): 213–29.

Canadian Council for Refugees (CCR). (2005). *Closing the Front Door on Refugees: Report on the First Year of the Safe Third Country Agreement.* Montreal: CCR.

Castles, Stephen, and Sean Loughna. (2003). *Trends in Asylum Migration to Industrialised Countries: 1990–2001.* United Nations University-World Institute for Development Economic Research (UNU-WIDER), Paper for Conference on Poverty, International Migration and Asylum Helsinki, 27–8 Sept. 2002.

Citizenship and Immigration Canada (CIC). (2001). *Immigration and Refugee Protection Act.* Ottawa: Citizenship and Immigration Canada.
- (2004) About the Department. Electronic version retrieved 17 Aug. 2006 from http://www.cic.gc.ca/english/department/index.html.
- (2006a) *Facts and Figures 2005: Immigration Overview: Permanent Rresidents.* Ottawa: CIC.
- (2006b) *Facts and Figures 2005: Immigration Overview: Temporary Residents.* Ottawa: CIC.
- (2007) *The Immigration System.* Electronic version retrieved 8 Aug. 2007 from http://www.cic.gc.ca/english/about/immigration/index.asp.
Fudge, Judy, and Leah F. Vosko. (2003). Gendered Paradoxes and Rise of Contingent Work: Towards a Transformative Political Economy of the Labour Market. In Wallace Clement and Leah F. Vosko (eds.), *Changing Canada: Political Economy as Transformation*, 183–209. Montreal and Kingston: McGill-Queen's University Press.
Hart, M.U. (1992) *Working and Educating for Life: Feminist and International Perspectives on Adult Education.* New York: Routledge.
Hou, Feng, and Garnett Picot. (2003). *Visible Minority Neighbourhood Enclaves and Labour Market Outcomes of Immigrants.* Ottawa: Statistics Canada.
Jackson, Andrew, and Ekuwa Smith. (2002). *Does a Rising Tide Lift All Boats?: The Labour Market Experiences and Incomes of Recent Immigrants, 1995 to 1998.* Ottawa: Canadian Council on Social Development.
Krahn, Harvey, Tracy Derwing, Marlene Mulder, and Lori Wilkinson. (2000). Educated and Under-employed: Refugee Integration into the Canadian Labour Market. *Journal of International Migration and Integration* 1(1): 59–84.
Li, Peter S. (2001) 'Immigrants' Propensity to Self-Employment: Evidence from Canada.' *International Migration Review* 35(4): 1106–28.
Macklin, Audrey. (2005). Disappearing Refugees: Reflections on the Canada-U.S. Safe Third Country Agreement. *Columbia Human Rights Law Review* 36(2): 365–426.
Osborne, Margaret. (2002). *Access to Licensure for Foreign Qualified Nurses.* Calgary: Alberta Network of Immigrant Women.
Oxman-Martinez, Jacqueline, Jill Hanley, and Leslie Cheung. (2004). *Another Look at the Live-in-Caregivers Program.* An Analysis of an Action Research Survey Conducted by PINAY, the Quebec Filipino Women's Association, with the Centre for Applied Family Studies. Montreal: Métropoles International.
Oxman-Martinez, Jacqueline, Jill Hanley, Lucyna Lach, Nazilla Khanlou, Swarna Weerasinghe, and Vijay Agnew. (2005). Intersection of Canadian Policy Parameters Affecting Women with Precarious Immigration Status: A

Baseline for Understanding Barriers to Health. *Journal of Immigrant Health* 7(4): 247–58.

Parreñas, Rhacel Salazar. (2001). *Servants of Globalization: Women, Migration and Domestic Work*. Stanford: Stanford University Press.

Philippine Overseas Employment Administration (POEA). (2001). POEA InfoCentre. Electronic version retrieved 8 Aug. 2007 from http://www.poea. gov.ph/html/gpb.htm.

Picot, Garnett, and Arthur Sweetman. (2005). *Deteriorating Economic Welfare of Immigrants and Possible Causes: Update 2005*. Ottawa: Statistics Canada, Cat. No. 11F0019MIE, No. 222.

Shah, Nasra M., and Indu Menon. (1997). Violence against Women Migrant Workers: Issues, Data and Partial Solutions. *Asian Pacific Migration Journal* 6(1): 5–30.

Shields, John. (2003). *No Safe Haven: Markets, Welfare, and Migrants*. CERIS Working Paper No. 22. Toronto: CERIS – The Ontario Metropolis Centre.

Shragge, Eric, Steve Jordan, Jill Hanley, Lauren Posner, Marco Luciano, and Charlotte Baltodano. (2004). *Learning to Resist-Immigrant Workers' Experience Preliminary Project Reports*. Work and Life Long Learning (WALL) in the New Economy: National and Case Study Perspectives and a FQRSC post-doctoral project, 'Organizing for the Rights of Undocumented Migrants.'

Spitzer, Denise L., Caridad Bernardino, and Ivon Pereira. (2002). *In the Shadows: Live-In Caregivers in Alberta*. A Research Report for Status of Women Canada, Canadian Heritage and Health Canada. Edmonton: Changing Together … A Centre for Immigrant Women.

Statistics Canada. (2004). *Immigrant Population by Place of Birth and Period of Immigration: 2001 Census*. Electronic version retrieved 8 Aug. 2007 from http://www40.statcan.ca/l01/cst01/demo24a.htm.

Wichterich, Christa. (1999). *La Femme Mondialisée*. Paris: Solin, Actes Sud.

16 Precarious Employment and the Challenges for Employment Policy

LEAH F. VOSKO[1]

Precarious employment represents a monumental challenge to the future of labour and social policy in Canada. There is a growing misfit between the nature of employment and the organization of employment policies, the consequences of which are particularly acute for workers who belong to equity-seeking groups, especially women, workers of colour, and recent immigrants.

The spread of precarious employment raises important questions about how best to imagine employment policy to meet women's economic security needs. In response to this challenge, this chapter explores three alternative models for reimagining labour and social protection in industrialized countries in light of the gendered rise of precarious employment. The first model aims to revive the 'standard employment relationship' (SER) – or the full-time continuous employment relationship where the worker has one employer, works on the employer's premises under his or her direct supervision, normally in a unionized sector, and has access to benefits and entitlements that complete the social wage (Büchetmann and Quack 1990; Mückenberger 1989). The second model proposes a new 'flexible SER' (Bosch 2004). Finally, the third model aims to move 'beyond employment' as a basis for labour and social protection (Supiot 2001). How do these models understand, and seek to redress, the disjuncture between contemporary labour market trends and the organization of employment policies? And how do they respond to women's economic security needs?

The chapter unfolds in four sections, beginning with a sketch of precarious employment in Canada with attention to its gendered character. With this backdrop, the next section describes the three alternative models for organizing labour and social protection, exploring how each understands and responds to the misfit between labour market trends and the organization of employment policies. Adding another layer to the analysis, the chapter then examines how each model approaches change at the level of the gender contract – or the normative and material basis around which sex/gender divisions of paid and unpaid labour operate in a given society (Rubery 1998; Fudge and Vosko 2001). This twofold analysis reveals that the most promising of the three models, the beyond employment model, along with elements of the flexible SER model, is best suited to addressing gender issues. This approach recognizes that devising employment policies to limit precarious employment requires not only adjusting the employment norms organizing policy but also embracing a gender contract characterized by shared work and valued care. The final section thus concludes the investigation by considering, through the use of a few examples, how insights from these models could inform policies aimed at limiting gendered precariousness in Canada and meeting women's economic security needs.

Precarious Employment: A Sketch of Gendered Labour Market Insecurity[2]

Growing numbers of workers in Canada hold jobs that offer low wages and limited social benefits and statutory entitlements. These precarious jobs are characterized by high levels of insecurity and weak employment contracts. They afford workers in them limited autonomy in their work and little control over the labour process itself.

Certain forms of employment are particularly likely to be precarious – such as employment through a temporary help agency, part-time work, and solo self-employment, where the self-employed person does not employ others. The distinguishing feature of these forms of employment is that they differ from the norm of the SER, which organized employment policy in Canada in the late twentieth century and 'functioned' (Bosch 2004: 618) to provide training, access to regulatory protections and social benefits, decent wages, and a social wage sufficient to support a presumed male breadwinner and his family. Of course, this 'traditional' norm is itself an institution of recent origin (Deakin 2002), having arisen in the period after the Second World War, and has always been of limited reach, having never extended to all workers. Instead, it was long dominant among men, first among white Canadian-born men in blue-collar jobs. The SER then was extended to white-collar workers, who were also initially mainly men, and later to some women, especially in the public sector (Fudge 2002). The SER thus owes its power partly to its associated gender contract. A male breadwinner/female caregiver gender contract grew up alongside the SER in Canada, and took sharp expression in the second quarter of the twentieth century. This contract assumed a male breadwinner pursuing his occupation and employment freely in the public sphere, with access to a SER and in receipt of a family wage, and a female caregiver performing unpaid work, possibly earning a 'secondary wage,' and receiving supports, such as social insurance benefits, via her spouse.

Even though the male breadwinner/female caregiver gender contract is waning, the SER remains shaped by social relations of gender, ethnicity, age, race, and immigration status. At the same time, there is increasing evidence that this norm, and the employment policy assumptions it engenders, is out of sync with the realities of the labour market. Full-time permanent jobs became less common over the 1990s and early 2000s, dropping from 67 per cent to 63 per cent of total employment between 1989 and 2005. Over the same period, forms of employment differing from the norm of the SER grew markedly. Solo self-employment and various forms of temporary employment expanded in the 1990s. While solo self-employment represented 7 per cent of total employment in 1989, it represented 10 per cent in 2005. Similarly, temporary employment grew from 7 per cent of total employment in 1989 to 10 per cent in 2005, a period in which the proportion of women in full-time temporary employment doubled.

These trends are significant since solo self-employment and part-time and temporary forms of paid employment are associated with dimensions of labour market insecurity. One such dimension is a lack of control over the labour process, a good indicator of which is the absence of coverage under a collective agreement. In 2005, while 34 per cent of workers in full-time permanent jobs were covered by a collective agreement, the comparable figure for those in part-time temporary jobs was just 22 per cent. Both men and women in part-time temporary and permanent jobs have low union coverage rates relative to those in full-time permanent jobs; yet women's high shares of part-time temporary and permanent forms of employment make them particularly likely to experience a lack of control over the labour process.

The movement away from the full-time permanent job has affected women and men differently. Men are still more likely than women to hold full-time permanent jobs: in 2005, 66 per cent percent of men versus 59 per cent percent of women held such jobs. Women, on the other hand, continue to participate disproportionately in forms of employment characterized by multiple dimensions of labour market insecurity, including part-time paid employment and self-employment, especially of the solo variety, as well as temporary employment.

Breaking down specific categories, such as temporary employment, reveals additional gendered patterns. Women are the majority (59% in 2005) of temporary employees classified as 'casual,' a group that mainly works part-time. In contrast, men constitute the majority of those in seasonal forms of temporary employment (64% in 2005), most of which are full-time, and many of which are covered by special measures under the federal Employment Insurance (EI) system.[3]

The distribution of forms of wage work across industries is also gendered. Consistent with the traditional norm of the SER, men in full-time employment are more likely than women to be in the goods-producing sector. For example, in 2005, 90 per cent of men in durables manufacturing industries, the prototypical example of the male industrial norm, held full-time permanent jobs, compared with 84 per cent of women. In contrast, the industry commonly labelled 'social services,' encompassing health care and social assistance, is the most common industry of employment for women who have any form of paid employment. It is also an important domain of employment for immigrant women from racialized groups (Das Gupta 2002). Yet women's participation in this industry is associated with women's precarious part-time and temporary jobs. Highly female-dominated occupations are also composed of large numbers of part-time and temporary employees. For example, in 2005, 20 per cent women employed in sales and services held part-time permanent jobs and 9 per cent held part-time temporary jobs.

It is well known that young people (aged 15–24 years) are more likely to hold precarious jobs than mid-aged people (McBride 2003). Among young people the likelihood of holding a temporary job grew in the 1990s and early 2000s, while the proportion with full-time permanent jobs declined. Although less well-recognized, gendered patterns are also apparent by age. While mid-aged men still predominate in full-time permanent jobs,[4] as well as employer self-employment,[5] very few men aged 25–54 years engage in any form of part-time employment.[6] The notable gender difference here is that women of all ages fill the most precarious forms of employment, alongside mainly young men.

'Race'[7] also intersects with gender in shaping precarious employment (Cranford and Vosko 2006). Domains of employment, such as the goods-producing sector and occupations unique to primary industries, where white male workers have dominated historically, are key contexts in which the full-time permanent job is still dominant, although with deindustrialization their numbers are shrinking. Racialized gendered patterns are also apparent in certain precarious forms of employment, such as temporary employment. Considering 'visible minority'[8] status along with sex, among women, visible minorities are more likely than non-visible minorities to be employed in part-time temporary jobs (14% vs 12% in 2003). Breaking the category 'temporary employment' down further reveals that a high proportion of visible minority women in Canada work in casual temporary jobs characterized by high levels of uncertainty, fully 35 per cent in 2003.

Precarious employment is growing in Canada and women, especially women confronting multiple forms of inequality, confront high levels of insecurity. This gendered labour market insecurity is a product partly of a series of fractures between the organization of employment policy, which takes the SER as a norm, and the realities of the labour market exacerbated by the drive for employer-centred flexibility. Employment policy typically assumes that workers meriting protection engage in employment relationships with a single employer, even though the reality is quite different. It routinely takes continuous employment as a norm, tying access to certain statutory benefits and entitlements to the duration of employment, often at a single job, despite the significance of various types of temporary employment. Employment policies also normally extend comprehensive social benefits and entitlements only to full-time workers. The three alternative models for organizing labour and social protection respond to misfits generated by these types of assumptions.

Three Models for Reimagining Employment Policy

Three approaches to organizing labour and social protection mark the terrain of reimagining employment policy.

Reviving the SER

The first model proposes a return to the SER. This model conceives of the employment norm as a 'leaky boat.' Pursued most actively in the United States, it seeks to redress the misfit between labour market trends and employment policy by plugging one of its most serious leaks, which is the profusion of situations in which an employment relationship exists but is unrecognized.

The best example of the leaky boat approach is found in the report of the U.S. Dunlop Commission on the Future of Worker-Management Relations (1994), which reported in 1994 on what it labels the growth of 'contingent work.' The Dunlop Commission Report embraces the idea that all adults should engage in employment, preferably full-time, and on an ongoing basis. It emphasizes private decision-making in the workplace as a means of providing benefits from health insurance to vacation pay, and it rejects calls to extend comprehensive labour and social protections to part-time workers. The model also authorizes the continued exclusion of workers, such as domestics and farm workers, on the basis of their occupational location, category of employment, or citizenship status (Commission on Labour Cooperation 2003).

The one significant area in which the Dunlop Commission seeks to modify the 'old' SER is in its call to extend the definition of who is an employee to some self-employed people on the basis of economic realities. This type of model aims to bring self-employed workers,[9] whose chances of profit and risks of loss are limited, into the ambit of employment policy (Dunlop 1994). This proposal resembles developments in the International Labour Code, which was expanded in 2006 to include a new Recommendation on the Employment Relationship. This recommendation encourages member states to 'combat disguised employment relationships,' and to '[facilitate] the determination of the existence of an employment relationship' through 'a broad range of means.' It also makes direct reference to 'multiple parties' in an employment relationship, highlighting the need for protecting workers in triangular employment relationships (ILO 2006: par. 4b, 11). The recommendation recognizes more fully the need for a modified basis of labour and social protection. Yet, like the Dunlop Commission Report, it only offers guidance to countries in addressing the most serious gaps in employment-related protections.

A Flexible SER

The second model encompasses efforts to forge what Gerhard Bosch (2004) calls a new flexible SER. Although there is no single identifiable prototype, this model has some affinities with Scandinavian approaches to employment regulation.

This model understands the misfit between the organization of labour and social protection and the changing nature of work as rooted in a series of five developments. The first development is the growing flexibilization of product markets. While the continuity and predictability of the SER were made possible by similarly structured and vertically integrated product markets (Deakin 2002b), the diversity of markets for products and services is leading firms to return to early industrial forms of hiring and firing, especially in service sector jobs with low levels of socially recognized skills (Bosch 2004).

The dual trend of rising educational levels and combining education or training and work, especially among young people, marks the second development. The notion here is that the expansion of the education system, and the consequent extension of the youth phase of life, contributes to a greater diversity of employment forms. As Bosch notes, 'temporary and part-time jobs have become standard, albeit temporary, employment forms that are not the last stop on an individuals career trajectory' (2004: 628).

A third development, and arguably a decisive factor in the dissolution of the SER, is the employment situation in OECD countries that face high levels of unemployment. At the same time, the fourth causal trend identified is, paradoxically, over-regulation. Here, the argument is that 'de-regulation of the SER is not the only problem, since excessive regulation, as well as the regulations governing other employment forms, can have similar effects' (Bosch 2004: 631). Spain is cast as an exemplar by adherents of this approach, who claim that the size of fixed-term work is a consequence of an 'SER that is too rigid' – or excessive regulation of permanent employment.

The fourth precipitating factor noted is the rising employment rates of women. For analysts calling for a new flexible SER, unlike the labour supply of men under a male breadwinner/female caregiver gender contract, the 'additional' supply of women must combine paid work with domestic responsibilities. This 'additional labour supply' calls for a greater diversity in the forms of employment encompassed by the SER. According to Bosch and others (Rubery et al. 2005), for women to benefit from the substance of the SER, its form must be more flexible.

Implicit in this diagnosis of the cluster of causal factors associated with the misfit is a normative commitment to social democracy: proponents of a new flexible SER aim to replace the SER with a more decommodified alternative, offering 'a flexible framework for self-organized diversity, in which the differing interests of individuals, firms and soci-

ety are balanced out and the social security system is lin⁄
ic efficiency' (Bosch 2004: 635). The objectives of the flε
cement a 'new bargain' between employers and workers ιλ
ated by the state, where equal employment opportunities and suppᴄ
for lifelong learning to improve so-called employability security and
increase flexibility in workplaces are added to the original functions of
the SER.

These additional objectives call for several interventions to establish the flexible SER: foremost is the development of public child care
infrastructure for children under 6 years of age and all-day schooling
for those of school age. Yet this institutional requirement is driven by
the recognition that 'an increase in women's employment that is not
accompanied by changes in the wider social environment is a phenomenon with the capacity to blow apart the traditional SER, albeit
one that is concealed by the decline of the birth rate' (Bosch 2004: 628).
This justification follows from Esping-Anderson, who in considering
prospects for a postindustrial gender contract, notes provocatively that
'we can abstractly imagine a world in which women begin to embrace
the typical male life cycle model, lock, stock and barrel. In this world
there would be almost no children' (2002: 126). Thus, Esping-Anderson's vision of an egalitarian project, defined effectively as a Scandinavian model minus sex segregation, entails 'women-friendly policy' that
includes affordable day care, justified on the basis that its provision is
'fundamental for mothers' capacity to remain employed' (ibid.). In this
vision, public child care is conceived more as a service for working parents than as a social goal.

A second intervention is the promotion of flexible work organization aimed at a synthesis of business efficiency and greater control over
time among employees. Additional objectives include lifelong learning,
with the emphasis on active transfers for those experiencing difficulty
in achieving 'labour market integration,' increased opportunities for
'choosing' working hours, and a shift to individual rights from derived
rights. Throughout the life cycle women are encouraged to build independent social protection through continuous economic activity (Bosch
2004).

The pillars of the new flexible SER include a degree of worker-cen-
tred flexibility in patterns of labour market behaviour, especially regarding working time at different stages of the life cycle. Under this
model minimum pensions are to extend protections against poverty in
old age (and presumably in temporary absences from the labour force),

as long as choices around working hours and form of employment in mid-age were socially justifiable.

As a prototype, the new flexible SER supports a diversity of employment forms without the insecurity typically associated with part-time and temporary employment. The employment relationship is to remain the basis of labour and social policy. However, its form is to matter less in its design, application, and enforcement.

Beyond Employment

The third model for reimagining labour and social protection rejects the notion of a SER, as well as many elements of the flexible alternative. It seeks to move beyond employment as a basis for labour and social protection.

Evolving principally out of European Union level proposals in the late 1990s and parallel developments in employment policy Germany, the Netherlands, and Sweden, this model adopts a vision of labour and social protection inclusive of all people, regardless of their labour force status, from birth to death, in periods of training, employment, self-employment, and work outside the labour force, including voluntary work and unpaid caregiving. It is concerned with spreading social risks and is attentive to transitions in the life cycle, such as movements from paid employment to retirement and from school to work. It also values civic engagement.

The approach to labour and social protection informing this beyond employment model assumes that every worker, over the course of his or her life cycle, should have access, as needed, to reductions in working hours while retaining access to comprehensive protections as well as income supports and, at the same time, the maintenance of regular hours in peak periods of labour force participation. It seeks to normalize working-time adjustments to accommodate shorter working hours in periods of weak demand, ongoing voluntary community activities, periodic skills upgrading, and phased-in retirement, as well as extended leaves, such as maternity and parental leaves.

This approach differs sharply from efforts to revive the SER, as it embraces a broad concept of 'work' that covers all people 'in both periods of inactivity proper and periods of training, employment, self-employment and work outside the labour market,' where 'work outside the labour market' includes training at one's own initiative, voluntary work, and care for others (Supiot 2001: 55). The idea, taking expression in the notion of 'statut professionnel' – that is, that 'an individual is a member of the labour force even if he or she does not currently have a job' – is to reject a linear and homogeneous conception of working life tied to the employment contract (Supiot 2001: x). Under this model, for example, instead of treating 'regular' part-time employment as a valid variation on the employment norm and calling for an extension of benefits, paid working time would be organized to better reflect life's different phases. Under this model, as Anxo and colleagues illustrate, individuals would 'consider their life course as a project in which they perform paid work with varying intensity depending on their circumstances and preferences,' and in turn, 'a new social system would have to offer citizens the possibility to design their own projects,' by which they mean that discontinuities would no longer be associated with precariousness (2006: 94). The problem with the current life course tied to the SER is that individuals making transitions incur significant risks and costs, largely in the form of income loss.

Employment policies adopted in Germany and the Netherlands in the early 2000s reflect this approach. For example, the 2001German Act on Part-Time Work and Fixed-Term Contracts confers a right to all employees with six months' continuous service whose employer regularly employs more than fifteen people to reduce work time (sec. 8). Its objective is to lessen unemployment and to allow employees to fulfil caregiving responsibilities and/or to engage in unpaid voluntary work, training, apprenticeship, or educational programs (Burri et al. 2003). At the same time, the Act also allows part-time employees fulfilling these criteria to extend their working time (sec. 9), and compels the employer to agree, unless this would conflict with urgent operational reasons or the requests of other part-time employees. The aim of this measure is to cultivate greater equality between workers by fostering a better balance not only among those who work part-time but also among those who work full-time.

The 2000 Netherlands Working Time Adjustment Act is even stronger than its German counterpart (Burri et al. 2003). It grants employees a statutory right to both reduce and extend working time, unless an employer can demonstrate that serious business reasons preclude the granting of such a request. Policy changes in both the Netherlands and Germany must nevertheless be approached with caution: while they are consistent with the beyond employment model governments' motivations for adopting working-time adjustment measures vary. So do the outcomes of such policies, such as the degree to which working-time adjustments are taken up and by whom. In the Netherlands, for example, there is debate over whether the higher take-up of such measures by women reflects genuine preferences or the resilience of social norms assuming that it is mothers who are responsible for child care.

Under the beyond employment model, 'social drawing rights,' the notion that people may draw on their prior labour force contribution at times when they are compelled to engage in other forms of labour or civic participation, are the proposed solution to the problem of minimum standards that approaches to labour and social protection organized around the SER are ill-equipped to address. These rights are imagined as 'a new type of social right related to work in general' (Supiot 2001: 56). These rights would not be exercised at the cost of social risks to the worker but based on a prior contribution to the labour force, indicating that employment remains central to the model.

A Continuum of Models

The three alternative models for organizing labour and social protection fall along a continuum defined by the traditional SER at one pole and the life course at the other pole. In its aim to plug the holes in a leaky boat, the revived SER model falls towards one end of the continuum. In contrast, the beyond employment model, in its emphasis on the life course, lies closer to the other end, since even though employment remains central to this paradigm, the goal is to spread social risks across the life cycle and throughout society. The new flexible SER model falls in between these poles. Like the beyond employment model, it supports negotiated working-time adjustments. Yet there are limits: for example, during career breaks 'only socially recognized activities, such as child-raising or further training, are paid for, while the realization of other individual preferences remains unpaid' (Bosch 2004: 633). Much depends, then, on which types of activities are defined as 'preferences' and which are assigned social value. Furthermore, by elevating the importance of lifelong learning as a means of maintaining employment, this model effectively assumes that so-called human capital is sound protection against uncertainty, a dubious assumption given the high levels of unemployment in the OECD countries that Bosch himself acknowledges. This conviction is evident especially in the model's emphasis on 'active' social transfers and on promoting work organization fostering business efficiency at the same time as time sovereignty.

The Three Models and Gendered Labour Market Insecurity

The continuum of models of labour and social protection interacts with a continuum of configurations (prevailing as well as imaginable) of the gender contract. This continuum is defined by an 'unequal work/undervalued care' contract at one end and a 'shared work/valued care' contract at the other end (Applebaum 2002). The male-breadwinner/female caregiver model, associated with the old SER, is the prototype of the unequal work/undervalued care gender contract. There are, however, other variations of this combination, where dual-earning is assumed while caregiving (paid and unpaid) is ignored, perpetuating de facto (and marginalized) female caregiver norms.

The shared work/valued care contract aims, in contrast, to reshape the behaviours, goals, and values of men and women by rewarding care, learning, and work in the public interest. Shared work encompasses a fairer distribution of work among people (Applebaum 2002). One aim is to improve access to the labour force for those (mainly women) who conventionally bear the responsibility for unpaid caregiving at the same time as their quality of employment. Another is to foster a more equitable distribution of socially necessary unpaid work. The flipside of this contract is valued care; as envisioned here, the notion of valued care does not refer to marketization but rather builds on Eichler's (1997) social responsibility model for care, which calls for an expansion of the public provision of services for those requiring care and improving the quality and quantity of employment for care providers in the public sector.

The three models take different places on this continuum of configurations of the gender contract. The model advocating a return to the SER proceeds on the basis that every adult should engage in employment, preferably full-time paid employment, and promotes a system of individualized labour and social protections. The gender contract implied by this vision is characterized by dual wage-earning and marginalized caregiving. The message behind the notion that 'every adult should work' is that women, taken as a homogeneous group, must be 'flexible'; they must bear the costs and dependencies associated with accepting forms of employment that enable them to accommodate caregiving. Consistent with this message, the Dunlop Commission took a positive view of the role of contingent work, when it came to women, suggesting that the 'flexibility' that 'contingent arrangements' provide 'helps some workers more of whom must balance the demands of family and work as the number of dual-earner and single parent house-holds rise' (1994: 61).

The flexible SER model takes a different view of the changing gender contract. This model recognizes that the increase in women's employ-ment that it prescribes could eliminate the SER as we know it, a trend already under way in various countries in the EU and North America, as well as in Australia, but masked partly by declining birth rates. It also views child care to be essential to socially embedding a new em-ployment norm, and worthy of greater state support than increases in child benefits. At the same time, in calling for a shift from derived to individual rights, where social protection for men and women is built primarily through continuous labour force activity, proponents of the new flexible SER model put their faith in equal opportunity. The path to women's economic security is formal equality or equal access to the market, rather than substantive equality. Esping-Anderson, in his call for the 'feminization of the male biography,' albeit a highly problematic notion, recognizes that a more equal domestic division of tasks is neces-sary, but he dismisses it as a realistic a matter for policy (2002: 124–6). Under this model, it is assumed that once child care is in place and once women no longer derive their rights as dependents, it is sufficient to treat men and women consistently, as if they are similarly situated. Yet, in making this assumption, the flexible SER model fails to address persistent gender divisions inside and outside the labour force, and neglects the fundamental issue of minimum standards. The pursuit of individual rights also neglects disadvantage suffered by equity-seeking groups, such as women, people of colour, Aboriginal people, and immi-grants, and issues of horizontal equity (Hepple 1994). If a flexible SER came into being, there is a danger that the associated gender contract could be characterized by dual, but largely unequal wage earning and caregiving that would lie a fair distance from the shared work/valued care end of the continuum.

The beyond employment model views a move from derived to in-dividual rights for women as necessary but insufficient. It offers open-ings for acknowledging the collective character of social disadvantage and discrimination. Indeed, it calls for recasting social rights based on a new concept of solidarity neither 'thought of as solidarity in the face of individual need nor on the basis of a closed list of risks' (Supiot et al. 1998: 227) but, rather, as a vehicle connecting social rights, such as group-based guarantees, to social equality. Solidarity, as it is imagined here, also aims to recover a state that is accountable and responsive to public needs. While its vision for the gender contract requires elaboration, this model endorses public universal and integrated caregiving, earning, and learning to avoid a system that is built along strongly biased gender lines (Supiot 2001). By placing public rights at the centre, the beyond employment model rejects policies compelling workers to trade off precariousness for the capacity to engage in unpaid caregiving and in training, locating it closer to the shared work/valued care end of the continuum of configurations of the gender contract.

Still, several of its central design elements are not fully in sync with the philosophical recognition of the value of work, broadly defined. As they are envisioned, social drawing rights are to be attained on the basis of a prior contribution to the labour force, highlighting an operational limit of this model. The need for respite for unpaid caregivers and supports to ease these workers through life-cycle transitions is well documented, as are the income consequences for these women in retirement (Townson 1997).

Limiting Gendered Precariousness: Policy Examples and Possible Solutions

Among the three models, the flexible SER model and the beyond employment model recognize that the lack of it between the nature of employment and the organization of employment policy rests on not only an outdated employment norm but on an outmoded gender contract. Both models depart from the vision of recuperating the SER. Yet the beyond employment model, and several elements that it shares with the flexible SER model, offers particular promise in advancing employment policy designed to mitigate precarious employment.

Two areas in which employment policy is not meeting women's economic security needs highlight several promising aspects of the beyond employment model: unemployment insurance, on the one hand, and labour standards and collective bargaining, on the other hand. The provision of supports for the unemployed is out of sync with labour market trends. In the mid-1990s, upon initiating a name change to Employment Insurance (EI), unemployment insurance coverage was extended to all part-time paid workers and holders of multiple jobs. On the surface, this move took account of the changing realities of the labour market. Yet it has had contradictory outcomes because a highly restrictive hours system is its centrepiece.

Under EI, new entrants and re-entrants to the labour force are required to work a standard 910 hours to qualify for regular benefits, whereas other workers need only 420 to 700 hours of insurable employment, depending on their regional rate of unemployment (Canadian Employment Insurance Commission 2000: Annex 1.1).[10] After the introduction of EI, many part-time workers were therefore insured for the first time but qualifying requirements under the hours system often make benefits out of their reach.[11] Women are more likely to be adversely affected by qualifying requirements for regular EI benefits because they represent the majority of part-time workers and because, on average, women's weekly hours are fewer than men's.[12] Women have also been affected negatively as workers that may become pregnant.[13] In contrast, full-time workers, a majority of whom are men, are mainly affected by reductions in the maximum number of weeks of benefits.

Policy-makers have extended EI coverage to part-time workers and holders of multiple jobs with one hand and limited their access to benefits with the other hand, confounding the misfit between employment policy and labour market trends: in 2004, just 32 per cent of unemployed women (down from 70% in 1989) and 40 per cent of unemployed men (down from 74% in 1989) who contributed to EI were eligible to receive benefits (Employment Insurance Coverage Survey, Special Runs 2005). All provinces experienced a decline in the ratio of beneficiaries to the unemployed after the introduction of EI and its hours system. Yet there are provincial differences. Notably, the especially low coverage rates in Ontario and British Columbia reflect two additional factors linked to an hours system assuming a SER – the magnitude of precarious employment in large cities and the number of 'new entrants' who face higher number of hours' requirements to gain eligibility for benefits, a designation affecting not only young people entering, and women with children re-entering, the labour force but recent immigrants who settle primarily in Toronto and Vancouver.

Furthermore, for the shrinking number of workers in jobs resembling the SER enough to access regular benefits, the levels and duration of benefits are often inferior to those available in the past. Benefits' inadequacy is a result of not only a low baseline benefit rate of 55 per cent (as of 2006) of insured earnings, but the introduction of a divisor rule counting weeks worked, and focusing on hours worked in weeks just prior to a claim, a period where hours typically decline among workers subsequently laid off, and tying the duration and level of benefits to the unemployment rate in a given EI region. This rule is highly disadvantageous for women, because their earnings and hours are, on average, lower and fewer than those of men and because women predominate in casual jobs.

The structure of the Employment Benefit Support Measures program, where training is addressed, is also out of sync with the realities of the labour market, and women's economic security needs in particular. This program functions primarily on the basis of individualized loans and grants, where costs for direct-purchase training are shared between individuals and the government. This model is limiting access to high-quality training for many EI recipients, especially women, who are less likely than men to have financial resources of their own since EI funds cover only a portion of program costs. One result is the return to short-duration and inexpensive training in traditionally female-dominated fields, where the returns are also lower and less secure.[14] Another result is that women constitute a smaller proportion of the total number of unemployed people benefiting from the direct purchase of training. Furthermore, since the mid-1990s, access to training dollars has declined for women's organizations delivering training for women in non-traditional occupations.

EI policy is a necessary, indeed an essential, aspect of employment policy that will always be linked to employment – and so it should be, given its goal of providing income replacement in periods of unemployment and promoting labour force attachment. However, it is possible to imagine a system that displaces a singular employment norm and embraces a gender contract that recognizes the social value of unpaid work, civic participation, and learning, and that de-emphasizes a static model of earning. One promising avenue in this direction entails supporting a well-resourced EI system (i.e., using surpluses in the EI fund), displacing a singular employment norm, assuming reduced working time for all people over the course of the entire life cycle, and fostering a reorganization of production for the market to reflect life's different phases.

The beyond employment model casts as central the need for freedom to work under different statuses – from employee to independent contractor status – without forfeiting social rights and entitlements (Supiot 2001). There are no sound reasons for extending inferior levels of protection on the basis of workers' patterns of labour force participation over the life cycle. Nor are there significant design impediments[15] to realizing this objective. Why should shifts in labour force status, on account of birth, and dying/death, and periods of training to upgrade one's skills lessen coverage and access to full regular and special benefits and supports for training?

If EI took account of such shifts in the life cycle and recognized a greater range of employment forms, there would still be the issue of evening out benefits across the life course. Under this system, benefits are prorated – but prorated benefits amount to neither equivalent conditions nor minimum standards. They do not confront the old SER. Given its broad definition of work, the beyond employment model also affords the possibility of imagining sufficient unemployment benefits for workers that do not rest solely on the nature of their labour force attachment immediately prior to periods of unemployment.

A second and extensively researched (see Fudge et al. 2002; Cranford et al. 2005) area in which labour market realities are out of sync with employment policy relates to the issue of which workers are covered effectively by labour standards legislation and have the right to organize and bargain collectively. This disconnect is manifest sharply among the solo self-employed, most of whom are excluded from such protections.

In the past several decades, the Canadian labour market has been characterized by a rapid growth of self-employment (Fudge et al. 2002; Hughes 2005). In the 1990s, solo self-employment drove this growth. Moreover, full-time solo self-employment, the largest subcategory, constituted almost half of total self-employment in Canada in 2005. The full-time solo self-employed are often depicted as people choosing independence, freedom, and autonomy over security (Lin, Yates, and Picot 1999), but many pursue self-employment because of a lack of available suitable paid employment or because of caregiving responsibilities (Vosko and Zukewich 2006). In return for pursuing full-time solo self-employment, a sizeable share of this group of individuals have low incomes, lower levels of extended benefit coverage relative to employees, and a heavy reliance on spousal coverage. The significant proportion of women in this situation,[16] and their male counterparts, also typically lack labour and social protections such as access to regular and special EI benefits and collective bargaining rights.

The beyond employment model recognizes that it may be 'particularly detrimental to women' (Supiot 2001: 181) to restrict most labour and social protection to what is, in the Canadian context, a narrowing group of employees. It highlights, instead, the necessity of embracing an inclusive approach to labour and social protection, taking into consideration 'work performed for others which is channelled through other kinds of legal or contractual relations' (Supiot 2001: 181), an insight that could legitimately be broadened to encompass self-employed workers (Cranford et al. 2005). The freedom to work under different statuses with full social protection and collective rights, as envisioned under this model, offers potential in limiting precarious own-account self-employment, especially among women. Similar approaches could be taken to improving conditions among temporary agency workers, for whom realizing collective rights is a challenge and for whom mechanisms are needed for accessing benefits and entitlements beyond job tenure. The flexible SER model is promising in this regard as well; however, its promotion of flexible work organization, designed to fuse business efficiency with control among employees, could impede collective representation.

Conclusion

There are risks involved in reimagining employment policy to limit precarious employment and meet women's economic security needs.

New and modified statutory entitlements and social benefits can only be made meaningful through strong (i.e., effective and enforceable) state supports. Inspiring elements of any alternative model are vulnerable to misappropriation, and it is critical, in particular, to be cognizant of the dangers of privatization. Attaining employment policy that promotes gender equity requires anticipating such pitfalls, as well as regulatory gaps and attempts to exacerbate these gaps. It also, of course, requires engaging in continual collective struggles.

None of the promising avenues canvassed here offer a panacea. The aim, rather, has been to offer frameworks for imagining. There are a variety of policy options for dealing with the misfit between the realities of the labour market and the labour protections and social supports initiated under previous employment policy regimes. The issue for women and equity-seeking groups ill-served by the current policies is the extent to which 'new' patterns of labour force participation, and the changes in employment relationships that they reflect and engender, can be recognized, and specifically, how policy can reflect an understanding of distinctly gendered patterns.

Notes

1 The research for this chapter was supported by the Social Sciences and Humanities Research Council (grant no. 410–2006–2361). Thanks to Marjorie Griffin Cohen, Gerald Kernerman, and Krista Scott-Dixon for their comments on early versions.

2 Data referring to 2003 and 2005 are drawn from the public use microdata files of Statistics Canada's *Survey of Labour and Income Dynamics* and *Labour Force Survey* respectively.

3 At the same time, men dominate in core segments that are racialized, such as seasonal agricultural work, many of which are underprotected.

4 In the 25–54 age group, 73% of men vs 66% of women held full-time permanent jobs in 2005.

5 In the 25–54 age group, 7% of men vs 2% of women engaged in full-time employer self-employment in 2005.

6 In the 25–54 year age group, 3.3% of men held part-time permanent and temporary jobs in 2005, in contrast to 17.3% of women.

7 'Race' is defined here as a social construct tied to racialization, a process of signification in which human beings are categorized into 'races' by reference to real or imagined phenotypical or genetic differences (Miles 1987: 7).

8 The term 'visible minority' is not taken as a conceptual or heuristic category. Rather, it refers to the specific variable defined by Statistics Canada as persons, other than Aboriginal peoples, who are non-Caucasian in race or non-white in colour. Many scholars use terms such as 'Black,' 'people of colour,' or 'women of colour' to reflect people's continual experiences with racism as well as the importance of identities of resistance. Thus, the analytical sections of this chapter use the term 'people of colour' to emphasize racialized social locations.

9 For a case for using the concept 'self-employed worker,' see Cranford et al. 2005.

10 Under UI, new entrants and re-entrants were required to work the equivalent of 300 hours (a minimum of 15 hours weekly for at least 20 weeks). Others workers needed the equivalent of 180 to 300 hours, depending on their regional rate of unemployment, many fewer than required under EI.

11 In 2004, e.g., 76% of unemployed workers who had previously worked part-time contributed to EI, but fewer than 20% of these contributors received benefits. The comparable figures for previously full-time workers were 81% and 55% respectively (*Employment Insurance Coverage Survey,* Special Tabulation 2005).

12 In 2005 the average number of weekly hours worked by men was 39.4 while for women it was 32.7; among those aged 25–44 years, men worked an average of 41.2 hours weekly, while women worked an average of 35.4 hours weekly (Statistics Canada 2006).

13 Under EI a woman needs 600 hours to qualify for pregnancy benefits, a problem for women lacking full-time employment whose children are born close together.

14 This sort of training is a central option for women, not only because of the introduction of cost-sharing but because of the bias towards easy-to-serve EI recipients and the legitimization of third-party agencies (for-profit and not-for-profit) as service providers under the Labour Market Development Agreements.

15 CPP/QPP, e.g., covers the self-employed, who pay both the employer and the worker contributions to this program.

16 In 2000 fully 45% of full-time own-account self-employed women earned less than $20,000 and had no benefits and/or no independent access to benefits (Vosko 2004).

References

Anxo, Dominique, Jean-Yves Boulin, and Collette Fagan. (2006). Decent Working Time in a Life-Course Perspective. In Jean-Yves Boulin, Michel Lallement, Jon C. Messenger, and François Michon (eds.), *Decent Working Time: New Trends, New Issues*, 93–122. Geneva: International Labour Organization.

Applebaum, Eileen. (2002). Introductory Remarks: Shared Work/Valued Care: New Norms for Organizing Market Work and Unpaid Care Work. In Peter Auer and Bernard Gazier (eds.), *The Future of Work, Employment and Social Protection: The Dynamics of Change and the Protection of Workers*, 91–8. Geneva: International Institute for Labour Studies.

Bosch, Gerhard. (2004). Towards a New Standard Employment Relationship in Western Europe. *British Journal of Industrial Relations* 42(4): 617–36.

– (2006). Working Time and the Standard Employment Relationship. In Jean-Yves Boulin, Michel Lallement, Jon C. Messenger, and François Michon (eds.), *Decent Working Time: New Trends, New Issues*, 41–64. Geneva: International Labour Organization.

Büchetmann, Christopher F., and Sigrid Quack. (1990). How Precarious Is 'Non-Standard' Employment? Evidence for West Germany. *Cambridge Journal of Economics* 14: 315–29.

Burri, S.D., H.C. Opitz, and A.G. Veldman. (2003). Work-Family Policies on Working Time Put into Practice: A Comparison of Dutch and German Case Law on Working Time Adjustment. *International Journal of Comparative Labour Law and Industrial Relations* 19(3): 321–46.

Canadian Employment Insurance Commission. (2000). *Employment Insurance 2000 Monitoring and Assessment Report*. Hull: Employment Insurance Commission, Human Resources Development Canada, Strategic Policy Labour Market Policy Directorate.

Commission for Labor Cooperation. (2003). *The Rights of Nonstandard Workers: A North American Guide.* Washington, DC: Secretariat of the Commission for Labor Cooperation.

Cranford, Cynthia J., and Leah F. Vosko. (2006). Conceptualizing Precarious Employment: Mapping Wage Work across Social Location and Occupational Context. In Leah F. Vosko (ed.), *Precarious Employment: Understanding labour market insecurity in Canada*, 43–66. Montreal and Kingston: McGill-Queen's University Press.

Cranford, Cynthia J., Judy Fudge, Eric Tucker, and Leah F. Vosko. (2005). *Self-Employed Workers Organize: Law, Policy, and Unions.* Montreal and Kingston: McGill-Queen's University Press.

Das Gupta, Tania. (2002). Racism in Nursing. Unpublished report for Ontario Nurses' Association. Toronto.

Deakin, Simon. (2002a). The Many Futures of the Contract of Employment. In Joanne Conaghan, Michael Fishl, and Karl Klare (eds.), *Labour Law in an Era of Globalization: Transformative Practices and Possibilities*, 177–96. Oxford: Oxford University Press.

– (2002b). The Evolution of the Employment Relationship. In Peter Auer and Bernard Gazier, eds., *The Future of Work, Employment and Social Protection: Dynamics of Change and the Protection of Workers*, 191–203. Geneva: International Institute for Labour Studies.

Dunlop, John Thomas. (1994). *The Dunlop Commission on the Future of Worker-Management Relations: Final Report.* U.S. Commission on the Future of Worker-Management Relations. Washington, DC: U.S. Department of Labor and U.S. Department of Commerce.

Eichler, Margaret. (1997). *Family Shifts: Families, Policies, and Gender Equality.* Toronto: Oxford University Press.

Esping-Andersen, Gösta. (2002). Towards a Post-Industrial Gender Contract. In Peter Auer and Bernard Gazier (eds.), *Future of Work, Employment and Social Protection: The Dynamics of Change and the Protection of Workers*, 109–26. Report of the France/ILO Symposium, Lyon. Geneva: International Labour Organization.

Fudge, Judy. (2002). From Segregation to Privatization: Equality, the Law and Women Public Servants, 1908–2001. In Brenda Cossman and Judy Fudge, eds., *Privatization, Law and the Challenge to Feminism*, 86–127. Toronto: University of Toronto Press.

Fudge, Judy, and Leah F. Vosko. (2001). By Whose Standards? Re-regulating the Canadian Labour Market. *Economic and Industrial Democracy* 22(3): 327–56.

Fudge, Judy, Eric Tucker, and Leah F. Vosko. (2002). *The Legal Concept of Employment: Marginalizing Workers.* Ottawa: Law Commission of Canada.

Hepple, Bob. (1994). Equality: A Global Labour Standard. In Werner Senen-
berger and Duncan Campbell (eds.), *International Labour Standards and
Economic Interdependence*, 123–32. Geneva: International Institute for Labour
Studies.

Hughes, Karen D. (2005). *Female Enterprise in the New Economy*. Toronto: University of Toronto Press.

International Labour Organization (ILO). (2006). *Recommendation on the Employment Relationship*. Geneva: ILO.

Lin, Z., J. Yates, and G. Picot. (1999). *Rising Self-Employment in the Midst of High
Unemployment: An Empirical Analysis of Recent Developments in Canada*. Ottawa: Statistics Canada Research Paper Series.

McBride, Stephen. (2003). Towards Perfect Flexibility: Youth as a New Industrial Reserve Army for a New Economy. In Jim Stanford and Leah F. Vosko
(eds.), *Challenging the Market: The Struggle to Regulate Work and Income,*
205–27. Montreal: McGill-Queen's University Press.

Miles, Robert. (1987). *Capitalism and Unfree Labour: Anomaly orNnecessity?* New
York and London: Tavistock Publications.

Mückenberger, Ulrich. (1989). Non-standard Forms of Employment in the
Federal Republic of Germany: The Role and Effectiveness of the State. In G.
Rodgers and J. Rogers (eds.), *Precarious Employment in Labour Market Regula-
tion: The Growth of Atypical Employment in Western Europe*, 267–85. Brussels:
International Institute for Labour Studies.

Rubery, Jill. (1998). *Women in the Labour Market: A Gender Equality Perspective*.
Paris: OECD.

Rubery, Jill, Kevin Ward, Damian Grimshaw, and Hugh Beynon. (2005). Working Time, Industrial Relations and the Employment Relationship. *Time and
Society* 14(1): 89–111.

Statistics Canada. (2006). *Labour Force Historical Review 2004*. Ottawa: Statistics
Canada, Cat. 71F004XCB.

Supiot, Alain. (2001). *Beyond Employment: Changes in Work and the Future of Labour Law in Europe*. Report prepared for the European Commission. London:
Oxford University Press.

Townson, Monica. (1997). *Non-standard Work: The Implications for Pension Policy
and Retirement Readiness*. Paper prepared for the Women's Bureau. Ottawa:
Human Resources Development Canada.

Vosko, Leah F. (2004). *Confronting the Norm: Gender and the International Regulation of Precarious Work*. Ottawa: Law Commission of Canada.

Vosko, Leah F., and Nancy Zukewich. (2006). Precarious by Choice? Gender
and Self-Employment. In Leah F.Vosko (ed.), *Precarious Employment: Understanding Labour Market Insecurity in Canada*, 67–89. Montreal and Kingston:
McGill-Queen's University Press.

Index

Aboriginal 9, 12, 36, 128, 152, 205, 386; citizenship 12; communities 139, 144; languages funding cuts 41n24; mothers 151; women with disabilities 38; working mothers with children 35, 41n18, 49, 172, 276. *See also* First Nations; Inuit and Indian

abortion 5, 6, 171, 361

abuse 96, 98, 139, 144, 146, 149–50, 154, 156, 171, 211, 239, 241, 300, 349; child 80, 145, 147, 152. *See also* violence

Act on Part-Time Work and Fixed-Term Contracts (Germany) 383

Action démocratique du Québec (ADQ) 58–9, 271, 288

addictions 9, 170, 242; counselling 339

Advocates of a Working Income Tax Benefit 301

affirmative action 157

Africa, migration from 355

age 31–2, 106, 313, 318–20, 326, 382; and employment 320, 376, 382. *See also* retirement; seniors; young; youth

agricultural employment 211, 366, 379

Alberta 19, 34, 52, 66, 121, 208, 288, 293

Anderson, Doris 40n10

antipoverty groups 304; policy 185

Anti-Poverty Law (Quebec) 53

Armstrong, Pat 14, 103

Asia 130, 140; human trafficking from 139, 144, 340; migration from 355

Assistance to Families with Dependent Children (U.S.) 186, 195

Association des garderies privées du Québec (AGPQ) 58, 63

Association québécois des Centres de la petit enfance (AQCPE) 63

Australia 42, 105, 144, 263, 386; JOBSTART subsidy program 192; model of home care 106; Public Employment Service 192; sex trade 332; support for adults to care for young children 229; welfare reforms 184

Axworthy Lloyd 304; Green Paper 304

Studies in Comparative Political Economy and Public Policy